Michael Moran was born and educate............................the twenties wandering the islands of Polynesia and Melanesia and later trained as an English teacher in London, studying the piano and harpsichord professionally. Posted for some years to Poland shortly after the fall of communism, he became fascinated with its history, people and landscape, and the music of Chopin in particular. A Fellow of the Royal Geographical Society and an incessant traveller, he is the author of the historical novel *Point Venus* and *Beyond the Coral Sea: Travels in the Old Empires of the South-West Pacific*, which was shortlisted for the Thomas Cook Travel Book Award. He lives in Warsaw.

'This memoir ... is in the tradition of Lawrence Durrell's *Bitter Lemons* and proves a well-crafted, spirited and original polonaise, triumphantly balancing humour with scholarship.' *Observer*

'Recalling something of W. G. Sebald ... Moran is a sensitive, intelligent companion, as able to capture the rapacious spirit and chaotic conditions of modern Poland as he is the mournful, savage ghosts of its past – the result is moving and absorbing.' *Metro*

'An entertaining document of the post-Communist period.' *Scotland on Sunday*

'This lively and intelligent book is stuffed with original material that is both fascinating and quite new to most people in the West. Moran has a taste for the baroque oddity, the outrageous eccentricity and the all-but-incredible historical anecdote.' *Times Literary Supplement*

'At its best, Moran's writing is richly atmospheric with real depth and sparkle ... [His] deep knowledge of the country and genuine engagement [make this] an absorbing ... ultimately rewarding travelogue.' *Independent*

'[Moran] presents a series of bite-sized historical chunks that add up to a good primer on Poland's complex history of dash and doom.' *Sunday Times*

'Moran writes well of the Polish concept of żal (regret after irrevocable loss); of Polish pride, honour and exuberance mingled with pessimism; and of the importance of the Catholic church and the family ... This well-written book offers some much-needed history lessons.' *Daily Telegraph*

'This superb introduction to Poland and the Poles is written with a keen eye for the ridiculous and powerfully communicates the surreal quality of the post-communist environment of the early 1990s ... This is not just a travel book, but also a journey through Poland's history, informatively and entertainingly re-told by a man with a real gift for storytelling.' *Good Book Guide*

'The author's prose captures the tragic undercurrent behind the scenes of bureaucratic chaos that made a misery of people's lives ... Moran's description of his tribulations at the Governement office ... could have flowed from the pen of a Dostoevsky ... This book has lifted the veil on one of Europe's most talented and inspiring people.' *Bookdealer*

'[A] thoughtful portrayal of a country that's grown in prominence over the last 60 years. Moran's two decades in the country give a fascinating insight.' *Big Issue (Cymru)*

A COUNTRY IN THE MOON

Travels in Search of the Heart of Poland

MICHAEL MORAN

GRANTA

Granta Publications, 12 Addison Avenue, London W11 4QR

First published in Great Britain by Granta Books, 2008
This edition published by Granta Books, 2009

A CIP catalogue record for this book
is available from the British Library.

1 3 5 7 9 10 8 6 4 2

ISBN 978 1 84708 104 9

Printed and bound in Great Britain
by CPI Bookmarque, Croydon

Dedicated to the numberless Polish children denied by history the joys of an adult life, and for those now living in freedom through a new Polish dawn.

CONTENTS

Map   x–xi
Acknowledgements and Author's Note   xiii
Polish Pronunciation Guide   xv

Prologue: A Death in Monte Carlo   1

1   The Peasant Self-Aid Agricultural   5
    Co-Operative
2   The Eagle's Nest   14
3   'Musical Genius etc.'   21
4   Warsaw the Phoenix   29
5   Remnants of the Old Regime   46
6   Testing Times   51
7   How to Buy and Register a Polish Car   62
8   Vistula – Queen of Polish Rivers   69
9   The Masculine Inanimate   91
10 Spring Loves   101
11 Johnny Fartpants   111
12 Frycek and the Prism of Reminiscence   119
13 The Little Shop of Horrors   142
14 Mozart in Warsaw   154
15 Dance of the Gnomes   160
16 Vistula – Of Dragons, Martyrs and Lovers   167
17 'Keep Away from Gin and Polish Airmen'   198
18 'Not Upon the Polished Road of Their   213
    Makers' Intention . . .'

19	The Lost Domains	228
20	'A Kind of Volcanic Explosion of Mankind's Spiritual Magma'	238
21	'Dog's Blood!'	244
22	Limited Company	254
23	Vistula – Teutonic Knights and Cherry Liqueur	260
24	'A Mixed Economy Kleptocracy'	278
25	'Only the Music of the Forest Playing'	286
26	The Moving Toyshop of the Heart	313
27	A Yellow Sleigh for the Departing Guests	319
28	Ghosts	322
29	Full Circle	328

	Brief Chronology of Polish History	337
	Select Bibliography and Recommended Further Reading	341
	Select Filmography	347
	Index	353

'Some thought it mounted to the Lunar Sphere,
Since all things lost on Earth, are treasur'd there.
There Heroe's Wits are kept in pondrous Vases,
And Beau's in *Snuff-boxes* and *Tweezer-Cases*.
There broken Vows, and Death-bed Alms are found,
And Lovers Hearts with Ends of Riband bound;
The Courtiers Promises, and Sick Man's Pray'rs,
The Smiles of Harlots, and the Tears of Heirs,
Cages for Gnats, and Chains to Yoak a Flea;
Dry'd Butterflies, and Tomes of Casuistry.'

> Alexander Pope, *The Rape of the Lock*, 1714
> Canto 5 (113-122)

'Poland might be, in fact, considered as a country in the moon.'

> Edmund Burke, 1772

'*bo lepiej byśmy
stojąc umierali,
niż mamy klęcząc
na kolanach żyć.*'
[better to die standing than to continue living on our knees]

> Words by Jerzy Narbutt from the
> Polish Anthem '*Solidarność*', 1980

'It's mud, but it's our mud!'

> An immigrant Pole now regretfully living in Germany

BALTIC SEA

Kołobrzeg

Kaszuby

Szczecin

GERMANY

R. Odra

R. Warta

●BERLIN

Poznań

Wielkopolski
National Park

Map of

Poland

Olszyna

Karkonosze Mts.

Wrocław ●

R. Odra

Mt. Śnieżka

Bystrzyckie
Mts.

Duszniki Zdrój

●PRAGUE

CZECH REPUBLIC

Author's Rally Route

0   50   100   150

km

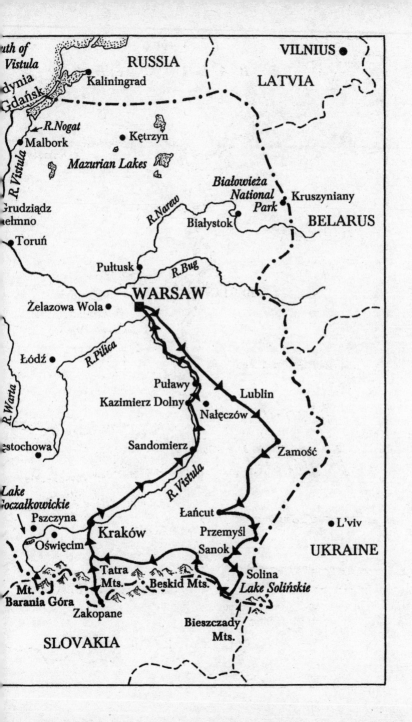

ACKNOWLEDGEMENTS AND AUTHOR'S NOTE

Writing about Poland when one is neither Polish nor Jewish and has no antecedents of either nation may be considered a foolhardy enterprise at worst and a significant challenge at best. In this book I recount my experience of travelling, working and living in Poland over a period of fifteen years as an outsider, a 'foreigner' following one of the greatest geopolitical transformations Europe has witnessed in the last hundred years. I have not had the temerity to judge 'from within' the contemporary outcome of the tortuous historical struggles of this psychologically complex, tragic and heroic nation. The casualty figures given throughout, in what the great Russian poet Osip Mandelstam called the 'wolfhound century', can only be regarded as approximations. Accurate figures will never be known as innumerable lives were brutally extinguished unremarked in the chaos of war. In my research I did my best to indicate at least the scale of the slaughter. Poland is still in a state of transition: political change is a rapid, even daily, occurrence. For this reason I have eschewed political commentary and concentrated on history, landscape, art, music, and the efforts of an individualistic people to come to terms with an unfamiliar world. This rich experience has been greatly enhanced by the friendliness, humour and knowledge generously given by many 'unprickly' Poles from many walks of life.

I would not have begun chronicling this extraordinary cultural journey had it not been for the faith of my commissioning editor George Miller. He felt it was a worthwhile project at a time when Poland had scarcely any profile in the 'new' Europe. His editing was detailed, constructive and well-informed, quite apart from his enthusiastic musical sympathies. I would like to thank Robert Mathews, who with his brilliant memory, humour and powers of observation reminded me of many details I had forgotten. Irena Dworzańska and Wojciech Potocki told me many moving stories of their lives as children growing up in Warsaw during the terrible years of the war, while Professor Włodzimierz Sobkowiak of the Institute of English Philology at the Adam Mickiewicz University read the text and made many constructive remarks on structure and language.

Dorota Banaszkiewicz and Anna Glińska from the Warsaw School of Economics shared many of my early experiences of the country and were mines of information on recondite subjects. The sardonic wit of travel writer and critic Robert Carver often lifted my failing spirits. The former HM Ambassador Charles Crawford generously facilitated many useful contacts at the British Embassy in Warsaw. The distinguished politicians Włodzimierz Cimoszewicz and Radosław Sikorski were generous with their opinions and made time for this foreigner writing in their midst.

Musically speaking, Professor Irena Poniatowska of the Fryderyk Chopin Institute gave me invaluable perspectives on the Polish mysteries contained within Chopin's music. David Winston's fine restoration of my Pleyel pianino and discussions of early instruments transformed my understanding of his sound world. The Warsaw Mozart Festival staged by Stefan Sutkowski and his Warsaw Chamber Opera was largely responsible for my having returned to Poland so often. Richard Berkeley, founder of the New Chamber Orchestra in Poland, made many constructive suggestions and supported me when I lost faith and felt the task was quite beyond my powers. Leslie Robinson, the cartographer, was tireless in pursuit of design solutions and accuracy with many difficult Polish names.

Lastly, but most importantly, words are quite insufficient to thank Barbara Adam, my inspiration, emotional support and Polish 'muse'.

Michael Moran
Warsaw
February 2008

POLISH PRONUNCIATION GUIDE

Polish words may indeed look daunting but the pronunciation is consistent and predictable. The appearance of the letter 'z' so regularly is intimidating when its appearance is so rare in English. Polish is a West Slavic language which uses the Roman or Latin alphabet rather than the Cyrillic which gives Polish a pleasant but sometimes misleading air of familiarity. I have used Polish orthography throughout apart from a few commonly Anglicized names such as 'Vistula', 'Warsaw' and 'Zloty'.

Vowels as pronounced in English:

a	as in	'drum'
e	as in	'men'
i	as in	'peas'
o	as in	'pot'
u	as in	'book'
y	as in	'pit'

Consonants are similar to English except:

c pronounced 'ts'
j pronounced as in 'yes'
w at the beginning of a sentence is pronounced as the English 'v' as in 'vessel' e.g. Weronika (*Veronica*) and at the end as the voiceless 'f' e.g. Stanisław (*Staniswaf*)

The accented letters and consonant clusters peculiar to Polish give rise to the most alarm. Here are the most common in an approximate form:

ó = 'u' so *Kraków* is pronounced 'Krakoof'

ł = 'w' in English so that *Stanisław* is pronounced 'Staniswaf'

ch = has guttural 'h' as in the Scottish 'loch'

ą = a nasal 'a' so that *Powązki* is pronounced 'Powonski'

ę = a nasal 'e' so that *Lech Wałęsa* is pronounced 'Lech Vawensa' (guttural 'ch' in Lech)

ś = 'sh' as in 'sherry' but not quite as strong

ć = pronounced as in 'cheek' so *Zamość* is pronounced 'Zamoshch'

cz = pronounced as in 'match' so *Czartoryski* is pronounced 'Chartoryski'

ci = pronounced as in 'cheers'

ń = a softer 'n' than in English as the 'ni' is pronounced in 'onion'

sz = 'sh' as in 'crush' so *szlachta* is pronounced 'shlachta' with the 'ch' as in guttural Scottish pronunciation

rz = as in 'pleasure' similar to the French *j* as in '*je*'

z = as in 'zebra'   Zamek (castle)

ż = as in 'leisure' similar to *rz*

ź = similar to ż but not quite as strong

szcz = this fearful cluster is pronounced 'shch' as in 'push-chair'

PROLOGUE

A Death in Monte Carlo

'Have you had your ampoule, Eddie?' asked Mrs Fischer in a tone accustomed to command. Her jet hair and impassive features under heavy makeup gave her face the appearance of a Kabuki theatre mask, although she was of aristocratic German extraction. She chose a glass phial from the variegated row arranged in front of her plate, worked industriously at the neck with the tiny saw, snapped off the top and poured the lurid yellow contents into a bowl of what appeared to be porridge for infants. She stirred and began to eat with evident satisfaction.

'Just about to, my dear,' replied the diminutive figure with a shock of white hair and heavy black spectacles. The swirling colours of the contents of his various ampoules mixed together festively. I found this *outré* activity faintly disturbing as I gazed down over the succulents and cacti of the *Le Jardin Exotique de Monaco* and the sparkling Mediterranean Sea

The year was 1968. I had the extreme good fortune not to have been conscripted to fight in the Vietnam War by the infamous 'birthday ballot' operated by the Australian government. I had decided to visit the 'family legend', Uncle Eddie, in Europe. A retired concert pianist, he was a dapper and glamorous figure with a marked resemblance to the Polish statesman and pianist Ignacy Jan Paderewski. Meticulously dressed by Savile Row and Jermyn Street, his sensitive, small-boned features and platinum blond hair swept back in 'waves of inspiration' had made him the darling of the Mayfair salons in the 1920s. Despite the physical disadvantage of having the smallest hands of any concert pianist (the travel writer H.V. Morton wrote a monograph on their miraculous powers) he performed Liszt with ease. He harboured a passion for the music of Fryderyk Chopin and also shared his neurasthenic disposition and that particular quality of *irritabilité nerveuse* that permeates his music.

Edward Cahill had risen to fame from humble beginnings in the dusty Australian town of Beenleigh, famous for the manufacture of a powerful rum. As a boy he was fascinated by sound and collected bottles and tins to give his first 'orchestral' concerts to audiences of small children in the dirt of the yard among the lizards of the Queensland bush. His earliest piano lessons were with the wife of the milkman. From such prosaic beginnings he could not possibly have imagined that he would play a glittering part in the musical life of Buckingham Palace and in the decadent world of the European aristocracy in the London and Paris of the 1920s. As a young man he was a laureate in numerous national piano competitions. The Australian soprano Dame Nellie Melba suggested he travel to Europe and wrote him a letter of introduction to her eminent social contacts in London. She once remarked waspishly: 'Better to be a lamp post in London than a star in Australia.'

Uncle Eddie spent the war years in Switzerland giving concerts for the internees of many nations. Polish officers hid their heads in their hands, shoulders shaking with sobs, as the polonaises and Funeral March of Chopin echoed in the vaults of the Swiss church at Büren an der Aare. His playing possessed exquisite beauty of tone, great sensibility, poetry and charm. His final concert in Paris under the patronage of Lady Diana Cooper (*née* Manners) had a glamorous audience of the French aristocracy that could have stepped from the pages of *À la recherche du temps perdu*.

He abruptly retired from the concert platform on a tour of Switzerland, having fallen in love with the privileged wife of a Swiss business tycoon who owned jute mills in South Africa. A curious *ménage-à-trois* evolved. They finally retired to the French Riviera, where he functioned as their personal secretary and 'pianist in residence'. Hypochondria and evangelical radio sermons ruled the household. At the time I was studying the piano intensively, hoping for a professional future in music. We had long discussions on musical culture and technique. We listened to recordings of the greatest pianists. He spoke of the wild originality and personality of his musical friends. He taught me much on his ancient Blüthner, but on this first visit I was full of youthful energy and in no mood to linger over bowls of invalid porridge and tales of Hermann Göring's lavish *fêtes champêtres* in Germany before the war, and I soon departed for a romantic assignation in Corsica.

It was many years before I visited Monaco again to console him in tragically reversed circumstances. His Swiss patrons had finally died in a Monte Carlo clinic after prolonged struggles, victims of the medical, legal and religious parasites that feed in the geriatric waters of that principality. Eddie had suffered a stroke under the strain of dealing with their illnesses. Drifting in and out of consciousness, suspended in that realm of heightened perception between life and death, he managed to speak with me of the high points of his glamorous concert career. He illuminated for me not only his own life but the entire age in which he lived.

With some difficulty he managed to extract a pledge from me to travel to Poland at some time in my life and visit those places Chopin frequented as a young man. He wanted me to better understand the patriotic roots of Chopin's music, as he felt it would be reflected in my playing. He implored me to scatter his ashes over the Mazovian plain near Chopin's birthplace at the hamlet of Żelazowa Wola, fifty kilometres from Warsaw. He died in Monaco in 1976 and, like Mozart, was buried in an unremarkable 'third-class' grave one bleak and rainy afternoon, the ground merely rented for a period.

CHAPTER 1

The Peasant Self-Aid
Agricultural Co-Operative

Many years had passed before I was able to keep that deathbed pledge to my uncle. My own concert career had foundered in my twenties. By night I had worked as a croupier under the painted Islamic ceilings of the sumptuous Crockfords Club in Carlton House Terrace and practised Bach and Beethoven by day. In the end I decided not to teach the piano but to follow a different life path in academia, although my passion for the music of Chopin remained undimmed. For many years I wrote and lectured on British culture, business and finance at a Swiss educational foundation, but I was beginning to feel restless, and cast about me for an interesting alternative.

I decided to accept a managerial posting to Warsaw (Warszawa). In the early nineties confidence had begun to return to Poland, hyperinflation had ceased and foreign investment and joint ventures were expanding in scope. The purpose of the joint venture was to introduce Polish companies to 'the joys of the market economy'. This posting would give me ample opportunity to explore Chopin's Poland, honour my pledge to my uncle as well as carry out my more official obligations towards business training in East Central Europe.

Initially I had grave reservations about applying for the contract. Hard information about daily life in Poland was unavailable. The customary unattractive preconceptions about the country were confirmed by everyone I spoke to. Hardly anyone wanted to visit Poland then, let alone live and work there.

'Michael, you are in rut. You are such a dull dog these days! Go to Poland – such spirited people! An adventure! The land of Chopin!' My mother was always forthright in her views and regarded my generation as rather wimpish. My upbringing had been sternly Victorian.

'All right, I'll apply for the post. Just to please you.'

Some time later, after dinner one evening, she vaguely asked, 'Did you post that application for project manager in Poland?'

'Yes, yes. I sent it off yesterday,' I replied impatiently. The buff envelope had been sitting on my study desk for a week.

'You're a little liar!' she looked at me with derision.

'What?'

'You didn't send it off, because I posted it for you! I came over yesterday while you were at work to check.'

'You did *what*?'

I was horrified.

I arrived in Poland one desolate January morning in the winter of 1992. Exhausted from walking around Warsaw airport attempting to follow signs in Polish, I foolishly climbed into a taxi and optimistically pointed out an unpronounceable suburb on my map. We headed towards the address along a road that ran beside the wintry Vistula (Wisła), which drifted past in various shades of grey. It was a desolate landscape of bare trees and frozen earth, snow on sand, ice forming at the jagged margins of water flowing beneath the ice sheets. It is an untamed river, the last large unregulated waterway in Europe.

The driver nodded with understanding at my fractured Polish but still proceeded to 'get lost'. Hours passed. Eventually we were driving in darkness across ploughed fields on the river banks. I presumed he was either a Ukrainian refugee or an ex-secret-police mafia agent, for whenever he asked directions people wilfully misunderstood him and shied away. I became convinced he was illiterate as the names on the map seemed of no navigational assistance. When we finally arrived at the training centre I asked him how much I owed.

'Five and a half million zlotys.'

I was aghast and offered him half the amount. Invective in Polish and English flew. I had been warned that Warsaw taxi drivers in those days habitually multiplied the fare by 1,000.

The training centre was some eighteen kilometres from the city centre, deep in a picturesque birch and pine forest on the banks of the Vistula. Private allotments for raising vegetables, known as *działki*, sported tiny, fantastical cabins. In the mid-sixteenth century the area had been a royal hunting park, but the village had been destroyed by the Swedish invasion a hundred years later. Nearby were the shrapnel-licked ruins of a small neoclassical palace built by Count Heinrich von Brühl, the powerful chief minister under the slothful and porcine Elector-King Augustus III. My first impression of the centre was that it resembled an abandoned military barracks.

I was met by my Polish counterpart, Dr Grabski, a surprisingly snappy dresser in yachting jacket and club tie but with disturbingly cold eyes, who enthusiastically showed me around. As we walked, he jammed matches in the energy-frugal, spring-loaded light switches that refused to remain in the 'on' position.

'That contract you signed is complete rubbish! We will invent solutions as we go along!' he burst out gaily.

Over strong coffee, confidences concerning the previous contractors were revealed. A 'mentally diseased' female teacher, after a romantic interlude, had attacked one of the personnel managers during a snowstorm and had bitten him on the neck and face as he attempted to escape her advances and leap from the moving vehicle. Former 'academic staff' had turned out to be shoe salesmen, a truck driver who had delivered oranges to Teheran and an unemployed actor who specialized in voice-overs for frying mushrooms. Now the Poles wanted a more professional group and were justifiably tired of being taken advantage of by cynical Western companies.

The building must have been one of the last conference centres in Warsaw untouched since communist days. Two architecturally sterile blocks were linked by a covered walkway. Decrepit and overgrown tennis courts with rotting nets lay to one side of a neglected Italianate garden that had once graced a charming summer villa. A three-legged dog nosed some promising rubbish bins. The reception area was dim, with unsmiling women behind a glass panel furnished with a tiny speech aperture that forced one to bend double to communicate. Anyone hoping to use the telephone needed to grasp the single red handset pushed through the gap on a short cord. Disconnection seemed inevitable and usually irreversible. The line became incredibly faint if it rained owing to the low quality, porous Russian cable insulation. A faint aroma of urine and boiled fish mixed with the kerosene used to wash the stairs. It mingled with stale cigarette smoke from overflowing ashtrays on perilously tall stands. Cats fought under the radiators and dogs ate scraps of lavatory paper on the floor. People rushed about distractedly carrying huge bundles of laundry in and out of private cars.

The corridors were decorated with curling photocopies of Polish medallions and photographs of onions and tomatoes. An enormous beige plastic bust of Lenin had toppled in one corner of an office while most of the light bulbs in the wooden candelabra had blown. Glass cases containing numbered lumps of coal and boxes of animal feed printed with cartoons of pink pigs lined the walls. Strips of fly-paper encrusted with generations of insects hung from the ceiling of the lavatories. Three times a day a truck arrived in a cloud of diesel to pump out the cesspit at the rear of the buildings, at which time a sweet, cloying odour wafted over the complex.

The view from the window of my room was of a flat asphalt roof garlanded with lightning rods linked by cables. Clouds of steam issued from every junction of numerous bent pipes. A wrecked chimney wrapped in rattling galvanized iron functioned as a nest for ravens. The courtyard below was illuminated by searchlights. Disconnected wires waved in the wind while dogs howled in the distance. Chrome-yellow curtains were printed with scenes of trop-ical Samoa or Tahiti that shuddered in the icy draughts. I stuffed the *Financial Times* around the gaps in the windows to stop the worst of the winter gales, an attractive pink border framing the industrial view.

The entire compound was surrounded by high steel fences. During heavy rain a mysterious white foam would emerge from the down-pipes and flood the entrance. Light switches were reversed in function, where 'on' was 'off', hot water taps produced cold water and vice versa, door locks would unexpectedly lock counter-clock-wise, wardrobe doors slowly drifted open, windows would spontaneously fall out of their frames, lavatory paper shredded half-way through the roll. (The lavatories themselves were marked with mysterious symbols to separate the sexes. They are powerfully sug-gestive and stimulate prurient thoughts.) I realized with a start one day that the tropical curtains in my room had been hung upside down. I began to believe I had stepped through the looking glass hand in hand with Alice.

The English Team anxiously awaited my arrival. Richard Trevelyan, a middle-aged English gentleman of marvellous wit but bruised emotions, had graduated in Oriental Studies from Brasenose College, Oxford. He wrote for the National Trust and lived in Mayfair, had a phenomenal memory, was a brilliant teacher and already spoke some Polish. He was a cultured and imposing figure with silver hair and a patrician air.

Geoff Ketley, an IT trainer from Bradford with a drawn face alert to disappointment and imagined slights, recently divorced and bitter, had suffered a deprived childhood which left him with a prickly temperament. He empathised strongly with injustice and the downtrodden. In his mid-thirties and a great walker, jogger, mountain climber and pot-holer, he was the first man to walk across Tasmania. 'When I see a mountain – straight up. When I see a pot-hole – straight down.'

David Mitts was an exceptionally tall, chronically indecisive young teacher with thick glasses and frizzy hair, a Morris dancer who had brought along 'the motley' and bells from somewhere in Dorset.

'There ... er ... on this contract ... seem to be three types of teaching hour – a real hour, a Polish hour and an English hour. I'm ... er ... treated like shit around here! I don't know which from what and how and what I should calculate.'

The twentysomething financial consultant, Nick Makin, was an Essex boy living in Battersea who held a black belt in karate and spoke obsessively about 'killing the Russian mafia' and his difficult life as an unemployed accountant. He had a severe problem with his class origins, accent and modest intellectual achievements.

'Ya know like, when ya come out the Barking Odeon on a Frid'y night lookin' for trouble ... like when ya got a piss-full, like ... this fuckin' geezer comes up to me ... heh – heh ... and says to me ... heh – heh ... Hey you big mouth ... university cunt ... heh – heh ... I says excellent, excellent, good one, good one ...'

On my arrival these 'consultants' recommended an immediate visit to the moribund British Club. It was the only nearby source of outside information in English. As I approached the dim veranda from pitch darkness, wild dogs threw themselves at the wire mesh fences of adjoining villas, snarling and foaming. An excursion to the club was strictly for the fearless.

'How long have you been out here?' I overheard a tweedy type ask another at the club.

'Oh, a couple of years now.'

'Terrible table manners, the Poles! Have you picked up any of the lingo?'

'No, not a bit of it! Too damn difficult and, anyway, I'm off shortly.'

'Damn shock the other day. A drunken chap just lurched out of the dark straight into the road in front of my car!'

'An entire drunken family staggered down the middle of my road – grandma, husband, wife, children. All careening about!'

'Really! Imagine if you were in Africa and struck one of the natives, one of those women who carry fruit on their heads!'

'Yes, damned difficult that . . . and the flies.'

'I say, I bought a pair of those Alpine sandals recently at a Polish market, or it may have been Ukrainian or Russian, it's all the same isn't it, out here . . .'

A formal welcome dinner was given by the President of the Polish company and his functionaries. When introduced to me he gave a slight nod and bowed from the waist, his heels coming together gracefully with a perceptible click. The Poles drank large quantities of vodka and briefly rested the frozen one-shot glasses in the top pockets of their suits. A toast was proposed by the President to the success of the venture.

'*Na zdrowie!*' ('Cheers!') echoed from the barren walls.

He made an inordinately long speech, simultaneously translated in whispers by Dr Grabski. The President, Dr Zaleski, was a curious mixture of qualities – a man of the old Polish school who possessed the studied, elegant manners of the trained diplomat. This seemed completely at odds with the physiognomy of his staff of 'gentlemen' who had more in common with boxers or racketeers than educationalists. He had been an important minister during the communist period and it struck me with a sudden humorous force that they were in adult education for the money.

The meal was modest but the vodka was free-flowing. Table manners were impeccable and *politesse* reigned supreme. Everyone waited to begin eating at the same moment and as guests we were always served first. One of the very first Polish words I learned with enthusiasm was *Smacznego!* (*bon appétit!*).

I was unexpectedly called upon to reply. I returned the toast and my mind raced over the little I knew about the country. I spoke of the noble history of the Polish people, the adventure of the visit, hopes for the future. More drinking ensued and then singing of the old war songs.

Apart from the unflappable Richard, who had been to public school and was inured to deprivation, the members of the team began to crack under the cultural differences surprisingly early on. At the outset these English expatriates posed deeper problems than the Poles. The food began the motivational rot – fatty sausage, tripe and chicken hearts, liver and tinned vegetables, blood sausage mixed with buckwheat and served with onions, stale bread, cheese curling on the plate, cold pasta with warm strawberry sauce washed down with a pink, faintly perfumed, gelatinous potato drink called *kisiel*.

Geoff had an instant character clash with Dr Grabski. He argued with him noisily on the dark concrete landing. Grabski was a nervous figure who kissed the proffered hand of the ladies in the chivalric Polish manner and had a Ph.D. in Linguistics. His particular dislike was inspecting the cesspit. He would finger his immaculate collar and ease his neck as he gazed down with horror into the murky depths. A man mercurial in mood, indecisive under stress, markedly panicky as he swung between low self-confidence and a sense of unfounded superiority. He often withheld details of staff meetings and then evinced critical surprise when one did not attend. Knowledge, under the former regime, was power and it could be an advantage not to share it, an attitude that persists. Sensing his weakness, Geoff urged me to 'Get in there and lay down the law. Grabski is a bastard. Hit him hard! Show him who's boss! Squash him down!' The neo-colonial British spirit readily rejuvenated.

'Take a low profile, old boy – no fuss – not now – keep the old head down early on. Culture and language, culture and language,' cautioned Richard.

'Listen mate, this ain't Cheltenham. This geezer wants a knock,' said Nick.

David said, 'Well, you could . . . perhaps . . . I feel we . . . you know . . . we might . . .' and moved his long Morris dancer's legs back and forth indecisively across the filthy carpet.

On a more optimistic note, we had expected that the Polish company trainees would be all male, but it turned out that they were mostly young women in their twenties. Eighty on each intake and they stayed for a month. I could scarcely contain my pleasure at this piece of news – cooped up in a remote forest conference centre during the winter with almost a hundred beautiful young Polish women – it could hardly be called hardship. The sad reality was that many were recently married, some with small children, and they shared their rooms in pairs. However there was little for them to do in the evening apart from go down to the coffee bar for beer and dancing, followed by gruelling parties in the rooms afterwards.

'We're in Room 233 and we've got vodka!' came the late phone call on my lime green melamine phone. Twenty bottles in the fridge for a party of thirty.

Poles have an enviable ability to make a festive occasion or a great party out of very few resources except the pleasure of simply being together and a few bottles of good vodka. Recent European Union regulations have meant the sad demise of the small 250ml size known affectionately as a *ćwiarteczka*. It was excellent if one required a 'stiffener' to start the day or cope with a punishing communist moment. Its passing has been lamented the length and breadth of the country. No more Poles cutting off their own heads with a chainsaw for a bet, as occurred recently during a vodka binge in a forest. No more nuns ploughing the convent tractor into lines of parked cars after intoxicating work in the fields. Poles sing, dance, joke, shout and laugh with an intensity unknown in the West.

It was customary to welcome the students in the Great Conference Hall that rose through two storeys in what they came to call 'The Prison'. Brass chandeliers burned before socialist realist mosaics depicting lyrically happy and healthy agricultural workers, Polish drillers with bulging muscles and grain gatherers with bursting bosoms. The re-crowned Polish eagle winged effortlessly above an array of defunct television monitors and electronic mixing equipment. No breakfast and no water were available the first day. The lights in the hall flickered ominously and finally went out during Dr Grabski's speech of welcome. We sat in darkness.

'That's a good sign! It means something is happening,' he commented.

Dr Grabski tended to overreact when any complaint was made. Geoff criticized the unstable tables in the computer room. (Signs such as 'Insert cassette and secure with chair' failed to build his confidence in the available technology.) It took all my diplomacy and tact to prevent the team from leaving altogether when the filters failed on the bore water supply, shirts were tanned in the wash and we were required to bathe in scalding brown water. The satellite dish, our sole contact with the outside world, was unable to rotate as the mechanism was jammed with jackdaw feathers. Clearly the Polish project was going to be a form of military campaign.

CHAPTER 2

The Eagle's Nest

My knowledge of Poland before setting out was limited to the conventional stereotype: grinding poverty; a grey country hacked to pieces during the Second World War; forests soaked in partisan blood and the site of unspeakable death camps; a depressing Soviet satellite. The collective European memory of this nation has been systematically erased by wave upon wave of invaders and occupiers. Yet by 1582 the Polish-Lithuanian Commonwealth stretched from Poznań in the west almost to Smolensk in the east and included Kiev and vast tracts of the Wild Plains of the Ukraine as well as most of what are now known as the Baltic States to the north. It was the largest and one of the most powerful realms of early modern Europe. Geography has always worked against the country's fortunes and affected the psychology of its people. The history of Poland and its fluctuating borders is one of the most complex in the region.

Until the twentieth century the vibrant colours of the Orient lived in a unique relationship with the grey melancholy of the Romantic north in the immense tracts of land between the borders of Western Europe and Asia patronizingly referred to in the West as the 'Eastern Marches'. The Roman legions had failed to subjugate this vast geographical area. The notion of Sarmatism, an ever-present perfume that lingers over Polish history into the present, deserves closer examination. In sixteenth-century Poland, alongside what was a common European aesthetic pursuit of the ideals of ancient Rome and Greece, the extraordinary and contradictory racial notion of Sarmatism came to rule the minds of the Polish nobility or *szlachta*.[1]

This exclusive, mythomaniacal, ferociously extravagant and xenophobic concept grew from the stubborn but rather illogical belief that the Poles were descended from the Sarmatians, an aristocratic warrior caste related to the Scythians with origins in Iran. Next to nothing was known of their culture and way of life apart from their passion for the horse, their legendary women warriors and their love of magnificent gold and jewelled ornament. Historically the nomadic Sarmatians from the Pontic Steppe had moved into southeastern Europe in the fourth century BC and settled between the Vistula and the Dnieper rivers. In their slow migration westwards they occupied variable expanses of what is now considered East Central Europe. The Ossetians of the Caucasus are their only living descendents.

Herodotus described the origin of the Sarmatians as the fearless progeny of young Scythian men and Amazon women. This picturesque and largely invented genealogical, cultural and militaristic heritage advantageously distinguished the *szlachta* from what they felt were the less attractive and inferior Slavic roots of the peasantry. Their mercurial and volatile temperament suited an imagined descent from wild nomadic horsemen and warrior women.

Over time the Sarmatian style developed into a fully fledged ideology of noble 'golden freedom' which completely permeated *szlachta* thought. However, self-serving arrogance caused a neglect of politics and gave rise to an exhibitionist philosophy of grandiose feasting and opulent Ottoman, Persian or Tatar display. Polish

1 *Szlachta* is a Polish term of unclear definition but in simplified terms may be considered as the nobility or noble estate. Joseph Conrad translated it as the 'Equestrian Order' in a letter to John Galsworthy in 1907. This culturally, economically and religiously diversified group were characterised by definite traditions, obligations, privileges and laws. Large by Western European standards, they made up some 10% of the population and identified themselves with the country itself. Some were fabulously wealthy, some comfortably off while others were landless and poor but all considered themselves as absolute equals. They enjoyed many privileges, were not obliged to pay taxes and were exempt from import and export duties. All were tremendously aware of their distinctive noble status. Despite being expected to defend the country as their duty, many displayed lamentable self-serving behaviour when Poland was under external threat. The *szlachta* contributed in various ways to the partition and the destruction of the nation, reducing it to a mere state of mind for almost a hundred and fifty years. The *szlachta* and all noble titles were abolished under the Polish Republic and Constitution of 17 March, 1921.

embassies became famous throughout Europe for their receptions. The populace of Moscow and Rome thrilled to hundreds of sumptuously caparisoned horses dyed cornelian and white with ostrich plumes and silver breast-plates. They gaped at running janissaries and camels draped in feathers burdened with the magnate's travelling library. Horses were deliberately shod with loose golden shoes that flew from their hooves across the cobbles into the astounded crowd.

Much *szlachta* wealth was worn on the person in the form of caps of fur and pearls, *żupans* of crimson damask, *kontusz* lined with silk and decorated with studs of gold set with precious stones – rubies, sapphires, garnets, and turquoises.[2] The assistance of at least one servant was required to tie the long, broad silk sash in cloth of gold or silver known as the '*Słuck* belt', decorated with delicate floral patterns. The men shaved their heads in a type of 'pudding-basin' style, occasionally leaving a long pony-tail dangling from the crown of a shaven skull. Despite fighting Turk and Tatar, these defenders of the faith, the 'bulwark of Christendom', perversely adopted the enemy's spectacular oriental costume and dazzling military accoutrements to the point where confusion of combatants sometimes reigned on the battlefield.

As a class the *szlachta* preserved their power and moderated their distrust of royalty by contriving to elect their king, a unique phenomenon in Europe. The establishment of the notorious *liberum veto* in the *Sejm* (Parliament) during the seventeenth century gave any single envoy the right to block any present legislation with the words, '*Nie pozwalam!*' ('I do not permit!')[3]. The *liberum veto* developed over time into an *idée fixe* and was increasingly abused by self-interested poorer *szlachta*. The notion of this 'golden freedom' had catastrophic results on the stability of the Commonwealth,

2 The *żupan* was a long gown worn below the knee made of a decorative, sometimes richly patterned fabric such as silk, worn only by Polish nobleman usually under a garment called a *kontusz*. Padded versions were worn under armour. The *kontusz* was a long coat-like garment also worn below the knee in soft wool or fabric heavier than that of the *żupan* and lined with silk or fur with slit sleeves that could be thrown over the shoulders in summer. They were normally in a contrasting colour or pattern to the *żupan* underneath and were generously cut with pleats to allow freedom for riding or walking. This uniquely Polish combination was worn from the mid seventeenth century to the early nineteenth century.

3 No legislation in the Polish Parliament (*Sejm*) could be passed without complete unanimity, a potent symbol of incipient insanity that was derided throughout Europe.

and 'leads many to conclude the Poles had parted with their senses.'[4] The great diversity of cultures and religions that lay within the realm was accepted as an established fact but the *szlachta* were riding the country to death. Foreign powers manipulated their pawns to exercise this veto in the *Sejm*. Politics and wealth were controlled by the most powerful families who flew at each other's throats given any opportunity.

By 1718 Russia had offered the Commonwealth 'friendly cooperation'. The first tentacles of domination that would finally suffocate the nation for the next two hundred and seventy years began their insidious work. By the mid-eighteenth century the power of the Commonwealth had degenerated to the point of its becoming the most chaotic and backward state in Europe. Through the continued use of the notorious *liberum veto* it had become the laughing stock of efficient European governments. The country was ruled and then lost by the elected Saxon King Augustus III, a regent 'obese, indolent and virtually incapable of thought'[5] who squandered his resources patronizing the arts in the creation of an opulent, magnificent but ultimately ruinous court at Dresden.

The decadence of the Polish-Lithuanian Commonwealth in the first half of the eighteenth century is personified by Karol Radziwiłł, a wealthy and eccentric member of 'the murky and stagnant pond that was the world of the *szlachta*'.[6] He was known to everyone as 'My Dear', his favourite form of address to all those he met. 'I live like a Radziwiłł – the king can do what he likes.'[7] In a drunken stupor he was liable to impulsively shoot 'like a dog' any dinner guest he considered disagreeable. His father, the Hetman of Lithuania (the most senior military commander next to the king), was similarly mercurial but laudably followed his violence by tearful repentance before the Virgin in his private chapel. (Besides attacking guests Karol's other favourite armed activity was shooting 'flying bison'. His servants catapulted these huge creatures into the air from massive launchers hidden in the primeval forest surrounding his

4 *The Polish Way: A Thousand-year History of the Poles and their Culture,* Adam Zamoyski (London 1987) p. 206

5 Ibid., p. 211

6 *Poland's Last King and English Culture,* Richard Butterwick (Oxford 1998) p. 73

7 Op.cit., Zamoyski p. 199

castle. Karol would take careful aim and fire. He was considered a crack shot and unfailingly brought down his quarry.)

By 1795 Poland had been swept off the map, a victim of colonization and lack of political vigilance, partitioned by Prussia, Russia and Austria, transformed into merely a state of mind. Thomas Carlyle described the country at that time as having 'ripened' into a 'beautifully phosphorescent rot-heap'.[8] The influence of Poland was extinguished. Before my sojourn I knew next to nothing of this history.

Since the eighteenth century at least, Poles have considered themselves predominantly Western and Christian, although this was not always the case. Echoes of Roman Byzantium remain. The result is their psychology often appears stranded in a world located somewhere between East and West. Perceptions abroad dwell almost exclusively on the murderous legacy of the Second World War and of forests soaked in blood. Some young Poles think Chopin is a type of vodka or an asteroid or an airport. I was asked recently by a young Australian Pole, 'What is communism?'

Being Australian and brought up in the New World, I have never been exposed to the conventional European prejudices and forgetfulness concerning Poland. My Irish ancestry and a volatile colonial background of congenital anti-authoritarianism and individualism has no doubt assisted me in a positive outlook towards Poland. I shared the misplaced lack of self-confidence common to the psychology of colonial nations. Betrayals by allies in wartime have a familiar ring to Australians. My inclination towards 'the demon drink', my own Catholicism and my admiration of the fearless Polish explorer of Australia Sir Paul Edmund Strzelecki helped me approach the country with confidence. As a youth I heartily agreed with Strzelecki when he wrote convincingly of his need to strenuously avoid being 'shut up hermetically within a dry circle of utility and most infernally inoculated with the disease of domestic felicity.'

The Poles I came to know later in England were quite familiar with the history of Western Europe. Anglo-Saxons on the other hand knew scarcely any history of Poland apart from the Nazi legacy of the

8 *History of Frederick II of Prussia, called Frederick the Great*, Thomas Carlyle (London 1858–65)

Auschwitz crematoria. In 1920 Joseph Conrad lamented 'I have long been aware of Western Europe's ignorance of the character, history and ideals of the Polish nation.'[9] The national characteristics of splendid excess, perversity and violent individualism were almost obliterated by the reductionist philosophy of Lenin.[10]

Edmund Burke, reflecting on the first partition of the country in 1772, considered this 'breakfast' as 'the first very great breach in the modern political system of Europe.'[11] On the final partition of Poland in 1795 he remarked 'with respect to us, Poland might be, in fact, considered as a country in the moon'. Not a great deal has changed to modify his view of the country despite accession to the European Union. Since Napoleon created the Duchy of Warsaw in the early nineteenth century the cultural heritage of the nation has been systematically packed up and stolen, destroyed or moved abroad in endless railway wagons. Lacking natural borders, reconstructed modern Poland is a shadow of the country which existed before the Second World War. Entire cities were lost, entire cities gained. A country that for hundreds of years had enjoyed the peaceful co-existence of Germans, Tatars, Jews, Poles, and Eastern Slavs among its inhabitants, one of the most culturally diverse and religiously tolerant nations in Europe, was paradoxically transformed into an ethnically homogeneous, massively 'Polish' nation. The Jews were murdered, the Ukrainians and Poles ethnically cleansed each other or were 'repatriated' in bouts of brutal borderland slaughter, the Germans simply expelled. The ancient territories of Galicia and Volhynia were erased forever from European memory. Nazi crimes and the ruthless Soviet policies that ensued continue to overwhelm wider historical thinking about the country.

The canvas of Europe in the historical imagination of those born after the Second World War remains partial. In March 1946 at Fulton, Missouri, Winston Churchill erected a metaphorical Iron Curtain across Europe and crystallized for an entire generation a mental map he assisted in creating. The conflagration effectively

---

9 Correspondence with Count Eustachy Sanguszko

10 Vladimir Nabokov pithily observed of Lenin to the critic Edmund Wilson, 'a pail of the milk of human kindness with a dead rat at the bottom.'

11 *The Annual Register*, 1772, i.2.

divided not only nations but the consciousness of Europeans from themselves, hermetically sealing the development of cultures and the export of talent. It disinherited the European mind. Invaders are masters of the liquidation of conscience as well as of monuments. The introduction of the lie as governing principle was perhaps the crime with the longest heritage in the years under communism. A molasses of bureaucracy was created in which one still feels as trapped as an insect in amber.

The English politician Enoch Powell observed that nations as much as individuals live largely in their imaginations. British history is an imperial history of many triumphs. That of Poland is a victim history of many heroic failures. The historical shortcomings of the Polish nation have long been obvious: the myths, mistrustfulness, patrician splendour and peasant shabbiness, xenophobia and impulsiveness, the fumbled victories, 'like a madman being led by the hand of an angel' as the German author Müller put it. A man who favours the rational, pragmatic and imperial temperament of the conqueror will not find much to sustain him in Polish history. But the rhapsodic temperament, the lover of charm and hospitality, the brave and reckless in life, the imaginative observer, the advocate of freedom will surely be satisfied. The lover of horses and horsemen, the patriot who treasures honour and fidelity above all, the romantic who favours the heroic gesture over the consequence, the burning emotion over the achievement, sincerity of intention over regularity of thought – such as these will mine a rich seam.

CHAPTER 3

'Musical Genius etc.'

– Joseph Elsner, from his third and final musical
report on Fryderyk Chopin

On an intensely cold day in January I began my first walk through
the city in the district known as Praga on the eastern bank of the
Vistula. The finest view of Warsaw is from this side of the river. I
strolled through the muddy and bleak Paderewski Park to the
'Russian market' in the *Stadion Dziesięciolecia* (10th Anniversary
Stadium). A faint air of criminality and exoticism haunted the largest
street market in Europe. Russians, Africans, Vietnamese, Tatars,
Belarusians, Ukrainians and Poles sold counterfeit perfume, furs,
cigars and caviar from kiosks and rickety tables. Russian military uniforms and equipment were draped about, as were labelled jeans,
imitation leather boots and hand-knotted rugs from the Caucasus.
Faces of great character and individuality greeted any prospective
purchaser of black market alcohol or pornography. In 1955 the arena
had hosted a celebrated Festival of Youth and later communist regime
festivities but the building was allowed to decay. This colourful and
atmospheric market will be forced to close by the end of 2007. The
site is likely to become a futuristic national stadium hosting a number
of matches for the European Football Championships in 2012.

Two elderly peasant women were scrubbing the filthy bollards of
the car park with steaming, soapy water. A Polish *Syrena* car (much
loved during the communist period) sported pink fake-fur seat covers
with two dustbin lids covering openings cut in the roof in an attempt
to turn it into a racy convertible. Nearby an AIDS victim was begging,

his body entirely enclosed in black rubbish bags, the small slits cut for his eyes covered by sunglasses. Primitive fears abounded in those days. In an underpass stinking of urine and daubed with graffiti old ladies were selling the most exquisite orchids, tulips, roses and other colourful, unseasonal flowers wrapped in cellophane and silver paper. Flowers are given on almost every social and public occasion in Poland. They shone against the winter monochrome and sterile communist aesthetic like beacons of friendship.

Crossing the Vistula was cold and windy. This strange slow river of silent pulse and wide sandbars gives Warsaw a unique setting. The skyline of the city and small developments along unregulated beaches continue to evolve but in the early nineties the townscape was a curious mixture of restored medieval steeples, Orthodox domes, eighteenth-century palace facades, a miniature electricity generating station and a very few modern glass towers perched on the escarpment above the polluted water. Thin chimneys striped in red and white belched smoke and sulphurous gases which threatened to obscure the Palace of Culture and Science. This edifice used to dominate the cityscape but has now been supplanted by glittering glass skyscrapers and luxury hotels. The city paradoxically turns its back on the Vistula. Neo-commercialism has now taken over with ever larger French hypermarkets spreading throughout the suburbs.

In this first foray I had a great deal of difficulty with the names of streets. A list of changed street names was published each week. When communism imploded, certain 'heroes' from the Old Guard lost their reputations and their names were summarily removed from signage. Great confusion reigned when perfectly respectable VIPs inexplicably lost their reputations and their monuments disappeared. A personality may be suddenly rehabilitated overnight and statues of controversial figures are still being unveiled from the detritus of selective memory. There is a move to alter street names once again, consigning even the 'faintest of communist collaborators' to oblivion. The cost and inconvenience to residents and businesses could be enormous. Poles seem to love change for its own sake.

After descending from the bridge I became lost in the labyrinth of socialist concrete that led to the elegant Ostrogski Castle, the seat of the Fryderyk Chopin Society. This small Palladian palace was destroyed by the Nazis at the time of the Warsaw Uprising but was rebuilt by the communists to its courtly late-seventeenth-century appearance. The original architect, Tylman van Gameren of Utrecht, brought Dutch classicism to many buildings in Poland when he settled there in the mid-1660s.

The museum of the Society is devoted to Chopin. The lower floor documents his life in the Russian-dominated part of Poland. A feeling of sick longing for his native land emanates from the rooms, his music possessing all the yearning of the exile, his lost country a phantom limb that accompanied him through life. Glass cabinets display letters, engravings, manuscripts and other memorabilia that miraculously survived the depredations of the Nazis and the Soviets. So many of his priceless autograph manuscripts, diaries, and letters have disappeared forever in the bonfires of conflict and war. Cossacks threw his piano from the window of his sister's flat. The extreme delicacy of the manuscripts that do survive make one feel Chopin was barely a corporeal being. He likened his own writing to cobwebs.

I climbed the marble staircase to the first floor, the walls decorated with frescoes in the Pompeian style. Here a letter from Hector Berlioz (whose music Chopin loathed) addressing him affectionately as '*Chopinetto mio*', there a letter from George Sand (Aurore Dudevant) declaring her love: '*On vous adore*'. One of the most notorious and talented women in France, she wore men's clothes, vented inflammatory political opinions and smoked cigars. She horrified and terrified Chopin at their first meeting but his later affair with her was both turbulent and productive. A copy of his famous portrait by his close friend and confidant the painter Eugène Delacroix adorns a wall on the landing. George Sand ironically remains a shadowy unfinished figure cut from the original double portrait and framed separately.

Small cards informed me this was the saucer belonging to the white china cup with painted scene and gilded rim from which Chopin drank chocolate during his visits to his cultured Polish patrons the Prince and Princess Czartoryski at the Hôtel Lambert in Paris. A rose had been carelessly cast on the keyboard of the Pleyel piano he had used. The smaller dynamic range and varied colours of the early instrument suit the inherent intimacy of his smaller compositions. 'I *indicate*, the listeners must finish the picture.'

On a satin cushion lay an inscribed pocket watch given him by the famous Italian soprano Angelica Catalani following a recital given by the child prodigy at the age of ten. Displayed under glass were the letters tied with a velvet ribbon that flowed from his blighted love affair with the beautiful sixteen-year-old Maria Wodzińska whom he met in Paris and planned to marry. His love was reciprocated but her parents erected barricades against this frail suitor who was so often in poor health. This package of joy and desolation was inscribed by the composer *Moja bieda* ('My misery').

The eloquent fourth Ballade in F-minor was playing as I moved along the cases containing plaster casts of his hands, his death mask and bunches of faded violets cast aside as if in grief. The accumulated emotion of many years of familiarity with his music affected me deeply. Uncle Eddie would have loved this museum. Each year the Kościół Świętego Krzyża (Holy Cross Church) in Warsaw is the site for a concert and ceremony to celebrate Chopin's birth on 22 February 1810.[12] Wreaths are laid at the plaque behind which lies the urn that contains his heart, brought from Paris by his sister Ludwika Jędrzejewicz. His body was interred at the Père-Lachaise cemetery in Paris. It is a small and remarkably moving ceremony. Many people move forward to lay single blooms or bunches of flowers while the organist plays a festive organ work. Two beautiful children, one a tiny three-year-old in a red bobble hat, laid a single tulip. This simple ceremony set the tone of nostalgia and melancholy for the day.

After I had laid my single red rose I walked to the monumental brick Cytadela (Citadel) on Żoliborz Hill, built by the Tsarist authorities after the November Uprising of 1830 against the Russians. I wanted to immerse myself in the historical source of so much of Chopin's anguished music. Tsar Nicholas I exacted a terrible revenge for being dethroned as King of Poland. The sledges and columns of prisoners soon began to leave for Siberia. The Citadel was built high on the Vistula escarpment to intimidate Warsaw and

12 The date according to the baptismal certificate but Chopin's family always claimed he was born on 1 March, 1810.

hold thousands of political prisoners for interrogation, torture and execution. By September 1831 the Kingdom had once again fallen under the Russian yoke and a distraught Chopin wrote in his Stuttgart diary in painful, dislocated sentences

> The suburbs in ruins – burnt down – Jaś – Wiluś no doubt died on the ramparts – I see that Marcel has been imprisoned – Oh God, have You not had enough of Moscow's crimes – or – or – You are a Moscovite yourself! . . . sometimes I only groan and express my pain on the piano – I am in despair . . .[13]

An undocumented tradition states that he wrote the 'Revolutionary' Étude in C-minor and the final tempestuous Prelude in D-minor while in Stuttgart after the fall of Warsaw. Princes and nobles were humiliated and Polish officers in their thousands were exiled to the Caucasus. Intellectuals, agitators and insurrectionists were executed on the steep slopes or in the fosses of the Citadel. The spirit of fierce resistance alternating with hopeless pain and despair are the womb of Chopin's patriotic music, not the salons of Paris.

It was snowing heavily and –6°C as I laboured up the Żoliborz Hill through the neoclassical 'Execution Gate' near the site of the gallows that had stood under a broad chestnut tree. A forest of crosses on the wooded slopes marks the place where thousands suffered a miserable death, particularly following the subsequent January Uprising of 1863. After this hopeless gesture tens of thousands of young people were marched to their deaths in Siberia. The nation never recovered. Many of the leaders passed through the Wrota Iwanowskie (known as Death Gate) and along Death Road into the horrors of Pavilion X.

The approach to the museum in winter is across a bleak, open area with snow-covered cannons, broken bricks and striped sentry boxes. A black wagon once used for collecting prisoners around Warsaw for transport to Siberia was parked casually at the entrance. The museum contains fascinating documents, tickets of incarceration, chessmen made of bread, prisoner's photographs (the Tsarist

---

13 *Fryderyk Chopin: A Diary in Images*, Mieczysław Tomaszewski trans. Rosemary Hunt (Warsaw 1990) p. 92

police would shave off *half* the hair, moustache and beard to mark a convict and so prevent easy concealment). So many men of brilliant intelligence and creativity perished here between 1822 and 1925. My friend Irena, who is a custodian, says she is aware of the metallic smell of blood in the corridors. Paintings, daguerreotypes and photographs record endless lines of tattooed, tattered prisoners – portraits of men of striking intelligence and sensibility – heading off on foot into the icy wastelands. The prisoners were forced to walk some five thousand kilometres from Warsaw to Siberia, a journey that took eighteen months, if you survived. Wealthy families riding on a sledge might be permitted to accompany the condemned men. At the Siberian camp men were chained permanently night and day to their wheelbarrow, sleeping with this ghastly succubus and finally dying upon it. I slipped on the frozen cobbles of Death Road.

Conventional prejudices against Chopin remain common. Later that week I was required to go to Polish Radio to record vocabulary for a bizarre system of language learning characterized by the Central European penchant for non-rational and physiologically determined methods of language acquisition. This method used a type of bio-feedback allegedly pioneered by East German Army brainwashing techniques. The learner lies on an airbed and dons a set of headphones and a pair of mirrored goggles containing red lamps. He then attaches a tube to his nose and all three paths are wired into a black box containing a tape player and wave generator. Hypnotic music, electronic beeps and a rich actor's voice are heard while the red lamps fade on and off in time with the learner's breathing.

We crammed into the recording engineer's Fiat 126p known affectionately in Poland as a 'Maluch'[14] and drove at suicidal speed to

14 The Polski Fiat 126p was manufactured in Poland from 1973 to 2000 under licence from Italian Fiat. They were hugely popular and eventually came to be referred to officially by their nickname 'Maluch'. This Polish word means a toddler but is sometimes used to refer colloquially to the penis. These inexpensive cars assumed an iconic status in communist Poland and featured regularly in comedy films with the car as the star. They were notoriously unreliable and I witnessed many groups of men pushing them or with their heads optimistically crammed in the engine bay, fingers pointing authoritatively and cigarettes dropping ash as the rain pelted down from leaden skies. A high-speed crash in one of these was usually fatal. Many jokes circulated about them. 'Why is that horse in the cart winking at us, Staszek?' 'Oh, he probably wants to pass.' 'Why are we driving along this wall, Staszek?' 'It's not a wall, you idiot, it's the kerb.'

arrive at a bleak communist building as it began to snow. The interior of the radio station had a 1950s feel to it: functionalist, pine-panelled and gloomy. We wandered along a labyrinth of endless, decrepit corridors to an antiquated studio containing heavy obsolete equipment with flashing lights and the whirring mechanisms familiar from Fritz Lang films. In the corners of the corridors were pieces of lavatory paper with rat poison placed in small conical heaps. Shiny pieces of tin patched the carpet. The technician talked on a lime-green telephone and set up the tape on a leviathan professional recorder. He told me the basement was used during the communist period for torture and interrogation sessions. Originally intended as the police headquarters, the building had never been used as such except for the lowest floor.

I met a female presenter from Polish TV smoking a cigarette in an amber holder and wearing a long, flared Russian coat, a fur hat, leopard-skin scarf and black boots. After 'Lara' divested herself of the Dr Zhivago apparel she retired with me to one of the recording booths behind a glass screen. Workmen passed the door carrying pails of cement. I giggled uncontrollably at the inanity of repeating such phrases as 'Pass me the red nail polish' and 'Please put my hair in curlers' which were then translated into Polish. I was also required to cluck like a chicken and bark like a dog.

The following evening a privately arranged piano recital at the Ostrogski Castle launched this futuristic learning system on an unsuspecting Polish public. There are many brilliant young Polish pianists who are desperate to play Chopin privately for a modest fee. As we were wandering around the museum during the interval, a 'gentleman' approached me and hissed close to my ear as I was gazing up at an elegant engraving of the composer.

'This Chopin, was he queer?'

'Most men of genius are a bit strange I suppose,' I replied, looking slightly puzzled.

'You not understand me. Chopin, was he a queer?'

'He had an excellent sense of humour.'

'Nein! This Chopin, was he . . . an fairy . . . an homosexual?' he spat out. I stammered something but was shocked into silence.

'Um. He was quite popular with the ladies as far as I know. Why do you ask?'

'Well, who was this George he was in the love? Living with George in Paris. There are letters here.'

'Well, actually George was a woman. Aurore Dudevant. She was a great French novelist.'

'Ah ha! They were then, how you say, dressing on the cross. Chopin looks as a weak woman,' he smirked.

'Well, George had a very strong personality, smoked cigars and was involved in politics.'

'Ach so! He is the feminine man and she the masculine woman. Now I know!'

I almost laughed aloud at this stereotypical view and murmured some bland response. It coloured the way I listened to the remainder of the recital as this militantly masculine individual squirmed in boredom beside me.

CHAPTER 4

Warsaw the Phoenix

Warsaw is the great survivor, the most representative capital of Europe yet perhaps the most unloved. This unpretentious, often desperately anti-aesthetic city reflects all the ideological, murderous and nationalist obsessions of the twentieth century. It is a city that has witnessed inconceivable examples of courage, heroic resistance and formidable reconstruction. An impossible leap of the imagination is required to deal with the scale of death and destruction and the statement of faith that followed. Now straining to become fashionable again, the city exhibits a Western made-up face to the world hoping for acceptance. My friends had thought me insane to leave the Palladian splendours of Bath. If you *must* go to Poland, why not historic Kraków? they cried.

It was the *intimations* of a glorious past that first attracted me to this city and this country. Signs, indications, ruins and reconstructions exercise my imagination in a way unknown in the immaculately preserved museums and scientifically restored monuments in the West. The history of Poland is a manifestation of *absence*, mysteries to be read from fragments, the residue of human action. Almost the entire movable cultural heritage of Poland has been systematically stolen, burnt or despoiled since at least Napoleonic times, going back even to the Tatar Golden Horde. The Nazis implemented a complete state-sponsored apparatus to facilitate the theft of artworks followed by their sale or destruction. Many survived only through displays of tremendous courage and patriotism. A chipped jewel, a dented monstrance, a military button, a captured Oriental tent, a shattered Teutonic castle on a timeless riverbank speak to me eloquently of resistance and sacrifice.

In 1820 William Wordsworth embarked on a tour of Europe and wrote a poem on contemplating the neglected ruins of Fort Fuentes on an eminence at the head of Lake Como.

O Silence of Nature, how deep is thy sway,
When whirlwind of human destruction is spent,
Our tumults appeased, and our strifes passed away

These lines describe so well a familiar feeling standing before a devastated Polish palace, *dwór*[15] or historic battlefield turned over to agriculture. 'That incorporeal Poland, Poland, that hypnotic phantom' as Tadeusz Konwicki put it in his remarkable book, *The Polish Complex*, an incisive portrait of the Polish psyche. I was privileged to experience the 'silence of nature' before the burgeoning tourist industry began to restore a lifeless splendour to what was once magnificent decay.

Warsaw brings into question the nature of memory itself and the responsibility one owes to a fading past. The continued existence of this city is a miracle and it would be churlish to criticize its mostly unlovely appearance. Between the wars Warsaw possessed one of the richest cultural and artistic scenes in Europe. The writers Isaac Bashevis Singer and Czesław Miłosz, both Nobel prize winners, worked in the capital. The concert pianists Artur Rubinstein and Ignacy Jan Paderewski performed in an atmosphere of champagne and cultivated outrageousness. The most daring cabarets such as The Sphinx, the Black Cat and the notorious Qui Pro Quo flourished in Warsaw to rival the most risqué cabaret acts in Berlin. Some considered it 'the Paris of the north'. The great painter of voluptuous and decadent nudes, Tamara de Lempicka, 'sexually voracious, theatrical,

15 The type of manor house which appears throughout Polish history, literature, painting and opera as a powerful symbol of civilized country life and the manners of the nobility or *szlachta*. The most uplifting Polish values had their origin and were enshrined in the *dwór* by literary exiles during the 'romantic' nineteenth century, a period distinguished by its resistance to the partitioning powers. The national epic *Pan Tadeusz* by Adam Mickiewicz presents the *dwór* as almost a living character in the poem. The lifestyle of the manor was accepted as the essence of the nation. The *dwór* released noble patriots for battle and was a source of the most powerful nostalgia for what was lost, looted or destroyed by marauding foreign powers. Most were later expropriated or demolished by the communists in the cause of 'social justice'.

stylish, smart and talented',[16] spent her formative years in this Warsaw café society. No city in Europe has suffered as much and no city demands of the wanderer at every turn such an intense ethical stance concerning human behaviour at inconceivable extremes. Warsaw has been destroyed and looted many times through its tumultuous history at the hands of the Tatars, Swedes, Germans and Russians but has always been rebuilt by its citizens. The city adopts the attitude of a Stoic in the face of the Russian proverb:

> You have no time to say Ooo Ooo
> Before the black bear sits on you

In a history increasingly bleached by time, the city suffered gross physical destruction by the Nazis, murderous repressions without parallel in revenge for the Warsaw Ghetto Uprising of April 1943 and the Warsaw Uprising of August 1944. The Warsaw Ghetto was the largest and most infamous of the Nazi ghettos where almost 480,000 Jews[17] died from either disease, malnutrition, execution or were murdered at Treblinka. In the Ghetto it was said that everyone had 'death in his eyes' or 'a skull instead of a face'.[18] The creation of it necessitated the displacement of over 200,000 Poles and Jews from their homes and businesses. A popular saying among Germans at the time was 'The Poles we hate instinctively; the Jews we hate in accordance with orders.'[19] The displaced lost everything.

The Nazis established the Warsaw Ghetto by decree on 12 October 1940 – on Yom Kippur, the Day of Atonement. It was divided into three main sections. In the 'Little Ghetto' wealthy Jews

---

16 *Tamara De Lempicka: A Life of Deco and Decadence*, Laura Claridge (London 2000)

17 Statistic from *Secret City: The Hidden Jews of Warsaw 1940–1945*, Gunnar S. Paulsson (New Haven 2002) p. 1 An extraordinary account of Jews in hiding with carefully researched statistics and many astounding individual stories of courageous Jewish resistance. See also *Words Outlive Us: Voices from the Warsaw Ghetto*, ed. Michał Grynberg trans. Philip Boehm (New York 2002) p. 1. This is a heartbreaking collection of first-hand testimonies of life in the ghetto. These eyewitness accounts were written by a remarkable range of people from all walks of life either in the ghetto or clandestinely outside, discovered in the rubble of Warsaw or passed through the hands of survivors. The grimmest of truths lies in the details that speak from pages that 'challenge us to imagine the unimaginable'. This is individual suffering by real people and not the sanitized, meaningless generalizations trotted out as contemporary 'history'. Indispensable if you have the courage not to turn aside.

18 Op. cit., *Words Outlive Us*, p. 145

19 Op. cit., Paulsson p. 240

and the intelligentsia lived well. The pianist Władysław Szpilman (whose memoir of the Ghetto, *The Pianist*, was an international bestseller) wrote of the Café Nowoczesna: 'This was the meeting place of the rich; dripping with gold and glittering with diamonds; this was where painted harlots, at tables bedecked with delicacies, seduced the wartime noveaux riches, to the accompaniment of popping champagne corks.'[20] He went on to describe the hunger and illness of the poor in the 'Big Ghetto', dead children lying uncollected in the streets. The third section was the industrial ghetto where the Jewish workers and their families were worked to death as slave labour.[21]

The Ghetto witnessed the departure of the packed cattle trucks from the *Umschlagplatz* (Shipment Square), the transport hub for the extermination camp of Treblinka and the Lublin labour camps. The Jewish police 'delivered' up to twelve thousand souls per day to the Nazis in the *Umschlagplatz* to die or work as slaves. Desperate parents drugged their infants and concealed them in knapsacks and suitcases which were often lost on the carts. Babies woke in the terrifying dark, buried alive, never to be seen again. Jews were driven to the overcrowded holding areas of the 'Hospital for Infectious Diseases', a building swimming in faeces, urine and blood 'as if designed by a satanic architect'. Cattle cars were packed with a hundred and twenty people in a space designed for twenty horses. And then the gas.

After a tiring day at the *'Umschlag'* one sadistic SS officer habitually drove around the Ghetto streets in a Mercedes sports car picking off strays with his revolver. Another asked a woman carrying a baby on her shoulder if she had had a difficult day's work. She responded positively to his gesture of concern. He then asked her if she would like a loaf of bread. She thanked him profusely for his generosity. As she walked away with optimism in her heart he took careful aim and shot her baby through the head.

20 *Śmierć miasta (Death of a City)*, Władysław Szpilman, compiled by Jerzy Waldorff (Warsaw 1946). This is the original unedited text of *The Pianist*, trans. Anthea Bell (London 1999).

21 An unparalleled expression in Western music of this suffering is the seven agonizing minutes of *Ein Überlebender aus Warschau Op. 46* (A Survivor from Warsaw) (1947) for orchestra and narrator by Arnold Schoenberg. In a text written by Schoenberg himself in English (a narrator living in the sewers of Warsaw), German (a violent Nazi sergeant barking orders to the gas chambers) and Hebrew (the prayer *Shem'a Yisroel*) he expresses how consolation in extreme adversity can come from song and prayer.

The Ghetto uprising in April 1943, led by Mordechai Anielewicz, was an act of inconceivable courage that has achieved formidable symbolic and moral stature. Yet after ninety per cent of the Jews had been murdered and the Ghetto destroyed and replaced by the concentration camp *KL Warschau* (where tens of thousands of Gentile Poles died) there remained in Warsaw 'the largest clandestine community of Jews anywhere in Europe, in fact probably the largest community of people that has lived in hiding in any city, ever.'[22] Some ten per cent of Poles in Warsaw helped Jews to hide, and many more provided food, clothes and money for their Jewish friends. Few were betrayed to the common enemy. Some 28,000 Jews hid on the Aryan side while so-called 'wild' Jews returned to the burned-out ruins of the 'wild' Ghetto and lived like rats.

An iconic moment of German–Polish reconciliation occurred in December 1970 when the then Federal Chancellor of Germany, Willy Brandt, spontaneously fell to his knees in a silent apology at the memorial to Jews murdered by the SS in the Ghetto. 'On the abyss of German history and carrying the burden of the millions who were murdered, I did what people do when words fail them,' he commented later. This kneeling figure became a symbolic image of the way forward for a mercilessly divided Europe. It was with a terrible irony, then, that late one summer afternoon I watched some young Poles swig alcopops in the holiday heat, adjust their iPods, kick and dislodge some ageing marble slabs on the *Umschlagplatz* memorial, laugh at an obscenely daubed swastika and pass by.

Abandoned by the Allies in thrall to Stalin, the valiant but hopeless Warsaw Uprising of August 1944 was fought against the SS and the *Wehrmacht* by the AK[23] in blazing buildings, cataracts of rubble and stinking sewers by adult, youth and child. For two months a kilometre-high pall of smoke and fire lay over the city. Some two hundred thousand of the most promising young people, many of

---

22 Op.cit., Paulsson, p. 2

23 *Armia Krajowa* AK or Home Army. This was the largest Resistance movement in Europe and was formed in February 1942. It was an extension of the Polish Armed Forces and as such possessed a strong political and legal framework. An armed uprising against the occupying power was considered its natural duty.

whom were teenage scouts, heroically sacrificed themselves for 'freedom'. Incandescent with rage at an upstart capital that dared resist his paranoia, Hitler ordered the systematic annihilation of the city and its inhabitants. Those not slaughtered in the burning tenements or immolated by flame-throwers were drowned in sewage beneath the streets or shot upon emerging from manholes, their bodies covered in excrement.

The Russians applied their infamous 'hyena principle' of waiting for the twitching corpse to die. The carnage of the uprising was witnessed from the district of Praga on the opposite bank of the Vistula by a cynical, complicit and anaesthetized Russian army before their eventual 'liberation' of the smoking ruins. To them the battle was simply a tactical element in their drive on Berlin and part of their longer-term strategy to deny independence to Poland. The aim of the insurgents was to valiantly resist in an expression of political and moral unity – the all too familiar Polish struggle for freedom and dignity. 'This was the revolt of a fly against two giants. One giant waited beyond the river for the other to kill the fly.'[24] Scarcely a shot needed to be fired over the lifeless rubble. Neither cat nor dog nor human moved there, only rats scurried among the dead.

> Your victorious scarlet army
> Has stopped beneath Warsaw's fiery clouds
> And like a vulture with a carcass sates itself
> On a handful of madmen, who are dying in the ruins[25]

Mention of the August 1944 Uprising inevitably unleashes a fiery response from Poles to this day. It was an action of profound controversy in which detail battles with detail. The resistance is celebrated in memorial services and symbolic re-enactments every year. Warsaw stops dead at 5.00pm on 1 August, the time the uprising began. Sirens wail, traffic ceases to move and people are frozen in time on the pavements. At night the war cemetery flickers with oceans of candles. It is impossible for a generation unaccustomed to

24 *The Captive Mind*, Czesław Miłosz trans. Jane Ziolonko (London 1953) p. 96

25 from the poem *We Await You* by Joe from 'Parasol' (the code name for an AK Unit). The poet Józef Szczepański was known in the AK by his code name 'Ziutek'. Poem trans. Norman Davies in *Rising '44: The Battle for Warsaw* (London 2003) p. 687

war or occupation to imagine the horror of those days. Recorded history sanitizes the most grotesque in human experience: even the magnificent, sometimes harrowing new museum devoted to the Uprising provides the visitor with an immaculate dry sewer of new bricks devoid of stench.[26]

My friend Wojciech Potocki, a Warsaw architect and painter, was just a baby during the Rising, but his father was an active member of the AK or Home Army. Like many elderly Poles his parents were unwilling to discuss the war with him but he remembers a few family stories. Before the outbreak of violence his mother used to wheel him around the streets sleeping peacefully on smuggled guns hidden in the bottom of his pram. He told me many stories, any one of which would be sufficient for life.

The AK had captured a German tank and were jubilantly about to board it when Wojciech suddenly began to cry in his parents' nearby apartment. His father came onto the balcony and called to his mother to come as the baby seemed particularly distressed. His mother reluctantly left her friends, irritated by this 'domestic' summons. Shortly after entering the building the booby-trapped tank exploded in a ball of fire as a member of the AK lifted the hatch, killing and wounding many nearby. The cries of her baby had saved her life.

On another occasion after an *Aktion* (an operation which involved the assembly, deportation and murder of Jews by the Nazis during the Holocaust) a German soldier was about to shoot Wojciech's father in the street. His mother begged for his life on her knees. The soldier kept raising his rifle and lowering it indecisively as the pitiful pleading continued. The soldier suddenly noticed a pet red squirrel in a cage on a balcony. In frustration, and unable to overcome his need to kill *something*, he shot the squirrel dead and stormed off shouting imprecations.

Finally, his father was stalking a German sniper holed up in the rubble of the city. He had crept up behind him when the German suddenly swung around and fired. A click indicated his pistol was empty. Wojciech's father then fired his own pistol but he too was out of ammunition. Both laughed and made their respective escapes.

---

26 In Andrzej Wajda's gruelling movie *Kanał* there is a powerful recreation of those Dantesque scenes of horror beneath the streets. The film accurately depicts the tragic betrayal, lies, disillusionment and heroism of human existence in time of war.

Wojciech believes the Warsaw Uprising was a complete waste of the finest in Polish youth and an act of profound irrationality and cynical manipulation. Yet his parents never regretted their actions during those terrible weeks.

After what many Poles consider the treacherous sell-out of the country at the Teheran Conference and the long-drawn-out Yalta accords, Warsaw experienced another half century of Soviet slavery as a reward for her Allied war effort. The paranoid NKVD (*Narodnyĭ Komissariat Vnutrennikh Del* or People's Commissariat of Internal Affairs) proceeded to shoot or imprison any surviving member of the Home Army they could track down who had been 'collaborating with' (i.e. fighting) the German enemy. Close to ninety-eight per cent of the Jewish population of Warsaw died during the Second World War and around twenty-five per cent of the Polish population. The war and uprising cost the city some 720,000 lives, half its pre-war adult population, 'undoubtedly the greatest slaughter perpetrated within a single city in human history'.[27]

After being almost completely destroyed by barbarian lust, the city miraculously revived in a wave of historicist nostalgia and selfless labour on an unprecedented scale. Poles began clearing the monumental mound of rubble that was Warsaw by hand. Over eighty per cent of the city had been destroyed. In the eighteenth century the Venetian painter Bernardo Bellotto[28] had painted many meticulously observed views of the city and the surrounding Vistula landscape which were used in a careful regeneration of the original appearance of the Old Town. (Many who knew both towns considered the new version superior.)

In addition to replicating the historical appearance of the city, Varsovians constructed a breathtaking and architecturally faithful reconstruction of the sixteenth-century Royal Castle. The destiny of the Royal Castle is that of the city itself. The statue of King Zygmunt

27 Op.cit., Paulsson p. 1

28 Bernado Bellotto was born in Venice in 1720 and died in Warsaw in 1780. He was a nephew of the famous Giovanni Antonio Canal (known as Canaletto) and he often rejoiced in being mistaken for his more illustrious relative, signing himself *Il Canaletto*. His superb vistas were similarly concerned with the interplay of elaborate architectural detail and atmospheric lighting. King Stanisław Augustus commissioned him to paint twenty-six scenes for the 'Canaletto Room' at the Royal Castle. Much of the post-war reconstruction of the Royal Castle and Old Town was based on the miraculous survival of his many detailed *verdutas* of the city.

III, the king who made Warsaw the capital of Poland, was blasted from the top of the nearby Kolumna Zygmunta III (Sigismund Column) by a tank in 1944. His image lying amidst the rubble and ashes of the city and then restored to its plinth became a potent symbol of death and renewal. The ruination of the castle was shockingly effective as demolition squads were allegedly advised where best to place the charges by prominent Polish art historians. Fortunately, thousands of original sculptural and architectural fragments as well as furnishings were secretly and courageously saved before the final annihilation and many surviving fragments were incorporated into the new walls.

Due to ideological communist barriers against this national symbol, reconstruction work did not begin until 1971. Special funds were finally established to which Poles freely contributed and many specialist craftsmen such as goldsmiths, stonemasons and carpenters offered their services and materials unpaid for many years. The rebuilding of the Royal Castle became a symbol of national unity and patriotic impulse. It was in the opulent ballroom of this castle that Napoleon made his celebrated remarks on the beauty of Polish women.

At the conclusion of the Second World War acres of sterile apartment blocks were constructed on the Mazovian plain outside the restored Warsaw Old Town. They were intended by the Soviets to provide quickly built, affordable accommodation for a desperate populace. During the rebuilding families were crammed into any single apartments that survived, some living like rodents in basements liable to collapse. Those who survived in the ruins were known as 'Robinsons' after the castaway Robinson Crusoe. Running water and lavatories hardly existed. Privacy effectively disappeared. My friend Irena told me about her family and survival in the ruined city.

'There were dead bodies everywhere under the rubble. There were murders for food. Chamber pots were used as cooking pots! My father was a baker and had been a prisoner in Dachau. He refused to talk about it. He baked bread and cakes in our wrecked apartment. Mother would then sell them around Warsaw. We Poles are passionate entrepreneurs!'

'Did many people do this?'

'There were lots of small businesses like that. The enthusiasm to rebuild Warsaw was enormous! Terrific spirit, really. Great sense of humour. We treasured small things in those days. Not like now. I remember with ecstasy the taste of my first orange! We could only get them at Christmas.'

The situation was quite unprecedented and workers descended from all over Poland and East Central Europe to rebuild the capital. Tragically the reconstruction of 'the people's city' was forced to follow the ideology of the Party. The soulless nature of the residential blocks was intended to crush the spirit and standardize the mind. 'This city is the capital of a people who are evaporating into nothingness.'[29]

The official policy was that buildings conceived after 1850 were not to be reconstructed. Many fine nineteenth-century buildings that had survived the onslaught were demolished in the frenzied utopian socialist vision. Puzzling ideological choices were made which mysteriously rebuilt the facades of aristocratic palaces now used as government institutions but destroyed beautiful *fin de siècle* architecture elsewhere. The Polish architect Edmund Goldzamt mordantly observed, 'The architect of a society engaged in the building of socialism is not only an engineer of houses and streets, but also an engineer of human souls.'

'Architects' were forced to produce blocks of apartments in bleak repetitive patterns that render many Polish country towns almost identical. Humorous, even embarrassing situations arose from carelessly entering an apartment that seemed to be yours unless of course the often duplicated locks had been changed. My Polish friends invited me to their small flats in these buildings where entire extended families of five or six were expected to live in tiny two- or three-roomed apartments the size of a luxury hotel room in London's West End. Paradoxically, after the passing of the communist regime, the consumerist god of the market economy has now erected similarly vast and barren edifices of more 'inventive' architecture. Larger and more luxuriously appointed certainly, some with beautiful communal gardens, but inspired by a similarly reductionist and coercive ideology. Hypermarkets abound, their huge acreage

---

29 *A Minor Apocalypse*, Tadeusz Konwicki (New York 1983) p. 7

serviced by girls in mini-skirts on roller skates. The uglification of
Warsaw continues apace.

With a waspish sense of humour the Giełda (Stock Exchange)
took up residence in the former Communist Party headquarters
and an equally black humour placed the Ministry of Education in
the former dreaded Gestapo headquarters in Aleja Szucha, an
address the mere mention of which injected terror into the hearts
of Poles and Jews alike. Prisoners were brought here for brutal
interrogation (often to death), from the Gestapo prison Pawiak.[30]
A custodian at the Pawiak Museum told me of a woman who
became pregnant in 'Serbia', the women's prison. For their amusement the Nazis dressed her toddler in a miniature SS uniform and
trained him to wander around the prison shouting *'Achtung baby!'*
('Attention, you hags!') Vicious dogs were regularly set upon prisoners for the amusement of the guards. Today Aleja Szucha is one
of the few unrestored Nazi sites that retain an authentic atmosphere of terror. The radio used to cover the cries of the tortured
seems to have only just been switched off. The notorious 'tram-
way' is ready for victims to be seated in rows awaiting their turn to
be tortured, forced to listen to the cries of their fellows. A Nazi
officer's cap and leather greatcoat hang on a hat-stand, an evil black
whip has been casually left on the desk beside a battered type-
writer. The stone floors are still stained with blood and there is a
strange smell about the place. One feels the SS may have just
stepped out for lunch.

The Old Town market place, deserted in the evening when I first
came to Warsaw, is now jammed on summer evenings with white
umbrellas shading beer gardens and cafés. Jazz pianists and accor-
dion players provide a warm and intimate atmosphere. Further out

30 This was a political prison built by Tsarist Russia in 1829–35 and designed by Henryk Marconi,
a member of the outstanding Marconi architectural dynasty who had been working in Poland since
the eighteenth century. The name Pawiak came ironically from its situation on pretty ulica Pawia
('Peacock Street') in the Warsaw Ghetto. Conditions were extremely severe with insufficient food
and summary executions. Here an estimated 37,000 Poles of the intelligentsia, politicals, members
of the AK and civilians unlucky enough to be caught in a round-up were executed. Around 60,000
were transported to concentration camps. After a period as the Gestapo prison and following the
destruction of the ghetto it became part of KL Warschau, the Warsaw concentration camp. The
archives were never found so details and accurate statistics are sketchy and constantly revised. Some
Jews from the ghetto were also fated to experience Pawiak before Treblinka. It was blown up by the
Nazis and a harrowing museum has taken its place.

in the residential wastes of the city, the monumentalism of the market has replaced the monumentalism of Marxism. The reduction of the individual to an economic molecule inspires rapacious investors to even greater efforts on the developmental blank canvas of the Mazovian plain. It is as unresisting to their advance as it was to the *Blitzkrieg* of the Panzer divisions and the Soviet rush to Berlin. The city has germinated towers of capitalist glass and steel draped in hectares of advertising hoardings. The market economy loves glass in the way the communists loved concrete. One of my first cultural shocks in Warsaw was the almost complete absence of billboards. Now colossal models recline seductively, overwhelming public spaces with parted lips and legs.

A stroll through Warsaw Old Town on a winter's night is a unique experience. Through flurries of snow, squares of golden light glow within 'medieval' facades. Remembering it is a reconstruction is a constant surprise and lessens the beauty only a fraction. Soft and quiet snow underfoot. Eddies of light form at the base of gas lamps. The old soul of Warsaw struggles to life like a magic lantern along the moat and Barbican fortifications. The illusion of an old city is maintained until the first frosty memorial stone bears witness to a horrifying site of torture and execution. The shortest walk becomes a lesson in the history of destruction.

In London or Paris the wanderer's attention is diverted by plaques celebrating famous artists, scientists, musicians and writers. In Warsaw grey chiselled stones of uniform pattern are set on walls riddled with shards of shrapnel and twisted steel or ornament the marble facades of a foreign bank or soaring new hotel. At this scorched wall 400 patients and doctors in a field hospital were immolated by the Nazis armed with flame-throwers; at that spot near a new Irish pub fifty Polish citizens were summarily executed.

The innocent bronze statue of the *Mały Powstaniec* ('Little Insurgent'), a child dressed in an oversized helmet bearing the crowned Polish eagle and wearing huge men's boots, drifts to frozen sleep on the bulwark of the Old Town walls, an automatic rifle slung over one shoulder. He commemorates the children and young people who died in the heroic yet tragic resistance to the Nazis in the Warsaw Uprising. 'But pity is superfluous wherever sentence is

pronounced by History,' wrote the Polish author Czesław Miłosz.[31]
Warsaw offers no escape from the terrible truths of humankind and
in this profound way is unparalleled in Europe. This is a tough city,
far easier to respect than to love. To walk here is to be moved to
melancholy at the folly and cruelty of human nature. Warsaw
inspires an exploration of the deeper heart.

Yet buildings and gardens of exquisite beauty are scattered throughout the messy reconstruction, buildings that inspire the imagination
in unexpected ways. Summer green dramatically transforms trees
planted in city courtyards, parks and gardens into bowers of mysterious beauty. Warsaw becomes unrecognizable from the barren
monochrome of winter. Pavilions may have fallen victim to war but
the grand terraces on the forested escarpments that lead down to the
Vistula remain.

In the mid-eighteenth century the last king of Poland was the
driving force behind the design of Łazienki Palace and Park. As a
young man Stanisław Augustus Poniatowski had come under the
influence of the cultivated and acerbic Welshman Sir Charles
Hanbury Williams, British Ambassador to Berlin and later St
Petersburg. Williams was a man of excessively contradictory traits
who belonged to the rakish set associated with Sir Francis
Dashwood of West Wycombe Park, and was a member of the notorious Hellfire Club. Members were considered politically suspect
and were rumoured to carry on debauched Satanic rites in the West
Wycombe caves. He treated Stanisław as a son and provided him
with a cosmopolitan perspective and excellent education in matters
of taste and women, encouraging (albeit for political reasons) the
beginnings of his ruinous affair with Catherine the Great of Russia.

As King of Poland, Stanisław Augustus developed into a man of
refined and subtle sensibility which was reflected in the artistic work
he commissioned from the Italian architects he brought to Warsaw.
He abandoned the severe Renaissance castle of Ujazdow and transformed the marshy ground of the former menagerie and hunting
ground into arguably the finest park in Europe – Łazienki Park
(Bathing Park). Stanisław Augustus heeded well Alexander Pope's

31 Miłosz op. cit., p. 97

advice to Lord Burlington to 'Consult the genius of the place in all'. The first Polish treatise on English landscape gardening was published by his gardener August Moszyński in French in 1774. The King commissioned and entertained in lavish Italianate *casini* scattered among groves of closely planted trees. He did not favour English grottoes and follies but built Chinese and neoclassical pavilions, sculpture galleries, orangeries and a Turkish ballroom that resounded to convivial laughter and the harsh cry of peacocks.

His obsession with theatricals and ancient Rome led him to construct an outdoor theatre on the island in the park in the picturesque style of Piranesi. The stage is planted with trees scattered among broken columns, crumbling walls and shattered pediments inspired by the ruins of the Temple of Jove at Baalbeck in Syria. The audience was seated in a Roman amphitheatre modelled on that at Herculaneum, separated from the actors by a narrow stretch of water. The uppermost parapet is surmounted by sixteen classical statues of playwrights. On a plinth the dying Gaul painfully raises his body at the water's edge.

At the heart of the park, where the formal French long water meets an English irregular lake, Stanisław August together with the court architect Domenico Merlini developed the exquisite neoclassical Palace on the Island. It is one of the most beautiful small buildings in Europe. Here, in the late eighteenth century, the King created his own particular 'Stanisławian' aesthetic by artfully merging many disparate European styles into his own aesthetic statement. Intellectuals and artists met in the dining room for his famous Thursday dinners to lament, debate and distract themselves from their embattled nation.

I visited Łazienki Park for the first time one winter afternoon. I had walked the length of a Agrykola Street over ice and frozen snow. Rows of gas-lamps stood at regular intervals like immobile sentries in the vapour. Haloes shimmered around the gas-mantles. The Palace on the Island floated disembodied on the frosted lake, immaterial and mysterious. The long vistas between avenues of limes and birch, spare and bereft of green, made a delicate study in shades of grey drifting into white, the trunks contrasting in shafts of solid black. Pavilions closed up for the winter slept in deep cold. An old park keeper was draping the statues in heavy brown canvas to protect them from the temperatures which can fall below minus twenty degrees. I crossed the stone bridge at dusk, passing before the equestrian statue of Jan III Sobieski crushing the Turk, this bridge the scene of many battles in uprisings against the Russians.

In spring Warsaw and the park are transformed in an explosion of new life. Chestnut trees with candles of creamy white dip into the water in the slight breeze around the palace beyond the lawns, ripples expanding and fading. Peacocks on heat strut about and bands of gaily dressed children flit and laugh. The grass is permitted to grow long and wild and is filled with buttercups, daisies and bluebells while carp sun themselves near the surface of the ponds. A man was feeding the delicate and nervous red squirrels.

'I have been doing this for years. I spend half of my pension on them!'

He had named each squirrel according to an injury it had received or a particular characteristic of its behaviour.

'This one is "Broken Tail" and that one, the oldest, is "The Pensioner".'

The dense and disorientating greenery of the Warsaw summer makes the park secretive and romantic. Gondolas with golden dragons and crimson canopies are punted across the lake before the palace. The forested park is imbued with the spirit of Pan concealing hidden trysts and forbidden relationships. In leafy alcoves Polish girls carelessly sit astride their lovers in achingly erotic poses and kiss. In autumn the air glitters with golden rain, tall trees arching like a cathedral vault. A restaurant with pink napery and dazzling glass nestles in the shade. In the sun of a bench beneath terrace pagodas of stained wood and white canvas a charming, intelligent old Polish patrician engages me in conversation.

'And what did you think of pan President Wałęsa's speech last night?' he asks.

'I speak Polish rather badly so I did not listen to it.' I apologize. He sighs.

'Ah. He speaks Polish rather badly, too.'

He turns out to be a retired military officer and we speak of the brutality of the endless waves of German and Russian barbarians who overwhelmed Warsaw. He rises, lifts his hat and leaves. This precious class of Pole will soon have entirely passed away.

Yet this Enlightenment gem was not destined to become the symbol of the city. Tall structures invariably become symbols of cities. Nothing compares in brutal physicality with that monumental creation of Stalinist paranoia and commissar prissiness, that inescapable monolith, that cake confectioner's nightmare known as the Palace of Culture and Science. Stalin 'gifted' the edifice to Poland in 1955 from a 'friendly Soviet nation' with a proud military opening ceremony accompanied by costumed representatives of the victorious medieval Knights of Grunwald on horseback.

One of the tallest buildings in Europe, 'Stalin's finger', as it was known, is a major piece of socialist realist art. Many beautiful buildings that survived the war were cleared to make way for it. Entire residential villages were constructed to house the workers. Designed to subdue the mind and enrage the heart, it is pasted with a duplicitous farrago of Renaissance and classical Polish architectural elements, some allegedly stolen from ruined Polish castles. The robustly impressive interior, lit by chandeliers, was created using marble from Georgia and Ukraine with mosaic floors, wrought-iron lanterns and ventilation gratings in the shape of complex rosettes. Within is a monumental warren of museums, cinemas, restaurants and theatres, a prodigious congress and concert hall, scientific research institutes, offices and even a swimming pool. A lift takes the awed visitor to a viewing platform with a spectacular panorama over Warsaw and the surrounding Mazovian plain. The eminent Polish writer Maria Dąbrowska wrote in her diary, 'All of Warsaw will now lie prostrate at the feet of this monster.' (Remarkably many Varsovians have fond memories of their time spent studying or working in the numerous departments of the edifice.)

The catastrophic architecture of Plac Defilad adjacent to the palace has never been properly addressed. Once a fun fair, it is now a car-park and covered market labouring under a marked air of improvisation. Another area bordering the palace is partially filled by the new *Złote Tarasy* or 'Golden Terraces', a huge futuristic office and shopping complex whose external appearance puts one in mind of bodies battling under bed-sheets of glass. Despite the general dislike of the Palace of Culture and its associations with a period of suffering and deprivation, it has become as inescapably representative of Warsaw as the Eiffel Tower is of Paris or Big Ben of London.[32]

Unlike many other regenerated cities in the country and despite the miracle of its reconstruction, Warsaw lacks a beating heart, an emotional core. Much of the population has settled there from elsewhere in Poland. Ravines of architectural sterility bore through the city. The charming Old Town, a mirror of history, attracts tourists but not large numbers of Varsovians except at the end of the working week in summer. Lazarus has been raised physically but lacks a soul. The great Polish patriot and journalist Jerzy Waldorf once observed that the most living part of Warsaw is the great cemetery of Powązki, one of the few places the Nazis permitted Poles to maintain undisturbed the secrets of their heroic dead.

Yet there is the excitement of expansion and rebirth in the air of this newly emergent business capital. The former depressing darkness has been dispelled from the streets and the once empty highways are filled with imported new cars. The city is regenerating itself at exponential speed with the help of the European Union and the sheer energy, ambition and humour of its inhabitants. A tall artificial palm tree has recently appeared on a central Warsaw roundabout in Jerusalem Avenue near a statue of Charles de Gaulle striding purposefully forward. The apparent incongruity of this tropical, almost Algerian, exoticism among the soulless communist buildings raises a laugh, but the palm conceals a deep and unrecognized symbolism.

The date palm is a rich source of life in the desert. Some produce fruit for almost eighty years. The new leaves that sprout from the spot where the dead fronds fall have given the tree a magical aura of indestructibility. As cars circle in their thousands, few Warsaw drivers would recognize this symbol of resurrection in the midst of their long-suffering city.

32 A highly entertaining book in Polish and English has been written by the journalist Agata Passent on the construction of the Palace and its particular significance for Varsovians, entitled *Pałac Wiecznie Żywy* (Long Live the Palace!) (Warsaw 2004)

CHAPTER 5

Remnants of the Old Regime

Back at the training centre, many of our trainees harboured deep resentment at being forced to learn of the so recently 'decadent' and 'inefficient' mechanisms of the market economy as it had been ideologically presented to them. They winced visibly and incessantly whispered asides as the English language and capitalist philosophy fell painfully upon their ears. History was a delicate subject and the mere mention of the words 'Jewish' or 'Communism' caused a chill to form in the air. A direct question except on the most innocuous of subjects would result in silence. This cultural trait persists. Poles react to direct questions of a personal nature as if under interrogation. Relationships are built more slowly here. Lives of fearful uncertainty and sudden reversals of fortune have made people cautious. Some trainees suspected there were informers within the group who might report their opinions to their superiors. Certain individuals were deferred to as spokesmen if a 'difficult question' was raised that required the expression of a prepared political position.

In the negligent and infuriating manner of former communists, staff were sent there unaware that they would eventually be facing a public examination in English. Poles rarely initiate communication and information flow is often one way. The trainees seemed crippled by confusion, lack of self-confidence and embarrassment and this matured into resentment of the West.

'We *have* come down from the trees, you know,' one remarked to me.

Animosity dissolved once outside the training rooms. It was as if the Poles juggled two contradictory traits, a public role and a private one. The woodland around the centre was a fairyland in winter and we had spectacular snowball fights across the wire net in the abandoned tennis courts. There was much drinking of *Żubrówka*[33] and long walks in the fresh snow in the luminous half-light of starry nights. The boys concealed themselves near trees and shook them violently as the girls passed underneath, showering them with snow. Wild shrieks rent the air. Drinking, dancing and breathless flirtatiousness in the *kawiarnia* (café) or on the banks of the Vistula around a bonfire proceeded nightly well into the small hours.

Curiously, the next morning one was ignored completely by the revellers as if intimacy had simply not occurred. There appeared to be no building up of emotional credit in friendship over time. I came to realize that with Poles there are many levels of intimacy in friendship, which is reflected in the language. Even Casanova experienced something similar when he visited Poland in the eighteenth century. On his return to Warsaw after his first Polish sojourn, Casanova was ignored by people he thought were his friends. He wrote despondently in his *Memoirs*, 'the Poles are always inconstant and changeable.'[34]

In the past Poles had been deceived so often by colonial powers they were understandably suspicious of what could be interpreted as simply another colonial adventure. Bitter experience has taught the East Central Europeans a habit of care and vigilance. Secrecy and the use of Polish as a language of refuge and national solidarity remain firmly entrenched. Not so long ago the Poles were forced to learn Russian, now it was English. Tomorrow could it be Chinese? Today this emotional insecurity has largely passed away as Poles realize the competitive, even dominant nature of their own talents in the European workforce.

---

33 Vodka flavoured with an aromatic grass eaten by bison roaming the primeval Białowieża forest in the far north-east of the country. I used to make my own – far superior to the commercial product.

34 From the highly entertaining *Memoirs of Casanova Volume 5e Russia and Poland*. The account of his Polish duel with Count Xavier Branicki is an absolute delight. Despite being forced to flee the country, this friend of King Stanisław Augustus Poniatowski remained proud of the incident all his life as it indicated to the nobility of Europe that he was a formidable force and as such a serious operative.

The psychological shock of the so-called 'fall of communism' is much underestimated by Western observers; the painful sense of lives wasted through devotion to a discredited ideal remains strong. In the Poland of those years there was little accumulated experience of the fundamentals of the market economy or of the process of parliamentary democracy. Much has changed as respect increases in Europe for Polish business acumen and Poles' strong work ethic. But the relative novelty of relying on personal strength of character and the necessity to accept personal responsibility for one's life and family continues to cause stress and distress. The old mentality continues to provide a safe house and refuge for older Poles. The elderly still voice nostalgia for the lack of crime, ease of state-subsidised holidays and the reverence for cultural values and solid education under communism.

'The wealth gap was not so great in those days. Thieves did not steal from those who lived in the same district!' my friend Irena told me. 'People were more generous and ready to share. There was a lot more socializing than today. I think people were happier when they had less and wanted less.'

An entire generation will need to pass before the nostalgia felt by many fades. Communism was an entire generation's reality, after all.

After the fall of the communist regime the system of social values was in a state of profound flux. Strong and honest opinions were not ventured in a climate of radical change, where more than the vestiges of the previous regime remained. The pathology of the system – economic inefficiency, secrecy, fear and apathy, paranoia and compulsion to intrigue – remained inextricably mixed with the new freedoms. The buoyant informal economy which enabled people to survive through their recent tortuous history and formed the foundation of much of life under communism has persisted into the 'new world'.

Working at the *ośrodek*[35] in the forest became increasingly a strain. Invidious comparisons with Western countries had to be avoided at all costs where a sense of awkward inferiority mixed with

---

35 An *ośrodek* is a residential conference centre. They were especially popular during the communist period as an opportunity for vodka parties, general mayhem and the odd love affair leavened by token ideological input.

dislike seemed to reign. There was severe ignorance and psycholog-ical resistance, particularly on the part of older managers whose families had perhaps been more economically committed to the ide-ology of the former regime.

'Tell me something about how you deal with customer relations in the company,' I asked a group of senior managers. After much consultation and whispering a large lady with heavily hennaed hair replied with some pride:

'When a customer rings the company and speaks to me ... he never rings the company again.' Nods of approval all round.

Meetings with the personnel managers of large companies were often necessary at the planning stage. Most were held in the ghastly run-down offices of the former government Department of Finance. Jennifer, my superior from Bath, was in attendance as a representa-tive of the British Council to ascertain needs and clarify the objectives of the programme. Two managers were present – the cus-tomary thug in a suit with gaps between his teeth and an aggressive middle-aged woman dressed in red who was furiously chain-smok-ing. I had the temerity to question the 'vague objectives' and 'lack of specificity in the programme'. There was a sudden explosion of emotional vitriol. Dr Grabski was simultaneously translating and matters became very heated indeed. The managers declared vehe-mently that they wanted practical assistance in the form of money for training and not advice that is too costly to implement from 'experts' who merely eat and drink all the aid revenue in the bars and restaurants of the luxurious Marriott Hotel.

'We know what our needs are! We don't want your analysis!' they shouted.

'We know what economic espionage is! Asking questions about what people do! Foreign companies will copy us!' accompanied by wild gesticulations.

The discussion, such as it was, degenerated into a venomous attack on the entire attitude and tenor of Western aid to developing Poland. I wished I had never come to the meeting. At one point the lady in red flounced out of the room slamming the door, resulting in the imitation baroque brass door-handle parting company with the door and shooting across the room. Dr Grabski was flushed with emotion and terror. My superior had lapsed into a crushed silence. We left in the pouring rain fairly shattered by this confrontation.

I returned to the centre with Jennifer via the long route, she stumbling over the gravelled tram rails in her Gucci pumps now covered in mud and the rotting remains of a dead dog. I chose this taxing direction to persuade her that we needed a company car. On the way we visited a supermarket where muscular women stood with folded arms. Shoppers were placed under a constant glare of surveillance if they failed to carry a minute wire basket around the shelves. Huge moustachioed Poles in lumberjack shirts moved along the shelves with their wives opening and sniffing the newly available cosmetics with inquiring glances. Alcohol was guarded in a room with bars the thickness of a lion's cage. In the suitcase department I failed to pick up a basket that could never have accommodated a suitcase.

'Don't you have shops in your country?' shouted a lady with bright orange hair.

At the bus stop a vodka drunk slid slowly down the pole and collapsed in a heap in the snow. The puppy he was carrying in his overcoat to keep himself warm whimpered and scurried away. In those days there were no bus shelters. The commuter waited in the threatening dark, driving snow or pelting rain, drenched by cars that drove through the deep puddles. Today one waits in a covered shelter under fluorescent lights surrounded by advertising hoardings. Under the dim lamps of the bus another drunk growled at Jennifer before putting his head between his knees and swaying from side to side.

CHAPTER 6

Testing Times

Jennifer decided that a car was a necessity. I showed her around the centre, the common room with its stained carpet and tumble dryer full of men's underwear churning away, filling the room with humidity. She fled the window and suggested an early dinner after taking in the panorama over the garden with its decrepit outdoor furniture, wrecked tennis courts, Frank the three-legged dog nosing the rubbish bins and the lake of raw sewage slowly freezing at the entrance.

We had a magnificent meal at the Zajazd Napoleoński restaurant – formerly an inn where Napoleon stayed en route to Moscow. Excellent restaurants were few, an extraordinary contrast to the food of almost every nation now available throughout the city. Geoff was quick to strip off his Goretex 'action trousers' while Richard adjusted his Oxford college bow tie. Nick kicked his trainers against the parquet flooring and David took his Willy Wonka flat cap from his mass of curly hair. I removed my Napoleonic naval overcoat and took Jennifer's Burberry scarf. A group of beautiful female musicians were playing some Telemann *Tafelmusik* on violin, recorder and harpsichord. A copy of Jacques-Louis David's equestrian portrait of Napoleon adorned the wall above our table.

'Where did you do your financial training, Nick?' asked Jennifer, managerially friendly.

'Da ya know the group the Lurkers?'

'Ah, yes. The South African banking concern Lelurk.'

'Na, na. London based group, London based group. Like I did

me teacher trainin' wiv a former drummer of the Lurkers. He always wanted to rejoin the band but I thought like I betta do somfink serious with me life. Great bloke.'

Jennifer fell silent and parted a small piece of sole from its backbone.

'Me grandfather went down the pits in Nottingham. He give up his accountant's job in an office and take up residence there in the fetid darkness.'

'Ah, I see. Yes, life can be so unfair.'

'Yeah. People fink I'm aristocra'ic. Tried to get a job at Coutts, but they wouldn't have me. Very pernikity they are, like.'

We were served the first course by a biochemist, the main by a mathematician and the pudding by a nuclear physicist. All had renounced their former professions for better pay as waiters. The conversation turned unaccountably to rivers. Richard spoke knowledgably about the source of the Danube and Geoff violently disagreed.

'Look, old boy, if it was the way you say, the river would be flowing uphill across the Hungarian border. Not normal in nature, I think?'

'Oh I see, clever clogs! No public school or Oxford, me. Comprehensive, me. You're such a bloody clever dick! Not frum south, me. North always bailin' out them frum down south!'

Jennifer stared open-mouthed at this unexpected eruption of class and regional resentment.

She returned that night to the Marriott in the centre of town in order to (so the Poles thought) indulgently spend more of the foreign aid money on cream cakes. Later in the evening, Geoff fixed a miner's lamp to an elasticized band around his forehead. A sure sign of anger. As I looked out of the window I could see the lamp bobbing distantly among the trees. He arrived back at the centre after this torture in conditions of −20°C looking pale and cadaverous. He had taken to running regularly through the snowy forest when angry and had been bitten by a Doberman while out jogging one morning. He was frantic about rabies and insisted I approach the Polish farmer who owned the animal and ask him to produce a rabies vaccination certificate. My Polish was hardly up to such an enquiry, nor would the farmer be likely to have carried out the procedure. I attempted to mime rabies to the secretary by barking and snarling but she interpreted my antics literally and leapt into a cupboard in terror. We inspected the wound. It was about a quarter of an inch long and superficial.

'Millions of viruses can get through there!' he shouted.

How would we get a doctor urgently? I had not addressed this contingency.

'The doctor comes to the centre on Monday, otherwise you will need to call an ambulance,' I was told by the resentful bleached blonde at reception. Her fingers were always bandaged from mysterious injuries.

I wanted to call the medical insurance company to determine our position.

'*Słucham pana.* ('I'm listening, Sir').'

I began to give her the number but she interrupted me.

'The number three is not working on the exchange. Does your number have a three in it?'

'No.'

'That's lucky.'

Investigation showed that we were not in fact covered by health insurance. It was a new Western idea. I did not reveal this. Geoff decided to trust to destiny and wait.

At the communal breakfast the next morning Geoff had come down to our usual fare of geometrically arranged cold sausage and curled-up cheese, jug of black tea and stale bread and jam. When he sat down he would neither talk nor eat, only mumble incoherently. David joined us and began to intently pull the small pieces of fat off his sausage, the meat held close to his bottle-end glasses and Nivea-encrusted face, as was his wont each morning. Richard arrived in a crushed shirt and Oxford cricket jumper, hair standing on end, with a cheery '*Dzień dobry*' (Good morning) in best Polish, smiling knowingly at all the girls with strong fathers.

'Pleasant to sleep with someone who has breasts!' He greeted us. 'I just found her in my bed after the other one had left.'

There was a grim silence around the breakfast table at this piece of intelligence. He was joined shortly after by two Norwegian girls wearing thin T-shirts without bras whom he had invited to Poland.

It became apparent that Geoff had a problem and we should all ask him what it was.

'Feeling alright after the dog attack?' I ventured.

'Well, since you ask, I can hardly open me mouth.' His hand felt his jaw which attempted to travel sideways in a 'freeing' motion.

'Must have lock-jaw. One of the rabies symptoms I've read about,' he mumbled.

'Really? Seems to have developed rather rapidly. Shall I ask Dr Grabski to call the doctor?'

'I'd rather die!' he said violently, then leapt up and left the dining-room.

He had taken to 'testing' his mountain-climbing equipment on the fixed pipes and heaters in the 'hospitality suite'. One evening, after we had repaired upstairs after dinner as usual for coffee and boredom, he suddenly exclaimed: 'Look at the strength of this!' impetuously throwing a hook at the radiator. It caught on the cast iron and he pulled the rope violently. The ancient heater designed by central planning parted company with the pipe-work and hot water sprayed high and low, soaking the carpet and scalding innocent Richard who was reading *Those Were The Days*, a nostalgic recollection of Auschwitz by the perpetrators. The accident required ponderous explaining in Polish to the elderly, vodka-soaked repair man.

'I once went camping for the Duke of Edinburgh's Award on Dartmoor,' Richard ventured after wiping down.

'Dartmoor? That's not camping, lad. That's bloody luxury! Southern softies! You should try proper camping in Yorkshire.'

Geoff attempted to impress us with finger pull-ups on the door frames which similarly began to part company with the walls. Sometimes I felt that working with these people was more like working on an oil rig than in education.

'Shall we imbibe a little culture?' Richard asked the team over a vodka one dull Sunday afternoon as the three-legged dog nosed the rubbish bins. 'There's an interesting palace at Wilanów. And some of the Sobieski-Stuart graves I believe.'

'How many K is it?' Geoff asked.

'I'm sure I have not the faintest idea.'

'Good one. Good one. Any nosh there?' said Nick in a burst of enthusiasm.

'Supposed to be a good restaurant out that way. Wouldn't mind a bit of wild boar, as grandma said,' Geoff cackled, suddenly adventurous.

'Well, I'm not sure. A piece of chicken might be fine or perhaps . . . have to wait and see.' David stood up and walked about indecisively.

And so it was that we set out on our first team expedition. Although we all managed to get on in a general sense, all the usual depressing cultural and class differences were made manifest that afternoon. It was the first and last excursion we ever made as a team.

The Palace of Wilanów (*Villa Nuova*), one of the most important Polish historical survivals, distils the essence of the martial Sarmatian spirit and opulent taste of the seventeenth century. Tiring of his noisy city castle King Jan III Sobieski initiated the building of this *château de plaisance* or country residence towards the end of the seventeenth century. The grand facade and spacious entrance court give it the appearance of a large Italian Baroque villa set within an elegant formal garden. Sobieski imported gifted Italian, French and Dutch sculptors, painters and stuccoists for his extensive decorative scheme. He set up a royal atelier which became the first Academy of Painting in Poland. The Italian formal gardens were laid out in baroque style with fountains, summer houses, statues and a grotto supplemented with orchards of apple, cherry, pear, plum, peach and apricot.

His bedroom was supremely masculine, the walls decorated with armour, crossed sabres and shields nailed to tapestries, his bed embellished with Persian and Turkish embroidered silks that were his spoils from the Battle of Vienna. By his death in 1696 the palace had become a fulsome tribute to his Sarmatian glory celebrating Polish military victories, particularly over the Turks at Chocim (1673) and Vienna (1683).

Sobieski's grand-daughter, Maria Klementyna Sobieska, was fabulously wealthy and married 'The Old Pretender', Prince James Francis Stuart of Scotland, in Montefiascone in Italy in 1719. They were recognized by Pope Clement XI as the Catholic King and Queen of England and provided with a palace in Rome and a villa in the *compagna* near Albano. She died a young woman of thirty-three and was buried with great ceremony in St Peter's Basilica in Rome. The career of their famous son, Charles Edward Stuart ('Bonnie

Prince Charlie'), shows much of the military *élan* and romance carried in his part Polish blood.[36]

The palace was extended over subsequent centuries by aristocratic families reflecting more feminine and refined decorative tastes. For much of the eighteenth century Wilanów was owned in turn by three wealthy and powerful women – grandmother Elżbieta Sieniawska, Maria Zofia Czartoryska and her daughter Izabela Lubomirska – all connoisseurs and resolute patrons of the arts. On a balustrade in the gardens four statues symbolize the four stages of love: Fear, Kiss, Indifference, and Quarrel. The property was pillaged by the Russians during Tadeusz Kościuszko's 1794 insurrection and a horrified Izabela passed it to her daughter Aleksandra, wife of the outstanding collector and scholar Stanisław Kostka Potocki. A magnificent equestrian portrait of him by Jacques-Louis David hangs within the palace walls. In a significant programme of decoration, Potocki returned the palace to its Sarmatian roots, founded an outstanding art gallery and magnificent library, and laid out an English landscape park. The Nazis finally stripped the palace, in the words of Heinrich Himmler, 'of all objects of artistic, cultural and historic value . . . whose security and appropriate treatment lies in the German interest'.[37]

The gallery contains a remarkable collection of Polish Sarmatian portraits and a unique collection of 'coffin portraits', a particularly Polish baroque genre. During the funeral ceremony a plain, almost expressionless painted portrait of the deceased was nailed to the coffin and interred with it in the grave or hung with heraldic devices in the church.

'How did you find the palace?' Richard asked the despondent group waiting on the stairs as we emerged into the sunlight.

'A bit steady,' said David.

'How about a cup of Yorkshire tea and some wild boar?' said Geoff.

'Excellent. Excellent,' said Nick.

*

36 The attraction Scotland holds for young immigrant Poles is revealed in the recent invention of a so-called 'Polish Tartan' in red and white with a thread of dark blue.

37 Document dated Berlin, 16 December 1939. See *Liquidation of the Effects of World War II in the Area of Culture*, Wojciech W. Kowalski (Warsaw: Polski Instytut Kultury, 1994) pp. 19ff

One weekend we discovered a note on the table of the 'hospitality suite' which informed us that the water would be cut off and there would be no food. 'Pails of water and sausage will be provided, of course' was the jolly message from Dr Grabski. Supplies of mineral water had ceased because 'it is too cold to deliver water' and anyway the delivery truck had broken down.

'Right. We're off for the weekend then. Not starving in this dump,' said David and Geoff in unison.

They returned from their walking tour of the Góry Świętokrzyskie (Holy Cross Mountains) but were completely inarticulate about their experiences. Geoff had met a number of remarkable Polish mountain climbers and to my relief was in excellent spirits and full of admiration. Perhaps he had simply needed to escape the confines of the prison and share his interests. They had no particular interest in Polish culture and we began to pursue our separate destinies in the country.

Nick had been to Kraków with his latest admiring Polish blonde.

'How did you find Kraków, Nick?'

'Good one. Good one. Kraków's a good crack.'

'Here, try some of this Czechoslovakian chocolate I bought in the mountains. Much better than the Polish muck.' Geoff threw Richard the remains of the bar.

'Actually it's not Czech. *Czekolada* means chocolate in Polish,' Richard pointed out.

'So smart! You can bloody well keep it! I don't like it.'

Back to the old prickly relationships then. Richard and I had remained in Warsaw, our sole source of food being the cardboard box of cold sausage, gherkins, stale bread and 'meat droplets in brine'. One pail of water had sufficed for washing and coffee. I felt a sense of close companionship with five drunken men I saw hunched melancholically over greasy soup at the Bar Mleczny (Milk Bar)[38] near the Barbakan in the Old Town, one with the solitary

---

38 A type of state-subsided canteen that served basic food such as dumplings, *pierogi* (a type of ravioli with a variety of fillings), soups, pasta and luminous jellies at extremely low prices for the poor, pensioners, students, the thrifty, the elderly and alcoholic social casualties. These 'Milk Bars', not unlike a 'greasy spoon' café in the UK, bars were looked upon with great affection during communist times and the few that remain are still popular and have smartened themselves up considerably. Under communism there was scarcely any tradition of eating out in restaurants. This is changing and many fine restaurants representing many national cuisines have opened in Warsaw. However, eating out is still normally reserved for special occasions.

English word 'Happiness' embroidered on the back of his denim jacket.

Dr Grabski was in a state of high neurosis as the exams for the trainees were to take place imminently. He told Geoff at the last moment that the exam he had spent hours preparing would not be required after all.

'Probably it will be too difficult for them.'

'Probably?'

Geoff was furious and stormed off into Warsaw Centrum clinging to the side of a tram.

'Why do you always take your rucksack, Geoff?' I asked as he bounded out.

'To keep both me hands free for grappling,' he replied viciously.

The English team were becoming increasingly unhappy in Warsaw and felt under physical threat. Nick was always leaping into a taxi spraying his personal defence gas canister to keep the Russian mafia at bay. We had all witnessed appalling violence on the trams as teams of thieves stormed the vehicle and relieved travellers of their wallets. Those that refused were thrown off and kicked in the head as they lay on the rails. Richard witnessed a knife fight in an underpass, blood arcing onto the concrete walls. I was worried that the project might be beginning to disintegrate and did my best to build a team spirit. I sympathized with Geoff on the academic front but tactfully failed to comment on this to Dr Grabski lest there be an overreaction.

The examination consisted of a written test and oral interview. The trainees took this remarkably seriously and it was clear a familiar psychological drama of punishment and redemption was playing itself out. The callous indifference of the communists to the private lives of ordinary working people was still in evidence. One trainee, heavily pregnant, had been told the previous day she was to sit a difficult exam in French and arrived to find it was actually one of the most difficult Cambridge University exams in English.

The candidates dressed up for the examination – the men in suits and ties and the women in glamorous and often suggestive clothes, plunging blouses and thigh-grazing skirts. A few wore characteristic 'Catholic' lace collars, carefully pressed, accompanied by pursed virginal lips. A great deal of superbly skilled cheating took place during the written papers. Exams were to be approached with strategic and tactical genius if a good result was to be guaranteed.

'Wojtek is clever at exams'

'Oh really? Does he study a lot?'

'Oh no. He always chooses the best position to see the others' work.'

There was a great deal of shifting to unnatural positions, craning of necks and fanciful movements of the answer sheets, which was considered rather a sport in Poland. One candidate euphemistically referred to the practice as simply 'the sharing of knowledge against a corrupt system'. Being an Oxford man, Richard became particularly upset, incensed might be a better word, at the constant whispering during the examination and scarcely disguised cheating. He was accused later of unfeeling cruelty because he had drawn attention to it. Such 'crude' forms of advancement were not for the managerial class however. They adopted far more straightforward systems of influence – bribery and utilizing their manifold *układ*[39] or connections. Such historical corruption based on influence rather than merit means that many managers today in government offices remain professionally ill-equipped to carry out their work efficiently.

Dr Grabski certainly behaved in a curious manner when we began to interview the candidates. He became another man, transformed into a figure betraying characteristics of the former regime, an interrogator. An urbane and charming European with an eye for the ladies, he became slippery and ingratiating. An atmosphere of danger entered the proceedings. From the beginning of our acquaintance I had thought his indistinct grey eyes were rather unsettling.

When the trainee entered the office, Dr Grabski made not the slightest attempt to relax the atmosphere but asked veiled questions

---

39 *Układ* is complex in its connotations and has accumulated different resonances since the passing of communism. It is a network of contacts and connections built up over time wherein an individual may profitably operate. A form of nepotism or 'the old boy network'. More recently it has attracted unsavoury notions of blackmail and dirty tricks in the urge to purge the state of SB informers who formed their own *układ*. The SB or *Służba Bezpieczeństwa* was the Security Service of the Ministry of International Affairs. Every society has its own form of *układ*, even Papua New Guinea, where it is called *wantokism* (preference given to members of your tribe, language or geographical group – 'one talk').

or made subversive remarks, unnerving and sinister. While doing this he would not look directly at the trembling victim but turn his head down and at an angle while fiddling with the edges of a burgundy velvet cushion on the settee. With studied deliberation he turned over a sheaf of papers. An uncomfortable atmosphere of damp fear condensed around the collar of my shirt.

'What do you do in the company?'

'We service the customers.' We both smiled at a common amusing error.

'No, no, my dear. What is your work at the company?'

'I'm a manager.'

'Correction, my dear – manageress.'

'Oh dear! Sorry!' the woman was covered in confusion.

'Yes. You shouldn't make such simple mistakes at your level! Shall we punish her for this, Michael? Probably not. She is a beautiful woman after all.'

I was entirely unused to the complicit yet charming smirk he then gave me. It made me feel an unaccustomed revulsion and shock at this notion of torturing a trainee.

A long pause.

'Why did you join the company at all?' he queried.

'Well, why I . . . do you mean, did I choose?'

'Yes.'

'I chose because I must to work after my father dead but are no possibilities of promotion. I am not so happy.'

'Yes. I see. I see. You start in the company when you're young . . . but then suddenly it's too late to change. Nothing else to do, *could* do, I suppose.'

Gestures of mock sympathy accompanied these remarks.

'Yes.'

'So, in fact I see you *lack the right connections* and *the most useful contacts*.'

He leaned forward with a smile for the sinner, charming and civilized, but smug at the perpetration of this social crime, this dreadful lack of acumen by the trainee. Information and access to information, the ability to *załatwić* ('arrange matters'), is so difficult in Poland and therefore has significant market value and adds prestige.

Another pause.

'Did you buy or sell today?'

'Well, both.'

'Please answer the question! Did you buy or sell?' (In a threatening *sotto voce*.)

He looked at me with a complicit sneer at the evident idiocy of the candidate and twiddled the velvet fringe.

'Well, in the morning I bought and in the afternoon I sold.'

'I see.'

I almost cheered this wonderfully improvised reply to an impossible question. There have been generations of practice in such evasions in Poland. Yet there is a degree of complicity in this terror between prisoner and jailer and both must play their part. I was reasonable and full of sympathy for the plight of my students and asked simple questions and made lightly humorous banter. Promotions depended on a successful outcome to this Byzantine conversation and they must negotiate a safe path through the traps.

The interviews complete and the papers rapidly marked, the results were reviewed and adjusted. Production figures were 'massaged' under communism as were examination results. This legacy will be slow to fade in Poland.

All the candidates were assembled and the results announced. This was followed by the ritual giving of flowers and chocolates, sighs of relief, speeches of thanks and hysterical dispersal in high spirits. There was a wild party that evening. I was given a large bunch of yellows roses, which were subsequently stolen.

CHAPTER 7

How to Buy and Register a Polish Car

Jennifer had allowed us to buy a car! All we had to do was register and insure it.

Buying a 'company car' posed few problems apart from arriving at dawn and defeating thirty-two Poles at 7.00am to clinch the deal. I chose one of the last examples of the FSO 125p to be manufactured, much to the disdain of the trainees, who felt I should have bought a new BMW or Mercedes. This attractive classic 1960s design based on a Fiat was twenty-four years old and the mechanicals thirty, the engine rugged and unbreakable, the body low-quality steel, the cabin spacious and the ride rough. I loved it. It was cheap and offered a low profit margin to thieves. Car theft in Poland at this time was of epidemic proportions. A popular spoof tourist advertisement in Germany read 'Come to Poland. Your car is already there!' This low-mileage example in ivory with towelling-covered leatherette seats belonged to an old Polish lady.

I found the unfamiliar requirement of my physical presence at every stage of the registration and insurance of the FSO a frustrating and ultimately ludicrous dilemma. Few bureaucratic tasks in Poland can be completed without being present in person, which makes everyday life needlessly laborious. The inheritance of a chronic lack of official trust means that any assertion requires documentary proof. A letter had to obtained, suitably signed and rubber stamped by the Director of the conference centre, declaring I would be a resident at this address for the period of my visa. The Director was out, but would soon be in. We waited. The heavy 'commissar' from the previous regime arrived in his colossal office decorated with acres of Persian carpet and a massive desk. He took a steaming glass of tea. He stirred. He came to a decision. We waited. He signed.

The secretary, Pani Jola, and a trainee named Kuba accompanied me the five kilometres to the Government Office in the Warsaw district of Żoliborz where the letter was stamped and officiated. This together with my visa enabled me to obtain a vital piece of paper the size of a small playing card called a *potwierdzenie* [Registration Document]. It was violently rubber-stamped five times and each stamp carefully signed. We then drove another kilometre to the Government Tax Office to pay the 2% purchase tax on the vehicle.

The scenes here were reminiscent of a wartime refugee camp. Two of 'our Poles' queued in different lines that snaked up and down the stairwells (an alternative queuer was necessary in case of mistaken information). In the past entire 'queue committees' were formed to maintain positions throughout the days and weeks required to obtain scarce commodities like television sets, washing machines and refrigerators. Pani Jola and I knocked on many doors to discover which office dealt with foreign purchase tax.

The Polish corridor is a unique phenomenon of bureaucratic subversiveness. In most government offices a crowded narrow passage without decoration opens up before the inquirer, a tunnel of horrors, a canyon of despair. The walls and closed doors are festooned with myriad scraps of paper in various states of wear and tear. They are of various sizes and denote changes of use or recent changes in government regulations. Supplicants perch uncomfortably on the edges of chairs and look up with pleading eyes as you pass, wondering at your destiny, seeking comfort in shared distress. Elderly folk may clutch tattered documents to prove they were slaves under the Nazi regime and are still claiming compensation from the German government. Marriage and birth certificates need to be reaffirmed if they are to be used in a legal context (this is not a requirement for death certificates).

Groups of demented petitioners clustered at various unmarked doors whispering wildly and reading notices, their eyes darting about like rats in panic. Pani Jola knocked, entered and loudly questioned the occupants until we found the correct room. Distraught

businessmen in long blue overcoats carrying briefcases were officiously rapping on doors and barging in, voices raised in protest,
flustered glances. Those with 'special arrangements' arrogantly
elbowed past. Warsaw inherited Prussian bureaucracy during the
partitions, followed by Russian and finally brought to sublime complexity under the Soviets, arguably the most bureaucratic nation on
earth. Women thrust screaming babies forward for preferential
treatment. Poles love children and will always give a mother priority. To triumph over the Polish corridor take a crying baby.

There is never an official reply in Poland, just a series of non-
answers. Success and the quality of information depend entirely on
the whim of whoever happens to be in control at the moment you
approach a government desk or shop counter. Officials feel bound
to answer even if it is with misinformation and feel no guilt if incorrect. To betray ignorance would be a worse crime. The cosy
protection of official guidelines or consumer legislation is denied the
applicant. Feeling insecure has become endemic, a drug, a need to
expect the worst. If matters are proceeding smoothly, throw a span-
ner in the works. A signature, a feeling of security, a degree of
finality unsettles a Pole and renders him prone to impulsive gestures. A leaf tumbled along by the wind of chance carries no
responsibility.

Pani Jola emerged after some time clutching a scrap of paper containing the tax assessment. From a kiosk some way outside the
building we had to obtain *znaczki skarbowe* (Government Tax
Stamps) for a trivial amount and glue them to the document. The
glue on the reverse of the stamp was uselessly thin so a pot of glue
with a brush had been thoughtfully provided. Much emotional
energy was expended over these accursed stamps that needed to be
obtained from distant locations and affixed to all official documents.

Kuba was already in the cashier queue and had moved along quite
significantly in the interim, so we joined him. The cashier operating
from behind a glass screen was a curious fellow who felt compelled
to ease his false teeth in an alarming fashion – shooting them out,
forward and down – all the while stamping forms, taking money
and giving change without once looking up.

We drove another five kilometres to the Registration Office for
Foreigners. I was helped into a parking space by one of the legions

of unemployed and alcoholics who 'assist' motorists to park in Poland. It is a valued occupation and there is much competition for the best spots.

'Dear Sir, I have just been released from prison and as a gesture of solidarity and reform I would like to look after your car whilst you are in the registration office. I will explain your unique problem to any officials that may pass by.'

How could I refuse?

We had to wait in another queue while foreign applications were processed. A Hungarian three-star General engaged me in laconic conversation in old-fashioned English.

'I see you are a foreigner, old fruit. What are you registering in this nightmare, my good friend?'

'A car. An FSO 125p. It's rather difficult.' I had already begun to sigh in Polish and look crestfallen at the floor.

'Ha! You are more than lucky – just a car!'

'Why?'

'I am registering a tank!'

'A tank! Do you have to register tanks?'

'Sure. That will give the bastards some problems!'

He laughed uproariously and proceeded into the inner sanctum. An hour passed before he emerged triumphant.

'They want me to put stop lights and direction indicators on the bloody thing!' He laughed again and wandered off.

None of the staff in the 'foreign' department spoke a word of any foreign language. Details were entered in a handwritten ledger and then transferred laboriously to the computer database. A secretary whose eyes appeared to be moving in different directions operated the computer slowly and resentfully. My signature strayed one millimetre outside the designated box.

'Is this a problem?' I asked when she drew my attention to this lapse.

'It could be. I will not be the one who decides.'

Kuba helpfully translated that I must obtain a screwdriver to remove the old licence plates and bring them up to the office immediately. The car did not have any tools.

'What is the Polish for screwdriver?'

'*Śrubokręt*.' Pretty straightforward as Polish words go.

After much effort I buttonholed a helpful man in the street who returned to his flat and emerged with a *śrubokręt*. We then discovered that the screws securing the old plates were rather poor quality and were rusted solid. No problem! The man disappeared and returned with a can of penetrating oil. This also had no effect so he returned with a hacksaw and set to work with a vengeance.

I returned to the office as the huge lady secretary was locking up. After much heaving and looking impatiently at her watch I was issued with two green registration plates and a small, pink document in a plastic slip case. I proudly rested the set on the dashboard beneath the windscreen. I was stopped almost immediately for driving without licence plates.

'*Dokumenty! Dokumenty!*' the police demanded severely.

Lunch back at the centre consisted of cold spaghetti with tinned strawberry sauce and a very large vodka.

Zbigniew was a manager with a big Ford car. He assisted me with the insurance procedure. We telephoned PZU (State Insurance Company) and with much difficulty obtained the address of the local office. The phone lines at the centre had gone faint as it had rained the previous evening. We drove up and down the street and came to the conclusion that number 34 was the vacant lot covered with long grass and filled with waste timber and bricks. Zbigniew asked for directions in a nearby motor accessory shop.

'Number 34 exists but it's 500 metres behind where it should be, near that apartment block. You can't see it from the road.'

The company did not cover foreigners. We were forced to find another private insurer.

'Just walk through the market, cross the footbridge over the motorway and then you will see a garden near the tram stop with a statue of the Virgin Mary. Well, it is not that building. It is the one next to it. Probably it is open now.'

As we passed the statue I said a quick prayer and sure enough we found a tiny office on the first floor. There was one small trestle table heaving with documents and telephones. We sat down. The impossibility of translating insurance terms and conditions from Polish into English proved almost insurmountable. We introduced French and German. The man was exceptionally friendly, patient and helpful. When you have a problem Poles are wonderful; it is when you do not have a problem that life is difficult. Problems need to be created to promote warm feelings. So often in Poland discomfort arises because matters are proceeding too smoothly, so a difficulty must be created to put everyone at ease. There is relaxation in uncertainty. At some point I decided to sign but I exerted too much pressure on the page and the table collapsed.

'*Przepraszam, przepraszam pana* (I am sorry, I am sorry, sir),' I mumbled incoherently picking up documents and telephones. I forked out millions of zloty with ease and negligence.

'The windows must be etched with a security number.'

'Really? Where do I have that done?'

'No problem! We have a machine around the back. Do you have the car with you?'

'No, because it is uninsured at the moment.'

'Well, I will issue the documents while you collect the car. We need to photograph the engine for security reasons.'

The tireless Zbigniew drove me back to the study centre and we then returned in the FSO, a round trip in traffic of about eighteen kilometres. I was feeling rattled and ill at ease – the desirable Polish emotions in dealing with bureaucracy.

The number from the registration document was set on a sandblasting machine and the mechanic set to work with tremendous energy, blasting numbers on every glass part of the car – windows, windscreen, headlamps, tail lights, indicators, side lamps, fog lamps . . . a virtuoso effort. He stood back and admired his work. As I wandered back to the office with this final certificate, I idly checked the engraved number against the registration certificate number. One digit was wrong.

'No problem! It's normal. We ask at office,' Zbigniew said.

'Could you come back next week?'

My humorous sense of the absurd had departed.

The correct number was blasted over the incorrect number, creating an illegible smudge. The mechanic lethargically resumed work, clearly despondent. Like any Pole he was desperately attempting to save face. The engine had to be photographed and the entire vehicle, the interior, even underneath the car, with a flash attachment. We repaired into the road where I had thoughtlessly parked the car parallel to a bus lane. The insurance man carefully timed his sally into the traffic so as to leap back neatly onto the pavement, cheating death by inches after taking each picture. We returned to the office and the final stamp descended. It was done. I returned to the centre in a perfectly legal car. It had taken three Poles and one Australian eight hours to complete.

'Thanks so much! *Dziękuję serdecznie* (I thank you from my heart). *Dziękuję pięknie* (I thank you beautifully). Let's have a drink!' I almost shouted.

There is an exquisite pleasure of a rare kind in possessing a complete set of legal documents for any Polish bureaucratic task. Exquisite. To this day I have never had the correct documents on my first visit to any government office. There is always something missing, despite the most meticulous planning and tremendous exercise of imagination. Break out the champagne! *Na zdrowie!*

'Why do you buy car? You said me you have no problems. Now you have problem. You have car in Poland. Is big problem!'

CHAPTER 8

Vistula – Queen of Polish Rivers

The purchase of a car had made us mobile at last. My plan was to explore the entire course of the Vistula from the source to the mouth whenever I had the opportunity during the course of the contract.

Over one thousand kilometres long, it is one of the last great natural rivers in Europe. First mentioned by the Roman author Pliny the Elder in his *Natural History*,[40] it flows virtually unregulated, often between long flood barriers, from the Silesian Beskid Mountains in the south of the country north to Gdańsk and the Baltic. By the spring, which extends into June, the trees were coming into leaf. Cyclists glided along the embankments.

On warm days I would arrive at my favourite sand island on the Vistula early in the morning when only solitary fishermen were about and the occasional traditional wooden boat fought the tide. I waded across shallow water through a gentle current, towing my airbed to a sand bar partly covered with low trees and shrubs. I ignored the more obvious signs of pollution bobbing past. In the distance an occasional red and white striped chimney or heavy power line reminded one of the destructive industrial past. The river has not been dredged and is not navigable along its complete length. The low banks, lined with white willow and black poplar, water chickweed and spindle tree, are criss-crossed by paths, the broad surface of the water broken by abstract swathes of white sand. Occasionally a cow wanders to the shore to drink and we are suddenly transported to

---

40 *ad flumen Vistlam a desertis Sarmatiae* (to the river Vistula in the deserts of Sarmatia). *The Natural History*, Pliny the Elder 4.25

the Suffolk of John Constable. Under a low spindle tree I unfolded my deck-chair, put the iced beer in the shade and read some Polish history as the slow, solemn tide flowed towards the 'Sarmatian Ocean', as the Baltic Sea was anciently known. Sunlight glittered from the ruffled surface and children's laughter drifted on the breeze. Bi-planes passed overhead and sometimes a glider performed lazy acrobatics in the thermals. At dusk swallows dipped and dived, lightly kissing the surface. I would stay until the voracious mosquitoes began to bite.

As the days of early summer passed in a haze I began to realize from my reading that this unassuming river was in many respects Poland itself, the bloodstream of the country, the very health of the nation reflected in the condition of its waters and their circulation. Not only were the finest Polish cities sited along its course but it had played a central role in history. The river was celebrated in heroic literature, played a strategic role in valiant military battles and created the romance of Napoleon's Vistula Lancers, his personal *Chevau-Légers Lanciers.*

On magical Midsummer Night, known in Poland as *Noc Kupały,* wreaths with candles that symbolize maiden virginity are floated optimistically down the Vistula by young girls. On summer days a tall, beautiful Polish girl with auburn hair habitually drifted into my view, sauntering languidly along the shaded path, her naked body berry-brown in those early days of sudden heat, wearing a minimal beaded thong. She would excavate a tiny cave in the sand of the river bank and build a dam or a castle before lying in the sun like a baking salamander. I was fascinated by her total lack of modesty as she lethargically smoked a cigarette and adjusted her long limbs to the sun. Without much difficulty I could imagine my naked Polish beauty lying on the bank, reed-thin and elegant, to be the legendary Mermaid of Warsaw, defender of the city.

The most popular version of the mermaid story is of a beautiful maiden who left the waters of the Vistula to rest on the sandy shore just below the present Old Town. She loved the picturesque spot so much she decided to stay. One day some fishermen noticed a strange swirling of the waters as if someone was tangling the nets and freeing their catch. They set out to capture her but the *syrena* so beguiled them with her beautiful voice that they allowed her to swim free. However a grasping merchant realized he could make a fortune exhibiting her talents. He captured her and locked her in a shed without water or light. One night her lamentable cries were heard by a young farmhand who rushed to her assistance with some friends and released the dehydrated beauty. Once more luxuriating in the stream, in a gesture of gratitude the mermaid promised to defend the town against attack. There are many representations of her lithe form about the city and the Warsaw Coat of Arms endows her with a sword and shield to protect her people.

But is this not too lyrical a sketch of an abandoned artery to be taken seriously? Are these not the etiolated musings of a spoilt Westerner who arrived in a ruined country at the conclusion of an extended process of desperate victimization, a country struggling to rise to its feet? The vigour of the country is reflected in the condition of the river. The clear waters of the eighteenth-century Enlightenment, the love of unblemished nature, had given way to pollution and neglect, war and the prostitution of nature to industry under communism. As I gazed into the deceptive eddies of the murky current I attempted to make sense of the archaeology of signs that Poland sets before the traveller. Nothing in this country is ever what it seems to the occasional visitor.

Deep within history the currents of the Vistula swiftly carried the ashes of Jews pulverized at Auschwitz-Birkenau, mingled the blood of resistance fighters with that of their enemies, killed fish with communist effluent, claimed lives through floods. But the river had also been a favourite playground in the past with pleasure steamers, sunbathers and healthy swimmers at recreational areas outside Warsaw such as Bielany and Młociny. The river was lovingly depicted by Polish artists in nostalgic landscapes. The greatest gems of Polish architecture had been constructed along its banks. The present return to civilized pleasures means that pollution is slowly being reduced and riverside cafés and sophisticated restaurants are opening once more in towns and cities along the increasingly balmy shore. The Vistula is a symbol of the neglected ecology of the country and its tentative recovery. I determined to explore its course, a path through the complexities of Polish history that would require more than one journey to complete.

*

From the first to the fourth century AD the ancient cultures of the Wielbark or Germanic Goths settled the lands of what is now Poland east of the Vistula and south of the estuary at the Bay of Gdańsk. Ancient myths and legends associated with the source of the river may have been present in their oral history intoned in stone-circle ceremonies and over burial mounds. We have gold and silver pendants, clasps, necklaces and jewellery of delicate workmanship from their necropolises to soften the image of barbarians covered by the 'skins of savage beasts' as described by Tacitus. The Slavic tribes of the *Wiślanie* and *Polanie* had arcane beliefs now lost in the clammy marshes and lakes of the Great Unknown of the east. Finding the fabled source of a river, its myths and mythologies may become a process of mystical reflection but in this case it is a lost world.

Fresh pine woods just below the summit of Barania Góra (Ram Mountain) in the Silesian Beskid mountains of Upper Silesia conceal the clear and healthy origins of the Vistula River. The source lies beside the Moravian Gate, a part of the Amber Road and the ancient pass for traders and marauders between the northern European plain and the Danube.

Crystal streamlets rushing over polished rocks collide to form the tinkling cascades of the Little White Vistula. This is joined by the Little Black Vistula and the Malinka in a small lake, finally breathing freely as the Vistula itself. I drank the pure cool waters of the first streams with delight, reflecting that by the time they reached Warsaw I would hardly touch the polluted flow with my toe. The Polish President's eyrie, a castle clinging to the hillside above the lake, has been much rebuilt in unromantic grey stone with a helicopter pad and orange windsock. In the Polish fashion, a new asphalted road up to the castle promptly ends at the upper boundary and resumes its impossible rutted, potholed surface further into the mountains. The river broadens through a series of soulless summer resorts to enter Lake Goczałkowickie, an immense reservoir of drinking water and a mechanism of flood control. The mauve vista of the distant mountains across the lake from the minor road following the shore is on a biblical scale.

*

'*Cyganie! Cyganie!*' a voice screamed down the telephone at 3.00am. 'The gypsies are attacking your car!'

Falling into my suitcase in the dark I attempted to rush outside but the doors were locked. I ran into the bathroom and climbed out of the window, appearing at the gatehouse lodge in disarray, ludicrously dressed in yellow pyjamas printed with classic cars.

'They were here, Sir, very close to the old Rolls-Royce! Perhaps there are damages. Here is my torch – we cannot see in this darkness.' I could make out a long cigarette burn where ash had fallen on the bonnet. No matter. The car had collected many noble war wounds over the years and badly needed repainting.

'Where are they?' I looked around, disconcerted.

'I chased them over the walls. They have run back to their camp in the valley. Don't thank me, Sir! Small beer to me, Sir!'

I returned to bed but not to sleep. Emboldened by having recently purchased the 'team FSO' I had perhaps foolishly brought my own classic car to Poland that first winter against the advice of everyone I knew. Their objections acted as a perverse goad and I was to repeat the adventure later in the summer in more reasonable weather.

The previous few days had been spent exploring Lower Silesia, an area rich in an increasingly forgotten German history. A feast of 'Wild boar in Ammonia' at a restaurant in the charming town of Jelenia Góra set me up to climb Mt Śnieżka (Schneekoppe). At 1603 metres it is the highest peak in the granite Karkonosze Mountains (*Riesengebirge* or Giant Mountains) of Silesia on the Czech border. Initially I got lost in the car, following narrow logging tracks covered in sheets of discoloured ice and melting snow, narrowly avoiding skidding off the edge into treacherous gullies. This landscape of magnificent pine forests has been ravaged by logging, pollution and acid rain to resemble the Somme after the Great War. Entire hillsides were covered with gaunt matchstick trunks and spiky pine branches stripped of needles. Carpathian birch and mountain ash stood grotesquely naked. The single German word *Waldsterben* means 'the dying of the forest'. A hidden factory spewed yellow smoke from a thin chimney. Poisons caused healthy trees to writhe into mutant shapes. What would a solitary traveller in a painting by the great artist of German Romanticism, Caspar

David Friedrich, have made of the desolate scene of 'the sacred fir forest, the national emblem of resurrection'?[41] Carved serpents consuming their own tails and gaping winged dragons adorn the astonishing Norwegian Świątynia Wang (Wang Chapel), making an ironic commentary on the devastation.

Deep snow obscured the path to the first station as I set off for the summit of the mountain. Wind from the Czech Republic screamed across the icy and precipitous track. Worn chains provided me a hand hold when I was unable to make any progress against the howling gale. At the first sub-station I avoided a dangerous path and swampy ground and bent lower to the wind. The immense expanses of snow on the Sudeten range and the forbidding, barren valleys on the Czech side stretched out before me. I was suddenly tapped on the shoulder. I swung round to confront a soldier in a green camouflage jacket carrying a sub-machine gun.

'Go back or come with me!' he shouted in what sounded like fractured Polish.

I had strayed over the unmarked Czech border and had great difficulty explaining my innocent error. The descent was worse than the ascent and I often lost my footing as the icy paths became torrents of rushing spring melt. Grasping the fragile chains and buffeted by winds funnelled along the Bohemian valleys I found it impossible to crawl around boulders to admire the Wagnerian vistas. Exhausted and hungry at the base of the mountain, I looked forward to 'Thigh in Flames *Arcadia*' and a large vodka at my favourite restaurant in Jelenia Góra before setting off at dusk for the castle of Książ.

The inaccessible fortress of Schloss Fürstenstein (Rock of Princes) in the foothills of the Sudeten mountains is a massive stronghold perched on an immense rock above a densely wooded ravine through which a cataract roars. The adjacent horse stud is famous for its pure-bred Arab and Anglo-Arabs. Zamek Książ was one of two castles owned by Baron Hans Heinrich XV, who married the remarkable Englishwoman Daisy of Pless. The other is Zamek Pszczyna, close to the Vistula in Upper Silesia.

I arrived at Książ late in the evening, driving through the Silesian

41 *Landscape and Memory*, Simon Schama (London 1995) p. 127

dusk and the depressing streets of the sooty town of Wałbrzych (Waldenburg). Hitler had planned a crazed rebuilding of the castle, the Red Army had plundered it and V2 rockets had been launched on England from the surrounding hills. *Lohengrin* was being broadcast direct from Bayreuth. Clouds scudding across the moon bathed the snowy towers in an unearthly light, a suitably Wagnerian setting for the Knight of the Holy Grail. I had gone to bed with dreams of boats, swans and the beautiful Elsa of Brabant until brutally woken by the telephone.

Polish castles often provide astonishing stories. One such history was the glamorous life of the largely forgotten Daisy of Pless, who lived at Fürstenstein before the Great War. Her diaries reveal a glittering world of privilege in an unremittingly Prussian atmosphere. After the drama of the night I wandered rheumy-eyed for breakfast at the unlikely named Bolko Café, dedicated to Duke Bolko I. Over a so-called 'Turkish' coffee I contemplated the engravings of unknown and severe Prussians that lined the walls.

The name 'Bolko' sounds faintly amusing to the English ear, a person one would be unlikely to take seriously. Originally this Polish Piast prince had fortified the castle to protect the trade route between Silesia and Bohemia in the thirteenth century. Since 1509 the stronghold had belonged to the Reichsgrafen von Hochberg und Freiherren von Fürstenstein (Counts of Hochberg and Barons of Fürstenstein). In more modern times the castle had been inhabited by a largely forgotten doyenne of Victorian society, Mary-Theresa Olivia Cornwallis-West, popularly known as Daisy of Pless. In 1891 she married the phenomenally wealthy 'smokestack baron', Hans Heinrich XV, Count of Hochberg and Prince of Pless. His wealth from the mineral resources of Silesia was rumoured to exceed that of the Emperor Wilhelm II himself. A handsome Prussian with a fine moustache, dressed in a uniform festooned with acres of braid, he maintained an immense household of postilions, coachmen, powdered footmen and liveried servants. At their wedding in London he emboldened her 'to become a good German'. Triumphal arches proclaimed 'Be Welcome German Eagle and Albion's Rose!'

They were to have three sons and a family life fraught with high drama and sadness. Daisy found the extreme formality of Prussian life claustrophobic, and felt that she had been sold to the Prince by her ambitious mother. Beautiful, perspicacious, a talented singer trained by a Florentine and an accomplished pianist, she was never passionately 'in love' with Hans but yearned desperately for her first love, whose humble social origins had been violently rejected by her mother. Homesickness for England made the cultural differences with Prussia a torture. '. . . one must simply make up one's mind not to think; but go on behaving like a *sensible* idiot.'[42]

King Edward VII christened the Cornwallis-West children 'the Wild West Show'. Fürstenstein and Pless attracted the cream of English and European aristocracy for extravagant shooting parties. Fancy-dress balls, motor trips and garden parties were staged in the summer. Winter delights included tobogganing and sleighs 'flying over the snow' drawn by swift Arab ponies. 'Masses of people' came for the sybaritic delights of Fürstenstein – the Emperor Wilhelm II, Emperor Karl of Austria, the Crown Prince and Princess of Prussia, the Duchess of Connaught, Lord and Lady Curzon, Prince Albert of Schleswig-Holstein, Grand Duke Michael of Russia, Vita Sackville-West, Guy Wyndham and his sister Lady Elcho. The xenophobic, frugal and moral Prussians were outraged by this flamboyant foreign cabal in their midst except, perhaps, the young Crown Prince William of Prussia who penned the jolly verse 'Always happy, no distress, when I visit Daisy Pless' in the Castle Pless Visitors' Book.[43]

As I journeyed along the Vistula through Upper Silesia in the shadow of the Silesian Beskid mountains, I encountered their other great Castle of Pszczyna (Pless). This mansion lies at the edge of a forest a few kilometres north of the river after it emerges from Lake Goczałkowickie. Once a fortified castle, its present appearance is a pleasantly coherent and restrained effort by the French neo-renaissance architect Gabriel-Hippolyte Destailleur (1822–93). During the baroque phase of the castle's long life, the composer Telemann spent glorious summers at Pless as a young *Kapelmeister* and composer.

Lawns roll down to serpentine lakes and a Japanese tea pavilion with low stone tables stands on a misty island. An ice house and

42 *The Private Diaries of Daisy, Princess of Pless 1873–1914* (London 1950) p. 135
43 October 1902

viewing tower, fig houses, a Chinese gate and a superb Palladian *dwór* lie at the edge of the park. The ensemble confirms Horace Walpole on gardening abroad: 'I should think the little princes of Germany, who spare no profusion on their palaces and country houses, most likely to be our imitators.'

The mansion possesses one of the most original nineteenth-century interiors on the continent. Bison heads, the antlers of thousands of fallow deer, mountain goats and stags, elks and rhinoceros horns fill all the considerable wall space. The Princes von Pless were certainly mad on hunting, if not actually mad. In 1914 tensions in Europe mounted. The Emperor Wilhelm II, staying at Pless, complained to Daisy of being fearfully misunderstood, at which moment she noted 'a tear fell on his cigar'.

Subsequently it was as the Imperial German Headquarters that the castle achieved prominence. 'Sister Daisy' worked for the Red Cross for the four years of the war but was persecuted as a sympathizer and spy. The Berlin press invented sensationalist tales about her, worthy of an operetta. '*The faithful friend of the Emperor* simply turns out to be *a traitor to our country!*' a rag shrieked.[44] The war on the Eastern Front was not as immobile as the trench war of attrition in the West. Forced to fight for the partitioning power that controlled their territory, Russia, Austro-Hungary or Germany, Pole tragically fought Pole. Some half a million Poles lay dead at the end of this slaughter in the East, many at the hands of their brothers.

Golo Mann, the popular historian and son of Thomas Mann, summed up the German Revolution of 1918 which followed the military collapse and laid the foundations of the Weimar Republic.

> The princes went. Hohenzollern and Wittelsbachs, Wettiner and Guelphs and Zähringer, the dynasties which for a thousand years had shared or decided, as they did in 1848, the fate of Germany – within two days they all vanished . . .[45]

Hans Heinrich was financially ruined when the wealthy region of Upper Silesia became an autonomous region of Poland by a deeply

44 *Daisy, Princess of Pless (1873–1943): A discovery* John Koch (Edmonton 2003) p. 256
45 *The History of Germany since 1789*, Golo Mann (London 1996)

controversial plebiscite in 1921. Daisy's life mirrored this collapse. She wrote to King George V of her misery as an Englishwoman married to a German at this moment of history. '. . . my husband is behaving vilely . . . I only implore you Sire for the sake of the old days to give me a minute's thought'. The poisonous atmosphere ended in their divorce in 1922 but the monies of his generous settlement had been eroded by political reversals and family scandals.

At a ball in Vienna Hans Heinrich XV met the beautiful Clotilde de Silva y Gonzales de Candamo and they were married soon after in 1925. Daisy's youngest son Bolko, although of fragile health, was a *bon viveur* fond of racing cars, parties, the company of beautiful women and, as it turned out, some rather dubious friends. To everyone's horror he became romantically involved with his mother-in-law despite being twelve years younger. As lovers they travelled openly together around fashionable Europe. To a punctilious Prussian aristocratic family the pressure of such a scandal was immeasurable and Hans Heinrich XV paid all their expenses in a vain endeavour to maintain his honour. The fraught marriage of Hans Heinrich and Clotilde was finally annulled and he insisted that Clotilde marry his son. In March 1934, Bolko was arrested and imprisoned on an obscure charge and his health began rapidly to deteriorate. Daisy paid all his debts and utilized the family friendship with Joachim von Ribbentrop, at that time Hitler's Minister Plenipotentiary at Large, to arrange his release. The intervention was fruitless, however, and Bolko died in June that same year.[46]

The multiple sclerosis which had plagued Daisy for years now bound her permanently to a wheelchair. Desperately unhappy, abandoned by everyone except her two surviving sons, she was restricted to living with a female companion in a couple of rooms of the gatehouse at Fürstenstein. The malevolent authorities at times denied her money for food and even fuel for heating. The Nazis evicted her and moved her into one of the villas in the park of the

---

46 For the extraordinary story of the marriage of Hans Heinrich XV and Clotilde de Silva I am indebted to *Księżna Daisy: Pani na Książu i Pszczynie*, Beata Górnioczek and Bronisława Jeske-Cybulska (Mikołów 2002)

castle at Wałbrzych (Waldenburg). The terrible wasting illness claimed her a day after her seventieth birthday on 3 July 1943. Harold Nicolson later wrote in *The Times*: 'In a world of snobbery, she remained natural. In a world become harsh, her cheerfulness and kindness were a beacon.'

The Vistula, mournful in the fog at this early hour, laps silently at the concrete ramp. Dew has crystallized to ice on the long grass as the clanking ferry makes its passage across the water. The hand-operated single-vehicle conveyance emerges from the gloom like a wraith. Driving is difficult and hazardous as the police force us to take a detour through the marshy and unhealthy land over a rutted track. However on the other side of the river the fog begins to lift, the frost a filigree of rime sparkling on the birch branches against intense blue. Soon the sound of locomotive hooters, trains metallically and rhythmically crossing points, distant machinery and barking dogs announces the dreary town and rail-head of modern Oświęcim (Auschwitz). These sounds, so banal and everyday, have gathered about themselves frightful associations. Richard, a particularly observant travelling companion, lapses into silence. The shock of this, my first visit to Auschwitz-Birkenau, is indelible.

The death camp always frightened me from the written accounts of its terrors and a childhood visit to the blood ditches of Dachau. Such is the power of this potent symbol of evil that I am apprehensive as I approach the gates. A shock, then, to encounter a pleasantly restored village, rows of innocuous red-brick barracks with a flight of steps to a porch, a dainty wrought-iron lamp, each block numbered as if for the delivery of post. The barracks are tidily arranged along a gravelled street lined with poplar, birch and chestnut trees and occasional concrete tubs of shrubs. In spring daisies speckle the lawns bright yellow and birds sing. But the barbed wire strung between concrete posts, the insulators, lamps and watchtowers make a grim frame. A toy town then with a heart of sadistic fire and a mind of cold stone. More sanitized today, the camp is a fine international museum and Holocaust study centre, a destination for the touring world and scholars of the Shoah, a reverent memorial to that 'voyage to the limits of a particular experience',[47] with signs carefully labelled in three languages. But on my first visit to the camp it seemed more threatening, a place redolent of the evil charm of the Nazis, a place with few visitors. Crude signs had been erected in almost grudging remembrance. Paradoxically this brought one closer to a barbarism beyond the power of language to engage.

On a similar spring day in April 1940 the nondescript farmer and former assistant to the commandant at Dachau concentration camp, *SS Hauptsturmführer* (Captain) Rudolf Hoess, began his official appointment to transform a former dilapidated Polish army barracks into a transit camp for Polish prisoners. Its ultimate function as a factory of death had not yet been conceived. 'I have never personally hated the Jews,' he later wrote fantastically in his autobiography.

The history of the horrors and development of the camp are described in minute detail in numerous sources but certain activities seemed to me particularly obscene. The playing of classical music in Auschwitz is shocking if one believes that art has any humanizing function. On misty mornings like that of our visit, squads of prisoners would stagger to work in the fog and return through the gate dragging their murdered, dead and emaciated companions back through the slush and slime. One of the six camp orchestras (one contained over a hundred musicians), perhaps directed by the conductor of the former Warsaw Radio Orchestra, might strike up Schubert's festive *Marche Militaire*. In Auschwitz it became a hellish *danse macabre*, utilized to maintain the prisoners' marching step. The orchestra played during the monstrous *Selektionen* when the healthy were separated from children, the sick or infirm, who were immediately despatched to the gas chambers. Amid the suffering one clearly saw 'the perceptible expression of its geometrical madness ... When this music plays, we know that our comrades, out in the fog, are marching like automatons; their souls are dead and the music drives them, like the wind drives dead leaves, and takes the place of their wills ...'[48.]

---

47 The Polish author Tadeusz Borowski was born in the Ukraine in 1922, survived Auschwitz and Dachau and committed suicide in Warsaw in 1951. His Auschwitz stories, written in a detached and laconic style, are the most gruelling, ironic and vivid expression of camp life on record.

48 Originally *If This Is A Man*, re-titled for later editions *Survival in Auschwitz*, Primo Levi (London 1996) p. 51

The SS had determined they would now dance to a ghoulish Nazi tune. A camp doctor, Margita Schwalbová, wrote: 'Auschwitz was a camp of absurd contradictions and insane inventions. One of its ironies was the music.' The ruthless logic once begun had to be carried through to an inevitable resolution.

Thomas Mann, agonizing over the relationship of ethics and aesthetics in his novel *Doctor Faustus*, perceptively refers to music as 'that curiously cabbalistic craft'.[49] The composer Adrian Leverkühn makes a Faustian pact with Satan, a dalliance with the 'poisoned butterfly' of music. For the Nazis, German music became the emotional confirmation of their rightness in exterminating the disgusting 'vermin' in their midst. All musical genres were performed in the camp, from the symphonies of Beethoven to the blackly humorous song *The Best Times of My Life*.

'A Hungarian at the piano, a virtuoso ... He played Mozart, Beethoven, Schubert, Bach. And then he suddenly played a funeral march by Chopin. And when he stopped, he sat without moving, hands on the keys. We all understood; we understood him and he understood us.'[50]

Music on the occasion of an execution made the anguish particularly acute. The fine women's orchestra at Birkenau (directed by the famous violinist Alma Rosé, whose mother was Gustav Mahler's sister) was particularly sought after by the musical connoisseurs of the SS after a demanding day on the selection ramp despatching women and children to the gas chamber. Dr Mengele liked to relax to the unresolved chords of *Tristan und Isolde* after a tiring day carrying out comparative autopsies on murdered twins. This psychopath once asked the cellist Anita Lasker-Wallfisch to play Schumann's deeply affecting *Träumerei* (Dreaming). Later she was to ask with savage irony, 'What *was* he dreaming about?'

The musicians themselves savoured a momentary island of peace, the performance of Bach a brief escape from a place worse than Dante's

49 *Doctor Faustus*, Thomas Mann (London 1968) p. 146
50 *Hefte von Auschwitz 5*, Jerzy Adam Brandhuber (1962)

Inferno. Their slightly better treatment often led to resentment from the other prisoners but composing, playing and listening to music enabled the physical and psychological survival of many of the damned. The suicide rate of musicians was among the highest in the camps as they were occasionally forced to play their entire family into the jaws of death.

The pseudo-scientific biomedical basis of the totalitarian state is what made the Nazis unique among absolute regimes. However, as one reads Nazi diaries it is the apparent 'normality' of those involved which truly disturbs. Hoess, ever the diffident and abysmally conventional commandant, arranged that an Austrian female political prisoner he fancied was employed as a servant in his luxurious family villa, 'a paradise of flowers', set some distance apart from the killing machines. He set her up in a love nest in the SS jail in the basement of the camp administration building. Hoess's sexual largesse also led him to thoughtfully set up a brothel near the main gate as an incentive scheme for prisoners with outstanding work records, known as the 'prominents'.

Blutordensträger (Bearer of the Order of the Blood) and cabinet-maker Felix Landau, serving on the execution squad, misses his lover and confides to his war diary, 'Now good night, my dear Hasi [bunny] ... My darling Trüdchen [Gertie], good night.' He frets she will not be strong enough to resist being unfaithful and might return to her fiancé. Later in the week he writes: 'As the women walked towards the grave they were completely composed ... Six of us had to shoot them. The job was assigned thus: three at the heart, three at the head. I took the heart. The shots were fired and the brains whizzed through the air. Two in the head is too much. They almost tear it off.' Felix reflects: 'Strange. *I am completely unmoved. No pity. Nothing.*'[51]

Auschwitz is an incubus with tentacles reaching into the present. Michel Lévi-Leleu decided to visit an exhibition in Paris of items from the Auschwitz Museum some sixty years after the closure of the camp. The keen eye of his young daughter recognized a battered suitcase that had belonged to her grandfather, a diamond broker deported to Auschwitz in 1943. The case had a tag inscribed with his address – 86 Boul. Vilette, Paris – and a handwritten

51 *Those Were the Days: The Holocaust As Seen by the Perpetrators and Bystanders*, Ernst Klee and Willi Dressen, eds, trans. Deborah Burnstone (London 1993) pp. 87–106

label: Pierre Levi – 48 Gruppe 10. The suitcase is a powerful refugee symbol and this example was authenticated and claimed by the family. Nonetheless the Auschwitz Museum, with the support of the Polish government, refused to return it. They justified ownership by asserting the case was a part of the collective memory of the Jews, a rare and vital piece of 'labelled evidence' proving the existence of the Holocaust. The law and the competing claims of collective and individual memory pose unique ethical dilemmas, a final twist of the historical knife.

One particularly grim irony of the Holocaust I discovered during my research was that the development of the pesticide Zyklon B or Prussic acid was supervised by a German Jew, the brilliant chemist Fritz Haber. Born in Wrocław (Breslau) in 1868, this gifted scientist and friend of Albert Einstein won the Nobel prize for chemistry in 1918 and among his many discoveries he was largely responsible for the development of German chemical warfare in World War I. He formulated the grotesque Haber's Rule, which is a simple mathematical expression of the relationship between the concentration of a poisonous gas and the duration a human must breathe it for toxicity or death to occur. $C \times t = k$ where 'C' is the concentration of the gas (mass per unit volume), 't' the duration of breathing to produce a toxic result and 'k' is a constant. His wife (also a chemist) opposed this research so vehemently she committed suicide with his service revolver after a dinner party one evening, shooting herself through the heart. A proud and patriotic German, he renounced Judaism but this did not save him from the wrath of the Nazis, and he was forced into exile in 1933. He died the following year a disillusioned man, never realizing that many of his relatives were to be gassed with Zyklon B.

The ravenous amoeba of Auschwitz I began to expand inexorably from modest beginnings, engulfing and digesting everything that came within its fatal embrace. As Jean Améry, a writer and survivor of Auschwitz-Monowitz, analysed the Nazi: 'With heart and soul they went about their business, and the name of it was power, domination over spirit and flesh, an orgy of unchecked self-expansion.'[52]

*

52 *At the Mind's Limits*, Jean Améry, quoted in *On the Natural History of Destruction*, W.H. Sebald (London 2004) p. 157

It is late afternoon as we drive towards Birkenau (Auschwitz II) and the early spring sun is losing its strength. The camp is almost deserted and a slight fog is settling over the wooden barracks. The brick watchtower or 'Death Gate' through which the single railway line runs is wreathed in a clammy mist. We pass through the former personnel entrance where trucks disguised as ambulances delivered the Zyklon B crystals to the gas chambers. Two guides are arguing loudly over the particular position of a crematorium.

'You never were here, I think! Go back to your books!'

'Show me your number, then!'

The elderly man rolled up his sleeve and thrust the tattooed number forward in the characteristic 'proving' gesture of former prisoners of Auschwitz.

'A high number! What would you know? Everything was blown up by then!'

They move off, gesticulating and shouting.

The immense size of the camp viewed from the main watchtower paralyses me as the banks of fog rise and fall. The neatly trimmed lawns of the present stretch ahead – a sanitized anachronism. 'Grass!' a shocked former inmate exclaimed on his recent visit. 'We would have eaten it!' As a form of torture, men were taken to the fields to cut the grass with their teeth.

I begin to distinguish various features. The wooden men's barracks of BIIa Quarantine, originally designed as stabling for fifty-two horses, are without windows, except for small ventilation shutters in the roof. At the peak of the killing over a thousand prisoners slept in each barrack, crammed into bunks or 'hutches', unable to turn on the filthy straw, a few overflowing buckets serving as lavatories. The stench of bodies encrusted with faeces was a nightly assault. A sign outside the latrines where men often drowned indicates a failed experiment in recycling. The Nazis hoped to use methane gas from the decaying excrement to illuminate the camp, power cars and other machinery. In contrast the guard dogs lived well in Auschwitz with a dedicated cook, green areas, warm kennels and a proper hospital. Hundreds of brick chimneys stand isolated like sentinels on the plain, the timber of the barracks requisitioned by homeless Poles after liberation.

The day is getting colder as we approach the infamous unloading ramp where in the spring and summer of 1944 the orgiastic killing climaxed. Marshalled quickly into interminable rows the Jews were 'selected' by Dr Mengele and other Nazi physicians to go straight to the gas chamber or to slave labour in the industrial sub-camps. Deceitful to the last, politeness and promises calmed the victims as they approached those infamous showers.[53] In less than eight weeks over 320,000 were liquidated. Many had already suffocated, crushed in the wagons and desperate for air and water, or overcome by the fetid heat.

> The train has been emptied. A thin pockmarked SS man peers inside, shakes his head in disgust and motions to our group, pointing his finger at the door.
> '*Rein.* Clean it up!'
> We climb inside. In the corners amid human excrement and abandoned wrist-watches lie squashed, trampled infants, naked little monsters with enormous heads and bloated bellies. We carry them out like chickens, holding several in each hand.
> 'Don't take them to the trucks, pass them on to the women,' says the SS man, lighting a cigarette.[54]

The Nazi regime perverted, perhaps forever, the sublime language of Goethe, Schiller, Heine and Hölderlin. Further on we stumble over the ruins of Crematorium II with its two underground gas chambers and five furnaces, each with three retort ovens which could dispose of over 1500 corpses in 24 hours. Rubble now covers the spot, commemorated with a few withered wreaths. In an effort to conceal their crimes the Nazis dismantled what they could and blew up the rest. Flowers and candles are pitifully placed on the collapsed roofs, unmelted snow lies in the interstices of the shattered concrete. Ashes and bones were crushed and 'taken in lorries to the Vistula, where they immediately drifted away and dissolved'.[55]

---

53 Hence the vicious irony of the title of Tadeuz Borowski's story *This Way for the Gas, Ladies and Gentlemen* (London 1976) set in Auschwitz-Birkenau. The Nazis were often polite as a point of policy to keep panic to a minimum.

54 *This Way for the Gas, Ladies and Gentlemen,* Tadeusz Borowski (London 1976) p. 39

55 *KL Auschwitz Seen by the SS: Autobiography of Rudolf Hoess* (State Museum in Oświęcim 1991) p. 100

The weather is closing in now and we are losing sight of the path in the fog but the camp draws us on. We wander disorientated through an area of pine trees to the foundations of the storehouses known as *Kanada*.[56] Here the stolen belongings of the prisoners were stored in overflowing warehouses before shipment to the Reich. Like the country of Canada, the name came to symbolize a place of fabled riches inaccessible to the prisoners. Women who worked here sorting clothes had a better chance of survival. Warmed with Jewish food, they could keep their hair and even fell in love.

By 1944 some 6,000 people a day were being murdered in the gas chambers. The *Sonderkommando*[57] extracted the bodies, covered in sweat, urine, excrement or menstrual blood, by thrusting hooks into the mouths of the corpses and landing them like game fish. They melted gold teeth into ingots and extracted diamonds from the colon. As incentives to their monstrous task, before being inciner-ated themselves, they were encouraged to wear silk underwear and shirts, utilize fine shaving brushes and perfumed soap, stomp about the mud in comfortable hand-made leather boots. During their brief lives in camp they ate off crested porcelain with silver cutlery, drank vintage Bordeaux and champagne, the wine catching the glow from silver candelabra. Feasts were laid out on damask cloths in the attics above the crematoria where they lived. The SS also frenziedly enriched themselves from *Kanada* despite theft being officially pun-ishable by death. Hoping to increase their sexual power some soldiers hid the genitals of newly butchered bulls amongst the stolen currency and pearls in their lockers. Eichmann told Hoess that the entire Swiss jewellery market of the time was dominated by the sales of the rare necklaces and fabulous gems stolen from the Jews.

Often accused of apathetic compliance, Jews did resist in Auschwitz as the extraordinary and largely unknown story of the Pole Witold Pilecki, an officer in the 13th Regiment of Uhlans, testifies. During the

56 *Kanada* or *Canada* (*Effektenlager*) was camp jargon for the 35 warehouses at Birkenau filled to bursting with the belongings looted from prisoners. Five days before the liberation of the camp SS men set fire to 30 of them, which burnt for days, but six partly destroyed storehouses survived with their contents.

57 The *Sonderkommando* were Jews forced under pain of immediate execution of themselves or their families to guide victims into the gas chambers, empty them of corpses and burn the bodies in the crematoria. They were gassed themselves on a regular basis to liquidate them as witnesses to crime.

Battle of Britain in September 1940, using forged papers and an assumed name, Pilecki allowed himself to be arrested in a Warsaw round-up by the SS and was taken voluntarily to Auschwitz with the incredible intention of setting up a resistance movement there.

The clandestine network was centred around the hospital and the labour office. The movement assisted many prisoners to work in 'better' gangs, perhaps with more food or working under a roof, which was one secret to survival. Working parties built secret links with resistance movements outside the camp. They took photographs and wrote reports concerning the murderous conditions, which were smuggled out. A secret radio transmitter was set up in the basement of Block 20, an area reserved for infectious diseases. This was a section of the hospital SS men were unwilling to enter. Typhus-infected lice were bred there and casually thrown on the uniforms of any SS officers visiting the hospital, some of whom were infected and died. These reports eventually made their way to London but were largely ignored or simply not believed.

The daring, even stylish, escape of four prisoners dressed as SS officers in a stolen Steyr 220 cabriolet in June 1940 was facilitated by the camp underground. By April 1943 Pilecki himself had decided to escape and personally take the news of the horrifying exterminations to the Commander of the Home Army in Warsaw, hoping for a strong response from the Allies. It would never come. Pilecki's escape from the Auschwitz bakery on a wet and gloomy night, assisted by Polish partisans crossing and re-crossing the Vistula by ferry, rivals some of the best escape tales of the war.[58]

The final flourish of the resistance movement was in the courageous revolt of the *Sonderkommando* during the final convulsive murder of Hungarian Jews in 1944. They managed to blow up Crematorium IV with smuggled explosives. The SS, armed with machine guns and dogs, shot around 250 fighting rebels and a further 200 prisoners were shot on the spot. After this violence it was suggested to Dr Mengele that 'this environment is highly unsuitable for scientific research'.

'What's wrong? Getting sentimental?' he answered coldly.[59]

---

58 Witold Pilecki's extraordinary story and that of the resistance movement in Auschwitz is told in detail in *Fighting Auschwitz: The Resistance Movement in the Concentration Camp*, Józef Garliński (London 1975)

59 *Auschwitz: A Doctor's Eyewitness Account*, Miklos Nyiszli (New York 1960) p. 171

Many survivors said humour and laughter were major ingredients in strengthening the mental perseverance that created the will to live, a defence mechanism that enabled these debased humans to retain a sense of identity. A television interview concerning life in Auschwitz as a slave labourer posed a question to a survivor.

'Why do you think prisoners always had to move quickly? The Germans wanted everything done as fast as possible. *Schnell! Schnell!*'

The survivor looked thoughtful for a moment and replied, 'Well, you know, the Germans are a very *sporting* people.'

The light begins to fail and fog swirls through the shattered window frames and the huge autoclaves of the *Zentralsauna* or Disinfection Block. We mistake it in the gathering dusk for a crematorium. *Ein Laus Dein Tod!* (One Louse, Your Death!) a poster with a skull and monstrous louse screams in Polish and German, symbolically identifying both Jew and louse as 'vermin' to be exterminated. The clothes and camp uniforms were deloused with the same blue crystals of Zyklon B used for gassing humans.

As we emerge from the *Zauna* it is almost dark and I realize we are lost in thick fog that has come down over Birkenau camp. We are probably locked in, as it is late and we have lost track of passing time. Richard is grimly quoting lines from Marlowe's *Doctor Faustus*:

Hell hath no limits, nor is circumscribed
In one self place. But where we are is hell,
And where hell is there must we ever be.

'Yes, Richard, but where are we now? Do you have any idea?'

'Let's walk towards the sounds of those trucks. It's probably the main road.'

We follow a path between the ruins of two more crematoria and a sinister pond looms up on the left. A crude sign informs us that the ashes of hundreds of thousands of Jews had been thrown into the dark waters. Mist lies heavy over it, broken branches of trees rising through the surface like supplicant palms. A dreadful silence descends. The clammy air, hooting of trains and distant barking of dogs shrouds me in terrible despondency. It is cold as we stand listening for a passing lorry but hear only distant machinery operating or sirens being tested. The atmosphere seems thick with ghosts.

We stand in the fog in silence near a perimeter fence blocking our way and listen again. Visibility is now down to about six feet. A car, this time it's probably a Fiat 126p judging from the high-pitched engine chatter and wavering headlights. We are relieved to find the main road rising out of the miasma alongside the quarantine barrack buildings and finally the savage silhouette of the 'Gate of Death' emerges from the gloom.

'*Nacht und Nebel* – Night and Fog indeed,' Richard mumbles.
'What?'

'*Nacht und Nebel.* It was a ruthless decree that caused political prisoners of the Reich to disappear into the night mist, never to be heard of again. Feels rather like that just now.'

The personnel entrance is not patrolled and with some difficulty we manage to escape. We drink a King's Ginger Liqueur to warm ourselves and reconfirm some degree of civilization after a journey through the underbelly of life. But hunger does not grip our stomachs in a vice.

Following this welter of blood, one feels compelled to ask questions that cannot be answered rationally. Did any Nazis feel some Nietzschean 'human, all-too-human' remorse, guilt or degree of moral unease at between 1.3 and 1.5 million deaths in this one camp?[60] Did any feel any regret for the misapplication of the German genius for science and organization; any horror at the first industrial application of recycling to the human body itself? Perhaps one did, perhaps many did. There were no whys in Auschwitz and therefore no remorse.

In his memoirs secretly written during twenty years in Spandau prison, Albert Speer, 'the good Nazi', Hitler's architect and Minister for Armaments, writes that he was warned by a friend 'never under any circumstances' to inspect the concentration camp in Upper Silesia. He failed to query his friends, Hitler or Himmler, on the issue of slave labour and extermination at Auschwitz. 'During those few seconds, while Hanke[61] was warning me, the

60 Auschwitz-Birkenau Memorial Museum estimate
61 Karl Hanke, *Gauleiter* of Lower Silesia

whole responsibility became reality again ... as an important member of the leadership of the Reich, I had to share the total responsibility for all that had happened. For from that moment on, I was inescapably contaminated morally ... I had closed my eyes ... Because I failed at that time, I still feel, to this day, responsible for Auschwitz in a wholly personal sense.'[62]

There is a renewal of Jewish religious and cultural life taking place in contemporary Poland. Music festivals of Klezmer bands in the Kazimierz district of Kraków, university courses in Hebrew, jazz performances, theatre and art exhibitions take place regularly in most major cities. The cornerstone of a Jewish museum and memorial has been laid in the former Warsaw Ghetto. After all, many of the most talented and creative minds in Polish artistic and scientific history were Polish Jews. Although the horrors should never be forgotten, the overturning of the prevalent vision of Poland as only a Jewish graveyard and nest of nascent anti-Semitism is slowly being supplanted by gestures of reaffirmation and reconciliation.

Leaving the camp our difficulties mount. It is hardly possible to drive in the heavy fog. I can scarcely see a foot in front of my face so Richard walks in the headlights and I follow slowly behind. He mistakenly leads me into a field along a track. An old tractor branded *Mengele* lies rusty and abandoned in a ploughed furrow full of water.

'Did you see that, Richard? Fancy naming a tractor after Dr Mengele.'

'His family owned the tractor factory. Didn't you know? He was a gilded youth.'

62 *Inside the Third Reich: Memoirs by Albert Speer* (London 1970) p. 376

CHAPTER 9

The Masculine Inanimate

The Polish corporate clients greatly feared 'company espionage'. They became infuriatingly vague when asked for the information necessary to formulate a programme – the communist mentality mired in suspicion was proving hard to shift. Course design was becoming so onerous that the team often threatened to leave for England. As the year progressed I felt my carefully constructed edifice was beginning to crumble. Geoff became resentful. He could be thoughtful and sacrificed much of his own time for the trainees but mutated into an aggressive bear when confronted with any authority figure. As an IT professional he criticized the language teaching staff.

'Just chatting – not a real job. They get it too easy.'

The Polish team were well trained and experienced. Most had learnt to speak with upper-middle-class English accents and quaint turns of phrase. They had spent five years at university studying English philology. They were always most supportive of our difficulties in adapting to a foreign country and made endless helpful suggestions and proffered many invitations. I asked Szymon where he was going for his summer holiday.

'Oh, me and the missus are popping down to the water meadows by the River Bug. We have a little place down there.'

Resentment of the native speakers began to build as they realized we were no better at English than themselves and in the case of Nick and Geoff a good deal worse. They also had to cope with two or three jobs to make ends meet. Our financial and computer expertise were superior but not for long. The Polish lack of professional self-confidence in those early days meant that as expatriates we were paid excessively well with air fares, accommodation, food and a car included. This unjustified discrepancy rankled. The disintegration of the project was brought about partly through the disproportionate cost of keeping us happy.

Our attempts to learn Polish met with mixed success under the friendly young professor from Warsaw University. He was incredibly patient and understanding and told us that Anglo-Saxons were the worst at learning Polish. The first problem was the alphabet. Polish is Western Slavic using Roman letters with accents rather than the Cyrillic alphabet of the East, which creates a dangerous illusion of familiarity. Polish is an enormously difficult language to master, up there with Vietnamese and Korean according to studies.

We began as a group class but Richard, with his natural gift for languages, tended to dominate and fly ahead, which upset the rest.

'Do you breast-feed?'

A timely utilitarian phrase betrayed his early mastery of the language and a suggestion of the object of his desires. Attendance soon began to drop off.

'The most important first phrase you must learn in Polish is *Nie ma* which means "There isn't any". You will hear this a lot so you must understand it. *Nie ma.* Could you repeat?'

'*Nie ma. Nie ma. Nie ma!*' we chorused.

Later in the week Richard was proficient enough to needle the others.

'I think you'll find that is the genitive, masculine, inanimate, Geoff, not locative animate,' he said over his steel half-moon glasses.

'Well, just get it out, says me. Life's too short for details. You're such a clever dick!'

Poles love giving foreigners tongue-twisters and watching or rather listening to their agony. Our teacher always finished the lessons with one from the poem *Chrząszcze* by Jan Brzechwa, a desperately demotivating experience:

'*W Szczebrzeszynie chrząszcz brzmi w trzcinie.*'

(In [the town of] Szczebrzeszyn a beetle buzzes in the reeds.)

'All those fuckin' Zs,' Nick mumbled in frustration and rudely walked out of the room.

'I need a haircut,' said Geoff. 'How do I ask for a trim?'

'*Proszę tylko przystrzyc,*' Mirek our professor obliged.

Everyone burst out laughing.

'Sounds like *Please give me the shits!*' Geoff laughed for a long time at that one.

'We'll ignore that. Actually, in Polish Scrabble the letter "Z" has the lowest score. Now isn't that interesting?' Richard smiled academically. 'Charles Dickens related that he had that very morning met a man whose name contained all the consonants and none of the vowels!'

I was usually paralysed into silence and frightfully self-conscious, positive that anything I said would be inaccurate, the wrong attitude completely.

One evening I got lost in central Warsaw looking for a restaurant called Troika, which specialized in Russian food and was situated in the Palace of Culture. I engaged a burly, forbidding former Soviet guard who was pacing up and down wearing a peaked cap and carrying a gun.

'*Proszę pani. Gdzie jest restauracja Trojka?*' I asked in my best Polish.

He looked at me witheringly and pointed in the general direction, grunted and turned on his heel, feeling for his pistol. It was only later that I realized I had asked, 'Excuse me, *Madam*. Where is the Troika Restaurant?'

Before I was beaten up, I decided to take private lessons with the eminent Professor Gronkiewicz at ruinous expense.

'In Polish language I believe there are twenty-nine consonants. But, my dear sir, my friend pan Profesor Czetwertyński from Lublin does not agree with me. He feels labial-velar semivowel and labial-velar approximant are same. I disagree most strongly with such heresy, my dear sir!'

He then unfolded a diagram of Polish vowels and consonants that might have been a wiring diagram for Concorde.

'Actually Professor, I would just like to make phone calls and book a restaurant. Simple things like that.'

'Ah, that is a long way off. You must take one step at each time.'

Needless to say, these lessons did not last long either. Polish is highly inflected (numerous cases and exceptions) so to say something accurately as a beginner is near impossible. To an Anglo-Saxon the very appearance of the words is intimidating. One madman I heard of had embarked on a translation of *Finnegans Wake* into Polish. He had already spent seventeen years translating *Ulysses*.[63] However if you make the effort to speak Polish in Poland a warm and communicative atmosphere is instantly created. Nowadays Poles tend to apologize for not speaking English rather than insisting as in the past, *'mów po polsku'* (speak Polish). I continue the struggle.

The English team lived in such close proximity to each other that tension rose, particularly when poor weather kept us indoors. I tried to distract myself with riding lessons at a nearby club. Poles are fine horsemen and I used to go out with Piotr, a former cavalry officer. Having a lesson in a field during a heavy snowfall was exhilarating – my part-Arab mare 'Habanera' steaming, the icy crystals striking my face, the hooves muffled by deep snow.

We had long given up going to restaurants together. 'What's this Polish muck?' was an inevitable question from Geoff. The 'Hospitality Suite' became a gladiatorial arena after every meal, particularly after supper before the trials of the *kawiarnia* and the girls. The spare room had been obtained only with great pressure on the Polish side. It was furnished with a wretched carpet, a rickety table and chairs, a washing machine and dryer, a refrigerator and a couple of defeated armchairs. When bored, Geoff would cut his toenails and leave heaps of clippings in the ashtray. Petty theft from the room was a constant annoyance. I brought this up on numerous occasions with Dr Grabski but he refused to attend to the serious security problems. We lost an electric toaster, an iron and a double-ring cooker. Richard had two calculators stolen. I became quite neurotic and attached padlocks to my cupboards. The team felt demoralized and perversely blamed me. The locking and unlocking of rooms each time you left even for an instant was an infuriating necessity. Many rooms were sealed with a piece of string between two bottle-tops filled with wax – one nailed to the door and the other to the jamb. I requested keys for the 'Hospitality Suite'. The next morning the lock itself had been stolen.

63 Maciej Słomczyński was far from a madman but a translator of genius from many foreign languages into Polish. He also wrote popular detective stories to keep the wolf from the door and facilitate his ambitious translations.

The vodka we kept in the freezer was a temptation to blue-rinsed Pani Roksana, who cleaned for us. During her work she would spray windows, mirrors and hinges with any aerosol she chanced upon and I often found my windows covered in spray starch. Hoover bags, broken glass and cigarette butts were emptied onto the roof when she thought no one was looking, slowly burying the dead pigeons that lay there. The right to sell or drown the kittens by the invariably pregnant team cat was also hers.

'*Koty wymiotują* (the kittens are vomiting),' she would declare and they would then disappear into the night, to the despair of the young female trainees.

After a decent swig of vodka, Pani Roksana would moisten and slide the label down the bottle in a pathetic attempt to conceal her pilfering. When the label disintegrated she took to replacing the guzzled amount with water, which froze solid.

When finally confronted she became breathless with palpitations. '*Pani Roksana jest "hooligan"!*' said Richard good-naturedly after one depredation. This sent her into gales of laughter for much of the morning and whenever she met him subsequently. Eventually we gave her a few bottles as she was, despite everything, rather a loveable soul at heart. Recriminations and absurd denials rang through the night among members of the team.

I had imported my favourite coffee from London: medium roast Kibo Chagga from H.R. Higgins (Coffee-man) in Duke Street. An extravagance but one of my very few gastronomic pleasures. I boiled bottled mineral water for the sacred brew but an argument erupted one evening about the 'poshness' of this approach. I suggested irritably that they boil the bore water. When Geoff made the Indian-manufactured instant Nescafé with this brown liquid I asked him how it tasted.

'A bit brackish. Nothing to worry me. Just get it down.'

'We're the lost legion out here. Abandoned on the Eastern Front,' commented David and continued with a plethora of complaints concerning the timetable, moving his long Morris dancer legs about and testing his bells. We drank a lot of vodka and I used to look forward to a heavy Saturday morning shot in a frozen glass. However as you drink your warm fingers take the edge off the cold and reduce the power blast.

'I really think we should invent the Vodka Glove,' Richard offered with a wry smile one morning.

'Another posh idea, I suppose,' Geoff said disagreeably.

'A miniature refrigeration unit could be built into the glove which keeps the external finger surface ice cold while keeping the hand warm.'

'Just get it down,' said Geoff.

The drabness of Warsaw added greatly to our depression. We often sprawled like sloths watching the snow fall. The low levels of illumination, the decaying architecture, the lack of neon signs, the vodka drunks staggering about after a 'hydraulic breakfast' at a *Non-Stop Alkohole* contributed to making a trip to the *Centrum* hardly worthwhile. Back then there were few decent restaurants as Poles only ate out on special occasions. Shops made little or no attempt to advertise and looked so uniform one could not be sure what they were selling until one was deep inside. The notorious *Pewex* shops offered a wide range of Western goods for hard currency and were popular with expatriates. Poles who hoarded dollars and high-ranking former communist *nomenklatura* were also permitted to use them.[64]

I often went to what I considered to be the perfect communist-era café in the Old Town called *Poziomka* (Wild Strawberry). The interior was dark and unwelcoming, gloomy and unchanged for years with faded plastic flowers and an elderly clientele. The coffee was strong, basic and served unceremoniously. The café had been a haunt of intellectuals and writers in the past and a refuge for insurgents under martial law. This establishment was not a place for the conspicuously successful in life but dedicated to those who had been

---

64 Originally the *nomenklatura* were an élite administrative subset of the general population of Communist Party members in the Soviet Union. In Poland, the *nomenklatura* did not always need to be Communist Party members but the Party needed to trust them. They had their own 'luxury' holiday centres and privileged access to ration cards enabling them to take delivery of a motor car or telephone more expeditiously. After the fall of the communist regimes in East Central Europe, many if not most of the *nomenklatura* held on to their administrative positions. Their perceived abuse of 'influence' and 'connections' to secure positions in the new system or well-remunerated positions in formerly state-owned industries remains the source of severe resentment and the subject of the investigative 'commissions' and process in Poland known as *lustracja*. However it was hardly surprising that the *nomenklatura* seamlessly adapted to the post-communist capitalist world. Similar financial goals are pursued without the ideological baggage which most Poles considered irrelevant anyway.

dealt a bad hand at birth. You could buy *half* a cup of coffee if you were too poor to afford a full cup, a truly great gesture of humanity in a heartless world.

An attractive exception to the general dullness was Nowy Świat or New World Street, the New Bond Street of Warsaw, lined with meticulously restored nineteenth-century neoclassical town houses that had belonged to past magnate families. Elegant boutiques were incongruously situated alongside robust hardware shops selling metal plate and washing powder. Many craftsmen still trade from small shops in Warsaw, making beautiful handmade brushes and brooms of every description, leather bindings for valuable books, violins, and locks. Watchmakers can repair any timepiece of any age while picture framers fashion antique frames with traditional sculpted clay mouldings of great artistry. Some of the last Jewish bespoke tailors and boot-makers using English broadcloth and Viennese leather continue to trade in these pleasant streets and hidden courtyards. The number of boutiques has recently expanded and fine pavement cafés in the Mediterranean style are shaded in summer by huge brewery-sponsored umbrellas. But something 'authentic' has been lost in this process of European standardization. An atmosphere of general equality has been replaced by the vanity and divisiveness of newly acquired wealth.

Markets made up of small kiosks sprawled around the base of the Palace of Culture. Plastic sheets laid on the ground by Ukrainians or Belarusians displayed pathetic small items for sale such as a single spoon, a clock, a cigarette lighter, three cigarettes and a frying pan.

After concerts I would visit historic Wedel for a cup of delicious hot chocolate served in elegant eighteenth-century surroundings. The chocolate was the only item available in these Adamesque interiors.[65] At the entrance, a heavy leather curtain parted to reveal a warm, welcoming interior. A charming old gentleman with a shock of white hair greeted one effusively and made obscure, amusing remarks in Polish as he took your coat and hat. A solitary cup of Polish chocolate was displayed in its own cabinet with a neatly printed price card underneath. This 'sacred object' was a triumph of

65 The neoclassical interiors of the Scottish architect and decorator John Adam were also popular in eighteenth-century Poland.

minimalism. The two 'drinking rooms' offered one a choice of mood, decorated as they were in neoclassical cool pale green or warmer rose doré. The waitress persisted in writing down your order even though there was only a single item to be had. This divine chocolate was so thick you could almost write your name on the surface.

The clientele were mainly lovers engrossed in each other and imbibing the wicked eroticism of the drink. Lingering over a cup of Wedel chocolate became one of Warsaw's greatest winter consolations. The rot of contemporary business pressure set in at Wedel when they began to offer a small *wafel* (wafer biscuit) with the chocolate in 1995. As Poland developed further under foreign investment the English company Cadbury installed the full commercial catastrophe of a drinks bar and food. The intimate chocolate house has now been relegated to the commonplace. As with much in contemporary Poland the romance of the East has gone forever West.

History reveals that Joseph Conrad's father, Apollo Nałęcz Korzeniowski, was a rather melancholic *szlachcic,* a 'knight' bearing the coat of arms Nałęcz.[66] He caused a 'patriotic disturbance' at Wedel when at the centre of intense insurrectionist activity in Warsaw against the Russian occupation of Poland. The fracas became one of a set of charges that sent the family into exile in 1862 at Vologda, an inhospitable frozen marshland five hundred kilometres north-east of Moscow. The four-year-old Conrad became seriously ill on the journey and his father wanted a halt in the transportation for medical treatment. The Russians, with characteristic fatalism, insisted that 'as a child is born only ultimately to die, the journey was to proceed at once'.[67]

---

66 In England or France a coat of arms 'belongs' to a person or family. Interestingly in Poland the coat of arms or *herb* is, as might be expected, quite the reverse. A family or person belongs to the coat of arms. Many families might share the same ancient coat of arms. The symbols on the *herb* are simple graphics possibly derived from the Sarmatian symbols of property known as *tamgas*, in turn derived from the Bosporans. A *szlachcic* possessed all the legal rights of the highest Western European nobility. In 1645 the Queen of France gave a ball at the Court of Louis XIV for the visiting *szlachcic* Krzysztof Opaliński, envoy of the King of Poland. Madame de Motteville was particularly miffed when Opaliński contemplated the flower of the French aristoctracy with an attitude bordering on indifference tending even to disdain. (For this material I am indebted to *Social Background of Sir Paul Strzelecki and Joseph Conrad*, Lech Paszkowski (Melbourne 1980) and *Black Sea*, Neal Ascherson (London 1995) pp. 238–241.)

67 Apollo in a letter to John and Gabriela Zagórski, Vologda, 27 June 1862

After the death of his adored and self-sacrificing mother, Conrad spent a long period alone with his father in this lonely and forbidding place. Here he absorbed his father's Latin and Polish-gentry sense of the Polish chivalric tradition and uniquely Polish notions of honour and fidelity to the national cause. 'My father read *Pan Tadeusz* aloud to me and made me read it aloud. Not just once or twice. I used to prefer *Konrad Wallenrod* . . . Later I liked Słowacki better.'[68] These moral characteristics often appear in his greatest work. Czesław Miłosz wished for a monument to Apollo in Kraków, 'portraying the man with the boy who owed him so much'.[69] He was often referred to as 'The Count' and Bertrand Russell observed that he was 'an aristocratic gentleman to his fingertips'. Others referred to his curious mixture of 'feminine grace and masculine incisiveness'. Throughout his life Conrad remained ambivalent towards the country of his birth, describing himself as 'a Polish nobleman cased in British tar'. Further, as an adult he was to observe 'Two things fill me with pride: that I, a Pole, am a master of the British merchant marine, and that I can write, not too badly, in English.' Conrad was eleven when his father died, an outcome which no doubt contributed to his dark and passionately tragic literary psyche.

Patriotism can take strange forms in Poland. Concert audiences at the *Filharmonia* were often harangued from the gallery by a curious personage I came to call the 'Polish Patriot'. A severe figure with shaved Sarmatian bullet-head and military bearing, formally dressed in white tie and tails sporting a row of miniature medals, he would make rousing speeches about Poland's heroic history. The audience would sit patiently through this Mussolini-type diatribe concerning the 'crime' of forgetting the Battle of Grunwald or the Warsaw Uprising. He once shook hands personally with the entire audience at the Warsaw Chamber Opera after making an impassioned speech concerning the massacre of Polish officers in the forest at Katyń. I have never discovered his identity. He has sadly disappeared from Warsaw concert life.

*

68 *Conrad Under Familial Eyes*, ed. Zdzisław Najder trans. Halina Carroll (Cambridge 1983) p. 199
69 Czesław Miłosz 'Apollo N. Korzeniowski: Joseph Conrad's Father' *Mosaic* VI/4 (1973) pp. 121–40

And so the 'inanimate males' sat in the disintegrating armchairs in a mood of disaffection, watching the dripping filter machine, downing vodkas, loading the tumble dryer with wet underwear and laughing and complaining about our situation. More often than not boredom and sexual promise inevitably drove us down to the *kawiarnia* to drink beer with a few of the more extrovert female trainees and dance for a couple of hours. The clouds of cigarette smoke, warm beer, dim lighting, deafening music, terrible coffee and all but naked nymphets, flirtatious in lacy skin-tight cycle shorts or microskirts, were at once wearing and enlivening.

'Look at that! Nice one, nice one. Heh – heh – heh. Excellent, excellent. Wouldn't mind giving her a portion. Heh – heh – heh,' Nick would invariably comment as a girl twirled and revealed most of what she had to offer.

The close erotic dancing is well practised, arousing and addictive, and I often went to bed very late. The closer you danced the more fulsome the compliments.

Conversation with the men, on the other hand, tended to be limited in scope and melancholically philosophical in a foggy, alcoholic Slavic manner. The barman was friendly but only had one tooth, which made understanding his conversation difficult. His mother, an aged crone, attended to the kettle that heated the brown bore water for coffee on an old electric ring. The boiling water was poured directly onto the grounds in the glass 'in the Turkish manner'.

We shared the training centre with some customs officers, who took to the old communist regime 'training course' idea with desperate vengeance. One might only have one or two 'courses' in one's life under communism so one made the most of them. On sleepless nights there would be an eruption in the early hours with wild stamping of boots on the ceiling, the click of high heels on the ceramic tiles, drunken vodka carousing, the old war songs or wild singing of *Sto lat! Sto lat!* (Live for a hundred years!) if it was someone's birthday. If I neglected to lock my door, drunken officers mistook my room for theirs and tried to get into bed with me. Some laughed maniacally and ran wildly through the forest. Furniture and stilettos flew from the windows into the garden like rain.

CHAPTER 10

Spring Loves

Poland has a wealth of stories of blighted love, perhaps the most tragic and moving of which is that of the refined Renaissance king Zygmunt II August (1520–72) and the sister of a Lithuanian magnate Barbara Radziwiłłówna (1520–51). The *szlachta* and the parliament were opposed to the marriage as she was a Calvinist and in any event they wished to diminish the power of the monarch. He married her in 1547 and assumed the throne in the face of considerable opposition. Within four years this most beautiful woman was dead in appalling circumstances. Suspicion fell on the King's own mother, Bona Sforza, 'a forbidding creature' who had been elevated to the malevolent higher echelons of intrigue and techniques of poison by her father the Duke of Milan.[70] Alleged to have been also implicated in the death of the King's first wife, many felt his mother, the Italian conspirator, had again been responsible.

None of us aspired to such Shakespearean drama but with so many beautiful girls surrounding us each day, involvements and flirtations were inevitable. Nick was conventionally handsome but curiously lacking in follow-through when any glamorous young Pole with endless tanned legs was 'showin' out' at the wild bonfire barbeques on the banks of the Vistula. 'Polish women have the best legs in Europe,' observed a journalist from Radio Free Europe to me at a party. Slavic women anticipate action and were confused by Nick's diffident English manner. When they invariably moved on

70 *The Polish Way: A Thousand-Year History of the Poles and their Culture*, Adam Zamoyski (London 1987) p. 85

and 'love' failed to flower he broke up his room with karate chops and shouts of 'Damn her, damn her!' Mirrors, furniture the window frames all received a beating. The door to his room would fly open, smashing into the adjacent wall of the corridor with a report like a gunshot.

'What is it, Nick?' I asked, rushing from my room.

'Just burstin' out!' he shouted and disappeared back inside.

Dr Grabski became particularly upset when Nick destroyed the glass plate on the photocopier. The Goethe Institute had generously gifted it to the centre when blue flashes from the old Agfa machine became dangerous and the print began to fall off the paper onto the floor.

David became mysteriously involved with a shy girl somewhere in the country but Geoff showed a surprisingly chivalric and professional side to his nature, amorousness being in decline after his recent painful divorce. Richard, our Oxford aesthete, was more interested in the younger trainees and even imported some talent. The less said about that the better. Soon he was spending a great deal of time with Ania, a gentle Polish blonde who adored him.

Clashes with Geoff were frequent, particularly over putting petrol in the 'team car'. He began a relationship with a trainee called Bogna, a rather unfortunate name to the English ear. She tended to stare unblinkingly through her thick glasses and rarely smiled. She was from Łódź and Geoff began increasingly to use the team car for visits to his *przyjaciółka* (girlfriend). One evening I carelessly said, 'Would you mind putting some petrol in it while you're out, Geoff?'

'I'm not paying for the bloody petrol!' he shouted aggressively and stormed from the room.

After my irritation faded I began to analyse what was behind his outbursts. I had failed to get him 'on side' in any supportive sense. He had also applied for the Project Manager position (in fact everyone had) but it was offered to me. He harboured significant resentment concerning this perceived failure. On numerous occasions he contacted Bath direct, side-stepping any authority I imagined I possessed. He was emotional and personal, tactless and blunt in his dealings with people. His wife had left him shortly before he came to Poland, which caused him to be understandably depressed, but this had created a deeply misanthropic attitude.

'What was your wife like, Geoff?'

'Fit bum. Fit bum,' he savagely replied in reference to their shared love of mountaineering. In addition he had disastrously miscalculated his salary. I greatly respected his professional skills and warm, constructive attitude to the trainees but he was not in any psychological state to contribute and compromise as a member of a team.

Nick had not had his driving licence long and was anxious to impress his 'goils'. He had not learned much from his lessons with his 'hard nut' driving instructor. The gorgeous Katarzyna, with the legs of a gazelle, climbed into the passenger seat. Nick careered through the garden of the centre, roses and geraniums flying, shooting out of the gates at high speed, taking part of them with him. Surely his instructor would have cautioned against wild driving?

'No way! That geezer says to me, "You wanna' get more aggressive, mate. Drive in a more aggressive way. If you see a bloke cut you up you say "'You fuckin' cunt, right, I'll show you ya' cunt!'" Zoooooom!'" Ya know, like that. Difficult for me 'cause I don't have the confidence. He's right really – heh – heh – heh – cunt! Be more aggressive, so I'm tryin'!'

I tried to avoid letting him anywhere near the team Polski Fiat from then on.

The team were working long hours and being cooped up in the forest far from the centre of town made everyone irritable. One needed a rest from the trainees, however cosmetically attractive. David tended to support Geoff against 'the management' but was so chronically indecisive one could not fathom his stance on any issue. His love affair turned out to be with an unhappily married Polish girl attempting to escape her husband. The agonies of travelling into the lion's den in the ancient town of Kielce preoccupied all his waking thoughts.

The team finally polarized and I had no idea how to heal the rift. The trainees loved Richard and he became tremendously popular because of his bow ties, tailored pin-striped suits, officer-and-a-gentleman 'Englishness'. This bred a certain envy among the others. The ugly face of British social class became increasingly obvious and as a colonial I did not play that game. I had attempted to adopt a team-based approach to tackling the difficulties. Consultation was encouraged at every step, asking each member to make his own contribution. My requests for individual initiatives in the face of the severe obstruction by the Polish clients fell on deaf ears. Despite the protestations of the management gurus whose 'revolutionary' books I had voraciously consumed before the project began, I discovered that many employees want authoritarian management. They are programmed to inequality. They need a target against which to vent their spleen. Certainly these particular Britons were far more comfortable with an aloof old-fashioned leadership style. In some ways this contract taught me more about the British than the Poles.

By Easter the team were on the point of walking out on the entire project in the same manner as the previous contractors. The trainees too were disappointed at the low quality of the services and food at the *ośrodek*. One of the bleached blonde female managers complained the lavatory seats were too small for her bottom and pinched it until the blood flowed. Difficulties were multiplying on the Polish side and Dr Grabski was apprehensive of losing his position. He had already become faintly uneasy as he instinctively detected the subtle shift in the power base that meant catastrophe and total loss under the communist regime. No one now spoke at breakfast.

Outside in the world spring had arrived and I hoped for some new life to be breathed back into the project. Perhaps the approach of summer would lift their spirits and romance might perfume the air. The Vistula was running high with melting snow and much of the beach had disappeared. The aspens and birches near the banks were swaying wildly, the new leaves nervously trembling. I struggled against the wind onto a short breakwater and looked upstream to Warsaw. The city has a unique position on the wide, silent river, the irregular sandbars in mid-stream covered in wild reeds and grasses. The tower of the Palace of Culture could just be made out on the horizon. Curved fishing boats with high prows struggled against their moorings. Sand dredgers clanked dully in the distance, giving an atmosphere of abandonment to the shore. Tall red and white chimneys smoked palely in the middle distance yet there was nothing unpleasant in this timeless human activity and industry. The view downriver was of almost undeveloped terrain and it was easy to imagine you were in some remote part of the country as water-birds pushed into the spring gales and young leaves dropped into the current.

May is a beautiful month in Poland. The air is clear and delicately fresh and the sun warm. Trees and plants burst into life quite suddenly with birdsong, flowers and insects in profusion. Łazienki Park is transformed from the monochrome of winter into a paradise garden and poplar seeds drift in the breeze like snowflakes. Lindens and oaks surge into leaf above buttercups and bluebells; entire fields of cornflowers and poppies come into bloom. Frogs set up a cacophony in ponds.

A great number of concerts are held in the park over spring and summer. The season of Chopin piano recitals in the open air had already begun in the rose garden. The instrument sat on a podium in the shadow of a monumental Art Nouveau memorial to the composer. Chopin is seated under a huge bronze willow blowing in a gale. The tree is shaped like a harp and symbolizes the renewal of life. He appears to be taking his inspiration from the landscape and listening to the wind. That particular morning a gale was blowing violently, scudding clouds rushed across the sun, the trees swaying furiously. The long hair of the pianist whipped about his face, his body obscured by dust billowing up from the path. The passionate rhythms of the *Polonaise-Fantasie* were buffeted by the gusts and I expected the entire ensemble of this extraordinary scene to spin off into the distance at any moment.[71]

That same afternoon a 'Renaissance Ball' was to take place at the

---

71 In 1908, some sixty years after the composer's death, a competition for a Chopin memorial was finally permitted by the Russian Imperial authorities. Wacław Szymanowski won the competition and his design was given the blessing of Tsar Nicholas II. World War I broke out before the bronze could be cast and the full-scale model was divided into two parts: one part went to Kraków where it ended up in a shed and the other was hidden somewhere in France. After the war the halves were miraculously reunited. The bronze was cast in Paris and the monument finally unveiled in 1926. After World War II broke out the Nazis, fully realizing the inflammatory patriotic nature of Chopin's music, banned performances throughout Germany and the occupied countries. They blew the monument up in May 1940. After the war a tiny model, cast in Rome in 1923, was discovered in the bombed basement of Szymanowski's house in Warsaw by his sons. The monument was cast again in Warsaw and unveiled in May 1958. It was erected in the former orchard in Łazienki, the site its creator originally envisaged for it. The career of this memorial is a wonderfully representative Polish story of conception, destruction and valiant reconstruction. (Information derived from *The Monument of Fryderyk Chopin by Wacław Szymanowski: Concepts and Reality*, Waldemar Okoń (Indiana 2004))

Palace on the Island. The intimate ballroom was transformed by the spring warmth. This fine example of Polish neoclassicism pulsed with light reflected from the stucco and marble sculptures. I attempted to decode the grotesques on the walls that resemble the Raphael *Logge* in the Vatican. The cultured King Stanisław Augustus commissioned the decoration from the Polish artists Jan Kamsetzer and Jan Bogumił Plersch. He was clearly preoccupied with the fatalistic role of women in the lives of men, hardly surprising when you examine his blighted affair with Catherine the Great of Russia and the terrible consequences for Poland. After her demeaning treatment of him at their famous meeting on the Dnieper in 1787, thirty years after their affair foundered, the Prince de Ligne wrote acerbically, 'He spent three months and three million to see the empress for three hours.' The sunlight from the water of the canal shimmered on the frescoed walls.

The musicians, dressed in Renaissance costume, were seated in a mirrored, orchestral gallery. Sixteenth-century dance music was imaginatively interspersed with dramatic elements – the richly costumed dancers talking, eating fruit, courtly love-making, a little tiff now and then, some couples resting while others danced, arbitrary entrances and exits. Bars of sunlight flecked their hair. Outside the palace windows peacocks with iridescent plumage strutted on the balustrades beyond the statue of the Apollo Belvedere.

My first romantic assignation was sadly not in Łazienki but at a sanatorium in the country. The beautiful Zosia, a blonde Pole with electric blue eyes, claimed vague descent from the darker side of the aristocratic Radziwiłł family, something to do with the prince and the windmill owner's daughter. She was a Lecturer in Linguistics at Warsaw University and fluent in beautifully accented English. We had first met at the wild welcome party. It was the first time I had experienced the frisson of close Polish dancing and the electricity of that first encounter did not fade. We often chanced to meet at prosaic language conferences, which developed into more regular assignations. Zosia was a mixture of a dreamer with a vein of strong practicality and an overriding sense of family loyalty and honour. Her young son and daughter were a major cause for concern. The early clandestine meetings were a torment of guilt for her as she felt that she was in some way violating the sanctity of the national myth of femininity, that of the Polish Mother.

Our favourite rendezvous during winter was at a romantic café in the Old Town called *Pod Krokodylem* (Under the Crocodile). The name came from the wooden carving of a crocodile being ridden by a cherub placed under the vaulted roof of the old wine cellar. Deep alcoves with wrought-iron grilles lit by single candles gave the interior a mysterious and seductive ambience as the snow fell outside. Polish whispered in my ear seemed inordinately romantic. The coffee and Hungarian cake were excellent and we spent many hours engrossed in conversation and lost in silence. The bucolic decoration of the medieval façades would glitter dimly through the gathering dusk. Horses and carriages, their hooves and wheels clattering over the cobbles, set out for unknown destinations with lovers snuggled under rugs, lanterns rocking and candles flickering in the freezing fog.

Zosia was married to a government minister who had fully embraced the dream of the new businessman of the period – international flights, private drivers with traffic priority and blue flashing lights, French cognac and a significant *układ* or multitude of former communist connections. She told me her love had been destroyed by anger and resentment. Moral disillusionment had grown from his completely different philosophy and style of life. Certainly she was entirely lacking in malice towards her fellow man and was so refreshingly 'normal' as to be outstanding as a person. Polish women have a deserved reputation for beauty, loyalty and (dare I utter the word in these benighted times) virtue.

She lacked that sadness in the eyes for which many Polish women are renowned. But then she was from a generation that had never known the horrors of invasion and war. When we met it was like drinking champagne; a feeling of optimism in the future coloured her moods, something lacking in the former generation whose lives were moulded by suffering and loss. With Zosia I would experience a different Poland to the classic accounts of lost domains and noble sacrifices. We both suffered moral scruples that kept us circling each other for months which naturally strengthened with the denial of the sexual heat growing between us. At that time I did not want more than an adventure but we had dangerously more in common than the sins of the flesh. We both loved Polish landscape, architecture and poetry despite much being lost in translation as I struggled with the language. I feared assassination or at least a beating if we were discovered – the Russian mafia were relatively inexpensive in Warsaw in those days, at twenty US dollars for that type of 'physical operation'. The name *Pod Krokodylem* increasingly gathered significance.

The drive from Warsaw the weekend of our first assignation was atrocious – a typical Polish early spring: sludge, sleet, freezing rain, hail, light snow and then, approaching the town of Nałęczów, dense fog. This formerly fashionable *Belle Epoque* spa was melancholy and gothic in this dripping season.

I met Zosia outside the Baroque gates of the Małachowski Palace in a forbidding atmosphere of drizzle. Her husband, the formidable Dr Krasiński, in response to her mild heart arrhythmia, had booked her into the cardiology unit of one of the numerous sanatoria scattered about the town. The palace overlooked the Spa Park and a picturesque rivulet burbled through the lawns beside the ancient trees. Fog swirled around the lamps and lit the paths in a ghostly light. Zosia was unable to find me a room in the 'palace resort' as it was booked solid, so the decision was made to stay with her clandestinely at the clinic.

I arrived at the sanatorium like a furtive spy and hurried past the rooms of starched nurses. Disguised as a doctor in a white coat I rapidly climbed the stairs clutching a sterile blood-transfusion pack which had a cross and caduceus clearly displayed on the plastic case. My urgency indicated a vaguely medical mission. The pack was a useful passport and I was not challenged.

We discovered in a heart-stopping moment that a mutual friend was on duty that evening, so as a diversionary tactic Zosia had a coffee with her in the canteen. I lay on the bed in her minimalist room that smelt faintly of disinfectant, watching an old romantic comedy on television about two young people who fall in love whilst competing in male and female construction teams to rebuild central Warsaw after the war. He is the fastest of the bricklayers and she, a 'socialist Cinderella', abandons a promising dancing career for her handsome, muscular lover, an ideologically correct mate in the workers' state.[72]

---

72 *Przygoda na Mariensztacie* ('An Adventure at Mariensztat') – a romantic comedy of the communist period. Mariensztat is an attractive part of the Warsaw Old Town.

We spent our first night together. Zosia's blonde hair fell in waves over those ice-blue eyes and caught between her lips. We felt a great deal more than we had anticipated and dreaded the inevitable and painful sundering when I would be forced to leave Poland at the conclusion of my contract. Quite early on we felt we were losing control of the adventure. We awoke the next morning to the intoning of the Latin Mass being said by a priest to a group of the afflicted in soul in the common-room next door.

I waited for her to return from her surgery consultation. Elderly cardiac patients wandered up and down the corridors of the clinic, blowing, puffing, cyanosis creeping over their skin. Trolleys rattled past the locked door of the room. Such provocative assignations as this appealed to Zosia's sense of the theatrical, a quality she shares with many Poles. An illicit meeting in a hospital was not at all the romantic ambience I had in mind when I set out from Warsaw, but I admitted it was a useful place to suffer a romantic seizure.

'Nothing wrong. I must be overexcited!' she said after her medical examination.

The town has a micro-climate with pure air and high humidity which has led to its renown as a cardiology centre – this accounts for the fog and invasive damp. It is said that 'Nałęczów heals the heart'. Patients suffering from sexual neurosis are also sent here to recuperate. The town lies in a beautiful river valley, almost invisible in mist at this time of year. A strange medicinal calmness pervades the place with groups of slow-moving convalescents wandering about. There were a number of Russian artists painting and drawing under the trees. A woman from Belarus with flame-red hair and dressed in a tight silver mini-skirt was working in oils. I wandered in her direction and she instantly engaged me in conversation.

'I am a famous artist, dahlink,' she said in a heavy, deep-throated Russian accent. 'I want to paint the picture of this beautiful, handsome man that is you.'

Unused to such forthright female compliments, I instantly complied.

Zosia had managed to obtain a room in the palace. The concierge took an active and inquisitorial interest in my arrival, but I hurried upstairs with an air of authority. The exterior is in an attractive baroque style, but the interior was a disaster, ruined in that anti-aesthetic communist way which rendered everything the ideology touched lifeless and arid. The furnishing of the room was of the type found in an assassin's temporary accommodation. The beds were unmade, the atmosphere stifling with staleness, covered in dust and the carapaces of dead beetles.

In the late nineteenth century Nałęczów became a fashionable resort in much the same way as Zakopane in the Tatra mountains of the former Austrian Galicia in the south. At the turn of the century, a sparkling array of cultural and intellectual luminaries rested or lived here – Henryk Sienkiewicz (the Nobel prize-winning author of *Quo Vadis*) and Ignacy Jan Paderewski were frequent visitors. The writer Bolesław Prus (author of a remarkable novel, *Lalka* or 'The Doll') drew inspiration from the people and countryside. The town was also a centre for insurrectionist and radical social solutions. The 'B. Prus Inexpensive Baths' were famous.

In the late afternoon we sat on the rose-garden terrace of the Prus house listening to the fountain and admiring the landscapes on the wall of the drawing room. Delicious grilled trout was served as the light began to fade and the waitress lit a candle which illuminated what remained of the white wine. We kissed furtively. I read aloud to her of the healing mineral spring nearby called 'Źródło Miłosci' (The Source of Love).

CHAPTER 11

Johnny Fartpants

Frequent and unexpected change is the most predictable aspect of
life in Poland.

'You have fraudulently claimed for mileage in a 1550cc car when
the car you drive is your wife's 650cc Maluch! You might explain
this anomaly,' quietly knifed the new administrative director, Mr
Fukowski, his head bent over a ledger, pencil poised above the
neatly ruled sheets. Dr Grabski looked aghast and commented to me
in English as Mr Fukowski understood not a word of the language.

'You see the Security Service methods they use to crack me,
Michael. I am on the rack to make me mad like King Lear. I'm
taking *Valium*.'

The car episode was merely one of a daily list of 'transgressions'
for which he was being 'punished' in a war of attrition and psychological manipulation. He had often spoken of the insidious erosion
of his authority. Ultimately driven into a fury by piecemeal hound-
ing he had suddenly resigned. No more gazing into the bowels of
the cesspit or sharing sunflower seeds with Pani Jola. A consummate
professional in his work, but thoughtless and self-absorbed in his
personal relations with the Polish staff, I found to my surprise I
could not help liking him. He seemed to have the best interests of
'the foreigners' at heart and I had little to complain about.

Dr Grabski came in early one morning and in a mood of unexpected vengeance removed all his papers and reference materials.
The mess he left behind was desperately unfair to the Polish side
but then he had always been disdainful of their professional abili-
ties. All our joint developmental work had been spirited away and

I felt personally betrayed. The notion of 'corporate loyalty' is unknown in Poland. Individuals hedge, defend and exploit their own positions at the expense of any communal project in hand. To survive financially most Poles hold multiple positions which erodes constancy and creates no allegiances. The following day he did not appear and the entire project began a slow descent into chaos.

Mr Fukowski had formerly been a celebrated bureaucrat in the Ministry of Education who had been encouraged out of retirement. He resembled a bereaved and fearful koala in spectacles. A chain smoker, he often appeared as flustered and as terrified as an elderly lady but as I discovered later to my cost, like all weak people, he could be dangerous and easy to underestimate. He called a meeting to explain his motives in cryptic language. We communicated in French, which was the universal language of diplomacy under the old regime. The modulated voice of this former *nomenklatura* guaranteed a secret 'understanding' of veiled intentions and *załatwić sprawę*[73] moving like a hidden current below the surface. The old guard share a '*nomenklatura* posture' consisting of an insinuating body language, clandestine gestures of complicity and inclinations of the head as the 'suggestions' are communicated. The meaning of his sentences became highly oblique and Kafkaesque.

'The scientific conference and its results have already been put into operation,' he commented, referring to the precipitate departure of Dr Grabski.

Vaclav Havel observed of the communist system that a man must silently tolerate all the mystifications, or at least cooperate with those who are operating according to the rules of mystification, or act as though the obvious lie is the truth and nod sagely.

There emerged quite suddenly the possibility of profitable 'Government Ministry contracts' as the vested interests of *układ,* the old *nomenklatura* networks, were given a new lease of life or perhaps had never died. Professionally Mr Fukowski came from a

---

73 The ability to 'arrange a matter' or perhaps better to 'wangle' a solution to a problem through a mixture of guile, persistence, 'connections' and subtle discretion. This behaviour was well established during the communist system and continues today among those in positions of influence and persists in some areas of ordinary life.

different era and clearly knew nothing of the new methodology of the current study programme. He recommended Course 901 on twenty long-playing records. One day he exploded: 'I want more typewriters! I'm selling all the computers!'

There had been a collision between the 'Old Guard' and an ill-conceived, ill-judged concept of what the nature of the 'new' market economy was and how it functioned. An idea of Western consumerism was embraced that took no account of the complexities of the production process and the ruthless world of free market competition. There was no real understanding of company structure, management skills, customer care or marketing procedures. The whispering cabals, vested interests, deliberately misleading information, lack of direction, clever and sharp observations, servile remarks and disagreeable wheedling made it almost impossible to work in any productive fashion.

Dr Grabski was replaced by a high-level university appointee whom I found charming and who did much to reduce my initial alarm. However she wished to remain in an academic ivory tower. Mr Fukowski arranged a meeting.

'I will allow you to speak with pani Profesor and I will leave the room so you may have a comfortable and frank discussion with her, maintaining the *discrétion* so necessary in such meetings.'

The professor was only to be present for two hours a week. The longer I examined the operation the more convinced I became that something was deeply awry and revenue was being siphoned off elsewhere. I always felt that the real agenda was being planned in the next room. Occasionally I would hear snatches of conversation or a persistent drone through a crack in the door, a shouted expletive through the wall. It was not long before I discovered we did not in fact have a contract at all.

An argument was brewing over airfares. The English team were insistent.

'The contract states the fares back to England are paid,' I pointed out firmly to Mr Fukowski.

'*Non. Non.* The airfares were given to you as a gesture of goodwill and *bienveillance.*' Mr Fukowski became the epitome of Polish charm and for that reason difficult to argue against.

'Oh really?'

'A Christmas gift from grateful Poles! Don't punish us, Michel!' I was disarmed at a stroke by the sudden appearance of a victim with myself cast as the devil.

A lack of accountability and commitment to firm decisions, contractual vagueness, impulsiveness, the attraction of the short-term deal rather than the long-term business relationship, the inability to foresee consequences, are still experienced by many Western companies working on joint ventures in Poland.

I pointed out the contractual anomalies to Mr Fukowski with some heat.

'You can sign the contract when it is finished, Mr Moran, if you are worried.' A beautiful example of the 'syndrome of incompleteness', according to the Polish journalist Marcin Król, and the irrelevance of legal constraints. In Poland a curious notion of 'social justice' determines that what is legal is often considered not moral and the illegal quite acceptable. Overcome by fear, an all-pervasive emotion under the old regime, Mr Fukowski scuttled to the lavatory in a panic and failed to emerge for some hours.

An inoffensive creature on first meeting, Mr Fukowski harboured a dreadful sting. In order to survive, many people who lived under the communist regime developed a mindset that was duplicitous and secretive, evasive and slippery. These habits have become ingrained in many businessmen and seem inescapable even after the exponential changes of the more recent past.

Examinations always provided an opportunity for some type of chicanery. One day in early summer I noticed Mr Fukowski wandering in the ruined Italianate garden with the overweight bleached blonde 'manageress', she whose large bottom had been painfully pinched by the small lavatory seats. They ambled lethargically by a rusty pipe that intermittently gushed water in the centre of a slimy pond, once an elegant baroque fountain, now attended by shattered concrete cherubs. This monstrosity of communist neglect was dutifully turned on every morning to create a civilized atmosphere conducive to study. Mr Fukowski had taken her arm and his head was bent towards hers with the characteristic *nomenklatura* inclination of complicity. I wondered what they could have been discussing, as romance was highly unlikely; probably an expression of *załatwić*. I had not long to wait.

'*Monsieur Moran*, in this examination the managers will not receive any letter below the B grade,' he announced peremptorily.

'Well, if they fail that is most unfortunate. But that's life,' I answered brightly and naively.

'I repeat, *Monsieur*. You do not seem to understand. No manager will receive below the B grade. Also they will be examined individually.' Fukowski's eyes began to dart about in confusion. He was used to instant compliance.

'I want to test their communication skills in pairs. They will receive the grade they deserve from the results of the examination,' I answered firmly, but I was at last beginning to grasp the significance of his tone. 'From each according to his ability, to each according to his needs' according to Karl Marx.[74]

'You must understand this. *C'est très important.* I have assured pani Konopnicka this morning of the final results. If they are interviewed together they could blame each other for a poor performance.'

'But they have not sat the examination yet!' I was growing exasperated by this pressure.

'The grades have already been decided, *cher Monsieur*. It is the way with managers.'

I lapsed into silence and finally repeated that if they failed they would get an E grade. If they wanted to face the three examiners alone in dry-mouthed abasement so be it. There seemed to be a strange complicity of sweating it out between examiners and their victims. Many of them were not terribly bright as their managerial positions had been obtained solely through contacts. Their inability to master lessons simply illustrated this.

'*Monsieur Moran, permettez-moi de m'expliquer.*' He became suddenly softly conspiratorial. 'My son is hoping to receive a position in charge of the German language department of a company. *Nous sommes pauvres Polonais ici.* I'm sure you understand. *C'est très important pour lui.* I have promised the managers a soft examination. Foreign language at their age *c'est très laborieux, très difficile*. Their promotion depends on a good result. We cannot hurt them,

74 *Critique of the Gotha Program*, Karl Marx 1875 (Selected Works Volume 3, pp 13–30, Moscow 1970)

Michel. Do you want to hurt them and ruin my son? I think you are a good man.'

'*Je regrette infiniment, Monsieur. C'est pas possible.*' I simply could not bring myself to fix exam results.

A cloud passed across his face and there was a short pause as he fastidiously inspected his well-kept nails.

'Perhaps you can help me in another matter. There have been many complaints about the lessons of Nick.'

'*Vraiment?*'

'*Oui.* The material he uses in the class is not strictly financial.'

'What does he use that they don't like?'

'*C'est qui,* Johnny Fartpants?'[75]

'I have no idea,' I answered truthfully.

'*C'est ridicule.* The managers think it is a waste of time.'

'Well, I shall talk to him about it.' I attempted to keep a straight face.

'In addition, *Monsieur Makin* shouts at night and batters the walls. Everyone is awake. You are the English director, *Monsieur Moran*, and you must send him back to England. *Il n'est pas professionnel.*'

'Impossible. Getting a replacement now would be extremely difficult.'

'*Alors,* if the managers get the examination grade I want, we can forget this little matter of the Johnny Fartpants and *la violence*. Otherwise *c'est très difficile pour vous.*'

I fell silent and left the office after making some trivial excuse, in a fury at such unaccustomed pressure and the echoes of former communist corruption.

'Nick, what is this about Johnny Fartpants?'

'Good one, good one. They love it. And Batman and Robin.'

'Well, there've been some complaints. Not quite financial enough.'

'Um . . . well . . . ya' know, like, when I feel I can't stand this any longer, gotta get away from these geezers, so I get out and go to the

75 Johnny Fartpants was a character in *Viz* magazine and a teenage favourite in the 1980s. He suffers from acute flatulence that is both nauseating and destructive. Buildings have been demolished and people injured by his farts. As a decent boy he always apologizes for matters beyond his control.

barfroom and sit on the toilet, 'ave a bit of diarrhoea then go back wiv Johnny Fartpants in me lesson feelin' much better.'

Far more important than the excretal preoccupations of this 'financial consultant' was the advent of 'Black Thursday'. It was on this day that I learnt the Polish side was bankrupt. The offices in the centre of town were to be reduced to one room and a secretary. The President of the Polish side was to go onto half-time. The expensive Italian furniture purchased in a wild gesture of extravagance was to be sold, together with the President's car. The language laboratory was inexplicably taken away in a refrigerated truck. The banks had withdrawn their credit as they had discovered terminal errors in the granting of it. The President was ill in hospital with cardiac problems and had been ordered by his doctors not to speak. He ignored this in a typical reckless Polish style: theatrical yet admirable.

'I will rise from my bed and even though ill talk to the Mr President of the English company for limited periods, up to one hour in duration, as determined by my advisors.'

Andrzej, the accountant to the Polish company, and I held a 'crisis meeting'. He arrived smoking a cigarette, clutching two bottles of Warka Strong beer and a battered laptop. We worked out a solution involving a labyrinth of percentages to be purchased, shares to be allocated and dividends paid out to reduce the indebtedness. Poles have an extraordinary ability to create increasingly complex solutions to any problem they create. These improbable schemes continued for much of the day, fuelled by endless cups of coffee and cigarettes.

It transpired that various highly speculative and risky investments had failed. A shipload of Chinese fireworks destined for the celebration of the anniversary of the end of World War II had been delayed on the docks by a Gdańsk shipyard strike and ruined by rain and sea air. Investments in land in the south had unaccountably lost value. My superiors in Bath wanted none of what they considered to be 'Polish Pizza' and planned to recall me under the shadow of failure. They thought I was suffering from what was known in the days of the Empire as 'District Officer Syndrome' over my loyalty to Poland: 'You know, the natives only eat people occasionally in my district.' I had been reporting on the dangers threatening the project for months but reports from outposts abroad are seldom read sufficiently closely at head office.

'We may have to ask you to pack your bags and come home,' my superiors faxed with fluid ease. I could only contemplate the unpleasant failure of the project, separation from my Polish lover and considerable financial embarrassment to my employer and myself. The Polish staff were in a panic. Mr Fukowski was the image of a considerably distressed koala.

The *ośrodek* was owed money for student accommodation.

'Avoid the Director of the hotel,' he advised.

Polish staff were owed salaries.

'Avoid the other staff when possible and do not talk to them, Michel. *Ils sont imbéciles.*'

The trainees themselves knew little of the problems but experience had taught them to suspect that something was afoot. As I lay awake in the small hours under my Moroccan rug listening to the wind and the fugue of distant dogs, I had little faith that the project could be saved. A graveyard of broken promises stretched out before me.

CHAPTER 12

Frycek and the Prism of Reminiscence

In late spring, in a despondent frame of mind, I decided to raise my spirits with a visit to Chopin's birthplace at Żelazowa Wola, a hamlet about fifty kilometres from Warsaw. The flat Mazovian landscape was relieved by stands of trembling birch and pine; forlorn willows with gnarled boles lined the deserted roads. I had long anticipated this visit to what musically, for me, was an almost sacred place. I wandered through the still and muffled park. A subtle atmosphere of reverence is created here among the groves of trees, the serpentine paths winding between hedges and over the little bridge above the Utrata river. Long-leaved aquatic plants flowed like Ophelia's hair in the current. It was almost dusk as I made my way to the softly lit entrance of the *dwór*. I leaned against one of the columns of the porch and looked into the depths of the park over the still pond with the dim carp. The possible loss of the project and separation from Zosia seemed increasingly difficult to bear.

I stooped to pick up a weathered chestnut and idly polished it on my coat. An old piano tuner I knew in Warsaw gave chestnuts from this park to piano students at the conservatorium, telling them to hold them close to their hearts as they contained 'the spirit of Chopin'. He claimed he had also seen the disembodied hand of the composer appear on a banister in the *dwór* late one night after tuning the piano for a concert.

In the soft light of early evening the distant figure of a woman appeared at the entrance to the park, dressed in a dark coat of military cut, blonde hair caught up in a ribbon. I idly watched her enter through the wrought iron entrance gates and come towards me up the path. She came into focus only slowly, preoccupied as I was with melancholic thoughts. I was astounded to see Zosia materialize.

'What are you doing here?' I asked in amazement.

'*Kocham cię* (I love you), that's all. I want to be here and listen to Chopin with you.'

'How did you get away, for heaven's sake?'

'I told them I needed to escape the city and go to a concert. Simple really.'

Hands linked, we pushed aside the heavy brocade and leather curtain at the front door. Only about twenty-five people could be accommodated in the tiny room. A brass candelabra with the crowned Polish eagle resting between the branches stood on the small grand piano. Warm yellow light flickered on the portrait of the composer and fitfully illuminated the painted beams of the *dwór*. The young pianist, a French girl, had ambitiously chosen to play both sets of Chopin études. Her little dog lay under the instrument fast asleep.

A feverish and ardent battle began in the risen music, a mysterious sense of loss driven by angry despair, the nobility of resistance in the face of unavoidable tragedy. Chopin was rightly thought of as a dangerous inspiration to rebellion by various invaders and his music banned. The études perfectly express the sudden lack of resolve that possesses one in the face of an impossible obstacle, replaced just as suddenly by a forced emotional courage to struggle, even into the realm of the obsessional.

Such tumultuous emotions brought Zosia close to me that night. Certain decisions were subliminally made as she clasped my hand and gently pressed her thigh against mine. Chopin called forth all the feverish, lyrical underworld of the heart in these works. The years separating the listener from his death fell away, peeled, shed like the skin of a serpent to reveal a glittering, venomous and recalcitrant spirit, heroic and dangerous yet paradoxically beautiful and seductive.

We wandered the house after the concert to the flowered 'birth alcove'. Formal portraits of Chopin's parents stared down from the walls. His well-educated father Mikołaj (Nicholas) was born in the French province of Lorraine in 1771 although the family 'Chapin' originated in the Alps, changing their name to 'Chopin' to avert an alleged family scandal involving smuggling. In 1802 he found a position at Żelazowa Wola as tutor to the children of the profligate Count Kacper Skarbek who had fled from his creditors to Paris. In 1806 he married Justyna Krzyżanowska ('hair golden as wheat and serene, sapphire-like eyes'[76]) from an impoverished *szlachta* family and a 'mother's help' to the abandoned Countess Ludwika Skarbek. Justyna played the piano well.

A cloud hovers over the birth date of Fryderyk in a rather characteristic Polish way. The year 1810 is not seriously in dispute but the Chopin family insisted on March 1 while the baptismal certificate records a birth date of February 22. Celebrations in Warsaw occur throughout the week, which covers all possibilities. He was brother to three intelligent and talented sisters. The family moved to Warsaw soon after his birth into an apartment in a wing of the superb Saxon Palace where Mikołaj became a professor at the Warsaw Liceum (High School).

The Chopins were a highly respected, emotionally close and loving bourgeois family with strong moral and religious values that psychologically formed the selfless moral integrity of the composer. He wrote of his first Christmas spent alone in Vienna in 1830 (being alone at Christmas is a terrible experience for a Pole): 'I felt more than ever that I was orphaned.' From this separation originates the emotive Polish concept of *żal* that Chopin used to describe his own compositions. This complex word carries the connotations of 'inconsiderable regret after irrevocable loss . . . premeditation of vengeance',[77] melancholic nostalgia and bitter regret which at times can lead to a type of internal fury of protest.

At this time Warsaw was an extraordinary melange of cultures. Magnificent magnate palaces shared muddy unpaved streets with dilapidated townhouses, *szlachta* farms, filthy hovels and teeming markets. By 1812 the Napoleonic campaigns had financially crippled the Duchy of Warsaw. The French Ambassador commented, 'Nothing could exceed the misery of all classes . . . I even saw

76 Ferdynand Hoesick, Chopin's biographer.
77 Franz Liszt

princesses quit Warsaw from the most extreme distress'.[78] Chopin spent his formative years during this turbulent political period and the family often escaped the capital to the refuge of the Mazovian countryside at Żelazowa Wola. Here the fields are alive with birdsong, butterflies and wildflowers. On summer nights the piano was placed in the garden and Chopin would improvise eloquent melodies that floated through the orchards and across the river to the listening villagers gathered beyond. To this day, the atmosphere is recaptured in summer when the windows of the *dwór* are thrown open for recitals and the audience wanders in the elegant gardens or leans on the railing of the small wooden bridge and gazes into the dreamy waters of the Utrata.

It was here in the dark garden of Żelazowa Wola after the concert, amid the spring flowers and rustling leaves of birch and aspen accompanied by the distant murmur of the Utrata stream, that I impetuously proposed to Zosia. Perhaps we could marry some time in the distant and difficult future that loomed ahead. Perhaps.

Chopin remained extraordinarily faithful to the impressions of his adolescence and youth. The lasting principles of his artistic vision were formed on his native soil among his childhood friends, teachers, romantic infatuations and family (in particular his mother) and on holidays in the Polish countryside among the peasantry. He was an ebullient young man and excellent company with a sharp sense of humour, fond of practical jokes and with an immense talent for caricature and mimicry. He could easily have become a professional actor. He loved the rough violin and openthroated folk music of Mazovia and was an excellent dancer, often playing the piano into the small hours at parties for the whirling couples, flowers resplendent on their folk costumes, performing the *Mazur*.

Largely self-taught as a pianist, he took elementary lessons for six years from Adalbert Żywny (1756–1842), an aged 'dusty' Bohemian violinist quite brown from his addiction to the snuff he carried in a pouch decorated with portraits of Haydn and Mozart. Żywny was

---

78 Quoted in *Chopin's Poland*, Iwo and Pamela Załuski (London 1996) p. 29. I have drawn on this as an excellent and detailed account of the development of Chopin in his own country.

a superb eccentric who seemed to have stepped straight from a *commedia dell'arte*. He had a large purple nose and few teeth, wore waistcoats cut from the auctioned trousers of the last king of Poland, an ill-fitting yellow wig and massive Hungarian boots. He rarely bathed, restricting himself to a brisk vodka scrub in the heat of summer. An excellent music teacher, he acquainted 'Frycek'[79] with basic harmony and counterpoint as well as introducing him to the world of Bach and Mozart, works that accompanied him throughout his life as models of the greatest achievements in music. 'Chopinek' composed his first *Polonaise* at the age of seven.

> The polonaise breathes and paints the whole national character; the music of this dance, while admitting much art, combines something martial with a sweetness marked by the simplicity of manners of an agricultural people . . . Our fathers danced it with a marvellous ability and a gravity full of nobleness; the dancer, making gliding steps with energy, but without skips, and caressing his moustache, varied his movements by the position of his sabre, of his cap, and of his tucked-up coat sleeves, distinctive signs of a free man and a warlike citizen.[80]

As a child prodigy he was considered to be 'the second Mozart' by the cream of the Warsaw aristocracy. The moody Grand Duke Konstantin Pavlovich, commander-in-chief and de facto viceroy of Tsar Alexander I to the Kingdom of Poland, often asked the *Wunderkind* to play for him to 'soothe a savage breast'. He was collected in a sleigh from his home in the Saxon Palace and drawn through Warsaw streets by four horses harnessed abreast in the spectacular Russian manner and taken to the Belvedere Palace. From his earliest years Chopin was exposed to the refinement and ease of the highest echelons of society. This remarkable social milieu formed both his temperament and musical tastes.

His second teacher, the neglected Silesian composer Joseph Elsner (1769–1854), one of the seminal figures in Polish music, taught him

---

79 'Frycek' is a diminutive form of Fryderyk. Much of the richness and intimacy of Polish comes from the use of diminutives.

80 The nineteenth-century poet and critic Kazimierz Brodziński

advanced composition, harmony and counterpoint. Chopin was to become the greatest master of counterpoint since Mozart. Elsner was not a frail little man living in a grubby Warsaw tenement: besides symphonies, piano works, quartets, cantatas and a number of masses, Elsner wrote thirty Polish operas and two ballets. An orchestral precursor to Verdi of great musical imagination, Elsner introduced Chopin to the art of *bel canto* song. Chopin's early love for the beautiful singer Konstancja Gładkowska flowered alongside his love of the voice, which later developed into a passion for Italian opera, in particular Bellini and Rossini.[81] Elsner constantly pressed Chopin to compose a 'patriotic opera' but failed despite the composer's enthusiasm for this art. Chopin's earliest composition for piano and orchestra was a set of variations on *Là ci darem la mano* from Mozart's *Don Giovanni*. Throughout his life his completed works were regarded as pale shadows of his improvisations. In 1821 a Warsaw taxidermist named August Brunner invented the strange *aeolomelodicon*, named after the Greek god of wind, which was a precursor to the harmonium. Chopin gave a virtuoso performance on it which so impressed Tsar Alexander I that he gave him a diamond ring.

Elsner also steered the young composer along the path of folklore. The mazurkas in particular, with their mobile rhythms of Polish folk music – the notorious *tempo rubato*[82] – are the unique outcome of an artistic sublimation of the music of his beloved Mazovian countryside.[83] When Chopin was accused of fancifully breaking rules Elsner replied 'Leave him in peace. His is an uncommon way because his gifts are uncommon . . . he will reveal in his

81 Joseph Elsner's great work, the extraordinary *Passio Domini Nostri Jesu Christi*, is scored for large forces of musicians including 14 solo voices, three 4-voice choirs, a piano and orchestra, military band and an enlarged percussion section. The autograph of the piece was discovered in the Berlin State Library. 'The Death of Christ' and 'The Earthquake' are in a particularly impressive *Sturm und Drang* style. The first complete modern performance was given in March 1999 in the neoclassical centrally-planned Lutheran Church in Warsaw by Warszawska Opera Kameralna (Warsaw Chamber Opera). Elsner was 'permitted' to dedicate the work to Tsar Nicholas I who was at that time King of Poland.

82 The explanation of *tempo rubato*, so characteristic of Chopin's style, is a thorny subject indeed, best left to the musicologist or an instinctive Polish virtuoso.

83 Yet there are very few examples of Chopin *literally* transcribing folk melodies into his sixty-odd mazurkas. A particularly interesting essay is 'Chopin's Mazurkas and the Myth of the Folk' by Barbara Milewski in *19th Century Music,* vol. 23, No. 2, 1999, pp. 113–135.

works an originality which in such degree has not been found in anyone.'[84] His succinct final report on his pupil observed, 'Szopen Frideric – Particularly talented. Musical genius etc.'[85] The limpid, untroubled and joyful nature of the early polonaises, mazurkas, rondos, sets of variations on Polish themes and piano concertos were written in the virtuosic *style brillant* fashionable in Warsaw. Now decidedly out of fashion, this style was characterized by lightness, delicacy, charm, sonority, purity, precision and a rippling execution resembling pearls – *le son perlé*. These works could only have been composed in a state of happiness and youthful 'sweet sorrows' living in his native land.

More a refined eighteenth-century classicist attached to the Baroque aesthetic than an unbridled Romantic in temperament, Chopin devoted himself almost exclusively to a single instrument. He explored the sound world of the piano, changing forever the way all later composers approached it. With the intuition of a great artist, the Polish harpsichordist Wanda Landowska called Chopin *'le Couperin du dix-neuvième siècle'* (the Couperin of the nineteenth century).[86] In a similar fashion to my uncle, I too moved away from the piano to the harpsichord for many years. I was particularly drawn to the Watteauesque world of François Couperin le Grand, Maître de Clavecin des Enfants de France at the court of Louis XIV. Both Chopin and Couperin express a subtle aristocratic melancholy, deeply exploring the sound possibilities of their instrument.

Chopin intensely disliked the music of most of his contemporaries

---

84 Quoted in the indispensable *Frederick Chopin as a Man and Musician*, Frederick Niecks, Volume I (London 1888) p. 40. Niecks also launches into an extraordinary diatribe against 'that loud, shallow talker Count Stendhal . . . *fanfaron d'ignorance en musique* . . . Beyle is an ignorant braggart, not only in music but in art generally . . .' Highly amusing in view of his incontestable literary genius. p. 74–75

85 A fervent nationalist political debate erupted in the late nineteenth century concerning the spelling of Chopin's name. Many right-wing commentators believed in the Polonization of his name to *Szopen* so that he would more purely represent the 'Polish race' in music. His distant *amour* Maria Wodzińska wrote in a letter to him in Paris from Dresden in 1835, 'We do not cease to regret that you are not called Chopinski: or that there are no other signs that you are a Pole because – as it is – Frenchmen may argue with us for the honor of being your compatriots.' The discussion of his predominantly 'French' or 'Polish' musical aesthetic rumbles on.

86 For further on points of similarity between Chopin and François Couperin see Jean-Jacques Eigeldinger, *Chopin et Couperin: affinités sélectives* in *Échos de France & d'Italie: Liber amicorum Yves Gérard* (Éditions Buchet/Chastel Paris 1997) pp. 175–193

except Weber, Hummel[87] and John Field. Like the double-faced mask of Janus he looks forward to the Wagner of *Tristan und Isolde* and backward to the late Baroque and Viennese masters. 'Everything *modern* escapes my brain,' Frycek wrote from Paris to his close friend Tytus Woyciechowski. Uninterested in the future or even the present of the tempestuous musical revolution that surrounded him in Paris, Chopin composed his works through what one musicologist perceptively calls 'the prism of reminiscence'.[88]

Part of the way through his studies Joseph Elsner recommended that Chopin 'take the waters' not far from where he was born in the small Silesian spa of Bad Reinerz (Duszniki Zdrój). Originally on the Prussian-Bohemian frontier, the village is now in the south-west of Poland on the border with the Czech Republic. Frycek's studies and intense partying into the small hours during his third and final year at the liceum had begun to affect his health. Headaches and swollen glands necessitated the application of leeches to his neck. The family doctors (there were a number) agreed his condition might possibly be serious. The idea gained in popularity with the Skarbeks of Żelazowa Wola (Countess Ludwika herself was suffering from tuberculosis) and three family groups set off at intervals on the arduous 450km journey by carriage from Warsaw to Duszniki Zdrój over rough roads serviced by indifferent accommodation. The route they took through pine forests and agricultural country now passes through industrialized towns.

Frycek arrived at Duszniki Zdrój on 3 August 1826, spending a day *en route* at the honey-coloured timber hunting lodge of Prince Antoni Radziwiłł, respected scion of the wealthy Polish family and

---

87 Chopin admired Johann Nepomuk Hummel (1778–1837) as a composer and a pianist above anyone apart from Bach and Mozart. His status as a pianist and pianistic 'devil' was legendary in Europe (members of the audience would stand on their chairs to improve their view of his double trills). Born in Pressburg in Austro-Hungary (today Bratislava in Slovakia) he was a prodigy and so impressed Mozart that he gave him free tuition, board and lodging in Vienna for two years. A friend of Beethoven and Schubert, a pupil of Haydn, it is all too easy to underestimate his extraordinary contemporary fame. The *style brillant* of Chopin's piano concertos and variations was much influenced by the glittering style of Hummel's piano concertos. When he visited Warsaw to give a concert, Hummel was greatly impressed by the young Chopin. Liszt's dramatic power defeated Hummel the refined classicist, whose music fell out fashion. His piano music (and the famous trumpet concerto) is having a resurgence today but his output has been unaccountably neglected.

88 Jean-Jacques Eigeldinger, *Placing Chopin in a Compositional Aesthetic* in *Chopin Studies 2*, John Rink and Jim Samson (editors) (Cambridge 1994) p. 102

a fine cellist, composer and singer. This delightful octagonal lodge is built in a beautiful region of forests and lakes. On a later visit he wrote, 'There were two young Eves in this paradise, the exceptionally courteous and good princesses, both musical and sensitive beings.' Of Wanda Radziwiłł, 'She was young, 17 years old, and truly pretty, and it was so nice to put her little fingers on the right notes.' While a guest Chopin wrote a polonaise for piano and cello – 'brilliant passages, for the salon, for the ladies'.

Duszniki as a treatment centre has not greatly changed. The Spa Park and the town nestle in the peaceful mountain river valley of the tumbling Bystrzyca Dusznicka. Fragrant pine woods flourish on the slopes and the moist micro-climate is wonderfully refreshing. Carefully stepping invalids negotiate the shaded walks that radiate across the park between flowering shrubs, fountains and lawns. Many famous artists visited Duszniki in the nineteenth century including the composer Felix Mendelssohn. In times past the regimented cures began at the ungodly hour of 6am when people gathered at the well heads. The waters at the Lau-Brunn (now the Pienawa Chopina or Chopin's Spa) were dispensed by girls with jugs fastened to the ends of poles who also distributed gingerbread to take away the horrible taste (it was considered injurious to lean towards the spring and breathe in the carbon dioxide and methane exhalations).

Chopin was reputed to have developed an affection for a poor 'girl of the spring' named Libusza. One tragic day Libusza's father was crushed to death by an iron roller and she and her brothers were made orphans. In his generous way 'Chopinek' wanted to assist the family and his mother suggested giving a benefit recital. Despite the lack of a decent instrument he agreed and in August 1826 gave two of his first public concerts in a small hall in the town.[89]

Since 1946 this event has been celebrated every August in a week-long International Chopin Piano Festival, the oldest music festival in Poland. The original building where he played has been converted into the charming *Dworek Chopina*, an intimate concert room. Many of the finest pianists in the world, established artists and even

---

89 Chopin's period in Duszniki Zdrój is derived from the excellent and detailed *Chopin's Poland*, Iwo and Pamela Załuski (London 1996) p. 85–95

child prodigies, including past winners of the always controversial Fryderyk Chopin International Piano Competition, have appeared in these Elysian surroundings.

The Duszniki festival attempts to maintain the intimate nature of the salon and the piano music is not restricted to Chopin. During the day there is time to walk in the peace of the surrounding pine-clad mountains, 'take the waters' if you dare, or visit splendid castles in the nearby Czech lands. Eccentric characters regularly appear there: the 'Texan' Pole who wears cowboy boots, 'Florida' belts and Stetson hats of leopard-skin or enamelled in blue, maroon or green. 'I jus' love it here but I jus' hate that goddam music!' (recitals are broadcast through loudspeakers over the Spa Park); the ethereal girl with the swan neck who seems to have stepped directly from a *fête champêtre* by Watteau; an old musician with long grey hair and voluminous silk cravats.

Under the guidance of the fine Polish pianist and artistic director Piotr Paleczny, I have experienced many remarkable musical moments at Duszniki. Grigory Sokolov, arguably the greatest living pianist, gave a magisterial performance of that radical composition the *Polonaise-Fantasie*. He recreated the tragic instability of Chopin's disintegrating world during his final years. The Ukrainian pianist Alexander Gavrylyuk, who lives in Australia, returned to the piano after an horrific car accident that threatened to leave him totally incapacitated. Miraculously recovered, he acknowledges his god to be Vladimir Horowitz and without apology emulates him both in his theatrical temperament and truly astounding virtuosity. The soulful young Russian Igor Levit is deeply involved with the music of Schumann. He movingly reminded the audience of the genesis of the 'Ghost' Sonata, written when the composer was on the brink of suicide in a mental institution and where after completing the final variation he fell forever silent. The great Liszt super-virtuoso Janina Fialkowska, a true inheritor of the nineteenth century late Romantic school of pianism, courageously returned to the platform after her career was brought to a sudden halt by the discovery of a tumour in her left arm.

A romantic late evening event, the *Nokturn*, takes place by candlelight. An eminent musicologist such as Irena Poniatowska might draw our attention to an obscure aspect of Chopin such as his friendship with the beautiful pianist, singer and composer of

Spanish descent Pauline Viardot or the influence of Mozart on the composer with the pianists illustrating her argument. In spite of the immense popularity of Chopin, this festival manages to recapture the essentially private and esoteric experience of his music, an experience one might consider had been lost forever.

The international competition in contrast places the composer squarely in the gladiatorial and political arena of the Warsaw Filharmonia. The competition is an extraordinary phenomenon where some three hundred and fifty virtuoso pianists play competitively for a month. Chopin's pupil Karol Mikuli described the playing of the composer as expressing 'energy without roughness' and 'delicacy without affectation', while his best pupil Princess Marcelina Czartoryska advised the performer to intuitively immerse himself *'au climat de Chopin'*.[90] Such illuminating remarks are lost on today's young tyros who utilize a limited dynamic range and articulation. The technical facility and power of young virtuosi is of a standard breathtakingly higher than ever before. Many give performances that would have rocketed them to instant fame and fortune seventy years ago. But in acquiring the necessary physical prowess, extensive repertoire and stamina demanded by the terrifyingly competitive modern professional concert career, many pander to the public taste. Much of the seductive charm and personal style of the great pianists who performed Chopin before the Second World War has been sacrificed on the altar of an increasingly esoteric musicology. As one of the French pianists on the jury said to me in frustration, 'Where is *la poésie* and *le bon goût* so prized by Chopin?'

Appearances can be distracting. One Russian competitor resembled Rasputin in appearance, with unkempt greasy hair and beard. He performed in a long black leather trench-coat and smiled vacantly at some mysterious member of the audience while taking outrageous liberties with the music. Glamorous and alluring Polish blondes seduced us with tone and *grand décolleté*, while Japanese girls were transfigured by 'angelic visions' and seizures of sentiment. We are very far today from the aristocratic poise, self-discipline and

---

90 *Chopin and the Technique of Performance*, John Rink in *Chopin in Performance: History, Theory, Practice*, (Warsaw 2005) p. 234

concentration of a Michelangeli, a Rubinstein or a Horowitz immaculately dressed, slightly adjusting their posture as the physical demands of the composition increase.

Chopin is one of the most difficult of composers to interpret and begs for a cultivated mind of sensibility and poetry with a proper understanding of his cultural milieu and noble historical style. But the world young artists have inherited is loud, cruel and violent, a world dominated by technology that prizes physical power, speed and the body above intelligence, morality and the soul. Many are simply too young for the pain and mystery of Chopin. Athletic training has turned them into acrobats of the keyboard participating in an Olympic sport of tempestuous brutality. C.P.E. Bach put it well: 'They overwhelm our hearing without satisfying it and stun the mind without moving it . . .'[91] The result is extremely destructive to music as an art. The great Russian pianists have taught us that an unassailable technique must be the foundation on which a pianist builds and matures, but Chopin is now erroneously viewed through the filter of Rachmaninov, Scriabin or Prokoviev rather than Mozart and Bach. Chopin himself loathed 'gymnastic' and exaggerated physical treatment of the piano. George Sand was once amused at his horror when he thought he may actually have been *sweating* in the summer heat at Nohant. '*Facilement, facilement,*' he often warned. 'Caress the key, never bash it!' Chopin would admonish.

The musical and cultural education of musicians in Poland is slowly being transformed. The country has produced some of the greatest composers and pianists of the twentieth century. Yet classical music has for a long time been unaccountably neglected in the educational system. The decades under communism separated many performers from the renaissance in 'early music' performance practice that took place in the West as well as other contemporary developments in music. Much of the charming Polish baroque repertoire gathers dust in Kraków libraries. The absence of a developed middle class means classical music remains largely a minority interest with restricted audiences.

91 *Versuch über die wahre Art das Klavier zu spielen 1753* (Essay on the True Art of Playing Keyboard Instruments), Carl Philipp Emanuel Bach, trans. ed. W.J. Mitchell (London 1949)

The situation has greatly changed since the fall of communism with fine baroque ensembles now playing on original instruments and a certain impetus towards change in education. There are promising new initiatives such as the remarkable Nowa Orkiestra Kameralna (New Chamber Orchestra). This foundation, orchestra and choir were established by the talented and philanthropic Anglo-Polish countertenor Richard Berkeley and the Polish conductor Paweł Kos-Nowicki. The orchestra performs rarely heard works of the Polish baroque and nineteenth century, as well as the standard repertoire. The educational wing stages opera workshops for children, training courses for music teachers and performers and music in hospitals for therapy. Berkeley writes with conviction: 'Music is where all human communication begins. Communication is what makes a civil society. An education system without music at its core is failing its children.'

Chopin possesses an unrivalled position as Poland's national composer and its musical *wieszcz*.[92] His music is the beating heart of the country. The great Polish poet Cyprian Norwid (1821–83) described Chopin as 'a Varsovian by birth, a Pole by heart, and a citizen of the world by talent'. Virtuoso brilliance, a supreme gift for melody and an air of sentimentality explain his immense appeal on a popular level. But more deeply the universality of Chopin lies in the sense of loss and nostalgia for his homeland. Contained within his intense music is patriotic resistance to domination, sacrifice and melancholy in the face of 'the bitter finales of life'[93] – all universal human emotions. 'Chopin's music was a kind of cultural battleground in the nineteenth century, prey to appropriation.'[94] What, then, is his significance for Poland?

Before leaving Warsaw Chopin was closely involved with the

---

92 There is no English equivalent for this Polish word – an approximation might be 'prophetic seer' or 'messianic messenger'. Adam Mickiewicz is considered a *wieszcz* through his national epic *Pan Tadeusz*.

93 *Russian Traditions of Chopin Perfomance*, Irina Nikolska in *Chopin in Performance: History, Theory, Practice* (Warsaw 2005) p. 249

94 *Chopin Studies 2* John Rink and Jim Samson eds. (Cambridge 1994). For some of the observations in the following paragraphs I am indebted to the essay *Chopin reception: theory, history, analysis*, Jim Samson pp. 1–17 and *Remembering that tale of grief: The prophetic Voice in Chopin's Music*, Halina Goldberg in *The Age of Chopin: Interdisciplinary Enquiries* (Indiana 2004) pp. 54–92

intelligentsia who espoused Polish messianic ideas. The national poet Adam Mickiewicz (1798–1855) played the role of *wieszcz* in poetry. The country was considered the reincarnation of the suffering Christ, a nation crucified by predatory foreign powers, the Polish pilgrim wandering far-off lands in exile. As a young man Frycek frequented the Honoratka café where the November Uprising was hatched. When living in Paris he was not politically active in the Polish émigré community but counted many committed Polish artists as his friends. Mickiewicz's poems inspired the Chopin Ballades, a unique type of dramatic, purely musical narrative. These works are in distinct contrast to so-called 'program music' (such as Vivaldi's *Four Seasons*) that has definite extra-musical associations. During a musical *soirée* in Paris the forceful poet roundly criticized Chopin for not being a more active patriot while he was actually improvising a piece at the piano. The composer seemed to physically shrink into himself as if struck a physical blow.

Poles treasure the mazurka, polonaise and krakowiak as do foreigners, but they contain hidden and secret signs known only to the soul of Poles. 'Only Poles can understand Chopin' is often declared to me with heat. Chopin often commented that the 'Polish element' was missing from the rhythm of otherwise excellent performances of his works. The patriotic hymn, the lament and the military march lie deep within the fabric of many of his compositions. The perfume of the Orient hovers about the nocturnes. Chopin often chose as the subject for one of his famed improvisations a piece that is now the national anthem of Poland, the 'Dąbrowski Mazurka' or *Jeszcze Polska nie zginęła* ('Poland Has Not Yet Perished'). The artfully concealed political message of this improvisation once elicited the remark from a diplomat, 'you should have thrown out a demagogue like Chopin!' There are powerful patriotic messages contained within his songs, ballades and particularly the *Fantasy in F minor Op.49* which contains among other things a reference to the insurrectionary song *Bracia, do bitwy nadszedł czas* ('Brothers, The Time Has Come To Battle').

His early biographer Marceli Antoni Szulc wrote of his compositions, 'they are native, immaculate and purely Polish'. The Counsellor of State to the Russian Imperial Court, Wilhelm von Lenz, wrote of 'his soul's journey through . . . his Sarmatian dream-world', and that 'Chopin was the only political pianist of the time. Through his music he *incarnated* Poland, he *set* Poland to *music!*'[95] The great pianist and statesman Ignacy Jan Paderewski, in an eloquent address given at the Chopin Centenary Festival at L'viv (Lemberg, Lwów) in 1910, said, 'he gave all back to us, mingled with the prayers of broken hearts, the revolt of fettered souls, the pains of slavery, lost freedom's ache, the cursing of tyrants, the exultant songs of victory.' He felt the entire Polish nation moved in the rhythm of *tempo rubato*. Finally Chopin himself wrote to his editor Julian Fontana in April 1848 with the hand of death already at his shoulder, 'There is no way horrifying events can be averted but in the end of it all is a splendid, great Poland; in a word: Poland.' Nearly a hundred years later, the Nazis understood his patriotic power; they banned his music.

Other nationalities harboured different conceptions of Chopin. The French reasoned he had a French surname, his career was made in Paris and his father was French. Concerning his music the emphasis was on poetic expression or as one critic mawkishly suggested, '[the listener] will weep, believing that he really suffers with one who can weep so well'. The Germans took until the end of the nineteenth century to remove him from what they considered to be the frivolous salon and incorporate him into the sacred canon of German classical music. A German commentator concluded in a fashion more characteristic of later predatory events: 'For the profundity with which nature has endowed him, Chopin belongs more to Germany than to Poland.'

In England his compositions – 'drawing-room trifles' and 'tuneful gems' – were considered 'easy' pieces for amateurs. Victorian ladies performed his more manageable waltzes, mazurkas and nocturnes on the piano, which had become part of the furniture of every respectable middle-class English home. In all European countries the vast majority of pianists in the nineteenth century were women. From this stems the absurd prejudice against the so-called effeminacy of his nocturnes and other 'small forms', the androgynous 'fairy voices' of an 'angel'. The conductor Charles Hallé observed that Chopin had become 'the property of every schoolgirl'. Perhaps the most misguided barb came from an English critic who lamented that the great novelist George Sand had become involved with 'the artistic zero' Fryderyk Chopin.

The extraordinary contemporary enthusiasm for his music in Japan, China and South Korea (where the majority of piano students choose his work above all other composers, and Asians far outnumber other nationalities in the Chopin competition) dates from 1945 and mass exposure to Western music. Some Japanese feel 'a sad depth within the brilliance', others that he possesses *yugen* (beauty, elegance and nobility), the essential qualities of Noh drama.[96]

In Russia the composer Balakirev perceived him as a Slavonic modernist, breaking revolutionary harmonic ground. His music was considered the expression of Slavic cultural nationalism, and in 1894 Balakirev initiated the first memorial to the composer erected at his birthplace at Żelazowa Wola. These Russian 'Slavonic' attributions paradoxically led to a renaissance of his music in Poland itself where it had been unaccountably neglected. This, together with the majestic example of Artur Rubinstein's performances, ultimately led to the establishment of the 'correct Polish' style of Chopin performance established through the perennially controversial Fryderyk Chopin International Piano Competition.

Paris in the first half of the nineteenth century recognized two broad schools of pianism. Balzac wrote in 1843 to his Polish mistress Madame Hańska, 'The Hungarian is a demon; the Pole is an angel.' The brilliant and refined style of Chopin, Field, Hummel, Ries and Kalkbrenner owed allegiance to the classical past. This contrasted strongly with the revolutionary Romanticism of 'The Thunderers', represented by Liszt and Thalberg. Judging by audience enthusiasm for loud and fast renditions we appear to have returned to the school of 'thunderers' with a vengeance.

Those who heard Chopin, 'the *Ariel* of pianists', or were his

96 Susumu Tamura, *The Reception of Chopin's Music in Japan* in *Chopin and His Work in the Context of Culture*, ed. Irena Poniatowska (Kraków 2003) Volume II pp. 467–473. A fascinating article on a mysterious phenomenon.

students regarded him as a unique human being in addition to his being a charismatic teacher and pianist-composer of genius. Like all the best teachers Chopin was a psychologically perceptive man who often improved not only his students' playing but their listening and entire mental attitude to the instrument. In his teaching he advocated Bach and recommended a study of the art of the finest Italian *bel canto* song. Many in Paris considered him '*le Bellini du piano*'. Emilie von Gretsch studied with him for two years and wrote of overcoming the 'perilous difficulties' of the *études,* concluding, after advice which had facilitated some extraordinary progress, 'I think he can read hearts'.[97] Listeners and students were much given to metaphysical hyperbole. In 1836 the young Charles Hallé, newly resident in Paris, wrote to his parents:

> I went to dine with Baron Eichtal where I heard *Chopin.* That was beyond all words. The few senses I had have quite left me. I could have jumped into the Seine . . . Chopin! He is no man, he is an angel, a god (of what can I say more?) . . . There is nothing to remind one that it is a human being who produces this music. It seems to descend from heaven . . .[98]

His student Countess Elizavieta Cheriemietieff wrote to her mother in 1842:

> It's something so ethereal, so transparent, that delicacy, yet his sounds [are] so full, so large . . . He's a genius far above all the pianists who dazzle and exhaust their listeners . . . It's a desecration, I find, to play his compositions; nobody understands them.[99]

Clearly Chopin was achieving something on the piano that was entirely new. He left behind an unfinished piano method of tantalizingly fragmentary insights.

Such effusions also point up the present dramatic shift in aesthetic

97 Op. cit., Eigeldinger p. 13
98 Op. cit., Eigeldinger p. 271
99 Op. cit., Eigeldinger p. 278

perspective of Chopin performance. Clearly radical changes in dynamic level, tempo and interpretative approach have taken place since his death. Closely allied to interpretation is the nature of the sound he extracted from the instruments available to him. He insisted that in the beginning a pupil develop a refined touch and beautiful tone before working on technique and velocity. A consideration of the instrument he chose to teach and perform on is a useful and educational corrective, confronted as we are by the ubiquitous black Steinway or Yamaha behemoths of the modern concert hall.

Before Frycek left Warsaw permanently he was familiar with all the finest European instruments. Early in his career he favoured Polish Bucholtz pianos and later those by the maker to the Austrian Imperial Court, Conrad Graf. Their light Viennese action and distinct 'fluty' tone was also preferred by Hummel. Liszt was known to demolish such instruments during the course of his recitals and required spares waiting in the wings. He bragged that he could be heard effortlessly in the back row at La Scala. Chopin had become familiar with the refined French Pleyel pianos before leaving Poland. He was to write from Paris to his friend Tytus Woyciechowski '*Fortepiany Pleyelowskie non plus ultra*', the last word in perfection. The tone of a Pleyel (upright or grand) has a seductive velvet quality to it, slightly diffuse, with light transparent trebles and a rich but clear mahogany bass. Liszt wrote of 'their silvery and slightly veiled sonority' and 'lightness of touch'. The puzzling descriptions of Chopin's playing, his refined nuances, inimitable *rubato*, cantabile melodic line and delicate ornamentation 'falling like tiny drops of speckled dew over the melodic figure', according to Liszt, make absolute sense with the light action and extreme sensitivity of the Pleyel. 'When I feel out of sorts,' Chopin would say, 'I play on an Erard piano where I can easily find a ready-made tone. When I feel in good form and strong enough to find my own individual sound, then I need a Pleyel piano.'[100]

Some months after returning to Bath at the conclusion of the Polish contract, nostalgia for my Polish musical experiences inspired

100 Op. cit., Eigeldinger p. 26

me to begin practising the piano again. I had always believed in the superiority of well-restored original instruments and in an attempt to assist my imaginative recreation of Chopin's sound world I purchased a restored Pleyel 'pianino' of 1844, a small upright much favoured by the composer. It was the type of piano he arranged to have delivered by donkey to the notorious Carthusian monastery at Valdemosa.[101] The Italian opera composer Bellini, Chopin's friend the French painter Delacroix, George Sand at Nohant and Madame de Balzac all purchased these delightful small instruments. His extraordinarily detailed notation reveal a composer obsessed with the nature of the sound he was producing.[102] Many of these indications can only be adequately realized on the very different instruments of his time.

In 1837 his friend Camille Pleyel suggested a trip to London to recover from his broken love affair with Maria Wodzińska. He travelled under the alias of 'Monsieur Fritz from Paris'. Naturally all was revealed the moment he touched the instrument at a *soirée* in Bryanston Square, at the home of James Broadwood, the English piano manufacturer. Broadwood became most solicitous of the fragile Chopin, particularly on his second, less successful, concert tour of England in 1848. The composer was debilitated from consumption and the damp climate (quite apart from the exhausting ministrations of his Scottish ladies). While touring, Broadwood would generously buy two train tickets for the comfort of the composer, one for his body and the other for his feet. Chopin felt that the English only 'love art as a luxury' and 'consider everything in

101 This instrument is a small upright or 'cottage' piano of six and a half octaves in an elegantly proportioned case of 'plum-pudding' mahogany with fine ormolu decoration. It was originally purchased in 1844 from Ignace Pleyel & Compagnie, Facteurs du Roi, by a certain M. Leveau Vallée of Rouen for 1,000 gold francs. During lessons the pupil would take the Pleyel grand and Chopin the pianino, playing the orchestral part of his concertos or variations. They are rare compared to the number of Pleyel grands that have survived. It was restored by David Winston of the Period Piano Company in England. His workshop is one of the finest in the world for the restoration and building of copies of historical pianos and fortepianos. He restored Beethoven's 1817 Broadwood previously owned by Liszt and now in the Hungarian National Museum in Budapest. He also restored the Pleyel grand pianoforte No 13819 that Chopin used in England. This instrument is now in the Alec Cobbe Collection of Early Keyboard Instruments at Hatchlands, the National Trust property in Surrey.

102 Chopin's high level of detailed thinking about sound is clearly revealed in the definitive Chopin urtext *Wydanie Narodowe* (National Edition) of his works still in progress of publication. His friends often spoke of his terrible labours composing at the piano. This edition is edited with reference to all available editions and autographs with minimal editorial intervention by Jan Ekier. Chopin's variant autograph sources and editions are a musical minefield.

terms of money'. He gave the final recitals of his life in London, Manchester, Glasgow and Edinburgh. He almost coughed himself to death in the pollution of 'beastly London' and was happy to drag himself away. The visit may have hastened his death less than a year later.

Many pianists and teachers ignore much of the highly sensitive detail in Chopin in favour of the roaring cataracts. After mastering the notes, 'Put some expression into it!' is often the exhortation. Chopin confided to Liszt:

> I am not suited to public appearances – the auditorium saps my courage, I suffocate in the exhalation of the crowd, I am paralysed by curious glances . . . but you, you can, since if you should fail to win over the audience you at least have the possibility of murdering them.

His anxiety in performance and the patronizing attitude of George Sand to her lover is clear from a letter she wrote to Pauline Viardot in 1841.

> The great news is that little Chip Chip is giving a grrrrrreat concert. His friends pounded the idea into his head so hard that he let himself be persuaded . . . This Chopinesque nightmare will take place in the Pleyel Salons on April 26. He wants no posters and he doesn't want anyone to talk about it. I've suggested he play without candles or an audience, on a mute piano.[103]

He also observed to his student Emilie von Gretsch, 'concerts are never real music; you have to give up the idea of hearing in them the most beautiful things in art.'[104] Chopin may well have been overjoyed by the way the modern Steinway effortlessly realizes the implied dynamic and latent dramatic potential of his compositions. But true passion is generated by limitation not realization. It is the very inadequacy of older instruments that gives them their unique creative tension. Exploring Chopin's music on an instrument he was

103 *Chopin and His Work*, Irena Poniatowska (Warsaw, 2005) p. 9
104 Op.cit., Eigeldinger pp. 164–166

known to love adds a vital dimension to understanding this apparently accessible yet mysterious composer.[105]

Frycek returned to Warsaw from Duszniki in much better health and began his studies at the Warsaw Conservatorium. In 1827 the doctors hastened the end of his adored sister Emilka – 'a flower blossoming with the promise of a beautiful fruit' – by bleeding her with a knife, applying leeches, mustard plasters and wolfsbane. The family were devastated by her death. Her mother never recovered from the loss. Chopin, by now a highly strung young man, managed a trip to Berlin to hear some fine operas and was enraptured by the *Ode to Saint Cecilia* by Handel. On the return journey at the tiny town of Züllichau (Sulechów) another legendary Chopin moment took place. His coach was delayed for lack of horses and to pass the time he improvised on a piano at the post office. Everyone round about was amazed and now the encores meant it was the turn of the horses to wait. Wine, cakes and sweets were handed around and glasses lifted to his health. None of the pretty admiring girls could have realized that a fatal bacterium had already begun its insidious work.

After a number of flirtations Chopin became infatuated with the daughter of the superintendent of the Royal Castle, a blue-eyed, blonde opera singer named Konstancja Gładkowska (the muse who inspired the ardent Larghetto from the Piano Concerto in F Minor). He wrote to his ideal, 'In my unbearable longing I feel better as soon as I receive a letter from you . . . I have nobody to whom I can open my heart.' As is the way of these things, Konstancja seemed more taken by the uniforms of two young dashing Russian officers than the glances and sighs of her admiring genius.

---

105 The young Polish pianist Rafał Blechacz, modest winner of the international competition in 2005, grasps the enigma of Chopin with Mozartian elegance, maintaining a delicate balance between emotion and reason. It is impossible for me to adequately examine the fascinating history of Chopin performance here. The recordings of the giants of late Romantic pianism such as Josef Lhévinne, Sergei Rachmaninov, Moritz Rosenthal, Josef Hofman, Vladimir Horowitz and Leopold Godowsky give at least some indication of the incredible *Fingerfertigkeit* (finger dexterity) of the late nineteenth century. They possessed exquisite beauty of tone with absolute delicacy and evenness of touch which scarcely any pianist today achieves with the same consistency. Above all they possessed great sensibility, poetry and charm. The modern pianist who came closest to the many descriptions of Chopin's own playing and is considered the heir to the 'pure' tradition was the Pole, Raul von Koczalski (1884–1948). This largely forgotten pianist and composer was a student of another Pole, Karol Mikuli (1819–97), who was one of Chopin's favourite pupils, his assistant and editor. Koczalski's remarkable recordings of Chopin are available on the Polish 'Selene' label as eight digitally transferred CDs. He devoted his entire life to Chopin.

In July 1829 he decided to broaden his musical horizons by travelling to Vienna. He gave two concerts there where he improvised and played his *Krakowiak* Rondo and variations on *Là ci darem la mano* to great acclaim – 'It goes *crescendo* with my popularity here.' By the autumn of 1830 Chopin realized he was chronically bored with the limited musical life of Warsaw. He wanted to return to Vienna, where he had been lionized by an adoring public, but was plagued by a fury of indecision. In September he had written to Tytus: 'I have always a presentiment that I shall leave Warsaw never to return to it; I am convinced I shall say farewell to my home forever.' It was finally decided he would go to Vienna for two months and a farewell celebratory dinner with family and friends was arranged for the night of All Saints' Day, November 1. He was to depart the next morning. *Zaduszki* or All Souls' Day is usually a day for praying and visiting family graves with flowers and candles. He could scarcely have realized that the choice of this date was an ominous sign he was never to return to Poland.

The day was fraught with activity as his sister packed his music while he called on friends and made his final farewells. He exchanged rings with Konstancja and arranged to exchange letters. She wrote in his notebook in verse 'Remember, unforgettable one, that in Poland they love you.' The political situation was deteriorating, which worried his family. The young man of twenty, already vaguely aware of some mysterious illness, was apprehensive of the unknown yet full of the optimism of youth. The sadness would be somewhat mitigated when his dearest friend Tytus Woyciechowski, who lived on the estate of Poturzyn near Lublin, joined him in Kalisz on the journey to Vienna. He wrote to him later, 'I long for your fields – that birch tree under the windows cannot leave my memory.'

He travelled in the coach with Elsner and some friends as far as the Wola gate, not so distant from the old election field for Polish kings. In a typically protracted Polish farewell they alighted shortly after leaving the city, the coach suddenly surrounded by a group of men. His old teacher had written a cantata which the assembled choir sang accompanied by a guitar, an instrument he particularly loved. The words implored Chopin to remember Poland and to hold the harmonies of the country close in his soul wherever he might be. At a final banquet they presented him with an engraved silver goblet filled with Polish earth which he kept by him till death.

There was something fatidic in those tearful last embraces. The coach rolled along the muddy road to Vienna leaving behind all he held most precious in the world, carrying into immortality the musical soul of the nation. 'You are to play Mozart in my memory,' were his last words in Paris to his friends the cellist Franchomme and Princess Marcelina Czartoryska. After his death in Paris in 1849, earth from the silver cup was sprinkled on his coffin as it was lowered into the ground. Yet his heart did return to Poland. Ludwika carried it back in a casket through that selfsame Wola gate where it was finally laid to rest in a marble niche in the Church of the Holy Cross.

CHAPTER 13

The Little Shop of Horrors

Despite the difficulties of daily work at the centre I was often invited to give lectures and attend conferences in other parts of the country. My paper at the Adam Mickiewicz University in Poznań was entitled 'The Little Shop Of Horrors: Western Business in the Polish Context'. The warmth of my reception by academics was always surprising, the Poles being almost embarrassingly grateful then that Westerners were prepared to assist their country.

Poles learn extremely quickly and misunderstandings concerning the market economy have now largely disappeared. Today a curiously blasé resentment and competitive edge greets the foreigner. In the forum of the European Union they have adopted a strong negotiating style to protect their national interest. No one anticipated the explosion of immigrant Poles to the United Kingdom, lured by the promise of higher wages and the need to escape the political theatre of the absurd.

I was staying in an arcadian lakeside setting at a stylish restaurant with rooms. Zosia had overcome her moral scruples to come to Poznań on the pretext of visiting friends and we managed to have a late romantic lunch together watching the water birds and later walking in the wooded park. Being rather a dreamer, she had a passionate love and detailed knowledge of the cinema and its illusions. Our affair satisfied her love of romantic adventure. She had always wanted to be an actress but financial difficulties after the premature death of her father, lack of self-confidence and the difficulties inherent in the acting career influenced her choice of more solid intellectual pursuits in the academic world.

She needed to leave in the early evening. I was deeply frustrated at the limitations of our relationship, the enforced separation dictated by her sense of responsibility to her children. Yet she truly believed we would be together permanently one day. We sat together at the luxurious bar, tortured, saddened by the melancholic jazz band playing 'Misty' nearby. A final snatched kiss in the car on a bleak former communist housing estate, the gloom punctuated by fluorescent strip lights. The darkness between the huge concrete residential blocks and caged cars swallowed her up and a terrible aridity took hold of my heart.

Poland always provides one with sudden, almost surrealist extremes. I often reflected that living here was like inhabiting a Salvator Dalí painting. Within a couple of minutes of returning to the hotel my sadness has dissolved and I was laughing again, this time at the expense of a Texan oil man in tooled leather cowboy boots engaged in a 'business transaction', probably worth millions, with a Polish *biznesmanem* at the terrace bar. A number of assistants hovered in the background.

'If you're talkin' sodium phosphate, boy, you're talkin' shit!' He moved his vast Texan hat to one side.

'Yes sir, shit, shit, *tak, tak, tak.*' (yes, yes, yes)

'Don't start that chicken stuff with me, boy! Listen up! What ya got here are ya di-oliphons!' – gesturing to a diagram sketched on a napkin.

'Yes, yes. Oilphons, oliphons. Understand you, understand.'

'Not oliphons boy, *di*-oliphons, *di*-oliphons. Git it?'

'I git, I git.' The Pole was clearly desperate and the Texan became more expansive despite the Pole's increasingly stricken expression.

'Look here, boy! Ya got all these atoms wrigglin' around and they're trying to lock onto each other. Ya got a carbon atom here and a hydrogen atom here and they're hookin' on just like a hooker! Ha! Ha! Can ya *see* that, boy?' He drew more sketches and the Polish businessman nodded with an absence of comprehension rare to witness.

I spent a couple of days after the conference wandering the city. Much was destroyed during the war but the Town Hall, with one of the finest vaulted Renaissance interiors in Europe, miraculously survived. The city is resplendent with fine churches and monasteries, particularly the ancient cathedral on Ostrów Tumski (Cathedral Island) strategically situated in the River Warta. The original Polonians founded a castle here in the ninth century and the first Christian prince of Poland, the Piast Mieszko I (c.922–92)[106] invested it as one of his seats, making the city particularly significant historically.

By the concluding years of the eighteenth century Poznań had become the major city of western Poland. Later, as a part of Prussia following the final partition of the country in 1795, it was known as the Grand Duchy of Poznań (Posen). The character of the partitioning power continues to be reflected in the areas over which Austria, Russia or Prussia ruled. Poznanians retain a distinctive Prussian reputation for logic and discipline. The careful division and ordered fields of surrounding farmland still manifest the Prussian temperament.

Much of the resistance to increasing German colonization was centred on Poznań and there was strong support here for uprisings in other parts of Poland. Following the armistice of the Great War, Ignacy Jan Paderewski arrived in Danzig in December 1918 aboard the British cruiser HMS *Concord* hoping to negotiate the premiership of the independent republic with the heroic, gritty and sombre President Józef Piłsudski. Paderewski travelled on to Poznań where he was greeted at the station with frenzied flag waving and a torchlight procession to his hotel. Here he made a speech which sparked fighting against the Germans and spread throughout the country.[107]

This was known as the Great Poland Uprising, one of only two successful Polish uprisings from the many launched throughout history. It led to the creation of the Second Polish Republic and the first taste of freedom for over two hundred years. However this event and the Treaty of Versailles laid the seeds of the Second World War in the tinder box of the Free City of Danzig (Gdańsk). Some of

106 This prince was a descendant of a dynasty that existed in Poland for over five centuries. 'Reputedly, Piast was a peasant. According to the Anonymous Gaul [a Benedictine monk d.1118] writing some 250 years later, he ascended the throne in succession to the wicked Popiel who, also reputedly, was eaten by mice in the dungeon of Kruszwica. He is thus a figure which links Poland's legendary past with its recorded history.' *God's Playground: A History of Poland* Volume I, Norman Davies (Oxford 2005) p. 52. There is now a Piast touring route in this part of Poland (Wielkopolska).

107 See the excellent biography *Paderewski* by Adam Zamoyski (London 1982)

the earliest workers' riots against the communist state erupted in Poznań in 1956. They were brutally repressed by the military with many protestors killed, wounded and imprisoned. Thus began the long and painful process of anti-communist resistance in East Central Europe which culminated in the fall of the Berlin Wall in 1989.

At my hotel I met by chance the BBC producer and author Catrine Clay, who was making a documentary about the thousands of Polish children between seven and fourteen who were cruelly stolen from their parents by the Nazis to be brought up in Germany as racially pure Aryans. 'They will be taught German. They will be inculcated with the German spirit so that later they can be brought up as model German boys and girls.'[108] We spent a day together and she showed herself to be one of the most understanding and compassionate observers of the all too human tragedies and redeeming loves of 'ordinary' people caught up in the horrors of the Nazi occupation.

We travelled together to the palaces of Kórnik and Rogalin. Kórnik is a rather unattractive English neo-Gothic style mansion with some remarkable Moorish interiors. Turkey did not support the partition of Poland and to show his gratitude, the owner and patriot Count Tytus Działyński built an extraordinary room for his armour collection based on the Courtyard of the Lions at the Muslim palace of the Alhambra in Granada.

Rogalin is a significant Palladian country house built for the Raczyński family in the mid-eighteenth century with fine neoclassical interiors. They bore the Nałęcz coat of arms shared by the Korzeniowski family (the family of Joseph Conrad). The baroque formal French gardens possess one of the most extensive collections of old oak trees in Europe, some as much as 700 years old. In the grounds there is an exceptional pink sepulchral chapel modelled on the famous Roman temple Maison Carrée at Nîmes containing the Raczyński family sarcophagi. This family played an important role in resisting the German cultural and economic incursions in the region.

---

108 The Trial of German Major War Criminals at Nuremberg. Sixty-Eighth Day: Tuesday, 26th February, 1946 p. 309

Count Edward Bernard Raczyński had a close connection with the United Kingdom, as Ambassador of the Polish Government-in-Exile. He remained in London after the war as an advisor on Polish affairs to the British government. In 1991, at the incredible age of a hundred, he married his long-term lover, and died in 1993. His remains were brought back to Rogalin and this great patriot was laid to rest in the family mausoleum with great pomp and ceremony. He bequeathed Rogalin and the famous Raczyński library to the Polish State. Catrine continued with her documentary filming and I headed back to Warsaw – but with a fatal detour, as it turned out.

After leaving Poznań I turned the rattling nose of the FSO towards Gniezno, the first capital city of Poland and cradle of Polish Catholicism and the Polish State. This sleepy town lies to the east of Poznań, the name derived from an old Polish word meaning 'nest'. The original settlement had been named by Lech, the legendary father of the country, who was thought to have settled on a hill where he saw the nest of a rare white eagle during the course of a hunt. The savagely beautiful legend of its death, the pure white of the feathers steeped in the slow spread of its red blood, became the national colours of this spiritually driven and tragic nation, the crowned white bird adopted as its symbol.

Pope John Paul II, on his subversive pilgrimage to Gniezno in 1979, recalled the birth of the Polish Catholic Church there in 966 when King Mieszko I was baptised in the Latin rite. He spoke to those labouring under communism of the myriad tongues of the Pentecostal experience which rendered the division of Europe at Yalta contrived and divisive. 'This Polish Pope, this Slav Pope, should at this precise moment manifest the unity of Christian Europe.' The cast for the historic morality play that followed had been assembled. Pope John Paul II was the man at the tipping point, the man but for whom recent European history would have been considerably different.

In the tenth century the missionary Bishop Wojciech (Adalbert), exiled from Prague, sailed to Gdańsk to convert the pagan Prussians. They beheaded him in 997 for his pains. The Piast Prince Bolesław Chrobry, soon to become the first crowned King of Poland, was much in need of a saint and purchased his body for its weight in gold and brought it to Gniezno. Wojciech was swiftly canonized as the patron saint of Poland and transformed into the object of a cult. The town developed into the centre for the coronation of Polish kings. Scenes from Wojciech's life are vividly depicted on the panels of two monumental bronze doors in the cathedral, one of the great Romanesque artworks of Europe. His relics lie before the high altar in a Baroque silver sarcophagus supported by six silver eagles.

After inward-looking religious thoughts at Gniezno I felt the need to walk in a forest or beside a lake so I set off in sunny weather to the Wielkopolski Park Narodowy (Great Poland National Park) situated on the left bank of the River Warta about fifteen kilometres south of Poznań. The minor roads were unmade and unsignposted, passing through bleak industrial villages and dense forests of birch and pine. The recreational area car-park was deserted, as was the landscape, except for an old man on a bicycle. A long avenue of trees lay before me. I put on my walking boots and set off.

The 'blue' hiking trail led to a lake edged with reeds and shaped rather like a heart. I sat on a tree trunk and passed the time enjoyably reading of the birth of Napoleon's love for the Polish Countess Maria Walewska, one of the great European love stories. She had grown up on the estate of Kiernozia in a small neoclassical manor house on the almost featureless Mazovian plain about eighty kilometres east of Warsaw. Grim family finances forced her into a marriage in 1804 at the age of seventeen with the wealthy and dapper Count Anastase Walewski, former Chamberlain to King Stanisław Augustus, but some fifty-two years her senior. She wrote 'the pink buds [of the sweetheart roses he gave her] looked incongruous next to his old wrinkled face and bald head . . .'[109] He lived in the nearby palace of Walewice, an elegant Palladian villa with beautiful gardens in the fashionable hybrid French and English manner. The statue of Mars and Venus at the edge of the brook would increasingly appear a premonitory sign of an historic affair.

November 1806 saw Warsaw joyously anticipating the arrival of Napoleon with his French troops. The crowds were jubilant and full of unquenchable optimism that independence would at last be

---

109 Quoted in the entertaining, moving and thoughtful biography *Marie Walewska: Napoleon's Great Love*, Christine Sutherland (London 1979) p. 32. This was the biography I was reading in the park and my account of the birth of their affair relies in part on this account.

restored. To a Pole a guest is considered 'God in the house' (sometimes one is even a victim of kindness), and poor families generously extended themselves to billet French soldiers. In an advance party ahead of the great man, Marshal Davout requisitioned Walewice as the Guard Brigade headquarters. November is one of the most unpleasant months in Poland with constant rain and mist, the overture to winter. Maria was distastefully contemplating crossing a lake of mud to reach the columned portico when a dashing young cavalry officer of much aristocratic refinement swept her up and carried her across to the paved entrance. This was Charles de Flahaut de la Billarderie, the natural son of the diplomatic genius Talleyrand and Countess Adelaide de Flahaut. Talleyrand, that champion of Polish independence, was still at Berlin but would soon be in Warsaw and Maria would be presented to him by his son. This impulsive gesture of gallantry would lead to a meeting that would change her life. The mud at Pułtusk on the River Narew just north of Warsaw had also bogged down Napoleon and his troops, preventing any clear outcome of the battle against the Russians. He decided to retire to winter quarters in the capital.

Maria Walewska reminded Talleyrand, a true man of the Enlightenment, of the sentimental and innocent '*têtes d'expression*' of the French painter Greuze. Perhaps it was her languid, slightly melancholic, blue eyes, blonde curls, perfect figure and pale complexion with just that ambiguous hint of erotic potential that fascinated men. At the reception for the Emperor at the Royal Castle in January 1807, Napoleon uttered his famous praise of Polish women as he came up to Maria: '*Ah, qu'il y a de jolies femmes à Varsovie*'. Reminiscing about the affair later on St Helena, the Emperor recalled noticing two unobservant rivals for her attentions, General Bertrand, whom he immediately despatched to the Baltic ('He never knew what hit him'), and the aristocrat Louis de Périgord ('I told Berthier to send him off to East Prussia . . .').

It was carnival time in Warsaw and at the Foreign Minister's Ball Napoleon insisted on partnering Maria in a complex *contre-danse*. His noble and penetrating gaze (Stendhal referred to it as '*ce regard fixe et profond à la fois*') scarcely disguised the fact he was an inelegant dancer. Maria received flowers and a letter next morning carrying the imperial seals depicting an eagle perched on a thunderbolt above the letter N surrounded by the rays of the sun. 'I saw no one but you, I admired only you; I want no one but you; I beg you to reply promptly to calm my ardour and my impatience.' The letter was signed 'Napoleon'.

This first unanswered letter was followed by another on a more personal note. Again no answer. Yet a third implored, 'Oh come, come . . . all your desires will be granted. Your country will be so much dearer to me if you take pity on my poor heart.' This cynical pressure appealed to her strong patriotic nature: the independence of Poland was at stake. She prepared to make the ultimate sacrifice – to lie back and think of Poland. Floods of tears accompanied her first reluctant 'interview' with Napoleon, she being an honourable married Polish woman whose moral standards were somewhat different to the 'wicked French'. Her husband, the aged dandy Anastase Walewski, would scarcely have stoked the fires of passion in this beautiful young creature. Her sensual nature was about to be awoken by the greatest man of the age. Napoleon soon took possession of his *douce colombe* and they became closely attached, she genuinely devoted and in love but forever emotionally confused by her intense patriotism. The details of their relationship emerge from the many surviving love letters she wrote to Napoleon. She would seal them with a scarab ring fashioned from shrapnel that killed his horse during the battle of Dresden in 1813.

Poland was intoxicated with the promise, the glory of Napoleon but he only offered them the vinegar of disappointed hopes. He used the country as a political pawn and sacrificed the valiant flower of its youth. His 'Polish wife' too was loved, admired but finally abandoned to his dynastic ambitions after reassuring him of his fertility with a son, Alexander. The boy was to become Ambassador to London and Minister of Foreign Affairs under the Emperor Napoleon III. Yet Maria – now addressed simply as *Madame* – always held a special place in his heart.

Princess Michael of Kent, recently researching at Malmaison (Napoleon and Josephine's residence outside Paris), wrote of a touching discovery. The Princess was pressing the curator for the slightest trace of Maria Walewska there. Reluctantly he descended to the basement and emerged with an old miniature. 'As he placed it in my hand, the frame fell to pieces, leaving me holding the tiny oval

painting. It was not made at her best moment – she was already ill
with kidney disease, her eyes slightly protruding, yet still young,
blonde and appealing. I turned the pieces over to reveal a small scrap
of paper. In an elegant hand was written, in ink faded to brown:
"Found by Prussian soldiers in Napoleon's carriage at
Waterloo".[110] One can only speculate at such moments on 'the
moving toyshop of their heart'.[111]

I closed the book and continued wandering along the shores of
Lake Góreckie and passed a remote farm building, white and low
with windows of prison smallness. Red berries glowed like tiny
flames in the lowering sun. The waters of the lake darkened from
azure to deepest indigo, the reeds at the water's edge a darker gold.
On my return a group of laughing children ran by. The light was
failing and the smaller lakes were turning black and sinister. As I
hurried back the trees seemed to arch over me in a menacing manner
and it was getting cold. Vague premonitions and floating anxiety
took over as I approached the car and all seemed well until I noticed
the smashed quarter light. The boot was empty. I had been robbed
of everything.

Any robbery is a form of negative violence and I sat in the car hit-
ting my head on the steering wheel, cursing myself. My conference
notes, my favourite Donegal Tweed suit, a tape player, English car
tools, training videos and an old suitcase that had travelled the world
with me were all gone. The thieves had thoughtfully left the car itself
and a tired pair of winter boots. Fortunately in a conditioned
response I had taken my passport and papers with me. My latest
notebook had gone. Documents can be replaced but one cannot
reconstruct a laboured-over felicitous phrase or recall an obscure
fact.

I rushed out into the road and flagged down a passing Maluch.
The driver promised to inform the police in the nearby town of
Mosina. Security was poor in Poland at the time and I had taken a
significant risk not only in leaving the car unattended but in walking in a forest alone. Theft was rife just after the fall of communism:

110 'Josephine's Garden', Orient Express Magazine Vol.19 No.1
111 Alexander Pope (1688–1744) The Rape of the Lock: Canto 1

Poles, Russians or Ukrainians, waiting like spiders in the forest to pounce on a victim. Cars had been stolen in broad daylight from outside our training centre near Warsaw, some set alight. Young children gathered around me protectively, offering me sweets. One girl rang the police again from her home nearby. These Polish children comforted me like angels in the cold dark until I told them to go home.

The familiar blue and white striped Polonez police car arrived in a shower of gravel. Both policemen were smoking cigarettes and pop music was blaring from the radio. They emerged with dull torches and asked me numerous questions in Polish, only some of which I understood.

'*Dobry wieczór panu.* [Good evening, sir.] You seem to have given yourself a problem.'

I must have looked confused.

'*Przepraszam panowie. Po polsku bardzo słabo.*' ['I'm sorry gentlemen, I speak Polish rather badly.']

'Don't worry. Please get into our car. Would you like a cigarette?'

They dusted the FSO for fingerprints. In the police car I noticed a deep pool of oil at my feet as one of them made futile attempts to contact his base on a static-infested two-way radio. The remoteness of the park, the cold, the moon and rustling trees, the barking farm dogs, pop music and smoking policemen created a perfect 'Eastern' European crime scene. They indicated I should follow them to the police station at Mosina and drove away at high speed after siphoning some petrol from my tank. The police were often short of fuel.

At the station they gave me coffee and obtained a sympathetic small boy with a huge dictionary to act as my 'translator'.

'I have been at a conference in Poznań. Lecturing on business in Poland.'

'We are so sorry when a good gentleman such as yourself comes to assist Poland in its development. We are sorry, my dear sir, for this experience. Terrible! You should never leave your car in Poland, even for a second!'

Through the boy I gave a detailed description of all the missing items and their value in millions of zloty. Much whistling through the teeth as this was typed up on an ancient skipping Remington, only the faded red half of the ribbon in use. After being triumphantly thrust in the face of the station commander, the document was laboriously copied out into a ledger by hand, finally to be written out yet again in illegible English for me to sign. The multiple translations led to some confusion:

'A red and black knitted nylon electric razor with pipe,' the boy read flatly.

'A brown tweed suit Donegal with old pen attachment and Irish black shoes.'

With a grim smile I recalled reading a comment of Napoleon's earlier on that blissful walk through the forest: 'From the sublime to the ridiculous is but a step.' The report was violently stamped in five different places and each stamp initialled. I tried ringing the training centre in Warsaw but was told by the switchboard operator over a background of barking dogs that I was not in my room and to ring back later. By now twelve police were working on the case and offering advice. Clearly it was the crime of the month.

My fingerprinting was methodical, my fingers and thumb rolled on an inked plate and pressed onto designated boxes on a sheet of paper. By now it was one o'clock in the morning and they suggested leaving the car with them and staying overnight at a hotel. They offered me a lift. The officer who escorted me to the police car was portly and sported a large Sobieski moustache. As I went to put on my seat belt he laughed uproariously, shouting, 'Nie, nie!'

The police car would not start. He summoned help on the two-way radio but again oceans of static defeated him. He sighed heavily and disappeared inside to emerge with a huge sledgehammer and gave the engine a terrific blow. It started. We set off through the deserted streets for the hotel with siren blaring and blue lights flashing. The elderly man in reception was asleep but suddenly wide-eyed and staring at this apparition and urgent request for a room.

The accommodation was frightful, with no towels, beds unmade and linen reeking of dry-cleaning fluid. The sink plug dangled from a piece of nylon fishing line. This was the perfume of communism, alright. I had not eaten since breakfast but nothing was available except Jim Beam bourbon. I tossed off a glass, soaked my contact lenses in the small amount left over (all my toilet requisites stolen) and lay on the bed listening to the rattling keys of the incoming drunks and their retching in the lavatory.

The ghastly breakfast, my stinging eyes and the robbery gave me a deep fit of the dismals (never soak contact lenses in bourbon). *En route* to Warsaw I passed through the town of Łęczyca which on that day matched my mood, having the atmosphere of a decrepit Mexican border town. A dust storm raged across the main square obscuring a run-down market of rotting fruit. Waste paper blew up against the walls of decaying buildings and remained stuck there. An elderly drunk lent himself an air of sophistication with a long, gold cigarette holder, his body swaying in the stiff breeze.

As I approached Warsaw the wind whistled through the shattered glass and the sun shone full on the driver's window revealing a palm print against the sky. The thief's fingers were extremely long with conical tips, like talons. It seemed his hand reached out for me even as I sped back to the capital. Certainly I received no sympathy for my losses when I returned to the centre.

'How stupid to go walking alone in the forest!' sighed Dr Grabski. 'Now look at all this trouble we have,' referring to my loss of lecture materials.

Most of the Polish staff and trainees, rather than commiserating, seemed amused by my losses.

'They have so little and you so much,' someone explained.

CHAPTER 14

Mozart in Warsaw

Warsaw is no slave to the cult of celebrity (it cannot afford them) and hence the musical work to be performed is often the primary focus of attention rather than the performer. Many rarely performed works regularly receive an airing in Warsaw. The Ballroom of the Royal Castle is a superb musical venue and an aesthetically overwhelming room. Domenico Merlini, the distinguished eighteenth-century Italian architect from Brescia who brought Palladianism to Poland, designed it with the allegorical guidance of King Stanisław Augustus. New gold leaf glisters from every crevice in a blaze of mirrored chandeliers. It was here I heard the first performance for two hundred years of a recently discovered festive piano concerto in the Russian style by Ferdinand Ries, a close friend and pupil of Beethoven. A castle guard in a faux military uniform, complete with a square four-cornered Polish *czapka* (cap), invariably presents magnificent bunches of flowers to the soloists and gives a brisk salute.

The music of Chopin had been the overriding reason for my coming to Poland but it was with surprise and delight that in the space of six weeks I was unexpectedly presented with all twenty-two Mozart operas. The cycle was performed by one of the most remarkable opera companies in Europe, the Warszawska Opera Kameralna (Warsaw Chamber Opera). Warsaw is the only capital city in the world where such an historically accurate Mozart cycle, together with much of his instrumental music, is performed on original instruments every year in summer.

Warsaw is no great distance from Vienna and *Die Entführung aus dem Serail* (The Abduction from the Seraglio) was produced in May 1783 by a touring German company for the birthday of King Stanisław Augustus just ten months after the Vienna première. *Don Giovanni* arrived in the capital to play in the National Theatre before the king in October 1789 with the same Italian Domenico Guardasoni company that had premièred the opera just two years before in Prague with Mozart conducting. His operas were performed in Warsaw well in advance of Berlin, Paris or London.

The city has had a distinguished operatic heritage since the early baroque period when it was the only capital other than Rome to have had an opera theatre that hosted famous Italian soloists. Many works were especially written for the Warsaw stage during the seventeenth century. The volatile Tarquinio Merula[112] wrote a theatrical duet called *Satiro e Corisca* for King Zygmunt III Vasa performed in Warsaw in the summer of 1626 some ten years before public operatic activities began in Venice. The Warsaw Chamber Opera continues this tradition with a magnificent annual Monteverdi festival where all the composer's operas and staged works are performed.

The story of the Warsaw Chamber Opera and its artistic director Stefan Sutkowski is a remarkable tale of courageous survival and musical exploration under communism. Born in Warsaw between the wars, he fled the capital just before he was about to be arrested by the NKVD. He told me he had lost his 'two best uncles' during the conflict – one in the Katyń forest massacre of Polish officers by the Soviets in the spring of 1940 and the other during the Warsaw Uprising of August 1944. After the war he studied the oboe and musicology at the University of Warsaw and set up the first early music ensemble in the country, the Musicae Antiquae Collegium Varsoviense.

In 1961 he and some theatre friends discussed the possibility of performing a chamber opera. Under communism such an ambitious cultural endeavour was an audacious project as they were completely

112 Tarquinio Merula (1595–1665) was a seminal composer, organist and violinist during the development of the early baroque, who composed in the Venetian style of Claudio Monteverdi and Giovanni Gabrieli. A native of Cremona, he came to Warsaw in 1621 for five years at the behest of the Swedish King of Poland Zygmunt III Vasa ('the longest and possibly the most incompetent reign in Polish history' observed Adam Zamoyski). The king's political ineptitude and his generous support of the arts may well be connected. Merula's private life was as much a shambles as his compositions were formally adventurous.

isolated from important historical source materials lodged in Western libraries. At the time he was playing in the National Philharmonic Orchestra, which often travelled abroad. This enabled him, unlike his trapped compatriots, to search for an appropriate operatic score. In Vienna he discovered almost by chance the score of the comic intermezzo *La serva padrona* (The Servant Mistress) by Giovanni Battista Pergolesi,[113] which he liked and brought back to Warsaw.

The birth of the Warsaw Chamber Opera took place with this intermezzo in 1961 played first on television and then in the Royal Theatre in Łazienki Park. The company was given a small grant, which was withdrawn without explanation after three years by the communist Minister for Culture. For the next seven years it became Sutkowski's private theatre, funded and sustained by dogged perseverance and self-belief, an unprecedented situation in communist Poland.

'I had to convince the commissars that Bach's B-Minor Mass was a masterpiece worthy of performance!' Sutkowski told me.

The cost of staging productions brought the company close to despair and collapse. Few people had money for anything in those days, let alone the luxury of chamber opera. They decided strong measures were needed to raise funds.

One morning half a dozen representatives of the company waited on the pavement outside the entrance to the Ministry of Culture on Krakowskie Przedmieście Street, contemplating alternative possibilities for action. Culture Minister Motyka's car drew up and as they crowded around it menacingly one whispered theatrically but not terribly seriously in his ear, 'This is an attack upon the Minister,' hoping the irony of the threat would not be lost on him.

'So, alright, let's go in for coffee,' he replied, notably quick on his feet. They had finally achieved their longed-for meeting with the Minister.

After talks the company found themselves operating as a state theatre under the administration of the Ministry of Culture. But for years they were forced to wander Warsaw in search of a permanent

113 Giovanni Battista Pergolesi (1710–36) spent most of his composing life at the Neapolitan court. In 1733 this intermezzo was performed to great acclaim as part of *Il prigioniero superbo* (The Proud Prisoner), an *opera seria* which has faded into obscurity. Chopin loved his music.

stage. The authorities finally allocated them a fine neoclassical building (once a church) fallen into disrepair. After eleven years of redesign and procrastination it opened in 1986, on the twenty-fifth anniversary of the foundation of the opera company. The auditorium seats 160 and the resulting intimacy is perfect for operas originally conceived for the court or theatres far smaller than today. The company, under the talented theatre director Ryszard Peryt coupled with the vivid scenic imagination of Andrzej Sadowski, produced the unprecedented first Mozart festival of twenty-five stage works in 1991, the bicentenary of the composer's death.

'I call my opera house the ambassador's club!' Sutkowski told me enthusiastically. He has a loyal following in the Warsaw diplomatic corps and is considered an institution in Warsaw.

Zosia, pale and blonde, was dressed in a short black evening dress and a fine gold chain the first night we spent at the opera. The festival was soon to become one of our favourite places of romantic assignation in Warsaw. We would sit in the small conservatory, among paintings of operatic composers and ornamental fig trees, drinking coffee from tiny porcelain cups. The young singers could be heard warming their voices with fragments of scales, popular tunes or the arias to come. A moment's inattention might inadvertently allow a window to drift open to reveal a costumed singer adjusting his wig or a soprano applying makeup or adjusting her breasts in a corset before a lighted mirror. A violin or flute from the orchestra might be practising a particularly difficult leap. The atmosphere was intimate, perfectly eighteenth century.

My first experience of this theatre was with *Lucio Silla*, an *opera seria* composed in 1772 when Mozart was sixteen for the carnival season in Milan. The libretto for this unlikely triumph of virtue was by Giovanni di Gamerra, a writer fond of tombs and lugubrious plots, allegedly drawn towards necrophilia in private life. All Mozart's musical strengths are here assembled, waiting for a decent librettist and the darker shadows of personal maturity to take flight.

The orchestra at the Warsaw Chamber Opera is concealed beneath a proscenium stage. To one side a small apron extends slightly into the auditorium where a harpsichord and cello continuo play under dim lighting. In this intimate theatre the singers seem enormous in stature, the slightest play of emotion visible, the vibration of the voice clearly felt. This intimacy allows a penetration of the mind of the character in a uniquely disconcerting manner. In *Lucio Silla*, the role of Cecilio, a Senator who has been proscribed by Silla the Dictator of Rome, was composed by Mozart for a castrato. Here it was performed as intended by the remarkable Polish sopranist Dariusz Paradowski with a voice as close to a castrato such as Farinelli as is possible today.[114]

This rare voice has an almost shocking effect when first encountered but Paradowski is a consummate actor with the stage presence of a Nureyev and duly received the flowers and ovations of a star. The youthful operas of Mozart all possess castrato roles. In the Warsaw cycle visual links are established between each opera in regard to scenery, costume and direction. Voices can be variable but the ultimate coming together of the production is magical. Through these rarely performed works and brilliant productions of the most famous operas (*Don Giovanni*, *The Marriage of Figaro* and *Die Zauberflöte* are all packed with wonderfully naive eighteenth-century 'stage business') I was uniquely able to follow the astonishing evolution of Mozart's operatic inventions as his dramatic genius unfolded.

'Brother Mozart' had also been involved with Masonic ritual from an early age: he set a Masonic poem to music, dedicated to the doctor who had cured him of smallpox. Music is utilized in many Masonic rituals, which led him to compose for the brotherhood throughout his life. In 1773 Mozart was asked to supply the incidental music to the play *Thamos, König in Ägypten* (Thamos, King of Egypt) by Tobias Philipp Baron von Gebler. The play deals with the Masonic conflict between light and darkness. At Łazienki Park in the Theatre on the Island the Warsaw Chamber Opera created a staged version fused with the music of two later Masonic cantatas.

Shortly before midnight fluttering funeral candles were lit along the sinuous paths leading to the theatre from the entrance to the park. The orchestral pit lies before a strip of water which isolates the

---

114 A sopranist is a countertenor who is able to sing in the soprano vocal range. Much baroque opera originally written for castrati is now performed by this very rare male soprano voice. The even rarer 'indocrinological castrato' is different again from a sopranist in that he is a singer who has an hormonal disorder that prevents the larynx developing in puberty and the voice from breaking. Such a singer might have the range to perform the 'Queen of the Night' aria from *The Magic Flute*.

Theatre on the Island (inspired by the ruins of the Temple of Jove at Baalbek in Syria), where the actors perform, from the amphitheatre (modelled on ruins at Herculaneum) where the audience is seated. Trees were silhouetted against a fading summer sky and the leaves rustled in the light breeze moving over the shattered columns and pediments, the lake a dull mirror reflecting statues of the dying Gaul and Cleopatra. Together with the cry of peacocks on the balustrades of the palace, one was lifted onto a plane of rare classical beauty.

The overture began, music at once spiritually passionate yet graceful. Gradually the chorus, a semi-circle of black-robed hooded figures wearing silver medallions, emerged through the mist. Soloists in black robes entered with huge silver sculptures of mythical beasts reminiscent of Egypt or Assyria resting on their shoulders – a winged bull, a winged lion, an eagle and a winged human head. Behind them a sculpture had been assembled from cannons, the skeletons of horses, scythes, drums and the tattered banners of war.

A dense moral argument unfolded with the chorus carrying splendidly grotesque banners of the Seven Deadly Sins. A cauldron of flame was lit in the centre of the stage and the winged lion crouched behind it intoning in a mysterious tongue. A mime lit a trough of fire that flashed across the entire width of the theatre, coinciding with an explosion of cannon which caused the sculpture of war to revolve. The darkness, the ancient ruins, the wind in the trees, the panicked wood pigeons and the harsh cry of peacocks lifted this setting of the Mozart Masonic Liturgy onto a theatrical and spiritual level which was quite extraordinary.

We drank champagne with the artistic director Stefan Sutkowski under the stars and wandered out of the dark park following the trail of light of the now guttering candles. Great music creates a desire for itself, a desire for repetition like a profound sexual relationship. Such Warsaw nights at the Mozart festival sustained me through many of the reversals of fortune associated with that ill-fated project and irresistibly deepened my romantic relationship with Zosia.

CHAPTER 15

Dance of the Gnomes

The melamine lime-green telephone shrilled like a toy, leaping about on my desk. I stumbled out of bed and grabbed the receiver.

'*Halo. Słucham.*' (Hello. I'm listening.)

'*Telefon do pana z zagranicy.*' (Telephone call for sir from abroad.)

'I don't understand. Could you speak more slowly please?'

'Telephone call for sir from Zurich.'

There was a silence, a great deal of static, pops and then a faint voice. It had rained last night.

'Lustenberger.'

'Good morning, Herr Director Lustenberger.'

'You seem to have a problem in your Poland, Mr Moran.'

'My Poland? You could say that, I suppose.'

'I want to help these people, eh, but statistics for success in this country are not good for Swiss investors. Not good, eh?'

'No, I quite understand. But they are trying hard.'

'We know you are emotional about your Poland, Mr Moran. I will read out the ultimatum which you will pass on to the Polish side.'

An ultimatum at this hour over the telephone. Excellent.

'They are required to pay all outstanding amounts within seven days or we will withdraw our services. You will pass this on before I visit?'

'Visit? Are you coming to Warsaw?' I asked with some alarm.

'Yes. I will speak to the Polish side and the president, if he exists, and look over the operation.'

'Fine, Herr Lustenberger.'

'Thank you for your attention, Mr Moran.'

I looked out over the flat asphalt roofs and steaming pipes through the pink frame of the *Financial Times* crammed around the window. The corrugated iron on the chimney flapped in the wind and ravens croaked as I glumly put down the receiver. The pedagogical side was a complete success, so where had the money gone? I feared that the duplicitous qualities inherent in the former regime had never been abandoned. This combined with sheer ignorance of the basic principles of the market economy.

The Polish staff seemed unmoved by what could be our imminent departure but they too had had their fill of disappointment and justifiably envied our Western salaries. Mr Fukowski, the director of the centre, was a fossilized Luddite. He had recently accused us of bribing the accountant, Andrzej, to obtain his support. Why one would wish to bribe a debtor defeated my logic. Dr Grabski held a conspiracy theory that Fukowski intended to destroy the entire operation as part of some grand strategic plan. However, I knew the eleventh hour had been invented for Poland and hoped for a last-minute solution. Zosia and I were facing a bleak separation.

An unusually heavy fog had descended over Warsaw the day of his arrival, which gave the city the atmosphere of an espionage novel. I took him to my favourite haunt, the Column Bar at the Bristol. This fashionable hotel had been founded by Ignacy Jan Paderewski in 1900. The first sessions of the government of independent Poland took place here in 1918. Lustenberger was completely uninterested in my history lesson and fastened onto the meetings Andrzej the accountant had arranged for him.

The next day we were to meet the president of a company that sent trainees to the centre. Over glasses of tea and long formal speeches we were assured of our value to the project and a tantalizing future was presented. Dr Grabski was unaccountably present and gave a sustained fifteen-minute burst of superb Polish rhetoric. Lustenberger was inflexible and cautious. We then proceeded to the offices of the Polish side to meet the vice-president of the operation. His car had just been broken into and the radio stolen so he was in a high state of anxiety.

He was clearly unprepared for the meeting. Since the financial difficulties had begun, the actual identity of our Polish partner had become a grey, amorphous cloud without a structure, a vaporous organization impossible to grasp. There were rumours it might have been taken over by an estate agency. It was never possible to identify anyone ultimately responsible for decision-making.

'The ideal Polish institution,' the consultant professor to the project later observed.

Dr Zaleski, the unfortunately ill president of the Polish side, courageously rose from his bed to perform vital services for the organization on the telephone but never appeared in person. His illness made him a spectre in the negotiations, absent because of a serious heart condition but present as a phantom hovering over the proceedings. Andrzej covered the mouthpiece of the telephone at critical moments in the discussions and uttered in a deep Slavic monotone.

'Dr Zaleski is beginning to go unconscious from heavy drugs. We must now stop conversation. The nurses order him.' There was a great deal of whispering between the vice-president and Andrzej during meetings with the body language of 'the mob' much in evidence.

'It is not the way we Swiss do business, eh?' Lustenberger replied in a dry aside to me.

Aleje Ujazdowskie is one of the most elegant avenues in Warsaw and home to foreign embassies and formidable government departments. We were heading for an early morning appointment with one of the Secretaries of State. As the headlights of the car cut through the fog, I felt attractively counter-espionage, as if in a *film noir*. We entered a vast hall of 'Commissar Style' architecture with gigantic marble columns and an acreage of red carpet. Mighty corridors of numbered mahogany doors with no indication of function were set in towering walls bereft of decoration. Obsequious male secretaries motioned us through the heavily padded entrance to a high-ceilinged room furnished with a massive desk and capacious leather armchairs. Tea, coffee and cake appeared with well-practised sleight of hand.

The Secretary of State was a middle-aged, thick-set, almost athletic former *apparatchik* type catapulted into a post of responsibility clearly above his talents. He had heavily brilliantined brown hair cut in a 1960s style and wore a shiny beige pin-striped suit bulging over muscular shoulders and calves. His shrunken grey nylon socks had been washed until the tops were frayed, revealing an expanse of pale, hairy leg. The leather of the brown Italian loafers was badly scuffed, giving him the appearance of a pugilist from the former regime who had just popped in for an assassination briefing.

'I am great friend of former director who is now important Minister. He was very good at training centre, extremely. And Dr Zaleski and I am great friend who is so much known and respected in Warsaw community. It is very nice you here for possible contract with Prime Minister Office. We welcome you. *Witamy.*' The practised sycophantic tone was nauseating.

'We are pleased to be here. What type of courses did you have in mind?' Herr Lustenberger went straight to the point with more than a trace of impatience. He was similarly short and stocky, like a Swiss-German gnome, with hair standing up at the back uncombed and unbrushed. An excellent negotiator, collector of modern art and a classical baritone. A man easy to underestimate. The assistant to the Secretary of State was a little moustachioed squirt who spoke Polish with an affected lisp.

'I believe in *intensive* course of short period. Two day or three day *intensive* so we are not liking half-hour or one hour per week is not good but *intensive*, where man is in language some days. I think is good. *Intensive* in language for some days.'

I smiled graciously and nodded, taking another of the heart-shaped, chocolate-covered gingerbreads.

'Yes, an excellent approach. We could provide such a course from our extensive experience.'

Vague promises were made about a possible future contract without detail. I felt that cracks were forming in the *układ* as we made our way out through the vast halls of post-communist power.

'*Do widzenia. Dziękuję.* (Goodbye. Thank you.) Very nice of you to visit us in our country. Is good for you to make friendship . . . to help our people . . .' his voice trailed off.

He had been Secretary of State for a week.

After returning to the hotel Lustenberger took me to one side.

'Only ten of five hundred Swiss-Polish joint ventures are working properly in Poland, Mr Moran. Not good, eh?'

There is a characteristic lilt of rising intonation in Swiss-German English which can be maddening. Lustenberger was stupefied at the rudimentary knowledge of his Polish business partner. To his credit he patiently taught them how to keep accounts. Suddenly and unexpectedly pan Fukowski and Andrzej informed us that some more money had been 'discovered' and we were probably able to survive another few months. Their first set of figures had been 'a little inaccurate'.

'Where did this revenue spring from?' asked Herr Lustenberger.

'Well, they make some small mistakes and did not count some things. Now they count and is alright.' Fukowski smiled like a beloved uncle. The 'correct' financial figures were deeply buried somewhere beneath layers of confusion.

'I would like a guaranteed payment through your bank,' Lustenberger demanded, assuming he was in Berlin or Zurich.

'Poland has not this thing yet. We are sorry.'

Lustenberger remained silent.

The final meeting of his visit was to Pan President Zaleski's flat in a sterile, anonymous communist block near the airport. Andrzej, like most Poles, drove his rust bucket as if in the Monte Carlo Rally, narrowly missing impaling us on a Warsaw tram. The common entrance to the building, like most of the blocks in those days, smelt of wet dog and had not been painted for years. A plastic bucket was unaccountably chained to a pipe, and cigarettes had been extinguished on all the plastic lift buttons. Dr Zaleski opened the door to his flat and stood like some dreadful spectre before us. Pale, drawn and underweight, his eyes stared from deep in their sockets, his suit hanging off his spare frame. He looked at me as if I were the avenging angel. He was clearly terribly ill with heart problems and I could not but admire his courage in setting up this difficult meeting. His wife was charming and vivacious, behaving as if nothing was amiss. Napoleon made his comments on Polish women with good reason. A table had been carefully prepared with all manner of cakes, fine china and silver. Dr Zaleski sat down trembling and Andrzej sat beside him to do the translating for Lustenberger.

'It is very good, *pan Dyrektorze* Lustenberger, that you are here in Warsaw, but a pity under such terrible circumstances for us. We hope that in future you will be able to come with pleasure to Warsaw and not for the reason you are now here.'

Lustenberger replied in his lilting Swiss-German English.

'It is good for me to be here but I am unhappy that Dr Zaleski is in such terrible condition. But we are glad of the personal meeting to discuss the difficulties.'

Andrzej leaned over to me and whispered in breath reeking of cheap tobacco, 'Dr Zaleski will go unconscious quite soon from strong emotions and administration of heavy drugs.'

The atmosphere became frighteningly dramatic as they began to discuss the outstanding debt. Dr Zaleski made notes with a gold pen which he could scarcely hold in his trembling fingers. He was behaving like wounded game, maintaining a fierce pride as he bled and weakened. Mr Fukowski had his koala head right down, writing furiously. Mrs Zaleski was the perfect hostess, winging effortlessly above grim reality with impressive emotional control and poise.

'*Makowiec*? *Pierniki* from Toruń?' She handed round these popular Polish cakes.

'I will of course pay this debt. We are entirely responsible. I do not want you to imagine we would not pay such a debt. We are very aware of it and will soon be sending an official letter confirming the rescheduling of the debt. It is a question of Polish honour and fidelity.' Dr Zaleski seemed stricken with embarrassment and pain. Poles feel a need to save face that is almost oriental. I felt terribly sorry for him.

'We are very pleased this would happen. It would be very good this would happen. We have a guarantee from the financial director that he will monitor all the accounts. I would like a written description of the rescheduling and a business plan within ten days.' Lustenberger had adopted a demeanour of what might be termed 'compassionate frigidity' in the face of negotiation under duress. He remained tough yet surprisingly sensitive. Over the last few days in Warsaw he had adopted an almost educative role in the long humanist tradition of the Swiss. Having divided loyalties, I attempted to be diplomatic and even-handed, which pleased no one.

We made our farewells. As Andrzej drove out of the yard he ran over one of the broken bricks that littered the place. It flew up under the car and ruptured the exhaust. I was in the back seat and over the incredible racket I could just hear Lustenberger saying, 'Your Dr Zaleski is a very sick man, eh? But he exists, eh? He exists.'

I gave him a bottle of *Żubrówka* vodka that I had made myself by putting strands of bison grass I had collected in Białowieża forest into clear spirit. He said a perfunctory goodbye. For a moment I watched his gnomish figure heading back to Zurich, furiously biting a fingernail as he passed through passport control and never looking back.

I felt I would never know the details of the saga which led to this situation. The 'team' were dissatisfied with my report on developments and meetings with our great leaders. The return tickets to England for the long summer break were wrongly dated. One evening I noticed them burning my effigy on a barbeque fire and dancing around it, to the confusion of the Poles. Working on this project was like being trapped in a room and vainly attempting to decipher voices overheard in the next room. On my return to the centre the Vistula took on a dark and forbidding aspect under a cloak of heavy fog. I rang Zosia and told her we had a ten-day reprieve, maybe more. The relief of exiles washed over us.

CHAPTER 16

Vistula – Of Dragons, Martyrs and Lovers

The ashes of barbarism carried by the Vistula's slow current from Birkenau had not far to travel before encountering a city of refinement and high civilization, one that by some miracle had remained undamaged through the Second World War. Zosia had managed to escape Warsaw to spend a few days with me in Kraków over Easter and wanted to show me the former capital. I had arranged to meet her in the main square under the statue of Poland's most famous poet, Adam Mickiewicz. But on my first night in the city I was alone. My room faced the bastions of an Austrian fort overlooking meadows which opened out towards the ancient city. Dusk was falling, solitary figures were walking along the parapet and mist shrouded the silver birches.

The inscription *Cracovia Totius Poloniae Urbs Celerrima* (Kraków the most glorious town in all of Poland) was etched in 1619 by Matthaus Merian on an engraved panorama of the city. In *Poland Revisited* Joseph Conrad wrote, 'It was in that old royal and academical city that I ceased to be a child, became a boy, had known the friendships, the admirations, the thoughts and the indignations of that age.'

In 'the noblest and most famous city of Sarmatia' the kings of Poland were crowned and interred in the cathedral up to the early seventeenth century when the capital was transferred to Warsaw. Prosperous Kraków lay on an important trade route from the Baltic for merchants carrying precious amber along the Amber Road to southern Europe and from the west to Rus and on to fabled

Byzantium. In 963 a wooden fort was built on the Wawel Hill and an imposing chapel was later to become the monumental cathedral. A fortified town developed on the banks of the Vistula beneath the citadel, often sacked by the Tatar golden horde in the thirteenth century.

The 'Golden Age' of the city was under the dynasty of the Jagiellonian kings (1385–1572) during which the renowned University was established, famed for its chair in Mathematics and Astronomy. Kraków became an intellectual centre of some of the greatest humanists in Europe, prompting Erasmus to 'congratulate the Polish nation [which] can now compete with the foremost and the most cultivated in the world'. The wealth of the court and city burghers contributed to a magnificent artistic flowering. A complex artistic response was formulated here to humanist ideas and the Italian Renaissance that dominated Central Europe in the fifteenth and sixteenth centuries.

The Florentine Renaissance heritage is focused mainly around the Wawel. This enormous rock was originally an island in the Vistula but is now the site of the cathedral and castle. The city declined under the monstrously destructive Swedish invasions and occupation of the mid-seventeenth century but began to recover under the Austro-Hungarian Empire when the Congress of Vienna in 1815 made it a free city – the 'Republic of Kraków' – under the control of the three partitioning powers, Austria, Prussia and Russia.

Kraków was incorporated into Austria in 1846 and the ruins of some forty-eight Austrian forts surround it in three massive defensive rings constructed during the partition of the country in the nineteenth century. On the first of many journeys I stayed in the fort named Kościuszko which has been converted into the romantic hotel Pod Kopcem (Under the Mound). It was peaceful and strangely silent here beneath the curious Kopiec Kościuszki. This huge heap of earth is shaped like an inverted cone erected to honour the heroic insurrectionist Tadeusz Kościuszko. This quiet and refined man fought brilliantly in 1794 against the superior forces of the partitioning powers. He also fought alongside Washington in the American War of Independence and designed defensive military fortifications. The mound was constructed from clods of earth taken from battlefields on which he fought

(Racławice, Maciejowice and even from America). It imitates the prehistoric Krak and Wanda hills nearby. These *kopce* are constructed as memorials all over the country and have a profound national significance for Poles.

I climbed the mound while the setting sun pressed through the mist of early spring over forest, woodland and city forming a magnificent vista from the summit. Kościuszko's tattered cloak and Polish sabre lay in a mouldering chapel at the base of the path which spirals up to the apex. They are a melancholic reminder of ill-fated but courageous battles and insurrections. A huge chunk of Tatra granite on the summit is chiselled with his name and the long winding ascent gives the climber or pilgrim ample time to reflect on the fraught nature of Polish patriotism.

My first entry into the ancient city was in the half-light through the Brama Floriańska (St Florian's Gate) joined by a bridge to the spectacular fifteenth-century fortification called the Barbakan, a mysterious and brooding Moorish-influenced structure. The most fashionable street is ul. Floriańska, lined with luxurious boutiques and cafés. Kraków is more chic than Warsaw, the mist giving the sparkling interiors the feeling of authentic cosmopolitan life.

Nothing prepared me for that sublime moment in European architecture when the perspective of the main market square opens out before the viewer like a magnificent canvas. Next to St Mark's Square in Venice, it is the greatest square I have ever seen – numinous and immaterial, particularly at night. It is considered one of the world's greatest public spaces, certainly the finest in Europe, and has witnessed some of the greatest Polish state occasions. The splendid towers and spires of the Gothic Archpresbyterial Church of the Virgin Mary with its turrets, galleries and gilded crown carve into the night sky. The church is set at an angle to the Renaissance Cloth Hall (Sukiennice) at the centre of the square, which has splendid parapet walls decorated with grotesque heads, arcades and loggias. This building exhibits the earliest example of the 'Polish attic', which became such a characteristic feature of Polish architecture.[115]

---

115 The 'Polish attic' is a decorative parapet wall masking the roof of a building similar in form to that of the Italian Renaissance or Classical architecture. In Poland it was given a particular constructional function and became an ornate and striking feature unique to this country.

Whimsically placed on the square is the small Romanesque church of St Adalbert.

The square was completely deserted, its monumental scale then still unencumbered by brewery sponsorship and nightclubs. The pollution of the winter evening descended like a damp cloak about my shoulders and I began to taste the sulphur of the nearby huge steelworks of Nowa Huta and cough like a consumptive. Now that the communist pollution has largely disappeared, the square buzzes with the summer happiness and spirit of youth night and day. Elegant new carriages driven by glamorous girls dressed as coachmen and drawn by handsome horses unhurriedly wander the streets. The architecture and charming atmosphere of the city is strongly reminiscent of Secessionist Vienna. Kraków is another example of the national characteristics of the partitioning power, in this case Austria, enduring into the present. Many families have lived in the city for generations and were not displaced during the war, unlike the murdered and transported citizens of Warsaw. A haunting trumpet signal called the *Hejnał Mariacki* still sounds hourly from the taller of the two church towers, originally warning of the approach of the Tatar horde. The melody is suddenly cut short as it was centuries ago by a Tatar arrow that lodged in the throat of the cornet player. This added significantly to the gothic feel of mystery that pervaded the desolate square. I felt dwarfed by these architectonic masses in the freezing fog.

I meandered up ul. Grodzka towards the Wawel. It was with a strange sense of trepidation that I approached this potent symbol of Poland's past greatness, the spiritual and patriotic heart of the country. The massive walls created a sense of awe as I stared up at the illuminated windows set in stone high above. Searchlights cut a swathe through the fog as a Polish sabre might wing through a Turk. It required little effort of the imagination to hear echoes of the dreadful tortures perpetrated by the Nazi Generalgouverneur Hans Frank, who set up his headquarters in this Kafkaesque castle.[116] This fortress and palace high above the Vistula was the first notable

---

116 *Kaputt* by Curzio Malaparte (reissue New York 2007) paints a revealing picture of the arrogance of the Nazis through their dinner conversations as Frank held court in Wawel Castle. Altogether a remarkable and largely forgotten account of certain aspects of the Second World War.

Renaissance building in northern Europe. On this particular night it was one of the most atmospheric buildings I had ever seen. Mist swirled about the curtain walls and towers so often laid waste by invaders. I walked around the base, along the deserted paths towards the dark-running river, past the threatening form of the bronze dragon outside its gaping cave (once a brothel), back and up to barred doors of barbaric proportions. As if drugged, I slowly made my way under the paralysing weight of history, making the circuit again and again, unable to leave off worrying my sense of awe or seeking the catch in the throat.

From a distance I could see Zosia waiting for me huddled against the cold under the monumental statue of Adam Mickiewicz. There are large statues of the greatest poet of Polish Romanticism in both Warsaw and Kraków although he never visited either city.

'Did you see the statue of yourself down by the river?' she murmured.

'What?'

'That big bronze dragon.' She giggled. 'Let me tell you the story of it. Every Polish child knows it.'

As we sat close together in the clammy yellow mist she told me of the most famous dragon in Polish folklore, the Dragon of Wawel Hill. The dragon lived in a cave on the banks of the Vistula during the reign of King Krak, the founder of the city. Each day the dragon would rampage through the countryside, killing people, sacking their homes and gorging on their cows and goats. He found young girls especially delectable and the people of Kraków needed to leave one at the mouth of the cave each month to appease his dreadful appetite. All the King's knights were consumed by the fire of his breath. Finally the King's daughter Wanda was the only young girl left. In despair the King promised the hand of his daughter in marriage to anyone who could defeat the dragon. More and more knights were consumed by fire. One fine day a little cobbler's apprentice named Dratewka accepted the test. He killed a lamb, stuffed it with sulphur and placed it outside the cave. The dragon was tempted by this tasty morsel but soon his stomach was burning with fire. He drank and drank from the river but nothing could quench this thirst. The dragon began to swell and after drinking half the Vistula he finally exploded. Dratewka and the King's daughter lived happily ever after. This myth has now been augmented by farce: a text message to the local gas company will produce a gush of flame on demand from the dragon's mouth.

Caught in a trap of passion rather like the dragon, my imaginative flight had yet to be elevated into a stable love. Intellectually Zosia was a generous, sensitive and knowledgeable travelling companion but I had an immature fear of becoming 'embroiled'. My emotions were in turmoil. I agreed with Telimena, a character in the national epic poem *Pan Tadeusz* who quotes the simple words of a song popular with Wilno University students in the days when Mickiewicz studied there:

> For the young heart a master still disdains
> And will not let itself be put in chains

The next morning the mist thinned over the city in the light of the rising sun. We breakfasted at the famous Art Nouveau café and cabaret Jama Michalika. Originally a shop opened by a confectioner from Lwów, this jewel was opulently decorated in the original Secessionist style I had hoped to encounter in Vienna but found only rarely in that city. The legendary satirical cabaret Zielony Balonik (Green Balloon) performed here (the name inspired by a hawker selling green balloons to children). The outstanding figure of Tadeusz 'Boy' Żeleński – paediatrician, poet and brilliant translator of French classical literature – was the moving spirit of the cabaret and wrote many songs of the French 'chanson' type influenced by the famous Chat Noir cabaret in Paris. A glass of Hungarian Tokay Szamorodni passed a ruminative and romantic hour in an unforgettable atmosphere of *fin de siècle* decadence.

The great castle on Wawel Hill situated above the Vistula has suffered many depredations over its long history. It is a miracle that anything is left of the structure or its interior. Much was built by Florentine architects in the sixteenth century. The passageway that leads from the parade ground opens dramatically into a courtyard of spectacular size and elevation. The design had an immediate impact on patrician buildings all over Poland. These are the most beautiful Italian Renaissance galleries in East Central Europe. The arcaded structure is in three storeys. The lower two are in the elegant spirit of the late Tuscan *Quattrocento* with arches and slim columns creating finely controlled pools of light and shade. The columns in the upper storey make allowances for native Polish custom and taste, a contrast to Italy in that the state rooms are on the uppermost floor. Tall, slender columns with central rings and decorative capitals or 'jugs' support the eaves and steeply pitched roof. This imaginative solution to the severe Polish climate is an aesthetic triumph. Jousts and tournaments were held on the crushed brick of the courtyard.

The Wawel castle possesses a unique collection of *'verdure'* Flemish tapestries (dominated by green foliage) assembled by King Zygmunt II August and known as the 'Wawel Arrases', which were famous throughout Europe. Despite plundering by the Swedes, the Prussians, the Austrians and the Nazis, the collection is still the finest in the world. The captured Turkish tents and accoutrements from the battle of Vienna in the Armoury are astonishing in their oriental opulence as is a similar collection in the nearby Muzeum Czartoryskich. Leonardo da Vinci's miraculous *Lady with an Ermine* and Rembrandt's meditative *Landscape with the Good Samaritan* are also to be found in this remarkable museum.

Imperial Russia and colonized Poland both had close historical connections with the Muslim world. European Christianity defended and indeed defined itself in constant wars against the Turks and Tatars, culminating in 1683 in the defeat of the Grand Vizier, Kara Mustafa, who was pursuing a *Jihad* or Holy War on the siege plains outside Vienna. The principal actor in this final Crusader battle was the Polish King Jan Sobieski III, the ultimate Sarmatian, born during a raging thunderstorm and Tatar raid. Fluent in half a dozen languages, richly dressed in furs and silks, silver half-moon heels to his Turkish boots and a jewelled scimitar, voluminous moustache and hair worn in the curious Sarmatian pudding basin style, he was in appearance the archetypal Polish Oriental. He had married Marie-Casimir de la Grange d'Arquien, brought as a child to Poland by the French Queen Marie-Louise. 'Marysieńka', as she is popularly known in Poland, was a formidable woman and they lived a passionate life whether together or apart. On campaign before the battle of Vienna among descriptions of 'characters' and military matters, he wrote in one of his many long, notoriously explicit love letters to her, 'I kiss you, embracing with my whole heart and soul all the beauties of you sweetest body.'

His legendary yet anachronistic, fabulously caparisoned heavy 'winged cavalry', known as the *Husaria*, were considered the finest horsemen in Europe. This spectacular force, which exerted an impressive psychological power over the enemy far in excess of their actual numbers, was derived from Serbian and Hungarian origins. Their steel armour was polished like silver and edged with brass shining like gold. Mascarons representing the Numean lion slaughtered by Hercules adorned their shoulders and engraved images of the Virgin Mary protected their breastplates. Officers rode in *karacena* or scale armour riveted with brass rosettes, the pattern revived from the ancient Roman *lorica plumata* seen in the bas-reliefs of Sarmatian warriors on Trajan's column in Rome. Leopard-skins lined with crimson satin were thrown over their backs, paws held in golden clasps. Eagle feathers set in wooden frames covered with red velvet arched above the rider's head attached to the back-plates of their armour or to Circassian saddles of embroidered velvet and precious stones. Conventional cavalry were understandably terrified at the appearance of these predatory beasts. The development of firepower and artillery gradually reduced their effectiveness as a fighting force against the marauding seventeenth-century Swedish forces of Gustavus Adolphus, however they remained effective against Turk and Tatar until being reduced to a purely ceremonial role in the eighteenth century.

This magnificent force, 'the bravest cavalry the Sun ever beheld',[117] lance-pennants fluttering, jewelled pistols and sabres glittering, swept down from the Kahlenberg Heights through the dark Vienna Woods upon a hundred thousand Turkish tents and the green banner of the Prophet. So spectacular was this charge that other soldiers engaged in the conflict allegedly stopped fighting to watch it.

No sooner does a hussar lower his lance
Than a Turk is impaled on its spike
Which not only disorders, but terrifies the foe,

117 *Scanderbeg Redivivus*, 1684

That blow which cannot be defended against or deflected . . .
Oft transfixing two persons at a time,
Others flee in eager haste from such a sight,
Like flies in a frenzy.[118]

Characteristically, after the swift defeat of the Pashas, Sobieski despatched the Vizier's jewelled stirrups by fast courier to his French queen and the Prophet's banner to the Pope but failed to press home his political advantage after looting the fabulous Oriental ostentation.

The cathedral on the Wawel Hill, 'the sanctuary of the nation' according to Pope John Paul II, is overwhelming in its complexity and eclectic mixture of architectural styles. The exterior is a picturesque plethora of appended chapels, turrets, spires, gilded and copper domes. This temple is the focus of the Polish nation and of the Polish soul. All the kings of Poland except two are buried on Wawel Hill and most had their coronations here. Many heroes of the tragic yet spectacularly courageous history of Poland are interred in the crypt. The most magnificent addition since the eleventh-century Romanesque foundation is the early sixteenth-century Sigismund Chapel. This family mausoleum, its gilded dome glinting triumphantly, is the finest Italian Renaissance structure north of the Alps, 'a pearl of the Renaissance'.[119] The Florentine architect and sculptor Bartolommeo Berrecci designed it to glorify the Jagiellon kings and it can favourably be compared to that of his contemporary Michelangelo who planned a similar, centrally-planned tomb for the Medici.

Despair on the part of King Zygmunt I Stary over the death of his first wife Barbara Zapolya in 1515 precipitated the building of the chapel. The interior transposes the spirit of Renaissance Florence and Rome unspoilt to Poland. The royal statues of King Zygmunt I Stary (died 1548) and his son King Zygmunt II August (died 1572) recline upon their tombs with flexed legs, resting their weight upon the right elbow, appearing to rise and greet us from sleep. The tombs

118 *Song of Vienna Liberated*, 1684 Wespazjan Kochowski quoted in *Polish Winged Hussar 1576–1775*, Richard Brzeziński (Oxford 2006) p. 46

119 The eminent German architectural scholar August Ottmar von Essenwein (1831–1892)

are sculpted in beautiful glowing red Hungarian marble from Esztergom and established the extraordinary tradition of recumbent sepulchral figures of the Polish Renaissance. The revolutionary tiered arrangement of father above son was conceived by the distinguished Florentine Santi Gucci, architect to one of the last Jagiellons, Queen Anna Jagiellon (died 1596).

We descended cautiously into the labyrinthine crypt of kings and heroes. Human mortality weighed heavily upon me as I dragged myself around. The Wasa and Jagiellon coffins with their sculpted or gilded crowns are sometimes grotesquely ornamented with skulls and crossed bones. The marble tomb holding the ashes of Tadeusz Kościuszko glows in purity while that of a king or member of a royal family is encrusted with dust. On the floor tiny coffins indicate the demise of royal infants. There is a celebration of death here that is at once unsettling and a proper extolling of the continuity of history, the superhuman struggle to maintain the Polish nation intact. Adam Mickiewicz merits his own small crypt set apart with a separate entrance.

Seized by the need to escape, we climbed the Sigismund Tower to view the panorama of Kraków and breathe some fresh air. The largest bell in Poland, called the *Zygmunt*, is suspended here and was cast from forty cannon captured from the Turks at the siege of Vienna. The great weight requires eleven men to set it ringing, but only on 'special occasions'. Oddly Poland's entry into the European Union was considered an insufficiently remarkable occasion to ring the bell as many reactionaries in the Catholic Church feared the onset of moral decay. The sun was setting in a lurid orange glow over the slow-flowing Vistula, ancient towers dissolving in the pollution vomited by the Nowa Huta steelworks. (Although there were sound practical reasons for building it close to the city, many Poles feel the satanic mills were constructed by the communist regime to precipitate Kraków's slow destruction by sulphurous acid.)

Zosia dressed in briefest black for our abandoned lovemaking that evening. Chilled Russian champagne and almond cakes renewed our flagging energy. Polish women are extraordinarily intense sexually, but that night my mind was crammed with royal histories, their arts and their departures. I fear I must have given a lacklustre performance. I was in search of something more dreamily romantic on this time-dressed, nostalgic evening. I wandered over to the window and pressed my nose against the icy glass. Through the heavy mist beyond the bastions of the Austrian fortress, the city lights twinkled like distant stars.

Sunday dawned and many elderly folk were laying flowers on graves in the nearby cemetery. Against the early morning chill elderly women wore buttoned overcoats with the ubiquitous woollen berets in mauve or grey and the older men rough brown caps that look as if a ferret had perched for warmth on their head. We walked around the bastions in the unseasonably warm sunshine and found a path that led towards the city. Sunday Mass fills Polish churches to capacity. The congregation spills onto the pavement outside listening to the prayers and homily of the priest on loudspeakers. Having reached the centre of the city, we sat in silence in the unaccustomed sun under the star vaulting of an ancient cloister and examined the heraldic devices on the well-head. The *Collegium Maius* of the Jagellonian University is one of the finest medieval university buildings in Europe. This gilded inner courtyard is tranquil and a strong atmosphere of medieval scholasticism saturates the institution with the spirit of Renaissance humanists.

While crossing the market square, Zosia suggested we go into the Kościół Mariacki and light a candle. The nave of the Gothic basilica is mighty in conception and the interior mysteriously gloomy with a powerful immanence. The choir and nave are decorated with paintings executed by the undervalued Polish history painter Jan Matejko. The church contains a wealth of important funerary monuments, stained glass and paintings. We had come to see the celebrated Gothic altarpiece of the Death of the Virgin. This wooden polyptych was carved in the late fifteenth century by Veit Stoss, a German from Nuremberg. Sympathetic to Italian Renaissance humanist ideas, he was one of Europe's greatest carvers, notably in lime wood. He was known in Florence and mentioned by Vasari. There are some two hundred painted and gilded figures to the front and rear of the folding retable. The most impressive section is the central scene with larger than life-size figures depicting the Death and Assumption of Mary. It took some twelve years to complete the strongly characterized postures, prominent veins and musculature in the superbly expressive hands, necks and faces of saints in various scenes from the life of Christ and the Virgin. The work is one of the world's greatest artistic masterpieces.

'Do you know the lovely story about the altarpiece?' Zosia asked.

'Not another story, Zosia! All right, let's have it!' I whispered in the dark.

'Don't be such a beast! It is a charming story about a child's yellow slipper from the medieval days that was found lodged in the carving of the altarpiece when it was being restored, I think in the nineteenth century. How this slipper came to be there is a complete mystery. A lovely novel exploring one explanation was written by Antonina Domańska. She imagined that after finishing his great altarpiece Veit Stoss was suddenly shocked to see he had forgotten to give the bishop a crozier. He asked a child to climb up into the carving and place it in his hand. While doing this one of the child's yellow slippers fell off. There was even a film made of this story.'

As it was a Sunday, the retable was fully open and lit, which meant the glittering polychrome filled the church.

We wandered south of Wawel around the dilapidated Jewish area of Kazimierz. Most of the buildings were ruined shells with tufts of grass growing out of the interstices of the bricks. Jews began to settle in Kraków in the late thirteenth century. A legend holds that King Kazimierz III 'the Great' was in love with a Jewish girl named Esther who lived in Kraków and accordingly in 1335 he founded the town of Kazimierz on an island in the Vistula near the city for Jews to inhabit. At first the town was joined to the city by a bridge known as the Pons Regalis which was the only bridge spanning the Vistula for some centuries. This became redundant when part of the river was filled in during the late nineteenth century and Kazimierz was joined to Kraków.

Within a hundred years pogroms had begun in Kraków itself and more Jews moved to Kazimierz to join the many Jewish immigrants fleeing persecution in Bohemia, Spain, Germany and Italy. During the sixteenth century the Jewish City became one of the greatest Jewish spiritual and scholastic centres in Poland and by the outbreak of World War II Kraków had some one hundred and twenty synagogues and over sixty thousand Jews. 'Cracow was one of the places where that life was most rich, most beautiful, most varied, and the most evidence of it has survived here.'[120] The Nazis laid waste the entire area and corralled the Jews in the ghetto of Podgórze. The movie *Schindler's List* was shot partly in the old ghetto area where from June 1942 the Jews, trapped like rats, were murdered at Bełżec or Auschwitz-Birkenau. Oskar Schindler's factory was located near the Płaszów forced labour camp south of the ghetto.

Some of the ruined synagogues and public buildings of Kazimierz are now being restored and a hybrid and lively modern atmosphere has become 'modern bohemian' with numerous 'Jewish-themed' bars, restaurants and music festivals. On Friday evenings and Saturday mornings (*Shabbat*) many Orthodox Jews now wander the streets and peaceful squares dressed in black, wearing large hats and long side curls. The sight of them in skullcaps effusively greeting each other in the courtyard of the Remu'h Synagogue or wandering the cemetery is a melancholic reminder of the loss of the great spiritual diversity and colourful cultures that made up traditional Polish life. A 'Wailing Wall' made up of tombstones smashed by the Nazis is one of the most moving sights in the country. A spiritual peace of a rare kind now inhabits the narrow streets of Kazimierz.

Estimates put the number of people with Jewish roots now living in Poland at around fifty thousand. A thirty-minute daily programme in Hebrew is broadcast by Polish Radio. Poles brought up as Catholics have discovered with surprise that their parents or grandparents were in fact Jewish. A Jewish cultural renaissance is in progress in Poland but the crushing weight of history stifles wider knowledge of these fledgling gestures of renewal.

The Vistula meanders north through Kraków across the flat and fertile plains of Małopolska (Lesser Poland), once part of Austrian Galicia, containing some of the most ancient towns in the country. Great meadows and scattered villages form a rural landscape of charm rather than drama. Such land poses no natural barriers, no obstacles to invading armies in quest of territory and plunder. Unlike many nations of Europe, 'the Poles have had nowhere to

---

120 Henryk Halkowski, a rare Krakowian Jewish survivor, quoted in *Upon The Doorposts of Thy House*, Ruth Ellen Gruber (New York 1994)

hide'.[121] As I passed through, work on the flat agricultural land (*pole*) from which Poland derives its name was being carried on much as it had been hundreds of years ago. In the middle distance lone farmers walked behind single horses ploughing long, narrow sections of land. There was a slow-motion, timeless quality to their movement as they looked up at the passing car with faint curiosity, the traces dangling in their hands. Horses pulled carts of various types through great stands of birch and pine anchored to the plain. Old tractors ploughing larger fields seemed like an improving lesson by a socialist realist painter from another era. People are only visible as dots in the meadows. They rise up to glance at the traveller just as the original inhabitants might have apprehensively scanned the horizon for the swelling dust of a Mongol raid.

The Vistula matures as it flows towards the Baltic. At Baranów, near the ancient town of Sandomierz, the river was once many kilometres wide and the primeval high banks can still be seen. The elegant symmetry of the white rectangle of a Late Renaissance castle rises from the flood plain and water meadows. The red tiled roof, the four corner towers with copper-sheathed helmets and a bucolic Polish attic lift the spirit after crossing the endless deserts of communist concrete that torture the landscape.

This imposing residence was built as a testament to the refinement and literary tastes of the noble Andrzej Leszczyński who also assembled a notable library here. The ensemble speaks of an Italianate Polish Renaissance of great opulence. Granaries once lined the banks of the river as Baranów exported grain. Many talented Tuscan artists came to work for prominent Polish magnate families in the Kraków area during the mid sixteenth century. The Florentine architect Santi Gucci and his circle were probably the architects of Baranów, which was completed in 1606 just before Andrzej's death. The estate passed to his highly educated and well-travelled son Rafał, who studied under Galileo. In 1621 Rafał had taken part in the legendary defence of the Polish camp at Chocim on the Dniester in Bessarabia (present-day Ukraine), surrounded by a Turkish army three times larger commanded by Sultan Osman II. The Polish cavalry yet again smashed the lines of besiegers.

121 *God's Playground: A History of Poland*, Volume I, Norman Davies (Oxford 2005) p. 24

As the Turk drew close, and with marvellous speed
Arranged his pavilions in endless array . . .
On fearsome elephants with trunks and pointed ivories:
Each bore thirty archers in lofty towers . . .[122]

This victory led him to transform Baranów into a *palazzo in fortezza* using a military architect. Battles during the Second World War left it stripped of its treasures and ruined. The communists continued the devastation of this hated symbol of privilege by filling the cracked rooms with sacks of grain, the cellars with potatoes and beetroot and the galleries with straw and hay. A military unit was installed in the upper rooms and rooting poultry in the cellars below. Poles are among the finest restorers of ancient buildings in Europe and have rejuvenated the entire fabric of the building.

The fluctuating borders and fluid frontiers of Poland throughout history remind me of my days as a medical student glued to a microscope observing the expanding and contracting membrane of a cell. A short distance from Baranów lies ancient Sandomierz, perched on an escarpment above the confluence of the San and Vistula. The architecture of the town and the landscape of the Vistula are in perfect harmony. Our accommodation however was reminiscent of the aftermath of a Tatar sacking.

'All the ambassadors stay with me. The Swiss ambassador has just cancelled, and the German ambassador loved my modest collection of antiques . . .' the châtelaine of our accommodation assured Zosia and trailed off vaguely as the forest of clocks chimed.

I suppose the painting in dubious taste at the head of the stairs went some way to explaining this assertion. It depicted Adam as a naked body-builder with a huge penis holding hands with a full-breasted Eve, both inanely facing us from the primitive jungle. A stimulating sight to work up an appetite before breakfast. Our room was a brilliantly contrived catastrophe, an achievement of dilapidation thankfully rare in present-day Poland. Just after the fall of communism, however, plaster was falling off the walls, mould growing on the window-ledge and curtains, death beckoned from naked

122 From the brilliant national epic poem *Transakcja Wojny Chocimskiej* by Wacław Potocki (Warsaw 1965) trans. Norman Davies in *God's Playground* Volume I (Oxford 2005) pp. 347–8

electrical wires in the bathroom, the tiny shrunken towels would not have done for Adam's parts and two creaking single beds protested at the slightest erotic movement. The menu offered 'Poultry Stomachs à la Nelson (100 gms)', 'Potatoes in Intestine (100gms)' or 'Inflamed breast of hen (100gms)'. Chopin waltzes played on an endless loop. We headed off to the 'Hernia Snack Bar' mightily relieved.

Throughout history Sandomierz has suffered depredations of every description, razed on many occasions by rampaging armies. In 1241 and again in 1259 the Golden Horde of Batu Khan fired the wooden buildings. Considered a rival to Kraków in beauty, the Polish spirit of reconstruction raised the town from the ashes on numerous occasions. The last Piast king, the powerful reformer Kazimierz III Wielki,[123] rebuilt Sandomierz much as we see it today with a defensive castle, strong town walls, a cathedral and a proper street plan. It was said Kazimierz found a Poland of wood and left it one of stone. The town grew in prosperity from the grain and timber trade along the Vistula but in more modern times it faded away and Polish miners have had to shore up the foundations to prevent the entire place sliding into the river.

After strolling the medieval cobbled streets around the sloping market square and superb Renaissance town hall, nothing could have prepared me for what the baroque cathedral contained. It is all too easy to imagine that the period of 'rational' modern history one inhabits facilitates objective judgements of past 'irrational' religious passions, that their intrusion into the secular present is largely negligible. I was suddenly brought up short by an eighteenth-century painting, actually series of paintings, hanging under the Gothic vault that telescoped time, forcefully reminding me that the fear of Muslims, Jews and 'infidels' has changed but little in this part of Christian Europe over hundreds of years.

I thought I had left anti-Semitism behind at the gates of Birkenau, but here in the cathedral of Sandomierz, only two hundred kilometres distant, the Medusa of racial violence rose again. I was confronted with the medieval insecurities of the Catholic

---

123 Kazimierz 'the Great' (1310–70) was the only Polish king to ever be given this title.

Church concerning Jews and 'heretics' projected into the 'enlight-ened' eighteenth century. In January 2004 Pope John Paul II had an audience with Israel's chief rabbis, Yona Metzger and Schlomo Amar, where he told them he had 'striven to promote Jewish–Catholic dialogue and to foster ever greater understanding, respect and cooperation.'[124] Yet here was a painting portraying the ritualized murder of a Christian child by Jews that supposedly occurred in 1710. The painting was commissioned from the artist Carol de Prevot by the local priest, Stefan Żuchowski, and depicts events described in his book entitled *Proces Kryminalny* (A Criminal Trial). The book was published in 1713 as a reaction to the trial of Jews in Sandomierz accused of murdering a Christian boy. In the painting a Christian woman loses her child to the Jews for ritual sacrifice. The infant is tortured first by rolling him around in a barrel lined with nails, the blood is then drained from his body and in the final ghastly scene the corpse is devoured and later vom-ited up by a dog. The faces of the death-dealing Jews are transfigured with demonic enjoyment.

In the 1990s a Jewish–Catholic committee on reconciliation sug-gested that the painting be removed from the cathedral as it could stimulate anti-Semitism, a particularly sensitive issue in contempo-rary Poland. The painting remained but was re-titled from *Infanticidia* (*Ritual Murder by Jews*) to *The Alleged Infanticidia*. In his book on the trial the priest Żuchowski 'follows the common cliché that Poland was a Purgatory for the clergy, a Hell for the peasants, and a Paradise for the Jews.'[125] Leaving aside the depraved desecration of the host, he details various grotesque medieval mur-ders of Christian children by Jews in the most bloody and perverted terms imaginable, giving his readers the cannibalistic shudders. 'Then they [the Jews] mixed the blood with apples and pears, and nuts and other fruit, and they ate it . . .'[126]

---

124 Quoted in *Jews and Heretics in Catholic Poland: A Beleaguered Church in the Post-Reformation Era* by Magda Teter (New York 2006) p. 1. Information on these paintings and the situation of Jews and 'infidels' in Post-Reformation Polish society is derived from this original and thought-provoking study. The author, Assistant Professor of History at Wesleyan University, is well acquainted with Sandomierz, the hometown of her father.

125 Ibid., p. 97

126 Quoted in Ibid., p. 115

This painting however is just one in a series of sixteen large bloodthirsty scenes arranged along the nave, four depicting the martyrdom of Catholics in Sandomierz and twelve depicting martyrdom in the general history of the Church. In 1260 Muslim Tatars slaughtered the Dominicans from the Church of St Jacob in Sandomierz (numerous beheadings, grotesque tortures and limb severings in this one) and in 1656 the Swedes blew up the castle (included among the flying bodies is a Pole still mounted on his horse, both believed to have been blown clean across the Vistula, landing uninjured on the other side). Each of the twelve paintings in the *Martyrologium Romanum*[127] series represents a month in the liturgical calendar with thirty or so martyrdoms contained in each painting. To assist identification in this farrago of bloodletting, each saint is helpfully numbered and linked to a list of names in gold below the picture. Clearly even as late as the eighteenth century the Polish Catholic Church felt threatened by the 'full catastrophe' of Jews, Turks, pagans, heretics and schismatics quite apart from simple sinners. Contemplating these beheadings, spurting severed limbs and monstrous tortures, the visual link with the present activities of Muslim fundamentalist extremists is inescapable. At moments like these the compression of human time and significance to a pinpoint is at its most depressing.

After a beautiful drive north along the Vistula, Zosia and I were soon strolling through the clammy dusk of Good Friday along the terraces which line the banks of the Vistula gorge. We were becoming more deeply involved and this location could not have been a more romantic spot for love to flower. The royal town of Kazimierz Dolny is magical, a gem of the Polish Late Renaissance. Known as the 'Pearl on the Vistula', it was settled during the fourteenth century and became particularly wealthy in the sixteenth and seventeenth centuries as it lay on the trade route from Lwów through Zamość to Warsaw. Grain, timber, salt and hides were floated down the Vistula

---

127 Generally speaking the *Martyrologium Romanum* (Roman Martyrology) is a list of Christian martyrs compiled for each day of the year and read during the daily Office of Prime. The first edition was published in Rome in 1583 and the third edition approved by Pope Gregory XIII was imposed upon the whole Church in 1584.

on great rafts to Gdańsk. Landed patrician families made fortunes in Kazimierz Dolny.

The remarkable quality of light in this enchanting place has attracted *plein-air* painters from all over Poland. Students from the Academy of Fine Arts in Warsaw studied and painted here between the wars, attempting to establish a national style. The banks of the Vistula are dotted with Renaissance granaries of beautiful simplicity decorated with Flemish gables. The effervescent light reflects from the river onto buildings of white Vistula stone – the round tower of a ruined castle, a Renaissance parish church, a baroque Franciscan monastery. Kazimierz is built into a dramatic and picturesque forested ridge, the golden light of evening revealing a panorama reminiscent of Italian pastoral landscapes by Claude Lorrain. Hiding among trees on the terraces are small wooden houses with charming verandas and mossy tiled roofs, their chimneys smoking from wood fires. The broad river lined with birch and aspen moves with an undemonstrative power.

We crossed the small market square flanked by extraordinary late Renaissance facades. The houses of two prosperous merchants were completed around 1516 with exuberant and whimsical plaster decoration. St Christopher holds a tree complete with its roots as a staff, carrying a minuscule Christ on his shoulders and standing on marvellous lobsters. He and St Nicholas share space with allegorical scenes and fantastic animals. This chaos is gloriously immoderate and witty, indiscriminately applied without regard to scale or function. A moment from the Jewish past returned to life when an old man with a black skullcap and a long white beard began busying himself with carpentry on a balustraded veranda high above the square.

In Poland I feel strongly surrounded by the atmosphere of religion, particularly at Easter. During my first experience it was as though childhood religious feelings had burst upon me with renewed vigour. The haunting feeling of Christ in his grave lay heavy in the air. Easter is one of the greatest Roman Catholic festivals in Poland. In the Kazimierz parish church on that Good Friday rivulets of blood ran to the floor from the body of Christ twisted in agony on the cross. His tomb was guarded by a pair of weary firemen in brass helmets holding silver axes. Three nuns were fervently praying while others performed the Stations of the Cross. Candles had been overturned and crucifixes were lying flat. Outside the sun was setting behind an old wooden barn and trees containing the nests of jackdaws and rooks thrust into a reddening sky. This beautiful parish church built in two stages in 1586–9 and 1610–13 is decorated with elegant panels, rosettes and hearts in grey plaster. It is the finest example of the elegant Lublin Renaissance style which flourished in the south-east of the country in the seventeenth century.

On Easter Saturday the faithful bring *święcone* to the church. These are small baskets decorated with white flowers, green leaves and covered with a white lace napkin. They contain hard-boiled eggs, sausage, bread, cake, salt, pepper and other food which is blessed by the priest and sprinkled with Holy Water. The contents are placed on a plate on Easter Sunday morning and each member of the family takes a portion of blessed boiled egg and salt and extends individual good wishes. At Kazimierz Dolny traditional bread cockerels are sold at the bakers as well as bread in the form of crabs or pigeons. The religious intensity of Easter is unsettling to anyone brought up in the largely secular society of Western Europe.

Easter Day began with a peal of bells and a procession of little girls in white turning graciously and strewing flower petals before a priest carrying the monstrance containing the Eucharist. An enormous Easter breakfast was served with a delicious fermented yeast soup called *żurek*. Cold meats with wine were soon followed by smoked trout, steak, Easter cake and Bulgarian champagne. Replete, we walked off the feast along the banks of the Vistula towards the tiny fishing village of Męćmierz.

No sooner had we set off than the wind began to rise and the sky to darken, but the low rushing clouds and occasional sunshine were invigorating. The river lies in a flood-plain with islands of lush green and wide sandbars, wavelets running up energetically against the shore. On the opposite bank of the Vistula a ridge of rock is exposed like a scar on the landscape which terminates at the village of Janowiec. A monumental Gothic castle was erected here on a dark green wooded escarpment with little evidence of habitation. A squall began to engulf the fortress and sheets of torrential rain moved towards us. We hesitated, fascinated by the lightning flashing over the battlements until we took shelter under some low shrubs. A glow broke over the broad ruffled water and ghostly sandbanks, a suspicion of thunder rumbled in the distance. In the rain Zosia's blouse and cotton trousers clung to her body as we hurried along the muddy path and birds flew in wild arcs above the breaking wavelets.

The spring squall passed as quickly as it had arrived and the sun emerged. Long, green weed was flowing in the swiftly moving river current like the hair of a bather. The wooden, thatched houses of Męćmierz straggled in picturesque disorder along the roadside. A windmill stood vacantly on a promontory. The sweeping panorama is strangely reminiscent of Asia with the rich, nervous greens of early spring marooned as if in paddy fields. Forested cliffs patrolled by birds of prey aroused the noble Sarmatian Poland of my imagination. We crossed fields with isolated trees and copses before a final descent to the town through a gorge dusted with bluebells.

Easter Monday dawned cold, windy and wet. We were awoken by the screams of children splashing everyone with water, an Easter custom in Poland called Śmigus Dyngus or 'wet Monday'. The weather continued in changeable cruelty. Snow, hail and freezing winds were pushing fast-moving dark cloud that broke up on occasion into clear blue sky. We followed a bifurcation of the Małachowski Gorge along a track which led across meadows and wandered through fresh green orchards glittering with cool rain and ice, air filtered by sunlight. Unique fissures called loess gorges characterize the region, the deep sides sprinkled with tiny white, mauve and blue spring flowers. The steep descent led to a variety of 'cross-gorges' which led upwards in mysterious tunnels. Fallen leaves were densely packed underfoot in a thick carpet.[128]

This labyrinth gave way to a sealed road which led to the Soviet War Cemetery. Reminders of war are never far from any experience of beauty in Poland. The Soviet War Cemetery is an emotional place

---

128 'Loess is usually deep, fertile soil, rich in organic remains and characterized by slender, vertical tubes that are said to represent stems and roots of plants buried by sediment. When cut by streams or other agencies, loess remains standing in cliffs exhibiting a vertical, columnar structure.' Columbia Electronic Encyclopaedia, Sixth edition 2003

with many unmarked mass graves, each holding up to fifty bodies. There are a few single graves with the customary Russian porcelain plaques on the headstones with yellow plastic flowers and a photograph of the deceased – one a beautiful girl of nineteen. A squall of hail suddenly blotted out everything and we were forced to shelter. Sunshine again and then we were heading once more through sparkling fields, asking directions at a dilapidated farmhouse with a dilapidated dog. Bright green moss, ice crust on the gnarled roots of trees, delicate flowers and clear, cool air.

The Vistula has witnessed and participated in most significant transformations in the history of Poland. But no period could have been more fateful and dramatic than the years leading up to the final partition of the country in 1795, when it was erased from the map of Europe by the cabal of Austria, Prussia and Russia. At the time of the First Partition in 1772 there were scandalously few dissenting voices in the Sejm (lower chamber of Parliament). Jan Matejko, the great nineteenth-century Polish history painter, captured a moment of extreme emotion when the Deputy, Tadeusz Rejtan, threw himself to the floor at the entrance to the parliamentary chamber, crazily tore at his clothes to expose his breast and shouted 'kill me, stamp on me, but do not kill the Fatherland.' As the Polish Commonwealth began to disintegrate further, nationalist movements strengthened in opposition to King Stanisław Augustus. He was powerless to resist the increasingly manipulative Russian 'protection' and internal Polish betrayal. The terrible word 'collaborator' began its uniquely evil work.

The principle of the election of kings preserved the power of the *szlachta* and reduced their pathological fear of hereditary despotism. This idea may well have been derived from the election assembly of the Crimean Tatars known as the *quriltai.* As many as fifteen thousand armed horseman of the nobility with their private armies and retinues of magnates would assemble on the Election Field at Wola near Warsaw. Any foreigner or citizen, provided he was Catholic, could present himself for election together with his supporters. The Marshall of the Crown would gallop between the pavilions of candidates urging, cajoling and persuading in an atmosphere of chaos. Duels, battles, cavalry charges and deaths were common. The final decision was arrived at through what might be termed 'collective intuition' and a great shout would go up as the decision was reached.

Catherine the Great, once the king's lover, had greatly influenced his election to the Polish throne and was now increasingly pulling the strings of policy. 'It must be true that love in a sovereign is quickly replaced by ambition, for that same Catherine soon destroyed her own work, and overthrew the monarch she had so carefully protected.'[129] Stanisław was a man of high artistic refinement and sensibility who preferred the company of women, spoke six languages fluently, read widely in the French *philosophes* and did not drink. He wholeheartedly embraced the Enlightenment and catalysed a cultural renewal in Poland. This polished cosmopolitan 'upstart' was unlikely to find much favour among the xenophobic, hard-drinking, hard-riding Sarmatian poorer *szlachta*, who espoused a growing revolutionary patriotic cause. 'He was certainly no hero, but behind the languid frivolity lurked a strong sense of purpose and love of his country . . .'[130]

In 1772 Jean-Jacques Rousseau published *Considérations sur le gouvernement de la Pologne*. He advised the Poles with great prescience, 'If you cannot prevent your enemies from swallowing you whole, at least you must do what you can to prevent them from digesting you.'[131] The French Revolution was sending ripples along the Vistula as far as Warsaw. A major indigestible fragment of Poland for Russia was the Constitution of 3 May 1791, the first written constitution in Europe. Stanisław Augustus was triumphantly carried shoulder-high through the streets of the capital upon its proclamation. Based on Enlightenment principles, it

129 *The Memoirs of Elizabeth-Louise Vigée-Le Brun*, trans. Siân Evans (London 1989). Marie Antoinette's favourite portraitist, this superb artist fled the French Revolution at the age of 34 disguised as a peasant with her six-year-old daughter. She was to become one of the most successful women artists in history with a vivid, luminous and refined palette. She survived by painting portraits of the European aristocracy and travelled extensively to all the major European courts. The *Memoirs* paint an intimate, gossipy and revealing portrait of aristocratic European life following the Revolution. In 1791 she said of the seductive Polish Countess Anna Potocka 'this countess is one of the prettiest women I have ever painted'. She painted Stanisław Augustus II, King of Poland, in 1797 dressed in a burgundy velvet cloak but kept the picture for herself as they were such 'good friends'. She also painted him in the dashing costume of Henry IV wearing a medallion of the Freemasons of which he was a Brother.

130 *The Polish Way*, Adam Zamoyski (London 1987) p. 236

131 Quoted in *God's Playground: A History of Poland* Volume I, Norman Davies (Oxford 2005) p. 281

created a hereditary monarchy, reformed the government and limited the powers of the *szlachta*. The day is still a public holiday in Poland, marked by military parades, folk dancing, and re-enactments of the King's proclamation by actors in the forecourt of the Palace on the Island in Łazienki Park in Warsaw.

In response Catherine massed her troops and precipitated a year-long war. In 1793 the defeated Poles were forced to rescind the constitution, Prussia and Russia gorged on more of the country and the Second Partition came into being. The atmosphere became revolutionary as the banks collapsed and cities began to starve. In March 1794 Tadeusz Kościuszko, the Polish General who had contributed so significantly to the American War of Independence, arrived in Kraków and declared an Act of Insurrection in the main square.

Strategically inconsequential battles often achieve mythical status in Polish history and so it was in April 1794 with the Battle of Racławice fought outside Kraków. Led by Kościuszko, furious peasants armed only with scythes assisted by artillery and regulars successfully forced the Russians to withdraw, capturing their guns. An astounding panoramic picture of this victory in a purpose-built rotunda in Wrocław (Breslau) covers 1,800 square metres of canvas with cannon, bushes, carts and 'blasted heath' erected between the viewer and the canvas. It was painted towards the end of the nineteenth century by Jan Styka and Wojciech Kossak together with some assistants.

The peasants subsequently became a potent symbol of heroic independent Poland, but as usual the vested interests of the landowning *szlachta* meant they would not agree to join them in united resistance. The combined forces of Prussia, Austria and Russia completed their Polish repast after Kościuszko fell seriously wounded, allegedly crying *'Finis Poloniae!'* in a posture worthy of Horatio Nelson. In reprisal the citizens of Praga, the Warsaw district on the opposite bank of the Vistula, were sickeningly slaughtered in their thousands, a bloodbath never to be forgotten.

This insurrection, like so many other valiant bouts of resistance in Polish history, ultimately failed through lack of cohesion. In 1795 the country was completely wiped from the map of Europe by the final partition, 'lying as if broken-backed on the public highway; a nation anarchic every fibre of it, and under the feet and hoofs of travelling neighbours'[132] but not forever. One can argue that Poland would not exist as an independent member country of the European Union today if these so-called 'heroic failures' and bloody insurrections had not taken place. As Marshal Piłsudski once remarked in a succinct expression of Polishness, 'Victory is to be defeated but not to surrender.'

In January 1795 Catherine exiled Stanisław Augustus to Grodno (now in Belarus) for two years. He left the Royal Castle in tears upon abdication, stopping his carriage after crossing the Vistula by raft to contemplate his lost capital for two hours, much to the chagrin of the impatient Russian general 'accompanying' him. In an access of *sensibilité* upon hearing the news of Catherine's death in November 1796, Stanisław again wept despite her past cruelties towards him. Tsar Paul transferred the ex-sovereign to the Marble Palace in St Petersburg.

On the evening of 10 February 1798 the former king of Poland dined with, among others, his 'good friend' the French painter Elizabeth-Louise Vigée-Le Brun. After a pleasant supper and conversation touching on the paintings collected by his English agents (later to become the nucleus of the Dulwich Picture Gallery), her artistic eye detected a change in his physiognomy. She remarked to the Marquis de Rivière that she had detected 'an extraordinary mistiness about his eyes' and predicted 'The King will die very soon.'[133] Her prediction was sadly fulfilled two days later when he collapsed and died of a stroke. Stanisław Augustus was buried amid great ceremony in the vaults of the Church of St Catherine in St Petersburg. Tsar Paul walked beside the hearse with a drawn sword pointed to the earth. The king's body was, after many travails, finally buried in St John's Cathedral, Warsaw, in 1995, almost two hundred years after his death. This cathedral was the church of his coronation and the church from which he celebrated the Constitution of 3 May.

132 *History of Frederick II of Prussia, called Frederick the Great*, Thomas Carlyle (London 1858–65) vol. viii p. 105
133 Vigée-Le Brun, op. cit., pp. 208–209

During these massive political upheavals increasing nationalist fervour found favour among the intelligentsia. The spirit of the Enlightenment had created a class of Romantic revolutionaries who felt Poland's sovereignty was under threat. Political opposition and cultural rivalry centred on the town of Puławy, an old river crossing, situated on an escarpment above the Vistula some hundred kilometres south of Warsaw. The activities of a cousin of the king, Prince Adam Kazimierz Czartoryski, and his intelligent and flirtatious wife Izabela Czartoryska, became increasingly significant in the world of culture and politics.

This political party of related magnates were known rather ominously as *the Familia*. Adam Kazimierz had been groomed for high estate but fortune, lack of worldly ambition and a bookish temperament worked against his election as king. Mounting intrigues and rumours led him to gradually withdraw his political support from the largely unrealistic reform policies of his uncle Stanisław Augustus during the 1780s yet all the while maintaining his cultural loyalties. Izabela was born in 1746, the daughter of the Saxon General Jerzy Detloff, Count Flemming. This remarkable woman, although not conventionally beautiful, was a vivacious and promiscuous creature, an excellent musician and painter who had a passion for gardening. Like many of her set, she was closely acquainted with Freemasonry. Her progressive salon at Puławy attracted all manner of prominent Polish writers, musicians, architects and painters of the time.

The first Picturesque 'English' gardens began to appear in the countryside around Warsaw not long after those in France and Germany. In the world of fashionable Warsaw, Anglomania was in full swing. This was reflected in the taste for English coaches, mahogany furniture (Izabela Czartoryska had a fine collection), porcelain and clothes (Stanisław himself dressed in the English style but was predominantly French in his cultural tastes). The Scottish architect Robert Adam inspired some fine interiors. French remained the language of choice among the magnates and wealthy *szlachta*, spoken in their preferred cities of Paris, Vienna and St Petersburg.

The Czartoryskis travelled to England in 1768–71 and after their return Izabela immediately began to lay out an irregular 'sentimental' garden at their Powązki estate near Warsaw. She and her Saxon architect, Szymon Bogumił Zug, modelled it on the Jardin Anglais of Le Petit Trianon at Versailles designed for Marie Antoinette. Izabela placed herself temperamentally within the French rococo and mounted extravagant *fêtes champêtres* and *fêtes galantes* at Powązki. (Sadly nothing survives of the estate as the area has now become the remarkable national cemetery.)

English landscape gardens are arguably the greatest contribution Britain has made to the visual arts in Europe. At Stowe in Buckinghamshire in the 1730s Lord Cobham had created a garden and parkland, part of which was dedicated to notions of patriotism and liberty. Judging from the gardens laid out at Puławy, known as 'the Polish Athens', it seems that Izabela Czartoryska on her own visit to Stowe was particularly impressed by the moral and political message of the Elysian Fields and William Kent's Temple of the British Worthies.

Political upheavals interrupted the peace of mere garden design. In the noble struggle for freedom in the absence of a Polish state after the partitions, the idealists and 'heroes' within the gentry and intelligentsia carried within themselves the spirit and soul of the nation. The final partition of the country destroyed Powązki.

After the final partition Izabela began to restore and transform damaged Puławy into a picturesque and elegiac English park with the help of the Scottish gardener James Savage. It became famous in Europe through the publication in 1782 of *Les Jardins, ou l'Art d'embellir les Paysages* by Jacques Montanier (the Abbé Delille). The centrepiece is the rather uninspired neoclassical Czartoryski Palace, the result of a number of remodellings since the seventeenth century. The park contained many different species of exotic trees such as thuja, catalpa and Douglas spruce as well as old lindens, white poplars and oaks. In 1798, perhaps inspired by the Temple of Ancient Virtue at Stowe, she commissioned a copy of the so-called Temple of the Sibyl at Tivoli near Rome to occupy a picturesque position at the end of an allée of lindens on the steep escarpment above the Vistula. The temple was designed in the decorative neoclassical rather than austere Roman style of William Kent by the eminent Polish architect and native of Puławy, Christian Piotr Aigner. He had been trained in Rome and inscribed the temple with a euphonious motto in Polish: *Przeszłość – Przyszłości* (The Past to the Future).

Under the glass dome of this temple, the optimistic and fiercely patriotic Izabela founded the first Polish museum containing national monuments intended to educate, sustain hope and strengthen the resolve of Poles in their struggle for freedom. The temple contained a casket with relics of the Polish kings, banners and weapons from the wars against the Teutonic Knights, Swedes, and Russians as well as trophies from Sobieski's victory over the Turks at Vienna in 1683. In Aigner's Gothic House completed ten years later she displayed foreign antiquities of European rather than Polish significance collected on her travels: memorabilia of Rousseau, Voltaire, Napoleon and Captain James Cook, including an armchair reputed to have belonged to Shakespeare.

Three great masterpieces of European painting hung there: Leonardo da Vinci's *Lady with an Ermine,* Raphael's *Portrait of a Youth*, both purchased by her son Prince Adam in Italy, and Rembrandt's *Landscape with the Good Samaritan.* The Raphael disappeared without trace after the Second World War along with hundreds of thousands of other items of the Polish cultural heritage stolen by the Nazis. Izabela intended to preserve the lost culture of Poland after the partitions and spur a cultural renaissance through historical associations.

In 1805 she published *Various Thoughts on the Manner of Garden Layout* with twenty-seven beautifully engraved copper plates. Palladian villas with 'English' gardens began to appear all over the country but few survive. One example that endured is the superb villa at Śmiełów near Poznań with elegant curved wings terminating in Polish pavilions with mansard roofs. The villa is based on Palladio's Villa Badoer at Fratta Polesine in the Veneto. It is the most romantic and atmospheric house I have visited in Poland. The day I encountered it the orchards were in flower, the roads lined with mauve and white blooms, the house encircled by lilacs heavy with blossom and bees. The noble Ionic portico is decorated with collections of banners, shields, cannon and soldiers in armour. Adam Mickiewicz stayed there in 1831 and later the Nobel prize-winning author Henryk Sienkiewicz. While staying with the Gorzeńskis, Mickiewicz by tradition drew scenes for his epic poem *Pan Tadeusz* from the country life he observed roundabout.

> Here a young gentleman, through gates unbarred,
> Drove in a two-horse chaise, then round the yard;
> He stopped before the porch and there descended;[134]

While a guest at Śmiełów he fell in love with Konstancja Łubieńska, an author and aristocratic sister of the châtelaine. This love affair matured into a close friendship which had a profound effect on the remainder of his life. Filled with the passion of resistance, as a patriotic Pole he was acting as an emissary from Paris on his way to the nearby Russian border at the Prosna River, travelling on a false passport in the name of Adam Mühl and carrying inflammatory letters from insurgents.

Over lunch in a Warsaw garden at Młociny with a descendant of Izabela Czartoryska, I talked of the experience of aristocratic families under communism. She attempted to explain the complexities of her family tree but I was left in confusion at the Polish custom of often naming sons with the Christian names of their fathers.

'Was there anything positive about the communist period, do you think?' I asked perhaps naively.

'Nothing,' she replied at once. 'They took everything from us including our house. Members of my family were put in prison. But worst of all, they destroyed all our documents, title deeds and papers. They annihilated our identity.'

'But couldn't your parents have helped you to regain it somehow?'

'You know, Michael, I have huge gaps in my knowledge of my parents and grandparents. They refused to talk about the war. It was so terrible they could not and now of course I cannot ask.' She seemed so crestfallen I felt an immediate wave of sympathy.

'What did you dislike most about communism?' I had asked this question many times and received many different responses ranging from bitter invective to rosy nostalgia.

---

134 *Pan Tadeusz*, Adam Mickiewicz trans. Watson Kirconnell (New York 1981) Book One lines 47–49

'They taught us to lie and to fear. Even now when I am confronted with an official form I am not sure whether it would be better to lie.'

'You don't trust what might happen?'

'Most Poles don't trust other people. There is suspicion everywhere! That's why the family is the most important focus of life in Poland – at least you can trust them. I try to predict the consequences of any answer. I can't help it. It's an automatic thing and really unpleasant. But I am optimistic about the future of Poland. Very optimistic.'

'So what do you think of the current *lustracja*[135] process?'

'I agree with it. I discovered recently that I was considered the best student in my year at college. Suddenly I was expelled without explanation. I thought I was no good academically for thirty years! Now I discover the real reason was that someone drew attention to my coming from an aristocratic family. It's good to know.'

'Has there been any success in Poland claiming property back?'

'No, is the short answer. There are still no laws at all to allow the return of private property. You can take a claim through the civil courts of course, but you must wait and wait in Poland forever if something goes to court . . .'

'Some former Soviet republics have returned confiscated property.'

'Yes, I know, but not here I'm afraid. Of course there is legislation for the return of communal property owned before the war by the Catholic and Orthodox church. And Jews have made many claims of course.'

I looked through the trees at a small dilapidated baroque palace nearby which I knew had been the subject of an endless process of litigation by an indomitable Polish woman living in England. Her father, a Polish officer, had been prominent in the army and was shot in the forest during the notorious Katyń massacre. The obsession of this woman to have her mansion returned led to more than

---

135 A contentious process of vetting that began with prominent public figures and extended an increasingly wider net to embrace over half a million Poles. A variety of middle-class professionals and many others from all walks of life were closely examined for suspected collaboration with the Security Services and other mechanisms and apparatus of oppression during the communist regime.

fifty court appearances until she finally had a brain haemorrhage and collapsed in the courtroom itself. She died without properly regaining consciousness. The mental scars of communism will take longer to erase than the physical blight.

CHAPTER 17

'Keep Away from Gin and Polish Airmen'

An English headmistress's advice to her girls
during World War Two

The architectural harmony and comfort of Bath had lured me home from Warsaw for part of the long summer vacation. However, after a couple of weeks wandering the Avon valley I was surprised to feel the claustrophobic familiarity of the 'dead blank' and yearned for the adrenalin rush of cultural exploration. Poland is transformed in the summer into an ocean of green. On impulse I decided to return and planned a modest expedition by car. Spectres on the lawless roads of Central Europe rose up in my imagination.

The car was packed with the necessary provisions – cases of Berry Bros. Good Ordinary Claret, bottles of the King's Ginger Liqueur and Blue Hanger whiskey, Bokhara rugs and a Moroccan bedspread to lift the sterility of any room. I felt I must push through the anxieties for the sheer pleasure of driving an old Rolls-Royce in remote regions with more than a hint of danger. There were persistent rumours of Russian mafia armed with Kalashnikovs hijacking cars.

I had decided to distract myself from dwelling on the slow death of the contract and take part in an international car rally around Poland, the first since 1913. My friends, mechanics, family, in fact anyone at all thought I was insane to take the old machine to Poland that summer.[136] But adventurous ideas of past Polish glamour had taken over. I had read the romantic story of one of the greatest Polish national heroes, General Władysław Sikorski, driving his rakish 1938 Rolls-Royce Phantom III Drop-head Coupé out of Poland through Romania to Paris ahead of the German invasion in 1939. He was to take up the position of Prime Minister of the Polish Government-in-Exile in the French capital before relocating to London.[137] The controversial Commander-in-Chief of the Polish Armed Forces, Marshal Śmigły-Rydz, reviewed troops and cavalry regiments in a Phantom II 'Allweather Tourer' until the Soviet invasion of 1939. He once memorably remarked of Poland's grim destiny: 'Germany will destroy our body; Russia will destroy our soul.'[138]

A clean and comfortable Scandinavian ship took me across the North Sea from Harwich to Hamburg. The autobahn to Berlin was easily found but shortly after the fall of the Berlin Wall extensive road works and diversions made entry into the city a navigational nightmare. From Berlin I headed along an old rutted motorway that lead to the German–Polish border at Olszyna (Erlenholtz) on the River Nysa Łużycka. The cracked ribs on the concrete set up a harmonic vibration until I thought the car would shake itself apart.

Driving in Poland is rather like taking part in a permanent running of the Targa Florio. Most of the time I drove moderately above the speed limit but was blasted off the road as if standing still. The painted wooden police cars placed at the side of the highway as if emerging from a cross-roads fool no one. Many Poles drive as if they were still enlisted in the Napoleonic Vistula Lancers and have

---

136 A modestly priced and completely underrated touring vehicle with a capacious boot and luxurious interior. The 1974 Silver Shadow in shell grey with light blue leather is unmolested and has never 'failed to proceed' in ambient temperatures ranging from 40°C to –25°C. Chassis Number SRH 18723.

137 This magnificent Drop-head Coupé (Chassis 3CM 81) has a dashing two-seater body by the glamorous coachbuilder Vanvooren of Paris. The first owner was the Pole Stefan Czarnecki but according to a Sotheby's catalogue of May 1969 the car was built to the special instructions of General Sikorski and delivered to him in Warsaw (*The Derby Phantoms*, Lawrence Dalton, RREC, Paulerspury, Northamptonshire 1991 illust. p. 394). It is now magnificently restored and resides in England. A Rolls-Royce Phantom II was also used by the Polish revolutionary and Chief of State of the Republic of Poland, Field Marshal Józef Piłsudski.

138 Quoted in *Poland's Politics: Idealism versus Realism*, A. Bromke (Cambridge, Mass., 1967) p. 26

simply swapped a horse for a car with all the crazy risk-taking and bravado that entails. Old buses converted into '24 Hour Non-Stop Alkohole' bars littered the roadside (petrol stations in Poland also sell alcohol). Half-finished mansion castles with medieval turrets were falling together in the Polish manner. The extremes of wealth are underlined whenever a working horse and cart are blown off the road by a Mercedes Benz driven at suicidal speed by a Polish entrepreneur. In recent years these working horses, to which Poland owes an immeasurable debt, have almost disappeared.

Dusk fell and, it being Sunday, vodka drunks oscillated to and fro into the path of the oncoming traffic. One I noticed in my mirrors appeared to fall over the parapet of a bridge into the river below. Two men stumbled out of the forest carrying a stuffed pheasant nailed to a board and were transfixed in my headlights like rabbits. My destination was the town of Żagań (Sagan) in Silesia, about 100 miles south-east of Berlin. I intended to visit the former German Air Force prisoner of war camp Stalag Luft III. It had witnessed two of the most notorious escape attempts of World War Two, popularly known from the films *The Wooden Horse* and *The Great Escape*. Here I hoped to join a reunion of survivors celebrating the 50th anniversary of the ill-fated escape of seventy-six airmen from the camp.

The ancient but now obscure town of Żagań is a good example of a once German but now Polish town remembered only for its World War Two associations. Yet the cultural and political history of Silesia is a powerfully rich and remarkable one, the heritage almost forgotten after the Polish borders were extended west to what was known as the Oder–Neisse Line after the Potsdam Conference of 1945. Poles refer to the region as the 'Recovered Territories' as it was under the Polish hegemony of the Piast Dynasty almost a thousand years before. However the cultural achievements of Silesian architects, painters, theologians, musicians, writers and poets, scientists and philosophers remain resoundingly German. The expulsion of some three and a half million ethnic Germans was deeply traumatic and continues to affect Polish–German relations.

Żagań had many distinguished owners including the Birons of the romantic but obscure Duchy of Courland and in particular the illustrious family of Talleyrand's favourite mistress, his young niece

Dorothée Talleyrand-Périgord. The French writer Sainte-Beuve wrote of her 'eyes of an infernal brilliance that shone in the night'. The palace which dominates the town was begun by the powerful seventeenth-century German statesman and soldier of fortune Albrecht von Wallenstein who purchased the fiefdom from Emperor Frederick II in 1627. To his cost Wallenstein used astrology as a guide in his military campaigns. In desperation he brought the mystical neo-Platonist astronomer and mathematician Johannes Kepler to Żagań in 1628 to take up the position of court astrologer.

By the mid nineteenth century Dorothée Talleyrand-Périgord was living in the chateau and wandering the romantic landscaped park. She created an international drawing room that attracted kings, artists, poets and musicians such as Franz Liszt, who gave piano recitals at the palace. Żagań subsequently became the capital of a small principality belonging to the Talleyrand family. The palace remained a sovereign part of France within Silesia until after World War Two. Marcel Proust wrote affectionately of the Prince de Sagan, whom he cast as a friend of Swann.

> A portrait detached from its frame, the Prince de Sagan, whose last appearance in society this must have been, baring his head to offer his homage to the Duchess, with so sweeping a revolution of his tall hat in his white-gloved hand (harmonising with the gardenia in his buttonhole), that one felt surprised that it was not a plumed felt hat of the old regime, several ancestral faces from which were exactly reproduced in the face of this great gentleman.[139]

I checked into a grotty hotel (with 24-hour guarded parking, one of the treasures of Polish motoring life) and noticed some of the survivors of the 'Great Escape' at dinner. What memories did the pitiless sirens and melancholic wailing of train hooters that night arouse in the RAF officers sleeping above me? Richard shared my interest in Poland as the greatest theatre of war in Europe and the following morning he arrived by train from Warsaw. He had

---

139 *Remembrance of Things Past: Cities of the Plain*, Marcel Proust. Translated from the French by C.K. Scott Moncrieff (London 1967)

recently met the Pole Staś Pruszyński at his restaurant Klub Aktora in the diplomatic sector of Warsaw. He was full of the story of how in 1955 a group of Cambridge students (now eminent ambassadors and writers), who later became known as the 'Cambridge Pimpernels', had smuggled the nineteen-year-old Pruszyński out of Stalinist Poland on the luggage rack of a train. 'I thought we were all going to Siberia,' one of them commented later.

Poland, considered the land of the Slavic *Untermenschen* by the Nazis, began to be destroyed as a state on 1 September 1939 following the almost farcical attack the previous evening by *Sturmbahnführer* Helmut Naujocks and his bevy of criminals on the German radio station at Gliwice (Gleiwitz). This 'unprovoked attack' on the Third Reich gave the Nazis the tawdry excuse they needed to invade Poland. The Poles put up a spirited resistance. It had been agreed among the Allies that the Polish role was limited to holding back the advance of the *Wehrmacht* until they could launch their offensive. The Poles courageously managed to do so but were effectively abandoned by France and Britain. Warsaw, Kraków, Poznań and other cities were bombed into submission. Much is made of the legend of Polish Uhlans attacking Panzer tanks but this mythical 'madness' only occurred if cavalry units were trapped by the *Blitzkrieg* with no other avenue of escape.

The Nazis had built a series of POW camps in the Żagań district and one of the most important was Stalag Luft III. Well run by the *Luftwaffe* with a degree of respect for fellow airmen, it was described by the Red Cross as 'Heaven in the Pines'. At the museum the few survivors of the 'Great Escape' were in ebullient mood, pointing out pertinent features on a model of the camp. The dapper Sydney Dowse, dressed in a camelhair overcoat, club tie, black astrakhan hat and gold-rimmed monocle was the epitome of the raffish Spitfire pilot and RAF officer baiting the 'goons' with an 'away run'. He escaped, was recaptured and sent to Sachsenhausen, from where he again escaped to safety.

'Are you from *The Times*?' he asked me with a pukka accent and patrician demeanour from a lost era.

'I thoroughly enjoyed the war. Every bit of it. Even captivity was a challenge.' The intrepid Bob Nelson, bearded and witty, had crashed in the deserts of North Africa and walked out alive after ten days, his only assistance from a solitary Arab who gave him water. While on the run from his Nazi captors, he would introduce himself as the famous maritime Englishman 'Nelson' and duly received tremendous assistance, as did his compatriot Dick Churchill for much the same reason. Planning the escape gave excitement to the insanely boring life of a POW. Winston Churchill referred to the hours of his own experience as a Boer POW as passing 'like paralytic centipedes'.

'Good God! Those are my glasses!' shouted someone bent over a display case of relics.

The warm, friendly but now frail Desmond Plunkett, map maker to the escape and inventor extraordinaire, was full of recondite information. Clive 'Nobby' Nutting had bought a Rolex Oyster Chronograph on mail order from Geneva while in the camp. The founder of Rolex, a German named Mr Wilsdorf, believing that an Englishman's word is his bond, assured Nobby he should 'not even think of settlement' until the war was over. He discharged his debt on return to London in 1948. Greatly missed by everyone was the mastermind, the professional escapee, South African RAF officer (and barrister and champion skier) Roger Bushell, who electrified the camp when he arrived in the summer of 1942.

The camaraderie of the survivors was infectious. Of the seventy-six who escaped from the North Compound, three made it to safety, fifty were captured and executed, seventeen were returned to Żagań, four sent to Sachsenhausen and two incarcerated in Colditz. They stood painfully silent before the obscene Gestapo photographic record of the execution of their compatriots – the blurred pistol, the Nazi cap and boots, the falling furry shape. Hitler and Himmler personally ordered the execution of the RAF officers, the Gestapo report reading 'the prisoners whilst relieving themselves' (taking the notorious *Pinkelpause*) 'bolted for freedom and were shot whilst trying to escape.' In a macabre and cruel gesture their ashes were returned to the camp in urns which are now in Poznań. This horrified the inmates who in response sewed black triangles on their prison uniforms. The Germans erected a desperate notice in the camp: *Escaping from prison camps has ceased to be a sport!* The *Luftwaffe* distanced themselves from a crime they felt had outraged their professional

code of conduct, recognizing it was an officer's duty to attempt
escape and if recaptured not to be punished. They magnanimously
allowed the prisoners to build and tend a modest memorial in the
surrounding pine forest.

A Polish Armoured Division based at Żagań presided over the
military ceremony. Lt-Commander John Casson of the Fleet Air
Arm, one of the leading lights in camp theatricals and son of Dame
Sybil Thorndike, read the roll-call of the dead, six of whom were
from the almost forgotten squadrons of the Polish Air Forces in
Great Britain. The crack of rifles in the sandy pine forest was deeply
affecting. Richard and I were the only English 'outside visitors' at
this astonishing ceremony. There was a scandalous absence of any
official or diplomatic British representative. Even the Swiss
Ambassador was present.

Poles have had a passion for flying since the Great War, when they
served in the air forces of the partitioning powers. They dominate
glider and acrobatic championships to this day. The most famous air
ace of the Austro-Hungarian Empire, Godwin Brumowski, was
born in Wadowice, formerly in Galicia and the birthplace of Pope
John Paul II. Constantly playing with danger he painted his planes
red and emblazoned a macabre shrouded skull on the fuselage. The
red and white chequer of another ace was adopted as the marking of
the Polish Air Force and remains in use.

The legendary Kościuszko Squadron of the Polish Air Force
was originally formed in Poland by two American airmen in 1919
with the consent of Marshal Piłsudski. Infatuated as a youth with
the valiant tales that pepper Polish history, Captain Merian C.
Cooper became a fighter pilot who later co-directed and wrote the
RKO picture *King Kong* (hardly surprising, then, those final
scenes when the gorilla clinging to the Empire State Building is
attacked by bi-plane fighters). Cooper and the fancifully named
Major Cedric Eric Fauntleroy created a Polish squadron with a
specifically patriotic emblem. The design consisted of the four-
cornered red cap worn by Tadeusz Kościuszko in the 1794
insurrection against Russia with two crossed scythes to symbolize
his support by the peasants set on a background of the stars and
stripes in recognition of his support of Washington in the

American War of Independence. This remained the emblem throughout the illustrious history of its later manifestation, Polish Squadron 303, the most formidable RAF Hurricane and Spitfire squadron in the Battle of Britain.

The *Luftwaffe* bombed Warsaw mercilessly. The city held out for three remarkable weeks. The Polish pilots defending the city were cruelly hampered. Their hundred and fifty obsolete P-11 fighters were almost useless against the two thousand planes of the *Luftwaffe* and the vastly superior Messerschmitts. The Germans wanted a 'correct war', but the Poles to their fury denied them this pleasure. The well-trained Polish Air Force fought like tigers using unique and courageously contrived close-encounter tactics. Superb flying skills in these miserable machines brought down an astonishing 126 German planes and damaged many more. Shambolic organization by their superiors contributed to their final defeat. The last sortie of this magnificent resistance was by a single plane patched with sticking-plaster from a chemist, the crew dropping hand grenades and firing at the German infantry with pistols. The apocalypse was consummated when Russia invaded Poland from the east.

Polish Air Force pilots were evacuated first to Romania and subsequently to France. Here they were unexpectedly greeted with resentment and Gallic *froideur*. In the phoney war that ensued, both Britain and France abandoned their most gallant ally, avoiding significant engagement with the enemy. The collapse of France deeply disillusioned the Polish airmen with a country whose military *gloire* they had idealized for so long as the cradle of Napoleon. A greater knowledge of history could have warned them of the likelihood of French opportunism.

Unquenchable spirit drove them to regroup in England against seemingly impossible odds. Determined to free their country, some resourceful airmen made their way crammed onto tramp steamers sailing from Casablanca. One arrived through Mexico and Canada, another via Brazil and the United States, yet others negotiated the deserts of Syria, a few stole aircraft and flew to Algiers, one disguised himself as a schoolgirl. In an escapade of perversity scarcely to be believed one Polish pilot dragged the three-metre-long wooden propeller of his downed aircraft across the entire continent to London, where it now resides in varnished splendour at the Sikorski Museum in Princes Gate.

The Polish Government-in-Exile was duly transferred from Paris to London with General Władysław Sikorski appointed as Prime Minister. It remained in power until the overthrow of communist rule in 1990. The 8,500 airmen, many older and more experienced than their British counterparts, were greeted upon arrival with frustrating diffidence. Patronized as recalcitrant children by the RAF officers, their already advanced flying skills were polished with long periods of (as they saw it) redundant training. They had cut their teeth on old aircraft requiring great flying talent – it was said they could scan more sky for the enemy than other pilots, having been trained to turn their heads through 180 degrees. The Polish ground crew were among the best. They tirelessly returned hopelessly damaged fighters to airworthiness and skilfully serviced the Rolls-Royce Merlin engine. A particular Hurricane or Spitfire would become a mechanic's 'personal love', lavished with all the technical affection for the machine he could muster. If lost in battle he would be emotionally devastated.

At first the Polish pilots were embedded in British squadrons. Learning at least some English was vital. The Poles were taught by a variety of unlikely teachers including the aesthete Harold Acton dressed as a Chinese Mandarin complete with pigtail. Radio directions were frustratingly practised on bicycles wobbling in pretend formation across the airfield.[140] Eventually the terrible losses suffered by Fighter Command forced the RAF to establish two dedicated fighter squadrons (later expanded to eight) of the Polish Air Force, the most distinguished and glamorous being Squadron 303 or the Kościuszko Squadron.

In their first week of combat in the Battle of Britain the brilliant score of forty kills by this squadron was simply not believed until their tactics were observed in person. 'My God, they *are* doing it!' exclaimed Group Captain Stanley Vincent as their Hurricanes dived almost vertically on the German bombers 'with near suicidal

---

140 An excellent Czech film, *Dark Blue World*, (2001) directed by Jan Sverák, gives a dramatic depiction (within a love story) of the training of a Czech Spitfire Squadron which was similar to the training and frustrations of Poles.

impetus'.[141] But they were fighting their own patriotic war with a different motivation to the British. The individuality and perversity of the nation were in the ascendant. The Poles had simply transferred to the air the élan and tactics of their famed cavalry. The terrified enemy bombers scattered in confusion like so many billiard balls to be picked off at will.

The dash of these airmen was also transmitted to the social scene, where civilians lionized the Polish officers in marked contrast to their generally stuffy reception at the RAF. Their continental manners, gifts of expensive flowers and gallant Sarmatian kissing of hands cut like a sabre through the married and unmarried ranks of adoring Englishwomen. Society hostesses 'adopted' entire squadrons and entertained them at the Dorchester and the Savoy. At their favourite watering hole in Northolt, The Orchard, the smitten women who 'escorted' a Polish officer to bed after dancing were affectionately known as 'Messerschmitts', as was the outrageous cocktail that weakened their resistance. One actress working as a volunteer driver for the cause was known as 'Speedy' due to her ownership of a white Jaguar and other attributes. 'In London waited lips as red as roses.' On speech day the headmistress of a girl's school warned her charges, 'And remember, keep away from gin and Polish airmen.'

Many Englishwomen commented in surprise that Poles actually seemed to enjoy female company, unlike their British male public-school contemporaries. Polish men do not feel it a weakness to respect women and give them precedence. The female attrition rate reached such a height that some British officers were said to pretend to be Poles, affecting fake Slavic accents ('I am Polish. I am very lonely'), kissing hands and sewing 'Poland' flashes onto their uniforms. A local commented meaningfully at their favourite pub: 'Rightly is they called Poles.' One Polish airman parachuted into the garden of a lovely young girl, landing at her feet. They were married three months later. 'On the ground they were gay and amusing,

141 Quoted in For Your Freedom and Ours: The Kościuszko Squadron: Forgotten Heroes of World War II, Lynne Olson & Stanley Cloud (London 2003). I am indebted to this fine account of the contribution of Polish airmen to victory in World War II. I also relied on another book full of highly entertaining anecdote and beautifully written: The Forgotten Few: The Polish Air Force in World War II, Adam Zamoyski (London 1995)

sometimes tragic and forever loyal,' wrote Group Captain Douglas Bader, himself a POW at Stalag Luft III.

Although children of the least imperial of nations, Poles are fighters without parallel, indomitable in resistance if they feel the independence of their country, their own freedom or that of others is under threat. In the face of Stalin's cynical intransigence and subsequently broken promise of free elections, Poland was sacrificed by allies of friable loyalties on the altar of political and wartime expediency. The brutalized population was despatched into the paws of the Brown Bear. During the Warsaw Uprising of August 1944 Polish airmen took a substantial role in the tragic attempt of the RAF to deliver supplies to the besieged city. Many aircraft and lives were lost in the smouldering rubble with negligible success.

It is well to remember when judging the behaviour of modern Poland that on the evening of VE Day, 8 May 1945, as hostilities ceased, 'London, liberated from more than four years of blackout, glowed with light ... In other European capitals – Paris, Rome, Copenhagen, Amsterdam, Oslo, Prague – lights also blazed brightly, as people sang, kissed, and danced in the streets. In the graveyard that was Warsaw, there was only darkness and silence.'[142] It is hardly surprising there is a lack of trust within a country where so many promises have been broken by 'friends'.

The war almost won, the vital contribution of Polish fighter and bomber squadrons would be soon forgotten. Still flying Lancasters in sorties over Germany, the announcement over the BBC on 13 February 1945 of the Yalta agreements hit them like a thunderbolt of betrayal. Churchill and Roosevelt had formally relinquished Eastern Poland to Stalin and transferred the remainder of the country to a Soviet communist government. Despite terrible losses Polish airmen continued to 'do their duty' but for what cause were they dying now? A number of former Polish prisoners of the Russian gulags in General Anders' 2nd Polish Corps committed suicide on hearing the news. The heroism and sacrifices of the Polish contribution to so many campaigns during the war were consigned to oblivion.

142 Olson & Cloud Ibid., p. 393

In many an officers' mess British fellow pilots cast their eyes to the floor in embarrassment as the treacherous news came over the camp radio. One British officer wept. The presence of Poles in England came in time to be resented by a majority of people and they were urged to return home. The arrival of the glamorous Americans had distracted and seduced many of their former admirers. The Polish Government-in-Exile was no longer recognized by Britain and the United States. A clear expression of sympathy with the Soviet ally had become paramount.

Most Poles elected to stay in Britain rather than go back to a wrecked and ruined country dominated by communists. Many of those who eagerly returned to their families were murdered, imprisoned or tortured during brutal interrogations by the UB.[143] The men in black hats and leather coats were hunting 'collaborators' or spies. A few Polish pilots succeeded in private business. Lest Stalin be offended, survivors were shamefully excluded from the glorious Victory Parade in London mounted almost a year after the conclusion of the war – many wept, relegated to being mere bystanders. A group of Polish officers who remained in Britain, assisted by public donations, arranged a dignified memorial to be erected at RAF Northolt in north-west London to the more than two thousand of their comrades who had sacrificed their lives fighting alongside Britain.

Recognition at anniversaries still eludes the Poles – their flag was absent from the celebrations of the fortieth anniversary of D-day and there was the recent hurried correction of the 'oversight' of omitting the insignia of the Kościuszko and Poznań fighter squadrons from the RAF Battle of Britain memorial on the cliffs of Dover. This for a squadron with more German kills than any other in the RAF.[144] Encouraging redress has been made at Bletchley Park, the former wartime government code and cypher school (Station X)

143 The feared UB, *Urząd Bezpieczeństwa* (Office of Security), was a part of the huge Soviet apparatus known as the MBP or *Ministerstwo Bezpieczeństwa Publicznego* (Ministry of Public Security). The UB's main function was to track down 'collaborators' and 'anti-soviet elements'.

144 Olson & Cloud Ibid., pp. 426–7 Statistics of aircraft destroyed tend to be unreliable and are often revised. The confirmed and probable score for Squadron 303 for the Battle of Britain was 126 and during the entire conflict totalled some 230 enemy aircraft. The 8 operational Polish Fighter Squadrons together destroyed a confirmed and probable total score of over 1,100 enemy aircraft during the course of the war.

in Buckinghamshire. An attractive memorial has been erected to the mathematicians of the Polish Intelligence Service who first broke the 'Enigma' code in 1932 and 'contributed to the allied Victory in World War II'. The brilliant mathematician Alan Turing developed an idea at Bletchley Park originally proposed by Polish cryptanalysts. The Kościuszko squadron continues its illustrious history today as part of the Polish Air Force in NATO.

Poland was the only country on the continent of Europe that neither surrendered nor collaborated with the Nazis from the very beginning to the very end of World War II. The treatment of the Polish forces in England and the country itself by the Allies is one of the low moral watermarks of the conflict. In any discussion I have had on this subject in Poland the 'betrayal' of Yalta still rankles among older Poles and has not been forgiven or forgotten. This wound surely contributes to the inherent scepticism, controversial remarks and 'difficult' behaviour of Poland within the enlarged European Union.

As the wreaths were being laid at Żagań I fell into conversation with a former NCO who had been a prisoner in the camp's East Compound and witnessed the other escape drama, that of the Wooden Horse. He told me that in his hut the eccentric and 'quite nutty' (as he put it) Wing Commander Roger Maw conceived the wooden horse inspired by Homeric accounts of the Greek infiltration of Troy. Maw was noted for inventive gadgetry and an ostentatious manner of dress. When flying a mission he believed he should dress like a foreigner so that he would not be noticed if he had to bale out. When captured he was wearing a bright yellow shirt with a large red handkerchief, grey flannel trousers, Egyptian sandals and pink socks. 'I must have been dressed as the wrong sort of foreigner,' he remarked.

Our plan was to return to the camp and examine the remains of Hut 104 where the entrance to the tunnel called 'Harry' in the 'Great Escape' had been recently uncovered. There was much good-natured argument among the survivors about the location of various buildings such as 'the cooler'. I looked into the historic hole at the mouth of the tunnel, now filled with bricks and broken tiles from the base of the stove. It was a remarkable sight to see my ageing boyhood heroes standing at the ruined entrance to the tunnel surrounded by the world's press. They began stepping out the tragically mistaken distance to the exit using a piece of pre-measured rope.

'How many have you counted, Johnnie?'

'Hundred and thirty-seven.'

'I make it a hundred and twenty-six.'

Sydney Dowse, the most extrovert and theatrical, although not the most popular, launched forth loquaciously about all manner of questionable features and distances. With his monocle he appeared a debonair and dashing RAF 'press on' type playing to the cameras. We retired to have lunch in an army mess tent. A German film crew were visibly discomforted by the endless stream of anti-German, Pythonesque jokes flying about. Genuinely depressing were stories of the chaotic evacuation of the camp during the bitter winter of 1945 in the face of the Soviet advance. Prisoners were forced to pull heavy sledges of food through blizzards and deep snow for fifteen miles. Exhausted, they were often forced to abandon some of it. A Nazi soldier was seen retrieving discarded supplies by a Nazi officer travelling in a motorcycle sidecar. The officer fell into an hysterical rage and shot the soldier dead. The RAF officers developed an intense hatred for German officers after witnessing such summary executions of their own men and came to regard them as 'a species of animal different from ourselves'. The *kriegies* then spent three days travelling by train to another POW camp, crammed into cattle cars fetid with vomit and excrement.

'Shall we try and find Stendhal's house?' Richard asked before we left Żagań. We were wandering in the tattered gardens of Talleyrand's chateau following our adventures with the RAF. To discover one of my favourite French authors had lived in Żagań was astonishing.

In 1813 Stendhal reluctantly accepted a minor appointment as Intendant of Sagan. He would have much preferred to seek happiness in the arms of a beloved Italian mistress in Florence or Rome. In his diary he muses on the nature of travel books. 'A travel diary should be full of sensations, a guidebook devoid of them.'[145] He

145 *The Private Diaries of Stendhal*, 28 June 1813 trans. Richard Sage (London 1955)

found this minor post so boring he borrowed a piano and hired a music teacher to perform Mozart. A cryptic diary entry and a document bearing the name Christiane Biel, unique in the region, indicates that Monsieur Beyle may well have fathered an illegitimate child in Sagan. But there was no mention of his 'having' a woman in the notes of conquests he habitually wrote on his braces.[146] Stendhal fell ill a mere seven weeks after taking up the appointment. Failing to find a cure by 'drinking an extract of aquatic herbs' he abandoned the post and travelled to Dresden. We wandered the streets looking for a plaque or some sign that might indicate his brief sojourn. Impatience drove us back to the chateau where we met two policemen.

'Do you know where the famous French writer Stendhal lived in Żagań?'

'We don't know any writers.'

'He's dead actually.'

'Oh, are you here for the funeral?'

---

146 *Stendhal*, Jonathan Keates (London 1994) p. 155. 'Stendhal' was the pseudonym of the French writer Marie-Henri Beyle, author of the immortal novels *Scarlet and Black* and *The Charterhouse of Parma*.

CHAPTER 18

'Not Upon the Polished Roads of Their Makers' Intention . . .'

–T.E. Lawrence, *Seven Pillars of Wisdom*

'*Na zdrowie*, Mike! Good vodka!'

'*Na zdrowie!*'

I downed another shot of my home-made *Żubrówka* vodka. I was sharing it amongst the other drivers of the Polish Automobile Club as we were interviewed under bright lights.

'Who is the President of the club?' I asked naively. They looked at each other aghast.

'Are you the President, Witek?' one driver with a ponytail asked.

'No, I'm not.'

'Are you, Staś?' This questioner looked like Orson Welles in a Bugatti T-shirt.

'No. Not me.' Everyone looked nonplussed.

'We don't know who the President is and we don't care! We are all leaders here! Do you want to be the President?'

I declined graciously.

Upon returning to Warsaw the problem of parking the old Rolls somewhere safe had become painful and I enlisted the assistance of the automobile club. They promised a space in the Technical Museum as an exhibit, but as usual it required a number of obstacles to be surmounted, not the least of which was the moodiness and whimsical nature of the curator.

'Perhaps he will decide against your car, Mike. You must contact him every time to go out and he may decide against it every day.'

There was a faint possibility of parking in the basement of the former communist party headquarters.

Zosia's husband generously offered me the use of a cramped underground parking space in the centre used by the official drivers of his ministry. Double steel doors led from the street to a courtyard and a red and white striped boom barrier. The guard lived beside it in a shack. A steep ramp led down to another padlocked steel door and a bunker about fifty metres below street level. The car was perfectly safe and I could have free access provided my romantic assignations with Zosia were never discovered. I dreaded to think of the outcome of Polish vengeance on my beautiful machine. I also felt morally uncomfortable about the whole situation. However, I put any reservations well to the back of my mind as there was no other viable alternative.

The first classic car rally around Poland for eighty years was to begin the following week and I had decided to take part. The last international event of this type was won in 1913 by Count Konstanty Broel-Plater in a valveless Benz. The Poles had an illustrious record as racing drivers long before the exploits of their fighter pilots. GP Bugattis were extensively raced in Poland by the wealthy aristocracy in the 1930s at the Lwów Grand Prix (now L'viv in western Ukraine) and in the Tatra Race in the Carpathian mountains. The female Polish grand-prix driver Maria Koumian drove her Bugatti to particularly glamorous public acclaim. In 1952 the German ace Rudolf Caracciola was interviewed at Monte Carlo. When asked which tracks he found most difficult, he answered: 'Definitely Nurburgring, next Monte Carlo, but no ... Lwów, yes Lwów in 1932 ... It was a difficult route, Monte Carlo is a mere velodrome. I remember Count Potocki, oh ... it's an old story ...'

The economic depression of the 1920s did for these great races but failed to demolish the élan of the drivers. The most famous Polish driver of the era was Count Louis Zborowski who raced at Brooklands in the 1920s and lived splendidly in the Palladian stately home Higham Park in Kent. He competed in Bugattis, Aston Martins and his own aero-engined monsters designed with his engineer Clive Gallop, one of the original Bentley Boys. He called each of the four examples of this car Chitty Bang Bang. Ian Fleming was inspired to write the story of the magical car *Chitty Chitty Bang*

Bang based on the Polish Count's romantic exploits the day his son remarked to him, 'Daddy, you love James Bond more than you love me.'[147]

Some sixty historic cars and motorcycles including marques seldom seen by Westerners set off from Warsaw on a course of 1500 kilometres. Richard was to act as navigator and my son Alexander had flown in from Lisbon to bolster his father's wavering resolve. We had first to complete a few bizarre driving tests in Piłsudski Square near the tomb of the Unknown Soldier – balancing the car on a pivoting platform and driving blind in a straight line with a green bag over the driver's head. The reception south along the Vistula was tremendously enthusiastic with people lining the roads throwing rose petals as if we were in the Mille Miglia road race. *'Piękny! Piękny!'* (*'Beautiful! Beautiful!'*) they called as I drove by.

The appearance of a neo-Gothic fantasy castle announced our arrival in Lublin, a city of rich intellectual, religious and cultural heritage. As is customary in Poland the Old Town is surrounded by sterile communist concrete. The Nobel prize-winning novelist Isaac Bashevis Singer paints an eloquent portrait of nineteenth-century Lublin in his powerful novel *The Magician of Lublin.*

The dusk descended. Beyond the city there was still some light, but among the narrow streets and high buildings it was already dark. In the shops, oil lamps and candles were lit. Bearded Jews, dressed in long cloaks and wearing wide boots, moved through the streets on their way to evening prayers. A new moon arose, the moon of the month of Sivan. There were still puddles in the streets, vestiges of the spring rains, even though the sun had been blazing down on the city all day. Here and there sewers had flooded over with rank water; the air smelled of horse and cow dung and fresh milk from the udder. Smoke came from the chimneys; housewives were busy preparing the evening meal: groats with soup, groats with stew, groats with mushrooms ... The

147 In the film the name *Chitty Chitty Bang Bang* comes from the noise the car makes. Actually Count Zborowski named his cars after a bawdy soldiers' song from the Great War concerning officers based in France. They would obtain a weekend pass known as a *chit* to go to Paris and enjoy the delights of certain accommodating ladies. The unusual name *Chitty Bang Bang* is thus readily explained.

world beyond Lublin was in turmoil . . . Jews everywhere were
being driven from their villages . . . But here in Lublin one felt
only the stability of a long-established community.

This original medieval trading city gave rise to its own characteristic form of Renaissance architecture and was one of the most
important centres of Jewish life in Europe. Most importantly it witnessed the signing of the Union of Lublin which established the
Polish–Lithuanian Commonwealth in 1569. In many ways this
republic embodied at a much earlier date similar political ideals to
those that inspired the formation of the European Union. It brought
together democratic principles, civil rights, constitutional law and
remarkable religious tolerance in the finest of political orders. In
1939 almost a third of the total population of Lublin were Jewish.
The largest Talmudic library in the world was located here and a
famous *Yeshiva* (high school) was staffed with distinguished refugee
Jewish teachers from all over Europe.

The scenes of innocently integrated civilization were swept away
forever by the horrors of nearby Majdanek concentration camp.
One exhibit in the fine museum is a barrack block crammed to
bursting with the discarded shoes of Jews. Without signage or commentary, choking with stale odour, this silent testimony to horror is
the most eloquent I have seen in Poland. Clouds of black ravens nest
in the trees, squawking raucously and drifting above the camp like
ashes carried by the wind. A synagogue has recently been renovated
in the city within the elegant yellow-ochre old *Yeshiva* building
where scholars used to study the Talmud. Exhibits for a museum are
being collected mainly from Christian Poles who preserved sentimental objects owned by murdered Jewish friends – a silver ladle,
some broken candlesticks, a powder box kept for sixty years by an
old lady. The mass killing of Jews was regarded by a majority of
Poles as a sign of the depravity of the German conqueror. An unremarked solidarity existed in the face of this common enemy as Poles
waited in fear of their own genocide. Scarcely any traces now remain
of the Jews of Lublin. Their absence haunts ancient courtyards, their
ghosts lean over the old wooden balconies.

The modern city is one of the most vibrant and attractive I have
encountered in the country. The reconstruction of magnificent

Renaissance town houses in the winding warren of streets and old squares is proceeding apace. In summer the streets and sidewalk cafés teem with Mediterranean bustle. A Jewish pub called Mandragora has been opened by a woman with Jewish roots who enthusiastically maintains many ceremonies associated with the culture and imports spices from Israel. The Catholic University of Lublin is the only such institution in East Central Europe and during the communist period remained a repository of Polish Catholic culture.

The following morning I turned the Spirit of Ecstasy towards Zamość, the *città ideale* of the Late Renaissance known as the 'Padua of the North'. An old wood-block print of this star-shaped fortified capital of the estate of Grand Hetman Jan Zamoyski had fascinated me since I had first seen it in the window of a Warsaw antique shop. We left Lublin early, mist rising from the fields, the landscape polished by moist light. The Lublin Upland is a largely unspoilt agricultural region between the Vistula and the Ukrainian frontier in the east, part of the European *latifundia* or great grain estates.

The old car was performing immaculately, wafting characteristically through the countryside with no apparent motive force. The quilted meadows were dressed in summer green. Enormous twin-spired parish churches dominated the flat landscape but one searched in vain for the village that financed their construction. Many single horses, a few harnessed in pairs, ploughed the fields. Surprisingly elderly men plodded behind the animals with the traces slung around their necks, grasping an implement of primitive design, pushing it deep into the earth. Women with their heads wrapped in colourful scarves were sowing seed in an ancient biblical manner, grasping a handful from a hessian bag and casting it in an arc with a wide sweep of the arm. Men dropped potatoes into furrows. These ancient *Polanie* or people of the fields unbend from their work to rise up in silhouette against the wide sky and clumps of birch and willow to gaze vacantly at your passing. I stopped at a village to buy warm fresh bread for breakfast.

No amount of reading prepared me for the exalted architectural impact of Zamość. The town was surrounded by characterless communist concrete but the elegant Baroque spire of the Old Town led me forward. Zamość is the perfect embodiment of the Polish

Renaissance-Mannerist style. The sides of the square are some one hundred metres long, lined with Renaissance houses above vaulted arcades with wrought-iron lamps and plasterwork. They provide cool shade in summer and protection from the severe winter. At night the square was eerie and mysterious with the galleries fitfully illuminated by gas lamps in the shadow of Renaissance pediments. The folk decorations of the Armenian merchants' houses were transformed into grotesque shapes that seemed to possess veiled threats. Hurrying silhouettes were muffled against the chill. Today the architectural spaciousness of the piazza has disappeared under a welter of sponsored brewery umbrellas and alfresco dining.

The city was designed and built in the late sixteenth century by Bernardo Morando of Padua as a work of art and the capital of the estate of Grand Hetman (Commander-in-Chief) Jan Zamoyski (1542–1605), head of one of the most illustrious Polish magnate families and arguably the most powerful Pole in history. A noble Sarmatian portrait of the Chancellor, a man of profound humanist learning who assembled one of the great libraries of Europe and studied at the University of Padua, hangs in the museum.

The city is an expression of the platonic ideal of community life built according to Italian Renaissance theorists intended to reflect the order of the cosmos, the divine music of the spheres. In the six-teenth century the market would have teemed with Jews, Armenians, Turks, Magyars, Ruthenians, Greeks, Italians and even Scotsmen as well as Poles. The city was on an important crossroads on the trade route through Lwów linking Northern Europe with the Black Sea. The city is a perfect realization of the Palladian *bello secreto* of musical harmony and architectural form. For this illustri-ous magnate, the capital of his 'kingdom' (half the size of Belgium) combined a centre of commerce and habitation, a massive fortress, a cultural *academia* (university), a place of religious observance and finally his residence. This 'Latin' capital is a unique survival in Europe.

The town was one of only two fortress cities that managed to withstand the Swedish sieges in the mid-seventeenth century. Although once an important trading hub, today Zamość struggles economically with unemployment as it is no longer on the way to anywhere. Colourful washing made bright splashes of colour above vegetable gardens in Italianate courtyards. Dogs and chickens rooted amongst the wrecks of old American cars. The Zamoyski Palace was turned into a military hospital in 1830 but is now being restored, the equestrian statue of Jan Zamoyski re-erected.

The Poles in the region around Zamość suffered a terrible fate during the Second World War. It was designated the 'First Resettlement Area' of the *Generalgouvernement* of the Nazis. This 'ethnic cleansing' resulted in the resettlement, execution and torture of some 110,000 Polish peasants and the clearing of hundreds of villages. Thousands of Polish children were dragged from the arms of their screaming mothers to be brought up with a new racial identity as Germans. The town was renamed Himmlerstadt and intended to be an outpost of German culture in the east. The Jews were transported to Bełżec and Sobibór extermination camps.

> Mounted police fell like a pack of savages on the Zamość Jewish quarter. It was a complete surprise. The brutes on horseback in particular created a panic; they raced through the streets shouting insults, slashing out on all sides with their whips. Our community then numbered 10,000 people. In a twinkling, without even realizing what was happening, a crowd of 3,000 men, women and children, picked up haphazardly in the streets and in the houses, were driven to the station and deported to an unknown destination. The spectacle, which the ghetto presented after the attack, literally drove the survivors mad. Bodies everywhere, in the streets, in the courtyards, inside the houses; babies thrown from the third or fourth floor lay crushed on the pavements.[148]

Thousands of Polish citizens of the town, including many children, were executed in the Rotunda, a nineteenth-century gunpowder magazine constructed by the Austrians. It lies in a memorial park south of the defensive walls. The road crosses the inevitable railway tracks near the local station and shunting yards. The building is a brick drum with an open arena in the centre covered in cinders. There are cells within the circular walls that are dank and dark,

148 David Mekler quoted in *Zamość Ghetto Aktion Reinhard Camps* (http://deathcamps.org)

reeking of evil and death. Many candles burn before memorial
sculptures but no cosmetic restoration has taken place here since the
war. The damp mould of decay catches in the throat as one wanders
about, spirits sinking lower and lower. The arena is entered through
the original Nazi wooden and barbed-wire gate painted with gothic
German script. Through the barred apertures one can see today's
children laughing happily in the sunshine, paddling in the nearby
lake, and running along paths dusted with wildflowers. The presence of the black night of the soul directly beside the golden
achievements of the Renaissance is a haunting and profound mystery. Poland is unique in these displays of light and utter darkness.

By chance we had arrived during a memorial service. The Polish
Air Force provided a guard of honour. Cinders crunched ominously underfoot. Torches were lit around the memorial as dusk
descended. Carbines were raised and the live rounds fired with a
tremendous flash, smoke and deafening roar, the reports tearing off
the walls in a terrifying amplified explosion that reminded one in a
physical way, like a punch to the abdomen, of Nazi executions. The
brick drum concentrated the sound painfully, acrid smoke filling the
nostrils, brass cartridge cases spinning into the cinders. I circled the
Rotunda looking at the forest of white crosses and the plaques
denoting the camps where the citizens of the 'Padua of the North',
the noblest expression of Renaissance humanism, had been brutally
exterminated.

From Zamość the rally passed through the Roztocze National
Park, the last home of the small, wild Polish horse called the Tarpan.
Sitting in the centre of an open field covered in yellow dandelions
was a tiny, blonde Polish girl with a red ribbon in her hair making a
crown of cornflowers and buttercups. A shaft of sunlight fell
through a gap in the trees creating a golden halo around her head.
Two peasant farmers without teeth engaged me in conversation and
leaped backwards into a pond in rustic surprise when I said I was
from Australia. The forests of huge fir trees (the largest in Poland
with a height of 50m) and magnificent Carpathian beeches give way
to spruce, oak, hornbeam and aspen. The superb lakes support a
huge variety of water-birds. There is an untouched wildness about
the landscape of the eastern borderlands of Poland that is intensely
romantic in its solitude. Yet in the midst of this natural lyricism

tragedy so often lurks. I came upon a car that had passed me at suicidal speed and which had now left the road and slammed into a
tree-trunk. The driver was slumped unconscious or dead over the
wheel, his face crushed and bleeding, his young wife or girlfriend
sitting by the roadside looking at him and weeping – an awful irrup-
tion of reality into my dreams. I stopped at a nearby farmhouse and
with great linguistic difficulty called an ambulance.

Some sixty kilometres from the Ukrainian border we reached the
great palace of Łańcut which also lies on an ancient trade route from
Western Europe to Ruthenia. After the 'cynical surgery' of the third
partition of 1795 this area became part of the Austrian province of
Galicia. We were directed to the usual rotting former communist
accommodation functioning at that time as a violin summer camp.
Łańcut hosts a famous annual music festival. What a contrast
between the beautiful melodies floating from open windows and the
dead flies in our freezing room, the urine running across the floor
from the broken pipes and blocked drains of the communal bathroom. This type of accommodation has happily almost completely
disappeared.

The crush of people around the cars obscured one of the grandest
aristocratic residences in the country and one of the most remarkable in Europe. The palace was one of the few magnate residences
relatively untouched either by the war or the communist period. In
the late sixteenth century a fortified country house stood on the site,
the stronghold of the brigand Stanisław Stadnicki known as 'The
Devil of Łańcut' for his reckless and predatory behaviour. In the
mid-seventeenth century the fabric was altered and expanded into a
palazzo in fortezza by the fabulously wealthy Lubomirski family.
During the Polish Commonwealth they were said to own 360 towns
and possessed greater wealth than many European royal families.
The ubiquitous Dutch baroque architect Tylman van Gameren
modernized the castle, adding the baroque towers with great
copper-sheathed cupolas as well as strengthening the fortifications
against the Turkish threat.

Elżbieta Lubomirska *née* Czartoryska was one of the wealthiest,
most beautiful and cultured women in Warsaw although she suffered from 'excessive sensibility' and a neurasthenic disposition.
Later in life she spent her time at Łańcut ensconced on a chaise

longue in a darkened room with her migraine headaches ministered to by a graceful young Turk. She had shared a sentimental and intellectual intimacy with the young Stanisław Augustus Poniatowski (the last king of Poland) and thoroughly put him through the grinder of jealousy and romantic despair. He wrote mawkishly in his *Mémoires*: 'she seemed to belong to a superior order of being'.[149]

Łańcut is reminiscent of a large English country house but rather more stylish and certainly less straight-laced. Elżbieta transformed the castle into a grand palace worthy of one of the greatest magnate families. A large garden was laid out in the English style and a Florentine artist created a sculpture gallery that displays Roman busts and antique marbles covered by a superb *trompe l'oeil* sunlit pergola covered in vines. Elżbieta's adopted son Henryk Lubomirski appears as an androgynous, cosmetically voluptuous sculpture of *Amor* carved by Antonio Canova. The Turkish suite pulsates in enthralling red, an opulent orientalism casting one back to the Sarmatian heritage of seventeenth-century Poland.

Elżbieta was a good musician and employed an Italian composer and a pupil of Haydn to be the *Kapelmeister* of her private orchestra. She created an exquisite private theatre and staged French plays by Marivaux and sketches (or 'Parades') written by her son-in-law Jan Potocki (1761–1815). This character straight from fiction was an ethnographer, linguist, early balloonist, mystic, oculist and author of the astonishing *Manuscript Found in Saragossa*, a labyrinthine weave of exotic and fantastical tales told by a young army officer.

The Potockis inherited the palace in the early nineteenth century and it 'became a byword for slightly vulgar show and manic entertaining'.[150] Emperor Franz Josef II, Afghan monarchs, Romanian princesses, Daisy von Pless, Madame de Staël and the Duke and Duchess of Kent were all house guests for foxhunts and shooting in company with assorted politicians, celebrities and the wandering refugee aristocracy of France. My concert pianist grand-uncle had taken a few lessons from the great musical pedagogue Theodor

---

149 My account of Elżbieta Lubomirska is derived in part from the superb *The Last King of Poland* by Adam Zamoyski (London 1992)

150 *Poland: A Traveller's Gazetteer*, Adam Zamoyski (London 2001) p. 132

Leschetizky who was born in the castle in 1830, his father being music master to the Potockis. In Vienna he was the renowned teacher of some of the greatest pianists of the age including Ignacy Jan Paderewski, Ignaz Friedman and Artur Schnabel.

The unique carriage museum has, next to a collection in Paris, the most extensive assemblage of private equipage in the world, including the elegant *calèche* reputed to have been used by Chopin. Sleighs of basket-work, gilded and upholstered in green velvet and deeply lined with fur, remind one of races across the winter ice in the novels of Pasternak or Tolstoy. The walls of the museum are ornamented with hunting trophies, including a rather unpleasant giraffe severed mid-neck and mounted vertically. The Potockis retained the palace until 1944 when the dashing Alfred Potocki was forced to load 14 railways freight cars with precious objects and despatch them ahead of the Soviet Army to Vienna, Lichtenstein and finally France. They were related to nearly all the crowned heads of Europe, which ensured the survival of the palace (assisted by a sign hung on the gate reading National Museum), but the communists forbade the return of its treasures to Poland. Despite the depredations of war Łańcut gives a unique and breathtaking intimation of the splendour and wealth of Polish magnate families.

We were treated to a fine chamber music concert in the *Sala Balowa* the first evening as part of the annual music festival. A number of priests, bishops, and archbishops had chosen to attend a performance of Pergolesi's *Stabat Mater* and Tchaikovsky's *Souvenirs de Florence*. The elderly Princess Potocka was present but seemed rather *distraite*. In this beautiful Aigner ballroom I could imagine an elegant past audience of Polish officers, ministers, artists and revolutionary writers dancing with radiant women in silk and jewels as guests of the Potockis. My body aching from a fast and reckless morning ride on their hunting estate near Julin was now bathed and relaxed. Under the chandeliers listening to a sentimental Wieniawski *Polonez* with the keenest pleasure, I recalled the forest rushing past, the pounding of hooves, the slight fear of the unknown as I too dreamed of a Polish mistress.

Early next morning we left Łańcut. The rally was heading into the far east corner of the country and suddenly took an unsealed road outside of the town. At the bottom of an incline, the ruts and undulations of a dry stream bed appeared to present no particular danger. I overcooked my approach speed and the car violently bottomed. The unmodified suspension is rather soft and I was forever clouting obstacles – hidden spikes, stones, culverts. A frightful roaring came from the engine. The underside was intact but I had struck a rock and broken the left bank of the exhaust manifold at the elbow. Experience has taught me that although they are strong, nothing is simple to repair on a Rolls-Royce. We were 900 kilometres east of Berlin and in deep trouble. Some Polish children, as usual, broke my despair.

'Excuse me, sir. Can we take a picture of your beautiful car?'

The rally support vehicle led the car like a wounded lion, growling and vengeful, to a local mechanic in the town. A man was welding a pair of enormous wrought iron gates from the Potocki palace. Sundry dilapidated sheds contained a riot of ancient lathes and other metal-working machines. His round, fresh-faced wife immediately offered me a hearty bean stew. I was despondently hunched over a bowl of it in the kitchen lamenting our lot with my son Alexander when Richard came in.

'Michael. Good news, old chap. There is a Polish mechanic downstairs who worked on Rolls-Royce cars in Chicago.'

'Get out! I'm in no mood for jokes,' I shouted ill temperedly.

'No, I'm serious. He repaired the car owned by the mayor of Chicago.'

'Richard, will you please stop torturing me and go away!' Jan the mechanic stood in the doorway of the farmhouse. He was a gangly, hyperventilating man with a cracked spectacle lens and a comforting smile who told me he 'spoke American'.

'No big video! I fix mayor of Chicago Royce-a-Rolls when mafia blow him up with a bomb. No big deal this repair. Józef he help me. No big video!'

The man working on the gates wandered in our direction and silently crawled under the car. Jan clearly knew a great deal about the rear of the vehicle where the bomb had exploded but seemed less certain about the engine compartment. Anyway it was now well out of my hands. The Poles had taken over. The repair become a question of national pride. Correct size tools were the main problem as my carefully assembled English set had been stolen in the Poznań robbery. The rally had continued on south towards the town of Sanok and left us to our own devices. The two-way radio of the *Kommandor* suddenly squawked.

'Krzysztof?'

'Yes. What's up?'

Squawk.

'It's Konrad. Where are you?'

'120 kilometres from Łańcut. Why are you asking?'

Squawk.

'We need some English tools for the Rolls-Royce immediately!'

'OK. I'll bring them in a flash! Like bringing blood to the wounded!'

Darkness. Torrential rain of a wild Polish summer storm. Vodka. Five men push a heavy car half into an ill-lit garage with a chicken coop and a crazy tethered Pekinese. The tools arrive but none fit the bolts as they have rusted slightly smaller over the years.

'No big video, Mike! My cousin has a factory and will make tool for us. I will measure with micrometer. We go home now for dinner. You sleep my place! It will be big party!'

We returned to his modest home for a vast meal which confirmed with a vengeance the adage that in Poland guests are considered 'God in the house'.

The next morning after a huge breakfast we returned to the garage and the tool was duly delivered. Its handmade appearance looked none too promising but it fitted perfectly. Each bolt was first hit a terrific blow with an iron bar and sledgehammer to loosen it. I became nervous indeed of the beautiful machine and moved from foot to foot with a furrowed brow.

'Go eat apricots from tree, Mike. You are make me nervous! Stop looking and worrying. We done this to Russian diggers and tanks. No big video!'

Mechanics seemed to be arriving from all over Poland to work on the car. Giving unsolicited advice is a Polish trait that can be helpful but can often be conflicting. Two Poles and three opinions, it is said. The exhaust manifold was soon off and they hot-welded the cast metal after truing up the faces by eye on a grinding wheel. An art in itself. Russian tank gaskets were trimmed and glued to the faces. The repair came together perfectly and by late afternoon the work was finished.

Jan was descended from Austrian stock who had inhabited Łańcut for many generations. While talking of the large number of priests in his family he took me on a tour of the 'hidden' town. First to the parish church where both mechanics had repaired icons, crosses and gates. The seldom visited dusty tombs of the Potockis were shown us by an old lady in headscarf, thick woollen socks and clogs. Then to the presbytery of a priest who had courageously concealed Solidarity activists hiding in the nearby forest in the crypt of his three-hundred-year-old wooden church. He had been arrested and tortured many times during martial law but had never become a collaborator, unlike many priests whose shady pasts are now being revealed. He lifted a lighted candle aloft for me to inspect the ancient polychrome decoration in the cavernous roof. This intelligent, articulate and handsome man with a hint of subversiveness was clearly a character from an unwritten Graham Greene novel. He had many pretty female callers while we drank tea, vivacious young ladies who became innocently flirtatious in his company.

Another celebratory night followed.

In the morning we were packing the car and about to leave when a voice erupted from the house.

'You don't leave, Mike! You must wait my brothers.'

I was getting impatient to rejoin the rally that was now hundreds of kilometres distant and camped by a lake. We waited. Seated in the car and poring over a map, I suddenly felt drops of water falling on my face. I thought it was raining. I looked around to see two priests, Jan's brothers, dressed in surplice and soutane, blessing the car with holy water.

'We come to bless your car for safe journey!'

Richard, Alexander and I were still not permitted to leave until we had consumed yet another enormous lunch. Some of my favourite Polish food appeared – *żurek* (sour rye flour soup with sausage and hard-boiled egg), *naleśniki* (pancakes with sweet or savoury filling), the fantastically popular *pierogi ruskie* (dumplings shaped like ravioli filled with savoury cheese served with chopped fried smoked bacon. The sweet variety with blueberries and slightly sour cream are superb) and *bigos* (a 'hunter' stew of sauerkraut and various types of meat, sausage and mushrooms). The meal concluded with coffee and *pączki* (a closed doughnut with sugar glaze filled with rose-flavoured jam).

An unaccustomed joy entered the proceedings. Jan and Józef charged us nothing for the repair or the two full days accommodation and food. We had experienced some of the finest qualities of Poles – emotional warmth and support in distress, solidarity, overwhelming hospitality and acres of food, the ability to improvise solutions in impossible circumstances and a final flourish of the Catholic Church. A big video indeed.

CHAPTER 19

The Lost Domains

The beautiful and seemingly innocent eastern borderlands region of Poland through which we were driving had witnessed some of the worst atrocities of the Second World War. The rally did not cross into Ukraine but some months before I had travelled independently to Kiev. At the Mikhail Bulgakov[151] house in the capital I was horrified to see posters of Ukrainian babies impaled on Polish bayonets. In a Warsaw museum I had seen posters of Polish babies impaled on Ukrainian bayonets. This shocked and confused outsider had been confronted for the first time with the fraught history of Polish–Ukrainian relations.

Poland's attitude to its eastern neighbours is at least as important as its relationship with the West since the country now forms the longest eastern frontier of the European Union. National myths and metahistories, accusations and counter-accusations, abound on all sides. The more one examines political frontiers the more one realizes they are an illusion and that the cultural borders lie elsewhere.

Refuting a myth is like dancing with a skeleton: one finds it hard to disengage from the deceptively lithe embrace once the music has begun, and one soon realises that one's own steps are what is keeping the old bones in motion.[152]

---

151 Mikhail Bulgakov (1891–1940) was a writer born in Kiev to Russian parents. He is the author of the masterpiece *The Master and Margarita*, a satirical fantasy novel. Banned but widely read in *samizdat* form it unflinchingly criticized the Stalinist regime and secured his place as one of the greatest of Russian writers.

152 *The Reconstruction of Nations: Poland, Ukraine, Lithuania, Belarus 1569–1999*, Timothy Snyder (New Haven & London 2003) p. 10. An award-winning, scholarly and brilliant account of the relatively unknown complexities and suffering of the nations of East Central Europe through World War Two as they approached membership of the European Union.

Compared with the war on the Western Front, the Second World War in the East was vastly more bloody, barbarous and cruel.

When the Russian army crossed the Polish frontier on 17 September Poland ceased to exist. Jews and Poles were vilified by both Nazis and Soviets. 'The 'racial enemy' of the one became virtually indistinguishable from the 'class enemy' of the other.'[153] The Soviet deportations of some one and a half million Poles in 1939–41 to the horrors of Siberian labour camps is well remembered in Poland but almost forgotten elsewhere in the light of the later better-publicized Nazi atrocities against Jews. The same story of cattle cars festooned with excrement and corpses, lack of food, summary executions and dismemberments but with the added inconceivable torture of mining in Arctic temperatures. This murderous policy resulted in the deaths of perhaps three quarters of a million Poles before the amnesty was granted in 1941 when Stalin 'changed sides'.[154] Accurate casualty figures in the chaos of war will never be known but let it never be forgotten that one in five Poles lay dead at the conclusion of that terrible conflict. Some six million Poles died during the course of it, of which almost three million were Polish Jews.

For their part, the Ukrainians suffered first from Soviet occupation in 1939, followed by the Nazis in 1941 (the *Wehrmacht* were ordered to live from the land), only to be reoccupied by the Soviets in 1944. In a gesture of the grimmest irony Ukrainian Jews fled the Soviets into the arms of the Nazis hoping for sanctuary only to find the Holocaust. 'War, occupation, hunger, reprisals, deportations, and genocide defined the situation within which Poles and Ukrainians lived for six long years.'[155]

Yet there was a marked absence of solidarity between them. The murderous behaviour of the occupiers markedly influenced their attitudes to each other. As ideas of establishing a Ukrainian nation state took hold, relations were blighted by bouts of vicious and bloodthirsty ethnic cleansing on both sides. In 1943 in Volhynia and

---

153 *God's Playground: A History of Poland* Volume II, Norman Davies (Oxford 2005) p. 329

154 Estimates of the number of deportations vary considerably. For more on this tragic 'forgotten holocaust', *God's Playground: A History of Poland* Volume II pp. 331–334

155 Op.cit., Snyder p. 155

Galicia (Western Ukraine) the Ukrainian Insurgent Army (UPA) accused all Poles of being 'Stalin–Hitler agents' and displayed the usual catalogue of human barbarity – entire villages wiped out, dismemberment, the burning down of churches full of worshippers, crucifixions, flaying alive and tearing out of hearts from the ribcage. Bloody Polish vengeance and brutality in the face of these atrocities resulted in the outbreak of the Ukrainian–Polish civil war late in 1943 – a war within a war. Hundreds of thousands of civilians died as a result and millions were displaced. As part of the Jewish Final Solution the Ukrainians 'collaborated' with the Nazis in the murder of some two hundred thousand Volhynian Jews hoping it might assist in the quest for national independence.[156] After Yalta, Poland lost the cities of Lwów (L'viv) and Wilno (Vilnius) and gained Wrocław (Breslau) and Gdańsk (Danzig). Between 1944 and 1946 some three quarters of a million Poles and Jews from the Soviet Ukraine were resettled in Poland. The NKVD insisted that 'whoever doesn't go to Poland goes to Siberia'.

In the other direction almost half a million Ukrainians, Lemkos and Boykos (Carpathian Mountain peoples from the far south-east of Poland or Western Ukraine)[157] were forcibly 'repatriated' to the Soviet Union by Polish communists assisted by Polish partisans. A delegate from the Council of Ministers in Warsaw commented in reply to Ukrainian objections, 'we have a tendency to be a national state and not a state of nationalities.' Such an attitude was the political antithesis of the multicultural ideals of the old Polish–Lithuanian Commonwealth. Mickiewicz would have been horrified. In early 1947 the appalling words 'final solution' were used once again but this time in regard to the Ukrainians by the Poles. 'Operation Vistula' was launched in the name of establishing a Polish nation state and resolving the Ukrainian problem 'once and for all'. Soviet agents were profoundly implicated in the planning. 'In terms of the number of people repressed, imprisoned, sentenced to death, and actually killed, "Operation Vistula" was the most massive exercise of terror

---

156 The complex and horrifying story of the ethnic cleansing of Western Ukraine 1939–45 and that of South Eastern Poland 1945–47 is exhaustively recounted in Chapters 8, 9 and 10 of Op.cit., Snyder pp. 154–214. Essential reading for 'Western' Europeans who wish to understand the national mentality of this part of East Central Europe.

157 Interestingly, the pop artist Andy Warhol was a Lemko.

by the Polish communist regime during the entirety of its existence.'[158] Some 150,000 Ukrainians were resettled west of the Vistula River and the centuries old regions of Galicia and Volhynia ceased to exist. 'Both ends of the gun are transforming: there is perhaps no experience so nationalizing as to have been both cleansed and cleanser. Such people have something to remember and something to forget, something to grieve and something to justify.'[159] The nation state of Poland had become 'crushingly Polish'.

Before Richard and I left Warsaw for Kiev simplistic warnings concerning the projected visit came thick and fast.

'There is an epidemic of diphtheria! Wash your hands!'

'The milk is radioactive. Fallout from the Chernobyl disaster! Don't drink it!'

'Kiev glows in the dark!'

'They'll murder you! You might not come back and then where will we be!' from the ever thoughtful Mr Fukowski.

The hospitality of the host family in Kiev was overwhelming and we were permitted the use of the old Institute of Physics Mercedes from Kiev University. Independent travel in Ukraine was rare. Cars and petrol were scarce, fuel being exchanged for payment in vodka in a complex barter system by the roadside.

Despite the destruction of the Second World War, the large complex of cathedrals, bell towers and caves known as the Kiev-Pechersk Lavra was breathtakingly beautiful. Founded as a cave monastery in 1051, it now houses the residence of the head of the Ukrainian Orthodox Church. Our elderly female guide gave a graphic account of the Mongol raid in 1240 led by Batu Khan who sacked Kiev. Whilst we gazed into a ragged hole above an entrance tunnel she rendered the screaming horses, tumbling walls, gouged eyes, boiling oil, skewered monks and general mayhem in a long and tremendous pantomime display lasting several hours.

After touring the city, we drove the ancient Mercedes through desperately poor countryside, past nightmare factories spewing toxic fumes, avoiding potholes that could swallow a truck, to the

158 Op.cit., Snyder p. 200
159 Op. cit., Snyder p. 207

forgotten but culturally rich town of Berdichev. This historic and seemingly deserted West Ukrainian town about 120 miles south-west of Kiev was once part of Poland. In the nineteenth century it was ninety per cent Jewish and the second-largest community in Russia before the Holocaust. Only remnants of this rich Jewish heritage remain in the town where the 'Final Solution' began its great acceleration in September 1941 with the murder of 30,000 Jews.[160]

In 1768 the fortified Catholic monastery was under siege to the Russians. The defending Poles were led by the dashing young cavalry officer General Kazimierz Pułaski (1747–79), dressed in a jacket of elk-skin and braid. Although surrendering after two weeks with fifteen hundred defenders he was a fearless upholder of the heroic Polish battle cry 'For your freedom and ours!' Pułaski was born at Winiary near Warka, about forty miles from Warsaw. The town is on the poetic Pilica river, which flows through acres of flowering orchards in spring. Incredibly Pułaski once rode from Paris to Istanbul with some youthful supporters to assist the Turks against the Russians in the hope they would advance the cause of Poland. The 'father of the American cavalry' was immortalized by a 'magnificent death' at the Battle of Savannah during the American War of Independence. Modern Poles inflamed by vodka in an access of heroic nostalgia still shout '*Na Berdyczów*!' ('To Berdichev!') and thump the table and stamp the floor.

For many generations from the fourteenth century the town with its impregnable castle was owned by the noble Polish Tyszkiewicz family. The great pianists Anton Rubinstein and Vladimir Horowitz[161] were born in Berdichev and some sources indicate Chopin spent time there. Despite strenuous enquiries, the town knows nothing of the birth in 1857 of one of England's greatest writers, Joseph Conrad (born Teodor Józef Konrad Korzeniowski),

---

160 *The Bones of Berdichev: The Life and Fate of Vasily Grossman*, John Garrard and Carol Garrard (New York 1996) p. 342. A passionate account of the rarely chronicled Holocaust in Ukraine. The mass graves at Berdichev have still to be exhumed. *Life and Fate*, Vasily Grossman (London 1985) is one of the great literary masterpieces of the twentieth century. It chronicles the many aspects of life under the Soviet totalitarian regime including the liquidation of the Berdichev ghetto in September 1941. Suppressed in the Soviet Union for many years, it is a Tolstoyan panorama of what Osip Madelshtam termed the 'wolfhound century'.

161 Some sources indicate Kiev as his birthplace.

although a plaque does celebrate the marriage there of Honoré de Balzac to the Polish noblewoman Countess Ewelina Hańska. Their love story is one of the greatest in French literature.

In 1832 Balzac was living in Paris and received an anonymous letter of appreciation from, at that time, impossibly remote Ukraine mysteriously signed *L'Étrangère*. His imagination aroused, an increasingly passionate relationship developed between the writer and the married Countess, carried on mainly by correspondence. Balzac was overwhelmed by his extended visit to her palatial though isolated Palladian mansion with its thousands of serfs and rolling fields of grain situated on vast Ukrainian estates at Wierzchownia near Berdichev. In *La Cousine Bette* he created the Polish nobleman Count Wenceslas Steinbock and wrote perceptively of Poles: ' . . . for if you show a Pole a precipice, he is bound to leap it. As a nation they have the very spirit of cavalry; they fancy they can ride down every obstacle and come out victorious.'[162]

All his fantasies of beauty, mysticism, nobility and wealth were satisfied by 'the only woman I have ever loved'. He was in childish awe of her aristocratic background: she was the grand-niece of Marie Leszczyńska, Queen of France, consort to Louis XV. However, seventeen years of tortured waiting were to pass before the simple marriage ceremony that took place early one morning in 1850 at the church of St Barbara in Berdichev, 'gleaming with snow and resounding with bells'. Both were ill – Mme Hańska with chronically swollen feet and Balzac was breathless with a serious heart problem and could hardly see. Barbey d'Aurevilly observed of Countess Hańska 'that she was worth of any folly . . . Her beauty was imposing and noble, somewhat massive, a little fleshy, but even in stoutness she retained a very lively charm which was spiced with a delightful foreign accent and a striking hint of sensuality . . .'[163]

Critically ill, Balzac returned by coach with her and a vast amount of luggage to Paris, a nightmare journey through the clinging mud of spring. He would sit in the rain watching sixteen men dig the coach

162 *La Cousine Bette*, Honoré de Balzac (1846) trans. James Waring (London 1991)
163 Quoted in *Prometheus: The Life of Balzac*, André Maurois (London 1965) p. 555

out time after time. Dresden, usually travelled in six days, took a month. He wanted to place her in the Aladdin's cave of a mansion he had prepared in the Rue Fortunée and sent messages ahead to his mother regarding the position of cushions, flowers and pillows on the beds. In a scene worthy of one of his own novels, just before his arrival his manservant had gone berserk: he had partly wrecked the glittering interior and was found crouched gibbering in a corner. With happiness at last within his grasp, at the height of his powers, the *Comédie Humaine* unfinished, Balzac died like one of own his ill-fated characters just three months later on 18 August 1850. He had written presciently 'I shall die the day before I achieve my desire.'

A great shout went up, bottles of champagne were opened and a silk tie with muffler motif presented when we finally rejoined the rally at Solina on the shores of a large lake, gateway to the south-east region known as the Bieszczady. The summer rainstorms were torrential and we had been forced to pull over on a number of occasions.

En route we drove through the seldom visited town of Przemyśl on the River San about seven kilometres from the Ukrainian border. The Renaissance burgher houses and baroque churches that survive on the winding streets that climb the hills remind one it was once an important and elegant Habsburg trading town on the way to L'viv. A vodka drunk with an amusing smile gave a slow, solemn turning salute as we passed. Twelve different languages were spoken here and newspapers published in four. From 1853 to 1899 a huge fortress was constructed which at the outbreak of the Great War was the main point of defence for the north-eastern region of the Austro-Hungarian Empire. The outer ring of forty-two forts was forty-five kilometres long and the inner ring is a unique survival in Europe.

The fall of the fort to a Russian siege early in 1915 implicated the notorious Austrian homosexual spy Alfred Redl. Born in L'viv in 1864 he was the father of many modern espionage techniques – secret recording of conversations onto wax cylinders, mail intercepts, miniature cameras, lifting fingerprints and shadowing suspected traitors. He rose to the exalted rank of Colonel and Chief of Intelligence for the Austro-Hungarian Army. He was considered honourable and highly intelligent, a model officer and an excellent comrade who frequented elegant society. His parlous financial affairs (he lacked the independent means indispensable for the Austrian officer class) and his need to conceal his sexual proclivities meant he was open to blackmail and the Russians successfully 'turned' him. He thoroughly sabotaged his own intelligence services before the outbreak of the Great War whilst simultaneously being hailed as a great patriot.

Austria has always respected titles and a blind eye was turned to his 'kept' lover, deftly introduced as his 'nephew', a dashing young cavalry officer named Lieutenant Stefan Hromodka whom he kept in a luxurious apartment, together with horses and a Daimler motor car. An unclaimed letter containing cash led to the unmasking of Redl, whose activities were a major factor in the defeat of Austria in the Great War. In May 1913 he was tracked to a hotel where officers of the General Staff confronted him and then quitted the room leaving a pistol on the table for him to do the honourable thing. Perfumed letters, women's clothing, pink whips, hair dye, photographs of male nudes in snakeskin frames and state secrets were found after the shot rang out and the whole matter was hushed up by a funeral with full military honours. It was explained that Colonel Redl was a victim of 'mental overexertion & severe neurasthenia'[164]

Passing on from Przemyśl through dense forests ringing with birdsong one comes upon a landscape that belongs to a slower, more rustic and carefree period. Hundreds of Poles were sowing seed in the fields, their rising silhouettes etched against the distant horizon. Narrow-gauge railway engines painted in bright red livery accompanied us beside the highway. Tiny tots climbed onto horse-drawn carts full of hay or grass, swinging onto the mounds of green with screams of pleasure, pulling at their white bobble hats, colourful scarves and knitted jackets. Well-dressed scarecrows wearing Russian caps dotted the freshly ploughed fields. The whole scene was medieval and bucolic, life moving to the rhythm of the seasons, preparing me for the castle that lay ahead.

---

164 The brilliant film *Colonel Redl* was directed in 1985 by the Hungarian István Szabó, starring Klaus Maria Brandauer as Redl in one of his most powerful and charismatic performances. The film was a Jury prize-winner at Cannes in 1985.

The Castle of Krasiczyn near Przemyśl is one of the unknown late Renaissance-Mannerist architectural gems of Europe – a building that is dazzling on first sight. This elaborate and exotic statement of the noble Sarmatian myth is an exuberant display of Polish Commonwealth excess. I was reminded of the 'sham chivalric' Bolsover Castle in Derbyshire that possesses a similar air of theatrical pageantry. It took some twenty years to complete the edifice for the powerful borderland noble Stanisław Krasicki. Based on the square, an assortment of refined Polish attics of great artistry are mounted on walls and towers and are among the most beautiful in Poland. The Sarmatian lifestyle of self-assertion and pietism are evoked by the *sgraffito* wall decoration of violent boar-hunting scenes, emperors and kings in Turkish costume, and by four towers of fantastical inventiveness named God, Pope, King and Nobility, the preoccupations of the *szlachta.*

The castle interiors were completely razed by fire and Russian barbarism during the Second World War. What remains of the once vast park contains a collection of exotic trees assembled by the Sapieha family in the eighteenth century – Polish larch, Podole smoke trees, Canadian hemlock and rare pines. The mentor of Pope John Paul II, Prince Adam Stefan Cardinal Sapieha, was born here in 1867. He operated a seminary in secret under the noses of the Nazis in Kraków where the future Pope was able to complete his training. The Sapieha family planted seven trees according to a charming old Lithuanian custom – an oak to commemorate the birth of a son and a lime that of a daughter.

Further on the sleepy town of Sanok is an unlikely place to possess the largest collection of Ruthenian icons next to the Tretyakov Gallery in Moscow. The early-fourteenth-century icons are fine indeed and one can follow the development of the school of Ukrainian icon painting through the centuries. Most of these icons had been saved from ruined *cerkwie*[165] after villages were destroyed

---

165 Even the definition of this word in English reflects the tumultuous history of the Ukrainian–Polish borderlands. Broadly speaking, the Polish word *cerkiew* or Ukrainian *tserkva* is used for a place of worship of the Eastern Rite Church whether Greek Catholic or Orthodox. The Polish word *kościół* or Ukrainian *kostel* is normally used for the Roman Catholic Church. Such distinctions and their allied passions could not exist in English. In Poland many *cerkwie* have become converted to Roman Catholic *kościoły* with attendant feelings of loss for Ukrainian Orthodox Christians in the local population, unacknowledged victims of the resettlements of Yalta.

during the war or abandoned during the resettlements and 'Operation Vistula' or simply neglected under communism. There is an extensive *skansen* in Sanok with many kinds of country buildings preserved following the region's turbulent and violent history. Another fine collection of Ruthenian[166] icons shelters among the windmills and wooden houses.

As we left the town accompanied by furiously running children, I realized that the reception of the car in Poland was unexpectedly positive, quite free of the usual negative associations of a Rolls. Boys fell off their bicycles as we passed and people rushed out of cafés to stare. Endless questions concerning engine capacity, petrol consumption and price followed my arrival anywhere. Much leaping back and low whistles at the answers. '*Jezus Maria!*' One 'Polish professor' gave me a detailed and impromptu lecture on the composition of the different metals used in the radiator since Sir Henry Royce began designing these cars.

'We are so proud that you bring it in Poland!'

I flinched when bystanders appeared to throw something at the car but it turned out to be flowers. Quite a contrast to the last time I had driven in it London when an Irishman in an alcoholic haze peed on the wheels while mumbling obscenities when I was stranded at a red light.

166 Ruthenian is a geographical and cultural term now commonly used to refer to Western Ukraine. Needless to say when dealing with this part of Europe a truly accurate definition is far more complicated than that.

CHAPTER 20

'A Kind of Volcanic Explosion of Mankind's Spiritual Magma'

From the Ukrainian guidebook to L'viv,
The Elegies of L'viv by Yuri Nykolyshyn

Many years after this adventure, waiting in the rain outside the Ukrainian Consulate in Warsaw to apply for a visa to L'viv (Lwów), I fell into conversation with a thin Australian pensioner wearing sunglasses and maniacally scratching his bottom. He assured me he was a resident of Sebastopol in the Crimea and was forced to travel for forty-five hours to Warsaw every three months to obtain a tourist visa to continue living there.

'Tolstoy wrote the marvellous *Sebastopol Sketches*, if I remember,' I commented somewhat pretentiously.

'Yeah. Sebasto's great, mate. There's a lot over there. I can live in comfort on me Ozzie state pension but not back home. Cunts.'

A woman emerged from the office and there was a flurry as more than one wet applicant attempted to enter and was roughly forced back into the rain by the burly doorman.

'Me marriage broke up in Sydney and I had a friend over there. Can't speak the lingo but always find someone to translate *words*.'

'Don't you find life difficult? Seems a bloody long way from Australia.'

'I've had me problems, mate. Fell down some stairs after more than a few vodkas and ended up in a Uko hospital with concussion. Had a fight and ended up in a Uko prison. This bloke spat in the street. I hate that. I comes up and says to him "You dirty bastard!"

and then I fuckin' decked him. Bang. Bastard. And I've got a bitch of a girlfriend. Gold digger. We went to this Uko health spa, a real shit-hole with flies and rats in the dunny.' My turn to enter. A welcome reprieve from one aspect of my heritage.

The girl behind the glass tapped officiously on the desk as I handed across my application forms. I intended to spend a day in L'viv, a magnificent although dilapidated city that had been Polish for some six hundred years but was now just across the border in Ukraine. It was lost to Poland as a result of the Yalta accords and modern Poles feel the loss deeply and visit it in droves. Although Ukraine became an independent state in 1991, the detritus of communist bureaucracy still hangs heavy in the air. I sighed audibly as the documentation seemed impossible to arrange from Warsaw.

'What's the problem?' she said aggressively.

'It seems a lot of trouble just for a one-day tour.'

'If you don't want a visa, you can leave,' she said and pointed to the exit.

The border crossing was a grim reminder of what Poland has left behind. Bored unshaven men stood in groups smoking while battered Ladas packed with 'families' and Polish goods stretched in impatient queues kilometres long. Resentful Ukrainian customs officers slowly gazed into faces and lethargically turned over papers and the contents of car boots. The crossing took about five hours, a great improvement on the three-day wait confronting the road traveller in the days of the rally.

L'viv is only seventy kilometres from the Polish frontier. Ukrainian nationalists believe it has been Ukrainian ever since Prince Danylo of the Ruthenian Duchy of Halych-Volhynia founded the city in 1256 and named it after his son Lev. It came under Polish domination in the fourteenth century and remained predominantly Polish until the first partition of the country in 1772 when, known as Lemberg, it became the capital of the Austro-Hungarian Kingdom of Galicia. Between the wars it was the second largest city in Poland. The commercial and cultural importance of the city, its former ethnic diversity and remarkably rich architectural fabric have put the medieval historic centre on the UNESCO World Heritage list.

Almost inevitably the first point of call was the Lychakiv cemetery, one of the most beautiful in Europe, a place where Polish–Ukrainian relations can be read like a historical novel loaded with all the tragedy of bloody conflict. Monumental Art Nouveau sculptures of power-ful rhythmic grace decorate many of the thousands of Polish and Ukrainian tombs of famous writers, mathematicians, insurgents and soldiers. The collapse of the Austro-Hungarian empire and the rise of nationalism in East Central Europe after the Great War resulted in 'a series of nursery brawls. In 1918–21 six wars were fought concur-rently.'[167] The Polish–Ukrainian War began in 1918 in L'viv where there was a majority Polish and Jewish population while Ukrainians dominated the surrounding countryside. This six-month-conflict for the control of the city was fought between the forces of the West Ukrainian People's Republic initially against local Polish self-defence units which were later supported by the regular Polish Army. Among the civilian defenders there were over a thousand high-school students and youths. Their great heroism and fighting ability earned these young people the name 'The Eaglets of Lwów'. A war cemetery constructed to honour them was unveiled in 1934 and became a potent symbol of Polish presence in the L'viv region and Eastern Borderlands.

During the Second World War tens of thousands of Jews living in L'viv were murdered by the Nazis or died in pogroms, the ghetto or in the nearby labour and extermination camp in Janowska Street. One of the worst Nazi atrocities occurred in the city in July 1941 when forty-five eminent Polish professors and members of their families were shot as part of the wholesale destruction of Polish cul-ture. The execution site was the Wulecki Heights, by a terrible chance visible to family members who survived the *Aktion*. The wife of the Professor of Mathematics at the Lwów Institute of Technology, Dr Antoni Łomnicki, described the scene of her hus-band's execution from her third floor apartment: 'I saw how they collapsed after each volley of shots. I stood there "frozen to the floor", semi-conscious, watching the spectacle.'[168] The brilliant

167 *God's Playground: A History of Poland* Volume II, Norman Davies (Oxford 2005) p. 292
168 *Mord Profesorów Lwowskich w Lipcu roku 1941* Zygmunt Albert trans. Jan Rudzki (Wrocław 1991)

Professor of French Literature and former guiding light of the Green Balloon cabaret in Kraków, Dr Tadeusz 'Boy' Żeleński, was shot on the terrible night of 4 July.

By 1959 Ukrainians made up a major proportion of the population, followed by Russians with Poles and Jews only a tiny minority. The Russians claimed it was a place where 'the proud veil of European culture masks the offensive face of a capitalist barbarian'.[169] The neglected cemetery to the Eaglets was desecrated by the Soviets in 1971 when war graves were bulldozed to make way for a truck park and garbage dump. After Ukrainian independence in 1991 there was a move to reconstruct this war cemetery.

In 2005, in a remarkable gesture of reconciliation, the Presidents of Ukraine and Poland attended the consecration and opening of the restored L'viv Eaglets Cemetery and unveiled memorials to the Polish and Ukrainian soldiers who had died during the Great War. This followed the support given by Poland to the 'Orange Revolution' in Ukraine, the popular demonstration against the compromised Presidential elections of 2004. 'The reconciliation of Ukraine and Poland is the last brick in the building of peace and harmony in Europe,' Mr Yushchenko, the President of Ukraine, said. He continued, 'Without a free Ukraine, there is no free Poland and without a free Poland, there is no independent Ukraine.' Mr Kwaśniewski, President of Poland, declared, 'We will build the spirit of peace, dialogue, unity and partnership.' This gesture has not been forgotten or forgiven by the Kremlin and has contributed significantly to the present testy relations between Russia and Poland.

The romantic decay of this once elegant city is reminiscent of Kraków or a crumbling Vienna. The most commanding building and focal point of the city is the impressive Opera and Ballet Theatre, a Viennese neo-Renaissance confection redolent of imperial Habsburg opulence and excess. Stone lions, potent symbol of the city, are everywhere – recumbent, asleep, smiling, snarling, holding a caduceus, rampant on dissolving palace walls towering

169 L'viv: A City in the Crossroads of Culture ed. John Czaplicka. Special Issue Harvard Ukrainian Studies, vol.24 (2000) p. 208

above narrow streets. The cobbled roads are almost undrivable, cars with wrecked suspensions rattle past, tram tracks stand dangerously proud of the surface. Beautiful girls in the shortest of skirts with long tanned legs and transparent blouses clatter past on killer heels sending out signals of wild sexual availability. Frenzied restoration is taking place with bulldozers, mad dogs barking at the wheels, sweating men laying millions of cobbles with iron mallets. Polish visitors wander their lost city besieged by swarthy beggars from who knows what nations, feet ingrained with dirt, who kiss hands and pluck at clothing hoping for money or food. Wasted babies are held out with a mother's whine and milky breast before the blackened Renaissance masterpiece known as the Boim Chapel.

Among the surprising number of world famous Leopolitans (citizens of L'viv) in the arts and science were Leopold von Sacher-Masoch, author of the 'sado-masochistic' *Venus in Furs*, the science fiction author Stanisław Lem, the film director Alexander Ford and the psychiatrist Wilhelm Reich. The electricity of the beautiful young women of the city convinced me there was something peculiarly energizing, even erotic, in the air of 'the secret capital' of Ukraine.

A blood-red sun was setting over the chaos of the Polish–Ukrainian border on our return. Bathed in an unearthly glow, queues of tireless women of all ages known as 'ants' were carrying plastic bags of tradable goods through the pedestrian gate – cigarettes, alcohol and clothing – crossing and re-crossing many times a day. Customs officers wandering about in camouflage gear and big boots and menacingly swinging black and white striped truncheons pointlessly herded them off the grass verge onto the hard pavement. I wandered over to have a look and was immediately accosted by a drunken, heavy-lidded officer. I smiled.

'Ah! Good evening. Do you speak English?'

'Yes, I do speak. What do you want and where do you go?'

'Just looking around. I'm going back to Poland!'

'You must go now from here. It is a . . . um . . . um . . . what it is?'

'International border?' I helpfully offered.

'Yes! international border. You must go from this international border instantly!'

A visit to the 'lost' city of L'viv forcibly reminds one that Ukraine, despite leaning towards the European Union rather than Russia, has a long road ahead before rejoicing in the freedoms and relative affluence Poland now enjoys.

CHAPTER 21

'Dog's Blood!'

The Bieszczady region in the far south-east is the Poland I always dreamed of before visiting the country, the rural region of my imagination. This was the destination of the final leg of the rally before the return section to Warsaw. Forests of pine and fir became increasingly alpine in character. Horse-drawn drays are as common as horses pulling ploughs in the fields. There are few cars and just the occasional whitewashed wooden farmhouse. Scattered about the deserted countryside, often only accessible along vague rutted tracks and hidden among clumps of birch trees, lie exquisite wooden *cerkwie* (*tserkvy*) such as that of the *Ascension* at Ulucz (Ulyuch) dating from 1510, the oldest in Poland but now a museum. The eighteenth-century *cerkiew* at Równia (Rivnya) is an exquisite work of art, the colour of burnt umber with a perfume of roasted resin. It was originally a place of Boyko worship with the characteristic three domes of that culture, clad entirely in wooden shingles of marvellous craftsmanship. It now serves as a Polish Roman Catholic Church. The *cerkiew* of St Michael the Archangel at Smolnik (Smilnyk) is hidden in a copse on top of a hill, a secretive and holy place, silent except for the soughing of the birches and the creak of a sun-dappled iconostasis.

Clouds settled in the dark green valleys and streamed through the pines in scenes of Wagnerian majesty. We were heading towards our isolated accommodation called Leśny Dwór (Forest Manor) in the remote village of Wetlina. As I began to unload the boot in the heavy rain strange cries rent the air.

'Psiakrew!' ('Dog's blood!')

'W mordę jeża!' ('Into the hedgehog's snout!')

'Wiwat!' ('Hooray!')

I swung round to see an exuberant figure with a bushy ginger beard, calf-length battered green cords, walking boots and socks, check lumberjack shirt and braces welcoming us in rather old-fashioned but delightful bucolic Polish. He seemed the perfect embodiment of the seventeenth-century *szlachta* type. I presumed he was the owner but he denied it ('I only do a few odd jobs around the place!') before wrenching my bags from my hands and carrying them up the flights of stairs to our warm timbered rooms in the attic. Tiny dormer windows opened onto a spectacular pine-clad mountain vista. Here was a family *dwór* of the old type with a drawing room and piano, veranda opening onto the garden, library and operatic arias playing softly in the background. I suspect the owner of the manor was a member of the intelligentsia who like many artists, writers and musicians adopted the notorious 'internal emigration' from the constraints of the communist regime years before. The following morning the summer rains began to clear and I decided to climb to the *polonina,* grasslands bare of trees that form the characteristic peaks of the low mountain ranges of the Bieszczady. As the tree-line was passed the vista was breathtaking, the fields covered in mauve wildflowers, the grass of the *polonina* long, delicate and a beautiful shade of pale gold, exquisite in the sun.

The long drive from the Bieszczady to the more famous winter resort of Zakopane in the High Tatra mountains of the Podhale region[170] was enlivened by a spell in the French 1929 BNC racing car (not unlike a Bugatti) in French racing blue with scarlet wire wheels. Richard took the wheel of the Rolls with verve and managed a *mandat* (fine) from the police for parking within a hundred metres of a military installation. In the Pieniny mountains we rode rafts made by lashing together groups of five traditional wooden boats. The journey passes through the dramatic limestone gorge of the Dunajec River which forms the Polish-Slovak frontier. The rafts are skilfully piloted through the white water by the *flisacy – górale* mountain men dressed in full colourful folk costume. Towering

---

170 The Podhale region comprises three mountain ranges: the Tatry, the Gorce and the Pieniny.

walls of limestone, pine forests and striking mountain ranges flashed past on either side.

This region too has remarkable wooden churches. The village of Dębno Podhalańskie has one of the finest shingled fifteenth-century timber churches in the country, the Church of St Michael the Archangel. The interior has survived with naive decorative carpentry and polychrome enrichment of every available surface. On the Sunday morning of our visit six elderly ladies in traditional costume of full, embroidered skirts, embroidered blouses and jackets, strapped felt boots and headscarves with flowers chanted the rosary in chorus, their breath forming clouds of vapour in the freezing air. Old gentlemen bustled about arranging the cruets for mass and ringing the bell.

We arrived at the Zakopane camp in the Tatra mountains in the early evening. The old car with its powerful engine had wafted effortlessly through the limestone mountain passes. We took our lunchtime picnic in the open meadows. The Tatra range is the highest in the Carpathians and the highest in Central Europe, divided unequally between Poland and Slovakia.

Two rest days would give the drivers a chance to do more fundamental repairs to their machines and explore the local area. Krzysztof was a huge Pole with a ragged beard and leather racing goggles wearing a Bugatti T-shirt and plus-fours with co-respondent shoes. His 1920s appearance reminded me that Zakopane had a distinguished history of motor sport. The famous Tatra Race was founded in 1927 by a group of aristocrats in the Kraków Automobile Club. This was a mountain trial for cars such as Bugattis, Mercedes and Austro-Daimlers driven by aces such as Rudolf Caracciola. The race was held on the roads between Zakopane and Morskie Oko (a well-known lake in the mountains called the 'eye of the sea'). The circuit was 7.5 kilometres long with many hairpin bends and a significant climb. Races like these were popular with drivers in the late 1920s as they required great driving skill and were not fatally destructive to the machines. The event fell victim of the Depression as did many other classic events of motor sport in Poland.

Krzysztof was replacing the blown engine on his 1936 DKW cabriolet with one sent down on the night train from Warsaw. There was a mass of loose wiring on the floor, the canvas roof had no struts, and the wrecked engine lay on the grass. He had a Polish car enthusiast's talent and heart of gold that effected the work in a mere twelve hours. A 1952 Polish *Warszawa* was having the entire rear axle replaced.

'I always carry a spare axle on the back seat!' smiled the driver.

The summers of 1913 and 1914 saw Vladimir Lenin in Poronin, a village not far from Zakopane, where he wrote many articles for *Pravda* while his wife attended a neurological clinic with heart problems and his mother-in-law made the tea. In the autumn of 1912 he moved from exile in Paris to Kraków, at that time part of Austro-Hungarian Galicia. 'The police in Kraków gave us no trouble, and our mail was not tampered with,' his wife Nadezhda Krupskaya wrote. Lenin indulged a childish enthusiasm for ice skating, at which unlikely sport he was apparently highly talented. As a Russian *émigré* in Zakopane he mixed with writers and intellectuals, walked in the Tatras and read newspapers and mail in the sun outside the post office.[171]

At the turn of the twentieth century the quaint and intimate health resort of Zakopane became a summer mountain retreat popular with artists, writers, musicians and Polish intellectuals. The region is one of the most beautiful in Poland. Spring witnesses torrents of crystal water and fields of brilliant wildflowers. Short leafy summers give way to golden Polish autumns. In winter snowy defiles and frozen waterfalls crack between craggy limestone peaks, while icy tracks lined with tall pines lead to intermontane lakes.

Dr Tytus Chałubiński, a physician from Warsaw, established a sanatorium in the town at the turn of the nineteenth century. He recommended the clear air, hot springs and also the spirit of the colourful folk culture of the highlanders known as the *górale*. He arranged excursions into the High Tatras with the vividly costumed local people acting as guides. They also provided festive entertainment in the evenings with singing and dancing to violins around the fire. His favourite guide, Sabała, was a legendary storyteller. The writer Joseph Conrad and the pianist Artur Rubinstein visited

---

171 I am indebted to *Lenin w Krakowie* [Lenin in Cracow], Jan Adamczewski et al., with an introduction by Walery Namiotkiewicz (Warsaw 1970)

Zakopane often. The composer Karol Szymanowski, arguably the greatest Polish composer since Fryderyk Chopin, lived at the beautiful Villa Atma. The fierce independence of the *górale* historically strengthened the resolve of Poles labouring under one or other form of foreign domination.

The town became cemented into the Polish cultural heritage with mythical status as the twentieth century progressed but has grown uncontrollably in size in recent years. It now attracts millions of visitors as the winter capital and prime ski resort in Poland. It has lost much of its intimate arts-and-crafts atmosphere but the highlanders staunchly attempt to maintain their traditions. Zakopane, nestling at the foot of Mt Giewont, remains the gateway to some of the most spectacular scenery in the country.

The tiny necropolis known as the Old Cemetery speaks eloquently of the Polish intelligentsia who lived in Zakopane. The tombs are decorated with beautiful carved wooden statues of Christ and other sculptures in the local naive folk tradition. Among the most eminent upper-class families living in the town was that of the Polish-Lithuanian Stanisław Witkiewicz (1851–1915). He was related to many legendary Polish patriots and surprisingly the family of the distinguished British actor Sir John Gielgud. He was also a cousin of the great military commander Józef Piłsudski. A fine painter and art critic, he created the 'Zakopane style' of sophisticated and decorative wooden architecture derived from the *górale* highlanders' humble dwellings, 'beautiful in a fundamentally Polish way'. He 'achieved the status of a national sage preaching a patriotic gospel of creative renewal through a return to native Polish arts and crafts'.[172]

He married a talented musician and they had a son in 1885 named Stanisław Ignacy Witkiewicz (popularly known as 'Witkacy') who was to become notorious for his outrageous behaviour and was widely regarded as a visionary genius in a number of disciplines – writing, philosophy, painting and photography. His father did not believe in formal education, writing to his son in May 1906: 'Try to wrench yourself free of the commonplace, vulgarity.

172 *The Witkiewicz Reader* edited, translated with an introduction by Daniel Gerould (Illinois 1992) p. 27

Aspire to great things, powerful feelings, people and women – naturally wonderful, exceedingly beautiful, heroic, noble – and not "dolts", not "dolts".'[173] Staś applied his father's advice with a vengeance.

One of the seminal twentieth-century intellectual friendships was forged in this magical place. Witkacy was a boyhood friend of Bronisław Malinowski who also lived in Zakopane (both of their mothers ran guest houses). Malinowski went on to become the 'father' of functionalism in anthropology, a British national and Professor of Social Anthropology at the London School of Economics. He enjoyed being referred to as 'the Conrad of anthropology'. Witkacy, for his part, became a famous avant-garde intellectual and philosopher of the Apollinaire type but a life spent mostly in remote Zakopane meant he never achieved a significant European reputation. This youthful friendship influenced them in manifold ways. They were both products of the fraught Polish intellectual climate of the time, fragmented personalities looking for a personal identity. Brilliant and talented in many fields, Witkacy as an agent provocateur was subject to violent and mercurial changes of mood. A Nietzschean in temperament, he nevertheless felt worthless, harbouring a compulsive need to distinguish himself. He was an excellent actor and took many extraordinary narcissistic self-portraits with an early camera. They portray a clown masking a tragic soul.

A horse-drawn carriage driven by a man in fantastically embroidered trousers took me along the Dolina Kościeliska, a valley cowering beneath craggy limestone peaks, the sun hovering behind their jagged line. Just before the outbreak of the Great War, Witkacy's fiancée, Jadwiga Janczewska, shot herself under a rock in this valley. She placed a bunch of wildflowers beside her in a symbolic gesture linking Eros and Thanatos (Love and Death). Fresh flowers have been placed at the spot ever since. She belonged to the radical and highly eroticized 'Young Poland' movement and such an histrionic act was only to be expected. Life among the intelligentsia in *fin de siècle* Zakopane was an incestuous business. A murky love

173 *Witkacy Life and Work*, Anna Micińska trans. Bogna Piotrowska (Warsaw 1990) p. 79

entanglement involving the 'scoundrel' (according to Witkacy) Karol Szymanowski was probably at the root of it. Szymanowski, 'a bird of paradise in the backwoods', wrote music of brilliantly inventive orchestration and ardent, almost painful, emotion. The ringing horse bells of my carriage, the rushing stream beside the path, even the little bag on the stick used to catch the droppings made for a scene from another century.

A peculiarly Polish dilemma at the outbreak of the Great War affected Witkacy and Malinowski as, by virtue of the partitions, they held allegiance to opposing sides. By September they had had a crisis of conscience and clashed over Poland's role in the war, 'Nietzsche breaking with Wagner' as Malinowski rather grandly observed. Both regarded Joseph Conrad as 'a traitor' for leaving Poland. As a Russian subject Witkacy decided to fight in the Tsarist army against the Austro-Hungarian Empire. He served with distinction as an officer in the glamorous Pavlovsky Regiment and witnessed the Russian Revolution at first hand in St Petersburg before finally returning to Zakopane in 1918. Malinowski, an Austrian subject, elected to continue his anthropological work in New Guinea. Witkacy slashed his wrists and cut his throat in the small Ukrainian village of Jezioro on 18 September 1939 upon hearing the news that Russia had attacked Poland. He wrote: 'Yet it is better to be gone in delightful madness, rather than in grey, dull tedium and torpor.' A feeling that many Poles share.

In the evening we listened to some colourful *górale* musicians make an attempt to teach a lugubrious Romanian band to play their mountain music with spirit and passion. I was roped into some wild highland dancing, whistling and stamping to the abandoned playing of a violin. *Górale* instrumental music, which is derived from song, has a small range and moves in short descending melodies based on musical ideas known as *nuta*. The music can be heard at weddings where the celebrations may last for days. The surprisingly festive playing at funerals is probably the most authentic as there is no commercial dimension. Funerals are considered a private 'return to the village' to which outsiders are seldom invited. The Romanian musicians with their dark moustaches were concentrated shamelessly on making money and took little interest in their talented tutors. They gazed at the diners with the dead eyes of poverty, rendered numb by endless repetitions of hackneyed tunes and disillusionment with their travellers' life.

The rally skirted Kraków to take in the astounding Wieliczka salt mine and a final party before heading back to Warsaw. The ancient mine has vast chambers – the Chapel of Blessed Kinga is 10,000 cubic metres in volume with chandeliers, altar and floor carved from solid rock salt. Gangways, immense shafts and slopes of salt with grotesquely weathered gnomes of rock salt render one speechless. Goethe regarded the mine more highly than the monumental wonders of Kraków itself. We rattled down in a miner's cage to our banquet in a chamber carved out of a solid block of salt.

'For Mike in his Rolls-Royce joining the rally again! A bottle of champagne and a surprise!' A four-cornered vermilion Krakowian cap with a peacock's feather was thrust on my head. The Krakowian band struck up wildly and I was grasped around the waist by a vast woman in folk dress and literally swept off my feet. A pimple on a pumpkin.

The car masterfully pushed through torrential rain to *Zamek Krzyżtopór* at Ujazd, the most spectacular ruin I have visited anywhere and unsurpassed as a Renaissance conceit. This was the largest palace in Europe before the construction of Versailles and considered the most beautiful in seventeenth-century Poland.

'Where the hell are we, Richard? You're the brilliant navigator!' (I can be particularly unpleasant when lost in a car.)

'I am doing my level best, Michael. You lack the Nelson touch, *panie*! It was *you* who suggested taking a shortcut. Fatal in this country. The map doesn't show the road.' There are many degrees of secondary road in Poland.

'The suspension is going to bottom and we'll smash the exhaust again!' We were moving around like an ocean liner over the corrugations.

'All right. Let me out and I'll walk in front of the car and guide you over the potholes.'

We proceeded in this fashion through the maze of craters at a snail's pace. Darkness fell and the castle became a lost illusion in the black countryside. A Maluch approached, its weak headlamps

scarcely penetrating the clouds of dust thrown up when it hurtled to
a halt.

'Need some help?'

'Yes! Is this the road to the Castle of Krzyżtopór?'

'*Pokażemy drogę! Jedźcie za nami!*' Richard went for the dictionary. ('We'll show you the road! Follow us!') They jumped into
their car and energetically waved us to follow them.

'Sorry if I shouted, Richard. I couldn't face another accident.'

'Hrmph.'

Another ten kilometres of terrifying trenches ensued until we
encountered a paved road. We were the last to arrive.

'Where were you, Mike? We worry about you! We want no more
of disasters!' They had clearly being drinking a lot of vodka. Lack of
space forced us to park within the pitch black ruins.

The castle had been built as a *palazzo in fortezza* by Krzysztof
Ossoliński, Governor of the Sandomierz province in the mid-seventeenth century. The conceits comprised four towers to represent the
four seasons, twelve halls for the months of the year, fifty-two rooms
for the weeks and three hundred and sixty-five windows for the days
with an extra window for leap year which was bricked up when not
required. The cellars had been turned over to stabling for some three
hundred and seventy Arab horses who fed out of black Carrara
marble troughs with gold fittings and could admire their reflections
in crystal mirrors erected to increase the light. The dining hall was
built over a spring and had a glass ceiling that was also an aquarium
with colourful exotic fish. Ossoliński died shortly after completion
of this Byzantine palace and was thus saved the agony of watching its
complete destruction and pillaging by the Swedes in 1655.

The local lighting had failed and a huge bonfire was burning in
the courtyard around which people were cooking delicious Polish
sausage on sharpened sticks. A sad group of elderly folk were playing lugubrious 1940s tunes on a platform in the dark. Alexander and
I decided to sleep in the car and Richard headed off to a comfortable
hotel some kilometres distant. The ruins dissolved in the misted
windows as the moon rose over this astonishing structure. As I
drifted off I thought nothing of the resident spectre, a ghostly horseman in hussar's armour I noticed standing on the walls defending
the castle.

Stiff after sleeping in the car, we washed in cold water and had a breakfast of leftovers. We may have arrived last in Ujazd but we were the first to arrive back in Warsaw at the Stadion Dziesięciolecia in Praga, which was a definite mistake. As often happens in Poland, publicity for the event had been poor. There were no spectators and plastic cups of warm sparkling wine made the conclusion a mild anti-climax. Our adventures in Łańcut were retold through loudspeakers to an empty stadium. The competitors did a lap of honour. In a doleful moment a man pushing a disabled youth in a wheelchair lifted him up to the driver's window of the car with enormous effort so that he might see the interior.

And so the first rally around the country for 75 years concluded, an adventure unlikely ever to be repeated in quite the same way. I would ship the car back to England reluctantly. The exploration of a reborn nation of romantic landscapes and magnificent castles, the adrenalin of driving a great car on the deserted Polish roads of those days far from help and without insurance, a lucky escape at the Palace of Łańcut, new Polish friends with their amazing hospitality and support in adversity – such experiences are given to few.

CHAPTER 22

Limited Company

'Jezus Maria! Sewage is pouring into the flat! What will I do?' Zosia shouted down the phone.

'I'll be right over.'

Under stress we never spoke Polish together. She had by this time separated from her husband and in a welcome and courageous expression of independence was living alone as a 'separated woman' in a small flat in a beautiful area of Warsaw called Królikarnia (Rabbit Hunting Park). The old communist block with rattling lift and smell of dog breath was built on an escarpment above long ponds and ancient trees near a neoclassical belvedere. For a few all too brief evenings we had enjoyed private bliss but now came the intrusion of a quintessential Polish situation.

Mayhem was raging when I arrived. Pieces of concrete were cascading into the bath from drilling above and the most terrible stench was coming from sewage leaking from pipes which appeared to have been joined together by a child. It had all started with a blocked pipe in the flat above. An alcoholic plumber (one of the few who had remained in the country) with two teeth appeared at the door. The electrician had already fused the lights three times.

'*Proszę pani.* We must pull down all the tiles in your bathroom, perhaps the bathroom itself!'

'Destroy it?' Zosia was more upset than I had seen her in a long time.

'*Proszę pani.* You must stop all the flats above you using the toilet! Immediately!'

'But there are fifteen floors!' She rushed out of the door and up the stairs to begin the long series of warnings. The puddles of sewage had not yet reached the sitting room but the threat of being overwhelmed was dreadfully present. The problem took weeks to fully rectify and taught me a great deal about exercising extreme caution when approaching any former communist construction or employing workmen from the 'old school' who require the assistance of vodka for their craft.

Zosia's bathroom was not the only area in my life under threat of disintegration. The next day I had a meeting with the dreaded accountant of the project.

'Well, let's jump in the car and drive to Bath!' Andrzej impulsively suggested in the style of a Polish cavalry charge.

We were discussing ways of stopping the disintegration of the project.

'It will only take us twenty-four hours!'

I was irresistibly reminded of the Polish hero Kazimierz Pułaski riding across the plains at the Battle of Savannah during the American War of Independence. Poles are fond of the big unconsidered gesture as a way of dispelling anxiety and saving the day. Brilliantly improvised solutions to problems of their own making. Sometimes this works, but not on this occasion.

We were drinking in a smoky *Minibarek* in deepest Warsaw discussing possible rescue plans over beer, sausage and cigarettes.

'No point in going to Bath, Andrzej. They expect *me* to dig them out of this mess in Warsaw.'

'Perhaps we could run Chopin Tours or a course for Catholics and Military Men. Make some real money.'

'Hmm . . .'

'Do you have any connections with the Know How Fund or the Phare programme? They have a lot of money. Perhaps we could get some out of them.'

The naiveté and arrogance of this remark took my breath away.

There had been a meeting in the forest prison the previous evening where Andrzej had revealed the details of the project debacle to the staff. Seated among the glass cases of coal, pig food and cow fertilizer a strange atmosphere of mutual contempt existed even before the meeting began. Poles are not great smilers but this was a particularly morose occasion.

'Bloody stupid teachers. My father was one,' Andrzej said impatiently to me out of the side of his mouth.

'All the managers are criminal and untrustworthy. Andrzej treats us like shit,' whispered Sylvia, one of the teachers, into my other ear.

One solution floated was the formation of a limited company. The words 'limited company' themselves rang with the success of the West. Everyone was optimistic. But so early in the arrival of the new freedoms of the market economy none of the staff had a clue how to go about forming one. At the same time no one wanted to lose face and appear ignorant. I felt great sympathy for the Poles being thrown in the deep end of the capitalist dream oblivious to the complexities of annual audits by chartered accountants, cash-flow statements, profit and loss accounts. Many of the senior managers were embarrassed to admit they did not know the difference between a credit and a debit card.

Mr Fukowski appeared with head bowed, filling in a form, sharpening a pencil with much deliberation, lethargically turning endless pages of figures for no apparent reason as if back in the halcyon days of communist bureaucracy. His finger followed a line of print laboriously down the page with heavy determination. Fukowski was an archetypal and superb *nomenklatura* bureaucrat, famous in the government ministries for his style, a star in his way. He never voluntarily communicated information. This particular evening he wore glasses with heavier frames than usual, brown tinted lenses and a slightly shiny blue suit – perfection of the type. Suffused with colour (a result of the numerous vodkas with the blue-rinsed cleaner before the meeting), he regularly buried his head in his hands and sighed heavily and audibly.

'The shares will cost ten million zloty each,' Andrzej offered brightly. 'Anyone interested?'

'Could we have some figures on which to base a financial decision, *panie Dyrektorze* Fukowski,' the teacher Katarzyna asked, ignoring Andrzej altogether. Małgorzata, the Director of Studies, sat with her eyes firmly shut and arms folded, head steadfastly to her chest, 'not listening'.

The bereaved koala slowly looked up unwillingly from his work as if distracted from a delicious eucalyptus leaf.

'Your presence here at the meeting is a mere detail. I am unable to reveal financial figures because of the dangers of economic espionage. I am sure you understand. Much has already been decided.' His deep voice was ominous in tone.

'No financial figures to form a company? An arrant absurdity,' Richard muttered.

Nick leaned over my shoulder.

'Yeh, well . . . I know this Pole who's an Arsenal supporter. The Gunners! Whoah . . .! Might go to West Ham next week.'

'*Panie Dyrektorze*, the figures must be made available,' Katarzyna pressed him tetchily.

'*Pan Michał* has all the information.' His head and finger resumed their slow perusal of the forms on the desk.

As he had never communicated anything of any substance to me I was shocked. I knew they wanted to renegotiate a non-existent contract for one of the staff. Half a teacher would work on credit, the other half in lieu of payment (whatever that meant in the real world).

'Well, actually I don't have anything on this.'

'Perhaps you would like to buy some shares in the company, *panie Michale*?' Andrzej asked, hopeful I would confirm the accuracy of his presentation for the others.

'What company? We haven't formed it yet.'

Buy shares in a company that was about to send me packing back to England?

Andrzej spoke in a dull monotone, flecks of saliva flying over the table and clinging to the corners of his mouth, translating for Fukowski like some dreadful machine. He expounded on the inner complexities of company formation in a partly hysterical and certainly desperate and agitated attempt to bolt together a solution. We began to veer wildly between the belief that everything was possible and that nothing was possible. He was aggressive and confrontational when questioned concerning procedure. Fukowski left for the refuge of the lavatory and we never saw him again.

'I really feel this has nothing to do with us, you know. What a shower he is, this chap. What *would* Jennifer say if she were here?' Richard maintained an air of patrician detachment in a crisis.

'Well, I dunno about dis den. Not too great. I jus' wanna know where I stand – and so does me dad! My landlord's climbin' the walls!' Nick's eyes began to dart about like a cornered rat. He had been actually thriving professionally in Poland and was genuinely upset at the imminent collapse. His accent did not attract the real or imagined class discrimination that lay at the root of all his anxieties in England.

'I said we should have squashed him down!' Geoff constructively chipped in.

'Yeah. Excellent, excellent. Good one, good one.'

The interminable length of the standard Polish meeting, with no chairman, no agenda, no structure, created deep anxiety about the future. The complex formation of a company and its operation within a market economy was imperfectly understood. According to Andrzej only part of the company would be responsible for the debt to the English side, which only added to the confusion.

The psychological shock of the dramatic recent changes in official ideology was evident on every face. The pace of change, the degree of change had made ordinary people tremendously insecure and removed self-confidence at a stroke. A friend of mine who was a Polish clinical psychologist told me many of her older patients were on the verge of nervous breakdowns faced with restructuring, redundancy or computer training. At the administrative level it was the collision of the 'Old Guard' with an ill-conceived and ill-judged conception of what the market economy is and how it operates. There seemed to be a belief that it was simply a style of clothing one adopted. Fear of the future was tangible in this reckless attempt to salvage something from the mess using 'exciting new concepts' from the West.

I imagined scenes like ours taking place all over Poland at that time. In smaller towns where huge communist factories had closed down, men and women have never managed to find another job to this day. There were many unremarked social casualties in those days, tragedies eclipsed by the surface glitter. During the present period of transition Poland continues to reap the legacy of an understandable lack of business, political and diplomatic experience and acumen. The patronizing tone and lack of empathy of many Western companies for Polish businesses floundering in this sea change was distasteful and opportunistic. Now Polish business practice has evolved greatly in sophistication and expertise. There is a newfound arrogance and absence of ethics in the deft manipulation of companies and their receipts. The corruption we witnessed in many Polish businesses has become endemic. Central planning was suddenly replaced with a form of market economy that failed to grow organically alongside any measure of moral accountability. A car crash had occurred with the survivors stumbling about the highway into the headlights of the oncoming traffic.

'I really feel you should take legal advice on this matter,' I said, but received blank looks all round. Anything remotely 'legal' meant years of waiting for a decision.

I took a long, melancholic walk along the Vistula. The river was flowing very slowly and ghastly pools of stagnant water were forming on the sandy shore. Fluffed-up gulls rode wavelets in the chill wind racing across the surface. The collapse of the project was distressing from a professional point of view but it would also separate me from Zosia, which was worse. We sat together in silence on the bed in my room gazing into each other's eyes in silence much as many other couples in Poland have done through history, threatened with separation by circumstances beyond their control.

CHAPTER 23

Vistula – Teutonic Knights and Cherry Liqueur

One of the most historically rewarding journeys one can make in Poland is to travel north along the Vistula from Warsaw to Gdańsk, following the ribbon of ruined fortresses of the Teutonic Knights to the awe-inspiring apotheosis of medieval strongholds at Malbork (Marienburg). The towns along the way bear the imprint of rich trade and development as well as massive fortifications.

Minor roads along the Vistula north of Warsaw pass deserted riverine landscapes with ruined cottages reminiscent of the seventeenth-century Dutch artist Jacob von Ruisdael. Near the north bank some twenty kilometres from the capital the once magnificent eighteenth-century Palace of Jabłonna, set in an English landscape garden, was tragically destroyed by fire in 1944 and is now restored. But the first sizeable structure on the river is a trailing ribbon of brick known as Modlin Fortress. The longest brick structure in Europe is partly the remains of a fortress built by Napoleon and his French military engineers against a possible Russian offensive into Western Europe. The six dilapidated forts overlooking the broad floodplain of the Vistula served as headquarters for Colonel Władysław Sikorski during the Polish-Soviet War of 1919–20 when the Red Army cavalry promised to expand their Revolution and 'water our horses on the Rhine'. The brilliant Polish victory by the commander and liberator of Poland Józef Piłsudski severed the Russian rear and cut their lines of communication. Known as the Battle of Warsaw or the 'Miracle on the Vistula', the future of European history was determined by the outcome for some twenty years.

One must first overcome the inner *Schweinehund*.

—Manfred von Richthofen, Air Ace of the Great War

I promise the chastity of my body, and poverty, and obedience, to God and the Blessed Virgin Mary, and to you, the Master of the Teutonic Order, and your successors, according to the Rules and Practices of the Order, obedience unto death.

—Oath sworn upon admission into the Teutonic Order

The crusades to the Holy Land are far better known than the Northern Crusades.[174] The Holy Wars of Outremer have a continuing mythical and presently inflammatory relevance but essentially the Saracens were victorious in that long and bloody battle. The crusades in North-Eastern Europe were not as spectacular but the changes and effects have been longer lasting. Western Christianity has managed to survive along the southern Baltic shore. A reborn Poland, Lithuania, Latvia and Estonia have all adopted the Western institutions of the enlarged European Union.

The evolution of the two Prussias (Royal Prussia and Ducal Prussia) is likely to give the non-specialist the vertigo of an historical bungee jumper and shall not be attempted here. Suffice to say the original Prussian tribes were neither Slavic or Germanic but of Baltic culture who had been resident on their extensive lands east of the Vistula for hundreds of years. They were more civilized and less sensationally godless than many chronicles would have us believe. The allure for Western knights of a cold wilderness peopled by barbaric 'pagans' is not overpoweringly obvious yet the lamp of Western civilization was forcibly lit in this darkness.

The monastic Teutonic or German Order was founded around 1190 during the Third Crusade as a small group of Hospitallers living under the rule of the Templars to care for German crusaders in a field hospital at the bloody siege of Acre. In 1198 they became a respected part of the Roman Catholic Church when Pope Celestine III permitted them by charter to reincorporate as a

---

174 Texts in English on the Northern Crusades are rare. The most authoritative and impressive is *The Northern Crusades*, Eric Christiansen (London 1997). Indispensable on the military history of the German Order is *The Teutonic Knights: A Military History*, William Urban (London 2003)

military order of monks now known to English speakers as the Teutonic Knights and the Poles as *Krzyżacy* or Knights of the Cross. The outstanding Grand Master Hermann von Salza was a close friend of Emperor Frederick II who assisted him in attracting substantial initial grants of land and funds for the Order. Later Papal Bulls gave them a free field of operations in Prussia with minimal accountability.

The discipline of the knight-brothers was extremely strict. They prayed at specific times throughout the day and were expected to fast when not eating their staple diet of eggs, milk and porridge in silence. In military fashion they were issued with two or four horses and a sword (none of which they owned), a limited set of clothing and a distinctive white mantle with a black cross. Concerning the vow of chastity, to 'protect us from lust', the *Komtur* (commander) of Königsberg (Królewiec, Kaliningrad) between 1289 and 1302, Berchtold Bruhave, masochistically trained himself in abstinence by sleeping for a year with the most beautiful girl he could find but without touching her. Others wore shirts of mail next to their skin until the flesh wept with pus. Spiritually the knight-brothers wanted to atone for sin and seek holiness in the outside world by avoiding the cloister. In our more secularized world view it is difficult to comprehend in any meaningful way the weird daily life and spiritual dedication of these military monks.

On the escarpment above the sleepy village of Czerwińsk nad Wisłą lies a fine Romanesque abbey, now a seminary. The wooden village houses straggle in disorder from the contemplative monastery gardens down to the riverbank. The river broadens at Płock. From the escarpment a magnificent wind-whipped panorama unfolds, the finest vista of the Vistula in Poland. This ancient town was for over five hundred years the seat of the Dukes of Mazovia. At Włocławek the river broadens further into a huge lake of sapphire blue with drifting white swans and clumps of russet reeds. Stands of willow, birch and pine line the shore while small wooden houses are built perilously close to the banks.

Little could the ambitious Duke Konrad of Mazovia have realized what he had unleashed when he originally enlisted the assistance of the Teutonic Knights at Chełmno (Kulm) north of Toruń in 1223 to put down a fierce retaliation by pagan Prussian tribes after some lacklustre crusading. In return for service he promised them the opportunity to build their own state from conquered Prussian land. Chełmno, once a member of the Hanseatic league, is one of the best preserved medieval Polish towns. It lies on the old Amber Road that carried the precious golden resin south from Baltic Gdańsk to Mediterranean Venice. Only the town walls remain of the Teutonic Knight's defences. The town hall is a jewel, the 'quintessential example of Polish Renaissance secular architecture'.[175] The play of light and shadow on the graceful Polish attic makes it one of the most beautiful buildings in the country.

Duke Konrad of Mazovia gave the Teutonic Knights use of their first castle on the opposite bank of the river to the city of Toruń (Thorn) shortly after. They darkly named it *Vogelsang* ('birdsong') as a reference to the final cry of a dying swan or tortured Prussian. This lively and formerly wealthy Hanseatic city was built on profits from the grain trade and is spectacularly sited on the Vistula. Minimal damage during the Second World War meant the medieval fabric has survived largely intact. In the early morning mist I wandered streets of ornate Renaissance facades munching the most delicious gingerbread on earth (the famous Toruń *pierniki*) while flower sellers scurried across the square almost concealed by their burden of blooms.

The Gothic town hall is a monumental brick structure of tremendous presence, the largest of its type in Poland. Here I learned of the realism of Polish portraiture that seldom flatters the sitter. King Louis I the Great of Hungary, also known as King Ludwig Węgierski (1326–82), is alarmingly depicted with his face covered in white powder, which he habitually wore to conceal the ravages of smallpox. Another represents in loving detail the palsied eye of a courtier. The Polish astronomer and polymath of genius Mikołaj Kopernik (Nicolaus Copernicus) (1473–1543) was born in Toruń some years after it laboured under the dominion of Royal Prussia. He studied at the famed Kraków Academy (where he may have been introduced to astronomy) and canon law at the universities of Padua, Bologna and Ferrara. One of the greatest single advances in human culture and science lies open before the awed visitor in a glass case at his

175 *Poland: A Traveller's Gazetteer*, Adam Zamoyski (London 2001) p. 47

birthplace – a copy of his great work *De revolutionibus orbium coelestium* which outlines the revolutionary heliocentric theory of the solar system. Less pleasant was the leaflet I noticed tacked to the notice board of Toruń cathedral urging the faithful to pray for the conversion and salvation of the Jews by citing a prayer of Pope Pius V at the Council of Trent in the mid-sixteenth century. In view of the tentative rebirth of Jewish culture it is with some surprise that one still unpleasantly encounters in souvenir shops throughout Poland comedic carved figures of stooped and bearded Hasidic Jews with hang-dog expressions draped in their *tallit* (prayer shawl), eyes popping with fear.

The fall of Acre to the Saracens in 1291 caused the Order to move its headquarters to Venice from where they finally abandoned their plans to recapture Outremer. The acquisition of Danzig (Gdańsk), the increasing success of the crusades against the Baltic pagans and the arrest and torture of the Templars on trumped-up charges of heresy by King Philip IV the Fair of France focused the mind of the Grand Master Siegfried von Feuchtwangen. In 1309 he prudently moved the headquarters of the Knights out of secular control to Prussia and Marienburg (Malbork) on the Nogat river just south of Danzig. It was to become the most prodigious Christian stronghold in Europe and impregnable until combat became airborne.

The original motivation of the Teutonic Knights was to extend the Christian world and not the German empire. Initially the knight-brothers were not very numerous, their necessary financial supporters being an increasing number of clever German burghers attracted to the Northern crusades for the very secular reasons of profit and land. The golden glow of precious Baltic amber was an irresistible lure to many, the strangest office of the Order being that of the *Bernstein-meister* or Amber Master. The Vistula remained the main artery of trade and travel through a trackless waste of impenetrable forest, swamp, lake and marsh. Hence the construction of this remarkable array of monumental fortresses to consolidate their gains.[176]

---

176 An excellent illustrated guide to the castles is *Crusader Castles of the Teutonic Knights* in two slim volumes. Volume I deals with the red-brick castles of Prussia 1230–1466 and Volume II the stone castles of Latvia and Estonia 1185–1560. By Stephen Turnbull, illustrated by Peter Dennis (Oxford 2003, 2004)

By the time I reached Grudziądz (Graudenz) on the old Amber Road on the banks of the river, the low-level flooding from the downpours had marooned willows and created ragged sand islands of low brush. The vista across the floodplain to the twenty-six granaries on the opposite bank deserved the palette of Vermeer to capture the richly textured brick, red-tiled roofs and clumps of cloud drifting in the blue northern sky. The Knights traded grain and other goods along the river in their own *cogges* or sailing ships. In Napoleonic times it was a strong fortress whose firing platforms totally dominated the Vistula. The town subsequently became a renowned Polish cavalry headquarters and training school. While searching vainly for the remains of the Teutonic castle (it had been demolished in 1801, I discovered later) the sudden clanging of a bell in a medieval street saved the old car by inches from being impaled Teutonically on the front end of a tram.

The minor road followed the broad, dark river flecked with foam to a set of locks in the form of a miniature castle at the confluence of the Nogat and Vistula. The riverine landscape has a subtle beauty with golden dried reeds, swamp, marsh and mixed forest of birch and pine. Water birds bobbed on the current and the occasional pair of storks noisily clacked their red beaks together in conjugal bliss (they mate for life) in an outsized nest precariously perched on a power pole.

Nothing prepares the eye or mind for the impact of the first sight of the fortress of Malbork (Marienburg). This tremendous structure, at once religious and military, is implacably ranged along the banks of the river Nogat. Monumental in worldly arrogance and powerful in its religious resonance, Malbork would have subjugated the mind and senses of any medieval witness to its construction. The stronghold of towers, battlements and spires forcibly convinces one of the invincibility of the Teutonic Knights. The High, Middle and Lower castles comprise the Grand Master's palace, chapels, refectories, monastery and administrative headquarters spread over many acres. The Knight of the Golden Fleece, Hue de Lannoy, Seigneur de Santes, said of it in 1412 '[It had] arms and provisions to maintain a garrison of a thousand persons for ten years, of ten thousand for one year.' It was the largest medieval castle in Europe. One cannot but be astounded that such manifest power could contain within it the megalomaniac seeds of its own destruction. The attraction of the excessive draws the German spirit like a moth to the flame.

Between 1329 and 1408 quite apart from the Germans and Poles, hundreds of Englishmen became involved in the Baltic northern crusades. The Lithuanian crusade even included Henry Bolingbroke, later to become Henry IV of England. For such 'guest crusaders' it was a cheaper and less dangerous road to the rapid redemption of their crusading vows. In light of the failure of the crusades in the Holy Land, the northern crusades were geographically more accessible, with the additional benefit that those who took part were granted full indulgences by the Pope. At times these crusades acquired the features of a crusader 'package tour'. Participants were offered an attractive spot of profitable looting combined with the religious adrenalin of fighting 'the pagans' hand to hand. Like all adventure tours it was seasonal and success depended on the weather.

The greatest legendary battle of medieval Europe – Poles call it the battle of Grunwald, the Germans Tannenberg and the Lithuanians Zalgris – took place on 15 July 1410. To Poles it has the significance that Agincourt has to the English. It began on the muddy fields and marshes between the modern villages of Łodwigowo (Ludwigsdorf), Stębark (Tannenberg) and Grunwald about 65 kilometres east of Grudziądz (Graudenz). The Polish forces were commanded by King Władysław Jagiełło (1362–1434) of Poland, athletic and still hunting energetically at the age of sixty-two. His small dark eyes would dart about calculating the strength of his forces. The flower of Polish chivalry champed at the bit, the quality of their plate armour and bascinet helmets reflecting the sun and their immeasurable wealth. The horses of the more powerful knights were splendidly caparisoned with embroidered coats of arms, as were the riders' tight surcoats and painted shields. Foot soldiers carried longbows, crossbows, battle-axes and swords. Trumpets tortured the air as they tied straw to their sleeves to distinguish themselves from those 'guest' crusaders fighting for the Teutonic Knights.

The Polish forces had previously joined up with the tremendously experienced 'pagan' Lithuanian Grand Duke Vytautas.

'Small, slim, energetic and fidgety'[177] he had tremendous experience fighting for and against the Teutonic Knights in addition to engaging the Golden Horde. The victorious outcome of this battle largely depended on his skill in the field. The armour of the Lithuanian army was Eastern in appearance with round, conical helmets tapering to a point and coats of mail. His Tatar (Mongol) contingent, dressed in weighty coats and leather boots, was commanded by Jelal-el-Din. This combined Polish–Lithuanian army numbered some 39,000 troops.

There was an historical inevitability about this clash of mighty forces. The Teutonic Knights fielded 27,000 troops, of which only about 250 were actually bearded knight-brothers mounted on heavy cavalry wearing the famous white mantle and black cross. Some were secular members of the order wearing a white mantle but with the Greek letter 'tau' in black. The lower orders wore grey and the 'guest' crusaders from all over Europe were robed in their own resplendent equipage. Most of the knights who fought for the Order lived on Teutonic lands but did not actually belong to the Order. Their weapons of choice were the crossbow and sword.

Both sides seemed reluctant to begin the fight. Jagiełło had to be dragged from prayer by his cousin that morning after hearing two Masses ('Brother! This is the day of battle, not prayer!'). In a gesture of operatic theatricality worthy of any great legendary battle of chivalry, the Grand Master of the Teutonic Knights, Ulrich von Jungingen, sent a messenger carrying two swords. He rode up the side of the hummock serving as King Jagiełło's observation post and violently thrust them into the ground, challenging him to fight.

The frenzied mêlée of screaming horses, hail of crossbow bolts and longbow arrows, fluttering standards embroidered with white lions, gold angels, black bulls and red eagles, flailing swords and groans of the dismembered lasted some eight hours. With the exception of one officer, all the high command of the Order were massacred during the battle or shortly afterward. Only one and a half thousand men from the original force struggled back to the

177 Quoted in *Tannenberg 1410: Disaster for the Teutonic Knights*, Stephen Turnbull, illustrated by Richard Hook (Oxford 2003) p. 23

refuge of Marienburg. The victorious Polish–Lithuanian army in pursuit then laid siege to the great fortress for two months but it never surrendered. Jagiełło was eventually to die far from the field of glorious battle in 1434 at the age of 72 from a fever caught after a cold night listening to nightingales. (The worst destruction at Malbork was in fact wrought by the Russians in 1945 when they believed Nazis were holding out within the walls and the castle was heavily bombed.)[178]

The legendary status of the battle tends to obscure the limited strategic significance it had on the history of north central Europe at the time. Within a year the Knights had reclaimed all the territory they had lost. But the Order had been mortally wounded. The battle drained their financial coffers and their irreplaceable upper echelons had been wiped out. In 1457 the great fortress was sold to the Czechs. The power of the Knights declined inexorably through the fifteenth century to the Thirteen Years War (1454–66) and their own *Götterdämmerung*. Much of the battlefield area is now a memorial with all the 'death positions' carefully marked and a splendid re-enactment of the battle takes place annually. The German Order continues today as an exclusively religious order.

Over the centuries the defeat of the Teutonic Knights at Grunwald has resulted in significant German historical denial and festering shame. Some nineteenth-century accounts held that the knights had brought culture and civilization to Poland, casting the victors as barbarians who had destroyed their achievements. In 1903 a monument was erected at Grunwald with the inscription 'In battle for German tradition and law, Grand Master Ulrich von Jungingen died the death of a hero on July 15, 1410.' At the outbreak of the Great War, the victory of Grand Marshall von Hindenberg in August 1914 was trumpeted as the Second Battle of Tannenberg. Prussian honour had at last been redeemed. A monumental Polish shrine was erected in 1961 to commemorate the 550th anniversary of the battle.

---

178 I cannot possibly do justice to the details of this great medieval battle here. The estimates come from a detailed and excellently illustrated account in English. *Tannenberg 1410: Disaster for the Teutonic Knights*, Stephen Turnbull, illustrated by Richard Hook (Oxford 2003). Another fine study of the conflict appears in *The Teutonic Knights: A Military History*, William Urban (London 2003) Chapter 10

The fate of the iconic painting *The Battle of Grunwald* (1878) by the great Polish nineteenth-century painter Jan Matejko (1838–93) speaks volumes for the profound significance to Poles and Germans of this ancient conflict, barely known further west. To view the tumult of battle in this monumental painting is to be thrown into the thick of it, one of life's great artistic experiences. The painting is some thirty feet long and placed in its own room in the National Museum of Warsaw. The impact on first sight is overwhelming. One can hear the clash of arms and the screams of men and horses.

Immediately after the Nazi occupation of Poland a manic search for the canvas was organised by Hans Frank, the Nazi Governor-General, as part of the programme of state-sponsored theft of Polish art collections. Joseph Göbbels offered a 10-million-mark reward for information leading to its recovery. The Nazis were convinced the painting was hidden somewhere in Lublin and many Poles were interrogated, tortured and shot by the Gestapo or transported to Auschwitz for protecting its whereabouts. In what is surely one of the most outstanding examples of Polish courage and patriotism, no one revealed where it was hidden, even under pain of death.[179] 'All battles are fought twice, once on the battlefield, then again interminably in the hearts of men.'[180]

At midnight I went for a walk around the fortress in the chill wind under a full moon. The castle was silent and deserted. I walked deep within the former moat, the walls of diapered brick towering above me like cliffs, oppressive and merciless. The stronghold is imbued with a vein of inflexible masculinity. The reconciliation of spiritual and earthly war is reflected in the stylistic unity of castle and chapel. St Bernard of Clairvaux believed that militant friars were combating

179 I am indebted for the account of the destiny of Jan Matejko's *The Battle of Grunwald* (1878) to the fascinating essay *The Political Censorship of Jan Matejko* by Danuta Batorska in *Art Journal*, Vol. 51, No. 1, Uneasy Pieces. (Spring, 1992), pp.57–63. Another patriotic Matejko painting mentioned in this article, also ruthlessly hunted down by the Nazis, was his *Prussian Homage* painted in 1882. This painting depicts the swearing of allegiance to the Polish King Sigismund I the Old (1506–1548) by Albrecht von Hohenzollern, Duke of Brandenburg, and last Grand Master of the Teutonic Order. The ceremony took place in 1525 in the Market Square in Kraków. The painting was concealed in Zamość in the crypt of the Church of St Catherine under an oath of secrecy. The work is almost as large as his Grunwald canvas and is now housed in the magnificent *Sukiennice* or Cloth Hall in Kraków.

180 Op.cit., Turnbull, *Tannenberg* p. 92

two Satans: the inner Satan fought through dedication to Mary and the strict observation of the vows of chastity, poverty and obedience; the outer Satan fought in battles against the forces of Islam or the pagans of the Baltic shore. The arresting atmosphere of decadent religious extremism saturates the architecture and reminded me of the mood of the haunting Palais des Papes at Avignon.

In the inner courtyard of the High Castle unearthly moonlight shone on a huge bronze pelican with spread wings perched on a wellhead beneath the great tower. She was 'vulning' (wounding) herself to feed her own blood to the young gathered around her, a potent symbol in medieval Christianity of self-sacrifice and the Passion. In the stillness under the stars I tried hard to imagine the daily life of these militant friars with their continual wars and sung masses but failed miserably. Murder, slavery, prayer and rape in the name of the conversion of the pagans is beyond my religious scope.

The history of Prussia is often identified with that of Germany and the Teutonic Knights. Over hundreds of years the history of the knight-brothers has been hijacked by irresponsible historians to support various nationalist causes. Hitler substantiated his perverted imperial philosophy of German statehood based on the Order and from it partially moulded the arcane philosophy of the Nazis. In creating the SS, Himmler attempted a resurrection of selected principles of the Teutonic Order and elected himself *Hochmeister* (Grand Master). The influential German historian and writer Heinrich von Treitschke politically distorted the motivation of the knights when he wrote, 'The full harshness of the Germans favoured the position of the Order amidst the heedless frivolity of the Slavs. Thus Prussia earns the name of the new Germany.'[181] The result was the displacement of over five million people and countless deaths in an attempt to regain the Slav lands 'lost' by the Teutonic Order and the restitution of 'disinherited' Germans. These wounds continue to fester even after the fall of the Iron Curtain.

The approach to the mouth of the river and the conclusion of my river journey was through featureless low-lying agricultural land.

181 Heinrich von Treitschke, *Das deutsche Ordensland Preußen* (Leipzig 1915); *Origins of Prussianism (Teutonic Knights)*, (London 1942)

The calm estuary of the Vistula is an anticlimax to the joyful tumbling at the beginning of its life in the Beskid mountains of Silesia. The crystal waters are no longer clear and have become heavily polluted on the long journey to the Baltic. The mouth of the river where it flows into the Gulf of Gdańsk forms a complex fan-delta. Small islands and shoals are produced from the sediment carried by the torrents of spring ice melt and the occasional storm surges. This low-lying area is a graveyard for coastal fishing boats. A bird sanctuary is waiting to be inundated by the rise in sea levels attributed to global warming.

The scream of seagulls next to my ear woke me from a deep sleep. I sat up violently and struck my head on the low attic ceiling. As Gdańsk is situated on the Amber Road, I thought it appropriate to stay at the Hotel Jantar (Amber Hotel) among the magnificently restored Renaissance and Baroque burgher houses. Exuberant strapwork, scrolls, swags of fruit, antelopes and bears in flight, drums and cannon and scenes of classical combat fight for space with portraits of Shakespeare. The gulls swept raucously away from their perch towards the Baltic as I poked my head out of the attic window and took in an unsurpassed view of the 'treasure of Gdańsk', the *Złota Kamienica* (Golden House), and the houses occupied by Polish kings when visiting the city. The high gables were reminiscent of Antwerp or Amsterdam, the convincing restored originality of these buildings reversing the extensive wartime damage caused by the 'liberation' of the city by the Red Army in 1944. The dilapidated interior of my room kept me at the window for some time.

The so-called 'Triune City' extends along the Bay of Gdańsk and comprises the great Hanseatic city of Gdańsk, the seaside resort town of Sopot with its faded *fin-de-siècle* charm and the industrial port of Gdynia. Gdańsk was a city of many privileges in a unique location with a complex history. Despite being dominated by Dutch and German traders attracted by the port facilities, the city remained strongly independent in outlook. The Teutonic Knights eventually relinquished it to Poland in the mid-fifteenth century. The city grew into one of the most famous centres of culture and commerce in Europe during the seventeenth century, producing fine work by goldsmiths and silversmiths, clocks and grandiose furniture (the famously huge carved wardrobes found in every magnate's house).

The city's high intellectual status produced the luminaries Daniel Gabriel Fahrenheit and Arthur Schopenhauer.

The Polish political pendulum swung energetically in Gdańsk. After the Second Partition in 1793 it fell to Prussia then briefly became a free city under Napoleon and again fell under the Prussian and German heel. The dithering at the Treaty of Versailles created the 'Danzig Corridor' under the control of the League of Nations. A compromise was reached when Danzig was created a 'Free City' having specific Polish rights which were deeply resented by German nationalists. Hitler lanced one of his many suppurating boils when the first shots of the Second World War were fired by the German battle cruiser *Schleswig-Holstein* into the Polish garrison at Westerplatte on a peninsula in the estuary of the Dead Vistula. The battle was the longest and one of the hardest fought of the German invasion.

At night the misty rain seemed to trap the city in a time-warp. Ferries and boats of all types lay at anchor, some boarded up in various states of disrepair. Dark shadows and ominous presences reared out of the deserted dark, the air strong with the smell of the sea. Ulica Mariacka is one of the most beautiful streets in the country with the features of 'old Gdańsk' preserved. Platforms on raised flights of steps (*przedproże*) cover basement shops glittering with amber and silver jewellery. Lead drainpipes descend from roofs to stone channels which terminate in the carved heads of dragons and gorgons out of whose mouths pour torrents of water when it rains. The appearance of this street in a downpour is breathtaking, the fountains forming two great streams which flow into the Motława canal. The nearby Gothic Kościół Mariacki (St Mary's Church) is the third largest in the world and accurately reflects the wealth of the Gdańsk merchants. Under the stellar vaults it contains the most tortured and intense crucifixion I have ever seen. The sculptor is reputed to have nailed his son-in-law to a cross to serve as a model. Couples hunched over café tables poured out their vodka dreams in *Goldwasser*, a vodka with glittering flakes of real gold suspended in the spirit. Floodlit steam rose in clouds into the powder-black sky over the Żuraw Gdański, a brooding wooden crane, the largest of medieval Europe.

The vast aluminium crosses of the Monument to the Fallen Shipbuilders towered above me, the symbolic anchors dissolving in the mist, the legs of the monument crumpled as if in suffering.

Gdańsk joggled the world's fickle telescope in 1980 when it focused on the Lenin Shipyard and the fearless opposition to Soviet policy being played out there. The fracture lines stretched back to 1970, when protests at heartless rises in the price of food just before Christmas resulted in a strike where Polish soldiers shot Polish workers outside the gates of the yard. The horror of Pole killing Pole struck at the very heart of the country.

By August 1980 the Polish economy had fallen into a parlous state, the rulers lacked self-confidence and Poles simmered under oppression and a bankrupt ideology. The powerful voice of the Gdańsk shipyards rose in protest at the sacking of a woman crane-driver. This strike galvanized the moustachioed Sarmatian figure of Lech Wałęsa to famously scramble over the tall gates of No. 2 entrance into the Lenin Shipyard. He leaped up beside the manager on the platform and shouted:

'Remember me? I gave ten years' work to this yard! You sacked me four years ago!'

Wałęsa injected a burst of energy into the faltering strike and transformed it into an occupation. The strikers pressed for an increase in pay, the erection of a memorial to the December 1970 martyrs, and various other conditions. Wałęsa demanded 'Solidarity'. He drove around the yard on an electric trolley, lobbying support in his inimitable fashion. By a hair's breadth the strike held together and its twenty-one demands survived. Poland embarked on an unprecedented ten-year confrontation with the Soviet Union, a great period in Polish history and a seminal one in the history of Europe.

Analysing *Solidarność* (Solidarity) as a trade union and political force and why it succeeded is a complex undertaking.[182] Communism in Poland was the most moderate of the Soviet satellites. Ideological propaganda was considered with derision by the majority of those who laboured unwillingly under it. By 1979 a social alliance had evolved that was unparalleled in the Soviet Union, invisible to most Western observers and unique in Polish history. Broadly speaking the success of *Solidarność* was due to a

---

182 The best account by far of the events surrounding the rise of Solidarity is *The Polish Revolution: Solidarity*, Timothy Garton Ash (revised edition, London 1999). The author had unique inside access to the events of that tumultuous time and wrote an account with verve, humour and political insight.

combination of the fearlessness, theatrical panache and strategic brilliance of Lech Wałęsa, his close associates and the strikers themselves. They were given unprecedented support by the intelligentsia and were spiritually strengthened by the religious scaffolding of the Catholic Church (the photographs of strikers kneeling on the asphalt to receive communion within the locked gates remain a provocative image of the period).

The visits of Pope John Paul II to Poland in 1979 and 1983 transfigured Polish consciousness and returned dignity to a humiliated people. He gave them the stamina and spiritual strength they needed to defy the imposition of martial law in 1981. Heroic 'Solidarity priests' emerged as a powerful force. The brutal murder of Father Jerzy Popiełuszko – strangled by agents of the Ministry of the Interior, his body dumped in a reservoir – further widened the fractures in the already cracked shell of the system. 'Without the Pope's leadership,' Wałęsa later observed, 'communism would have fallen, but much later and in a bloody way.'

Outside of Poland the emergence in the Soviet Union of Gorbachev's glasnost and later perestroika meant dissent within the empire could no longer be so easily suffocated. The attempts by the authorities to neutralize opposition appear naive at best and murderous at worst. The appeal to simple Polish patriotism was strong and on the many occasions when Wałęsa felt he was losing support he would cleverly invoke the uplifting march of General Dąbrowski's Polish Legions: 'Poland is not yet lost so long as we live . . .', now the national anthem. The long ten year bloodless revolution of a nature unprecedented in European history changed the complexion of the Soviet world forever. Vladimir Putin described the break-up of the Soviet Union with a degree of paranoia as 'the greatest geopolitical disaster of the twentieth century'. Paradoxically for Western observers, who still consider him one of the greatest heroes of our time, the charisma of Lech Wałęsa did not survive his transfer from shipyard to the presidential Belvedere Palace in Warsaw.

'How long do your guests stay on average?'

'Oh, about two nights. Usually they are business people,' the receptionist grimaced.

'Do you have families?'

'Oh yes. One or two nights.'

'That's not long.'

'Some individuals stay for a week.'

'Short stays, then, in the main?'

'Some families stay for two weeks.'

'A short holiday.'

'We have couples who stay for a month.'

'That would cost a lot.'

'Some individuals stay for two months.'

A beautiful example in small of the Polish spirit of besting someone at all costs; Dickens' Circumlocution Office in the Polish setting.

Zosia and I had managed a short break at a luxury hotel in Oliwa, between Gdańsk and Sopot. The famous former Cistercian abbey church is famous for its extraordinary late Rococo organ. The case is a fantastic winged framework of richly carved wood containing an ogival stained glass window depicting the Virgin Mary. There is an array of twenty-five music-making angels and putti with moving hands and musical instruments as well as a revolving sun and stars. Hearing and watching this organ in action is spectacularly entertaining.

The massive area under the control of the Teutonic Knights becomes obvious as one leaves the Vistula Delta. Moving west from Gdańsk into Pomorze Wschodnie (Eastern Pomerania) one encounters Poland's most undeveloped secret destinations – a region of picturesque lakes and rolling fields of golden maize. Avenues of limes trained into tunnels of green draw the traveller into the pine-clad hills. Engined boats are forbidden on the glassy surface of the water and a swimmer will feel his way like a water spider across a silent mirror of mercury. The area is known as Kaszuby or the 'Polish Switzerland'. It is home to a remarkable ethnic minority described, rather too cleverly, by Günter Grass in *The Tin Drum* as 'Not German enough for the Germans and not Polish enough for the Poles'. Their language is a curious mixture of Polish and German. The region is famous for honey and it was here I watched an apiarist put a handful of bees in his mouth and allow them to escape one by one from the corners. *'Proszę bardzo'* ('You're welcome'), he murmured self-effacingly after what for the onlookers was an agonizing performance.

East of Gdańsk and further into East Prussia one encounters the regions of Warmia and the superb lakeland playground of Mazury: blue water and white sails, tasselled reeds bending to the wind, sunsets over dark virgin forests. The Baltic seaboard is open and fresh with fine white strands but uninviting, rather cold, cloudy water. Windbreaks at resorts of faded glory at Sopot and Łeba speckle the beaches with all the colours of an impressionist palette. Further along the coast at the sleepy and atmospheric town of Frombork, Mikołaj Kopernik carried out many of the observations that form the basis of his immense work. His almost impossibly great mind flickered out here in 1543. Fishing boats are hauled up on the sand festooned with bright marker flags fluttering like Himalayan prayer banners.

'A man would stand on the floor, which would get hotter and hotter, until he was forced to leap from the window onto the sharpened stakes below.'

The toothless old man with a fascination for the gruesome was dressed in gumboots, a Breton beret and a jacket in the Black Watch tartan. A dog that had been waiting at the window was beside itself with excitement, running in ever-decreasing circles and barking madly. Zosia and I were at the obscure ruined Teutonic mansion-fortress at Szymbark at the head of a long lake, one of the most poetically eloquent and romantic of the knight-brothers' castles. Zosia had managed to obtain the key by first deciphering an almost illegible sign precariously balanced on a chair inside the gate indicating its whereabouts.

'Here a man was lowered into a deep pit, thus frightening him into confession.' Our colourful local demonstrated the position of the rope by rubbing under Zosia's arms and suggestively under her breasts. The palace was intact until 1945 when again as elsewhere the Russians suspected it of concealing Nazis and bombed it into the next world.

'You don't mind if I have a little drink! *Na zdrowie!*' Our 'guide' had produced some cherry liqueur and began swigging thirstily from the bottle.

A little further south-east is one of the best preserved moated Teutonic castles at Lidzbark Warmiński (Heilsberg), which the powerful Bishops of Warmia used as a fortified residence for some four hundred years. There is a fascinating collection of icons in the castle imitative of those by the Russian genius Andrei Rublev, taken for safety from the convent of 'Old Believers' at Wojnowo. This 'Old Rite' sect fled the reforms of Peter the Great, only two nuns being left alive when we visited this remarkable place. The passion for Teutonic castles was finally halted at a restaurant called Happy End, which seemed singularly appropriate as I was quite worn out simply contemplating the past power of the Teutons let alone fighting them.

CHAPTER 24

'A Mixed Economy Kleptocracy'

'Mosquitoes don't bite me, wouldn't touch me!'

Geoff was adjusting his cheap and cheerful sandals in the hospitality suite.

'I just wipe me contact lenses on the grass, me. No fancy cleaners!'

The fug was well established in the room, with underwear and socks tumbling in the dryer. He was planning a hiking and camping trip with his lady of the moment.

'Where are you planning to go, Geoff?' I asked.

'Not so posh as you in that bloody limousine. Kaliningrad. Sleep in a barn on straw if necessary.'

'Kaliningrad! There's not much to see there except industry. Did you get a visa?'

'Don't need a visa for Kaliningrad. I'll just jump over the fence.'

I was never sure whether Geoff was being serious.

'There was a fax for you, Mike. Have you read it?' Richard appeared concerned.

A curt message from Zurich asked me to press home the payment ultimatum. There was also trouble in Bath. I would be the sole representative on our side if the contract was to be renewed. Mr Lustenberger had tired of impossible alternatives to secure the debt and had decided to reduce the staff to a token presence.

Byzantine schemes and cabals greeted my return to the centre after the summer break. Alternative solutions flew across desks like so many billiard balls across the green baize. Whispers, huddles, sudden silences, the whole repertoire of historically practised secrecy now seemed to be everywhere. Most of the Polish staff felt we were an unnecessary financial drain on the project. The accountant Andrzej and the board on the Polish side had formed a new company in an attempt to salvage the project and reschedule the debt. This had bought them time as the legal process was agonizingly slow. Lies and half-truths flew thick and fast.

'We would not turn you out in the street, Michael. How can you think such a thing!' Andrzej uttered without conviction and a slight smirk.

'Things are in such a mess,' I said in despair.

'Michael, let me tell you something about the Poles. Imagine we are in Hell.'

'Well, that's not difficult.'

'All the damned souls are boiling in pitch in their various national pots and each has a guard to stop any sufferer escaping.'

'I'm not sure I'm in the mood for this, Andrzej.'

'Each has a guard except the Polish pot.'

'Oh yes. Go on. Why is that?'

'Because any Pole who tries to escape is pulled back down into the soup by the other Poles envious he is escaping. It's called solidarity!' Andrzej erupted into gales of laughter.

'Is that supposed to be funny, Andrzej?'

At a meeting held with superb Polish politesse we were informed that *pan Dyrektor* Fukowski was leaving without notice amid a litany of thanks and a catalogue of his 'achievements'. Flowers were duly given. The President looked terribly ill and I sympathized with his courageous attempt to come to the meeting and grasp the nettle of the market economy. As is often the case with presidents, he had not been well served by his minions. Effective communication is not conspicuously strong in the Polish character, which leads to many misunderstandings. The malaise infected groups of trainees, who left without even a farewell, an extraordinary omission in Polish culture, where farewells are normally emotional and protracted affairs.

I suggested the beleaguered English team begin looking for alternative employment as the already non-existent contract was unlikely to be renewed.

'Well, after that news I need a bracer! At the Elgin Hotel in

Darjeeling, breakfast comes with a half of Pol Roger to counteract the morning chill.'

'Here we go again. What's a bracer, then? Posh clever clogs frum down south as per usual!'

'Also called a stiffener. Similarly an iced vodka at 9.00am sets you up for the morning. I don't know whether I told you of my collateral antecedent Father Matthew, the Apostle of Irish Temperance. Anyway, he is credited with the introduction of the practice of drinking ether – quote "the liquor a man can drink with a clear conscience". All the effects of alcohol but a clear head again after fifteen minutes. Apparently the practice was so widespread that railway carriages used to reek of the stuff.'

'Well, that sort of sounds interesting,' said David.

'I'm straight back to Bradford I am. Out of this dump, back to the UK. We worked bloody hard! For what?' Geoff sucked fiercely at a tin of beer.

'Anyone for the Irish pub? Met this geezer the other night. The Duke of Chatham. A real aristocrat. We got on like, both bein' aristocrats.'

Richard continued unabashed.

'There were two problems associated with ether. It was difficult to drink because it evaporated quickly in the warmth of the mouth. The usual practice was to drink iced water and then down a shot of ether. Occasionally, it evaporated too fast in the digestive tract and caused violent eructations. The other problem was its flammability. In Russia an ether drinker exploded, killing three children and injuring fifteen.'

'Excellent. Excellent. Nice one. Nice one. Should take some to the Horrenda Club.'

Nick was often chased by irate Russians on the Warsaw club circuit.

David and Geoff finally refused to attend any further meetings, became severely demoralized and began writing letters of application. David thought he might head off to Qatar as working conditions and pay were excellent, and Geoff planned to return to Bradford to patch up his relationship with his children. Nick was going through a personal crisis. An English solicitor had stolen his Polish girlfriend (he habitually 'pedestalized' Polish women into madonnas, which is not at all what they wanted). The door to his room slammed open violently ten times a night, followed by beating on the walls at 4.00am fit to bring down the building. Everyone rushed into the corridors in alarm.

'Burstin' out! Just burstin' out!'

Nick attended all the meetings but seemed incapable of rational thought and dwelt on irrelevancies.

'What abou' materials then? Ya know like, what about 'em? My Batman and Robin films.'

Pani Jola asked him if he had borrowed some dictionaries and to please return them before he left. He now refused to speak to her in Polish.

'I ain't got nuffink!'

When she appeared sceptical, he stormed out.

'Well, I'll have a look in me room then!'

He returned to her office with four dictionaries, threw the heavy books across the desk and started to hit the walls, banging on the door, threatening to throttle the now trembling Pani Jola.

'He would be chock me! Ergh . . . ergh . . .' she told me in broken English with a graphic illustration of a choke hold.

I had a long 'pastoral' chat with Nick about why he might attract violence to himself and lash out in physical anger at reversals.

'When I see 'er, I wanna hit 'er like, ya know!'

The class system in England and his difficult upbringing were clearly playing havoc with his psychology. He said he might apply for a post at Bristol university. Richard on the other hand, urbane as usual, was planning a bit of teaching in Cambridge, punting on the Cam and high tea at Grantchester with his latest Russian nymphet who was studying sub-atomic physics at Trinity. That or a visit to India and his father's regiment, the Rajputana Rifles.

The accountant Andrzej, in a frenzy of improvisational virtuosity, continued to float hopeless marketing schemes and make outrageous promises in an attempt to save the project. Dreams of a businessman. Whenever he encountered an authority figure his demeanour changed dramatically to whispered asides, obsequious and oriental manners, the low masculine intonation of the Polish 'man of business' on the telephone. Any implication of subterfuge brought a faint smile to his lips, the relentless precursor of implied duplicity. Then Andrzej simply disappeared without notice.

In Poland communism led to a complete erosion of ethics in almost all transactions of life outside the family and the few other 'closed' social groups. The decay of the socialist economic system at this time had evolved into what one academic termed a 'mixed economy kleptocracy'.[183] The development of accountability, financial self-discipline, proper marketing strategies and the increased adoption of Western management structures have completely transformed the private business sector in Poland. But the communist mentality of absolute distrust and veiled intentions will be difficult to eradicate. Sceptical calculation has definite short-term advantages in the market economy and in dealing with state bureaucracy.

The cultivation of Byzantine defensive strategies was an imperative in Polish society if you were not a member of the Party. This need for concealment eroded the capacity for transparent communication in private business and the echoes of these habits remain problematical. Knowledge was power so the imperative was to retain it. This is hardly surprising considering the severe penalties imposed by successions of totalitarian invaders if one 'said the wrong thing'. Most of my correspondence during the course of the breakdown of the project remained unanswered, telephone calls were not returned whether in English or Polish. This situation has not greatly improved. Communism seems to have created a permanent climate of fear.

The present generation of young people raised in freedom are largely unaffected by the communist upbringing of their parents. They could be on a different planet to their elders, yet many could profitably relearn the charm, graciousness and sensibility that Poles were famous for throughout Europe before the Second World War. A completely different breed of young Poles is emerging who are excellent at languages, highly skilled professionally, ambitious and hard-working, who have a more cosmopolitan and internationalist outlook. They mercifully lack the crippling provincial xenophobia and devaluation of the work ethic of the past. Hopefully at least some of them will stay in Poland.

---

183 *The Decay of Socialism and the Growth of Private Enterprise in Poland*, Jacek Rostowski in *Polish Paradoxes* ed. S. Gomułka & A. Polonsky (London 1990) p. 198

The death throes of the project were prolonged by indecision on both sides. I overheard a phone call Nick made to Jennifer in Bath using his curiously contrived language.

'It behoves me to pass the information that you have made a miscalculation of my holiday pay. Could you do somethin' about it if and when?'

The final groups were examined and issued with their certificates. I felt wretched as the pedagogical side had been so successful. The edifice had foundered on disorganization, lack of forward vision and the seduction of short-term financial gain. The disparate groups engaged on the project failed to pull together as one, pursued individual agendas and lacked any sense of corporate loyalty. More emotionally the collapse meant separation from Zosia, which was dreadful to contemplate.

Our final barbeque party beside the Vistula was a happy affair with Nick playing his guitar and singing songs, kilometres of grilled *kiełbasa* (sausage) washed down with oceans of beer and vodka. The last groups of beautiful girls danced with abandon round the fire and taught us Polish songs. David and Geoff demonstrated some Morris dancing with much cracking of staves and tinkling of bells. The Poles loved it. I spoke to one of the female trainees, who was related to one of Hitler's Prussian generals. The family had returned to East Prussia their old home.

'Such a pity we are leaving the project. How do you feel about it?'

'Pass me a grenade,' she replied without blinking.

The highlight was the fun-filled burning by the English team of yet another but more ornate effigy of their team leader dressed in an old suit, shirt and tie. They performed a circular dance around it and shouted warlike Native American incantations as the straw burst into flames and his sadly drawn face melted.

The next day at the centre was strangely quiet. Rain began to fall after everyone had left for the airport. I felt like a general who had lost his troops. Despite the difficulties with the project and clashes there had been many satisfactions. Autumn was already turning the leaves to gold in the neglected Italian garden. One of the janitors was attempting to paint some white lines along the kerbing at the entrance. The paint adhered quite well in the rain, until he reached the end and looked back over his handiwork. The drizzle had washed it off and the remainder was slowly dribbling in a white river down the drain. He sighed heavily and his shoulders heaved as he returned to begin again. I could hardly avoid the parallels with my own situation. Now I was forced to wait alone for my own sentence to be passed. I refused to be cowed despite my lack of optimism and planned some final autumn excursions in a country whose spirit of renewal I had come to admire, even to love.

I travelled first to the village of Nieborów near Chopin's birthplace at Żelazowa Wola where my favourite Polish country house and pendant garden is situated, one of the great mansion and park ensembles in Europe. I knew it would console me. Eschewing the Radziwiłł mansion, I briefly sat on a garden seat with the admonitory and apt Latin inscription *Non sedas sed eas* (Do not sit down but go on).

About a mile from Nieborów, Princess Helena Radziwiłł created the astonishing garden of Arkadia over a period of forty years. With the assistance of her architect Szymon Bogumił Zug and the French painter Jean-Pierre Norblin de la Gourdaine, she evolved a picturesque and elegiac garden of allusions, one of the most extraordinary 'sentimental' eighteenth-century gardens in Europe. Changing vistas were evoked by the golden pastorals of Claude Lorrain and the dramatic classicism of Nicholas Poussin. The English Virgilian landscapes created at Stowe, Stourhead and by Alexander Pope at Twickenham played their part, while the magnificent German realm of Wörlitz exemplified the rule of Reason and Nature. Arkadia was conceived as an eloquent set of theatre scenes evoking the vanished joys and lost ideals of the Enlightenment. An inscription reads *L'ésperance nourrit une Chimère et la Vie S'écoule* (Hope nourishes a Delusion as Life slips away). 'Arkadia was all about memories, reveries, regrets and keeping civilisation and culture alive.'[184]

Lying on the grass in the sun it was not difficult to imagine

---

[184] For this all too brief description of Arkadia I am indebted to the brilliant scholarly essay *Arkadia, Poland: Garden of Allusions* James Stevens Curl in *Garden History*, Vol.23, No.1 (Summer, 1995), pp. 91–112

'Turkish' *fêtes galantes* on the lake among those 'crowds of vanishing, marvellous creatures'[185] languishing in the autumnal paintings of Watteau. Willows trailed leaves in the still waters around the islands, swans glided by while boats set sail for the *île de Cythère*. A world of intense impressions, melancholy, poignancy and reflective thought, an excursion particularly apposite in my present situation.

185 Charles Baudelaire

CHAPTER 25

'Only the Music of the Forest Playing'

–Pan Tadeusz

Shortly before I arrived in Poland in January 1992 a historic event took place deep within a primeval forest in Belarus. In a hunting lodge in the wilderness of Belovezha forest, Boris Yeltsin, Leonid Kravchuk and Stanislau Shushkevich officially dissolved the sixty-nine-year-old Soviet Union with the stroke of a pen. The old Polish–Lithuanian Commonwealth formed by the Union of Lublin in 1569 had finally been transformed into a number of nation states. I wanted to visit the primeval forest of Białowieża one final time. This wilderness in the north-east of the country straddles the Polish–Belarusian frontier known as the *Puszcza* Białowieska. For Poles the *puszcza* is hallowed ground and a symbol of national imperishability. This would be the last autumn excursion I made with Zosia before leaving Poland and I had something special in mind. She had never visited nearby Białystok, a city of remarkable ethnic diversity and home to a palace once known as the 'Polish Versailles'.

The obscure hotel I had chosen in woodland near the town was close to the border with Belarus, a low concrete barracks that could only have been described as Communist Gothic. Under the harsh sodium lights of the car-park, a Russian-registered BMW sat low on its suspension, the crazed blacked-out windows and scratched navy paintwork covered in mud. A forest of communication aerials added to a rakish appearance that exuded an air of powerful illegality. The exhaust crackled as it cooled. I parked my modest ivory FSO beside it.

After negotiating a number of impossible aluminium-framed doors opening in different directions I walked into *Recepcja* and was stared at sullenly from the bar by a 'criminal crew' of borderland Poles, Russians, Ukrainians, Belarusians and possibly descendants of the Tatars. Leering mouths full of gold teeth and cheap cigarettes. Indeterminate pop music was loud and gambling machines bleeped and winked red. The place stank of cabbage water and linseed oil. A couple of English truck drivers were talking loudly.

'Safely in Poland from Moscow, John, thank Christ! Once you cross that border, you sigh with fuckin' relief, mate.'

Conversation stopped as I approached the desk. As I was being checked in by a typical unfriendly *biurwa*,[186] the owner of the BMW coughed and splayed his gargantuan limbs over a sofa of split vinyl. He was an overweight mafia type in crocodile shoes, reeking of aftershave and wearing a tailored Italian suit. His wrists were festooned with heavy gold bracelets and a massive gold watch, fingers dripping with gold rings. He lazily stroked his 'moll', a slight bleached blonde. Two silent 'heavies' sat at the nearby table, one in a lurid mint-green shell suit and the other in casual mauve.

The road from Warsaw to Białystok is almost dead straight which gives a free-breathing open feel to the sparsely populated landscape. Golden birch glowed against deep green swathes of pine. The landscape has a definite eastern feel with moors, small lakes and forest buried in an autumn cloak of russet, yellow, and orange. The region reflects an astonishing diversity of faiths – Orthodox, Christian, Muslim and Jewish – exhibiting the remarkably broad nature of the former Polish–Lithuanian Commonwealth.

I had first visited Białystok alone in winter some months before. A chronically poor city, the remaining wooden houses were reminiscent of scenes from a nineteenth-century Belarusian novel. In the area of the old Jewish ghetto an old man, stubble-cheeked,

---

186 An insulting word used to describe the particularly morose and distinctly unhelpful female office functionary encountered everywhere throughout the communist period and unfortunately only slowly dying off.

with sacking leggings stretched over his boots and a hessian bag slung over one shoulder stared at me fixedly. Weathered faces, downcast eyes, bent backs carried buckets of coal or water into shattered tenements over the icy pavements. Women looked to have laboured all the feminine joy from their exhausted bodies. They ignored the fashionable contents of the new boutiques stocked with erotic Italian lingerie. Ancient crones stooped to gather cranberries abandoned by birds in the snow. Belarusians, Tatars, Russians, Ukrainians and Poles would have formed a fascinating ethnic mixture were it not for the crippling poverty, particularly among the old. The heroic Białystok Ghetto Uprising of August 1943 was the first in the Reich and doomed to instant failure, but the insurgents felt it was better to die fighting than in the gas chamber. Nearly all the sixty thousand Jews of the town were liquidated. Białystok has become far more prosperous in recent years and the pre-industrial atmosphere I encountered over a decade ago has disappeared forever.

The poverty could not have been in greater contrast with the French-inspired palace and formal gardens of the flamboyant Pałac Branickich (Branicki Palace) rebuilt in 1730 for Hetman Jan Klemens Branicki, Palatine of Kraków and Field Hetman to the Crown. The entire town revolves around the beautiful palace park, an oasis of calm. Little survives of an interior once furnished with the finest panelling, furniture, textiles and objets d'art from Paris. But there were more horses in Branicki's stables than books in his library. Charles Hanbury Williams, mentor to the young future king, Stanisław Augustus Poniatowski, visited the palace in 1752 and wrote: 'I was lodged in one of the wings & before my window there was drawn up every morning a company of Janissaries exactly dressed like those of the Sultan, & at 5 of the clock I was usually awaked by Turkish musick which is very bad.'[187] Branicki at sixty had married Izabela, the eighteen-year-old sister of Poniatowski, but she was soon in the loving arms of a younger man. Branicki went to great lengths to indulge King Augustus III in his notions of a good day's shooting.

187 Quoted in *The Last King of Poland*, Adam Zamoyski (London 1992) p. 36

Wild animals, brought in cages and released in the groves of this charming place, were forced to climb along wooden ramps with tall sides to the tops of trees which line the canal. There they found a pivoting trap which, by projecting them over the water at a height of thirty yards, gave the king the opportunity of shooting wolves, boars and bears in full flight.[188]

There follows a highly amusing account of a flying bear landing in the prow of a boat, throwing the aristocratic occupants into the water. All the creatures thrashed about together in a state of some distress to the mighty amusement of the monarch. It is hardly surprising to learn that Branicki with his own pretensions to the throne did so little to prevent the disintegration of the Commonwealth.

It was a Sunday morning during my autumn visit with Zosia and a service was in progress in the nineteenth-century Church of St Nicholas. A deep-toned choir and incense drifted through the darkness in the slow complex ritual of the Orthodox service. There are some two hundred thousand Orthodox Christians in the region, a quarter of whom are Belarusian. Dim candles fitfully lit the iconostasis and frescoed walls copied from the Orthodox cathedral in Kiev. Beards of great wisdom and chasubles of gold, ciboria draped in cloth of gold, surreptitious movements behind golden gates lined with mauve silk were in a mysterious communion with God.

We went to sit in an old coffee bar to drink the Polish variation of Turkish coffee.

'Weren't the forests around Białystok once part of Lithuania?' I knew Zosia's mother had grown up in the small town of Oszmiana close to Vilnius (Wilno), now the capital of the reborn Baltic state.

'Yes, but what a complicated story that is! It was a long time ago during the Commonwealth and the Grand Duchy of Lithuania. Before the Second World War Wilno was Polish. Do you know the opening of *Pan Tadeusz* by Mickiewicz?'

'You remember it?'

'Every Polish schoolchild knows it!' She quoted the beginning of the national epic in Polish.

188 Ibid., Zamoyski p. 36 from *Mémoires du Roi Stanislas-Auguste Poniatowski*, ed. S. Goriainov Vol. I, St. Petersburg 1914

Lithuania! My fatherland!
You are like health. Only he who has lost you may know your
true worth.

'Vilnius' in Lithuanian, 'Wilno' in Polish, 'Vil'nia' in Belarusian,
'Vil'na' in Russian and 'Vilne' in Yiddish. For almost five hundred years
the majority of the population of the city were Jews and Poles and it
had a predominantly Polish culture. Belarusian was spoken in the countryside. As the idea of the nation state developed, acquisition of the
ancient capital of the former Grand Duchy of Lithuania became a political and spiritual goal for a number of conflicting groups. 'In this house
of mirrors . . . local nationalists were absorbed in an image they desired
to see as distinct, pure and beautiful.'[189] The President of Lithuania,
Valdas Adamkus recently commented, 'From the Battle of Grunwald
to the Kościuszko Uprising, at all crucial moments of our common history, Poland could always rely on Lithuania, while the Lithuanians
could always count on Polish friendship.' Adam Mickiewicz conceived
of Lithuania as a land of different peoples but with an ultimately Polish
fate. He could not have imagined it as the culturally and politically distinct state it has become. He yearned for a more lyrical past.

As butterflies drown in golden amber
Let us remain, dear, as we once were.[190]

These beautiful lines are a perfect expression of nostalgia in the
face of the juggernaut of 'progress'.
'Zosia, what happened to your mother's family during the war?'
'My grandfather was a civil servant, so when the Russians invaded
in 1939 he was protected by his Jewish friends. Then under the
Nazis he in turn attempted to assist these same Jewish friends – doctors, lawyers and so on.'

---

189 For a full clarification of the profound complexities surrounding the contested claims to modern
Vilnius and Polish Lithuanian relations refer to the perceptive and scholarly *The Reconstruction of
Nations: Poland, Ukraine, Lithuania, Belarus 1569–1999*, Timothy Snyder (New Haven & London
2003) pp. 15–102. Snyder tactfully and tellingly avoids committing himself to any nationalist or partisan view of the mixed origins of the Polish national poet Adam Mickiewicz by captioning a
reproduction of the frontispiece to the 1834 edition of *Pan Tadeusz* 'Adam Mickiewicz (1798–1855),
European Romantic poet of the Polish language.'
190 Adam Mickiewicz, *Konrad Wallenrod* (1828)

'You mean Jews hid Poles? That's a new one!'

'Yes, of course! The friendships between educated Poles and Jews in the east was very strong. You should speak to ordinary people about what they felt, not listen to all those anti-Semitic arguments that followed some terrible isolated events.'

'Well, I really don't want to get into that, Zosia. Tiger country, really. You know how negatively Poles are represented in the West regarding the Jews. And then there was that terrible Jedwabne pogrom not far from here when fifteen hundred Jews were burned alive in a barn.'

'I know, I know, but it was an isolated event and all too horrible to talk about!' So many Poles I have met, perhaps understandably, lapse into silence whenever Jews and their terrible fate are mentioned.

'And then?'

'And then in 1944 the Russians came again. Someone informed on my grandfather and he was put in a Russian prison. He managed to get a message out telling my grandmother to leave. They were packed into cattle cars in the heat of midsummer and sent west. About one and a half million Poles were forced from Soviet occupied territory. The train often stopped in the stifling temperatures and the driver could only be persuaded to continue with bribes of vodka. My mother was only fourteen and her two sisters were eight and ten. Grandmother and the children decided to go to the terminus of the train at Zielona Góra (Grünberg) as far as possible from the Russians.'

'Where did they live?'

'Well, the Germans had all fled in panic leaving everything behind – books, paintings, furniture, crystal, their cars, as there was no petrol for civilian use. There was a lot of looting. They could move into any empty German house and my grandmother was so terrified she moved into the first one that had a Polish-speaking family living on the top floor. It was absolute chaos in those days. My mother and her sisters have been living in that house ever since.'

'But how did they survive? Where did the money come from for food?'

'Barter mainly. They only had a bag of peas and a goat to begin with.'

*

The extremes within the Polish temperament are reflected in the richly varied landscape which ranges from pristine primeval forest to the most polluted soil in Europe, a country where chemically damaged children seek rehabilitation in the mountains. It was the Polish trees that captivated me from the very beginning of my excursions around the country. The leaves on linden, birch and aspen have the tremulous, nervous movement of impressionist paintings. The rapid vibration is like a marvellous electro-chemical agitation. The branches sway lethargically, flexibly in the summer breeze above impossibly slender trunks. In winter the bare birch and pine forests on the Mazovian plain creak in a mood of melancholy solitariness, a haunting accompaniment to any wanderer in the snow. In the ancient forest of Białowieża the last herds of European bison roam amidst the chaos of the primeval bog together with lynx, eagle, roe deer, wolf, wild boar, red fox and elk.

The first encounter with Białowieża, one of the last lowland primeval forests in Europe and the home of the *żubr* or Lithuanian bison, is an experience never to be forgotten. In spring the birdsong can be deafening from trees whose new buds paint the forest with a wash of mauve. Storks repair their nests high on power poles or platforms thoughtfully attached to the eaves of houses. In high summer the forest floor is a profusion of wildflowers and butterflies in sunlit clearings. In winter irregular and mysterious animal tracks in the snow lead into the interior.

Zosia and I followed a long straight road that cut like a sword through the forest. The mists of autumn suited our melancholy situation. The road passed through golden woods of oak, birch, aspen, ash, linden and hornbeam, gradually giving way to gloomy stands of elderly pine and spruce, many trees over a hundred and fifty years old. The river valley of the Narew flows through marshy meadows scattered with willows where beavers gnaw at fallen logs. In a grove dedicated to Polish kings, a set of monumental oaks are twisted and gnarled into disconsolate form by the passing of six hundred years. The crowns of trees disappeared in the swirling mist, the entire region deserted and seemingly bereft of human life. The felt absence of the secretly executed began to insinuate itself once again into my consciousness as invariably happens when I am in a Polish forest.

The murderous joy of the hunter and the sweated panic of the hunted filled my imagination. King Władysław Jagiełło hunted here to build up a stock of food before the battle of Grunwald. Even the aesthete King Stanisław Augustus Poniatowski, not a man one would associate with blood sports, shot bears from a pavilion in Białowieża forest in the eighteenth century. Teutonic Knights, Russian tsars, Lithuanian princes and Sarmatian magnates pursued bison, lynx (their pelts used for the winged cavalry), bear and wild boar through the marshy and gaseous bog sparkling with iridescent dragonflies and spotted with luminous orange and scarlet fungi. The Nazis hunted men in glades of dappled sunlight. In homicidal saloons the Gestapo and NKVD sped along these same roads to torture human prey in groves of oak to the song of the barred warbler.

In a more lyrical present I have tried to shut out the persistent layers of memory that cloud my enjoyment of Polish forests, those bloody hectares of sand and pine. It is in a thoughtful mood that one strolls along tracks marked with the twin swords above a cauldron of flame, the device of memorials to partisan deaths. Nature herself remains indifferent and generous, cemented in a timeless present as bluebells flower, butterflies dance and birds chirrup in spring.

We visited the bison enclosure, the *żubry* a similar though different species to the shaggy auroch of legend hunted with spears by Sarmatian warriors. The Lithuanian bison is a chocolate-brown beast with a powerful muscular neck and massive head. Adults can weigh up to seven hundred kilos. They munch an aromatic grass used to make *Żubrówka* vodka, strands of which are sometimes placed optimistically under the conjugal mattress. They are quiet and still in the enclosure, distant and bored by the gaping children and camera-mad tourists. No longer do they charge the pavilions of royal hunters, eyes maddened red, the *mort* blown on the horn at the kill. Over four hundred *żubry* now roam free throughout the National Park, but like all the animals here they are sensibly wary of man and readily take flight.

In Białowieża, the Saxon King Augustus III of Poland, that indolent lover of fine art, energetically pursued his other great love, killing animals. Near Dresden he arranged to shoot 'geese, monkeys and hares dressed in costumes of Angelinas, Harlequins, Crispins and Caramuzzos'. At Białowieża one notorious day in 1752 after breakfasting luxuriously on cake and champagne the King and his party seated themselves on the platform of the pavilion for a day's shooting.

Wearing kid gloves the Queen ostentatiously opened a French novel in a fine binding. A trumpet fanfare sounded as the first bison were driven before the royal party along a narrow corridor. A great puff of smoke came from a heavy calibre rifle. Augustus III had despatched his first bull. The *mort* was sounded on the horn. The audience applauded wildly. The Queen looked up from her book, shot the second bull and 'looked indifferently at her victim going into convulsions, and directed her bulging eyes back to the pages of her novel. The Queen of Poland interrupted her reading twenty times.'[191] The kill that bloody September day amounted to forty-two bison (eighteen bulls, eighteen cows and six calves), thirteen elk and two roebuck. An obelisk inscribed in Polish and German was raised in Białowieża Palace Park to commemorate the immortal event.

In Warsaw Zosia had bought me as a parting gift a copy of a *hełm karacenowy* (helmet of Karacena armour). This type of 'scale armour' was unique in the history of European armour, more a seventeenth-century ideological statement of Sarmatism than a development in protection.[192] It was beautiful and ruinously expensive. I had brought this talisman with me to Białowieża. A man quietly passed riding a bicycle with a huge set of antlers strapped behind the seat. We parked the car and set off on foot through the trackless wilderness.

The clearing we chose after a light trek was dripping with moisture, the undergrowth a tangled mass of fallen trunks and rotting branches, vines, leaves and moss. A rude wooden cross with a

---

191 *The Białowieża Forest Saga*, Simona Kossak (Warsaw 2001) 240–245. This is a fine, emotionally committed account of the tortured history of this magical place and takes a partisan ecological stance. For the hunts see the invaluable *Mémoire descriptif sur le forêt impériale de Białowieża en Lithuanie*, Baron J. von Brincken (Warsaw 1828). The elegantly written and moving *Landscape and Memory*, Simon Schama (London 1995) 23–75 deals with the forest of Białowieża as a personal reminiscence and also in the wider context of landscape. The book is a magnificent and unique study, one of the great books of recent times.

192 Individual metal scales were sewn onto an elkskin or deerskin backing or riveted to a metal backing with gold or brass rivets. Sometimes this armour was decorated with mascarons of gilded lions' heads (associated with Hercules, who slayed the Numean lion). The scaled helmet had a coloured turban around the rim, a type unknown in the East or West.

wreath of barbed wire marked an execution site. The primordial chaos and confusion was reminiscent of the ruined walls of abbeys or cathedrals shattered by time. Fallen trunks breached stagnant black ponds like decaying castle ramparts.

> Who has explored in Lithuania
> The forests to the centre of their awe,
> Their deep abyss, the kernel of their thicket?[193]

I looked about me for a suitable 'altar' to place the helmet. Sedge was withering by brackish ponds of sluggishly flowing water drifting with electric green algae and a crust of rust. Mushrooms dotted the forest floor and a bracket fungus thrust from a tree trunk. The roots of perished oaks reared up from the marsh like placentas wrenched from the womb. A stump with clinging moss presented a perfect primitive table and I placed the *hełm* with its red silk turban on the soft, green surface. In front of the stump I laid a small Bokhara rug over the fallen leaves and we sat down cross-legged.

The silence was punctuated by the staccato tap of a frenzied woodpecker, occasional birdsong and the erratic pat of dripping water on the carpet of leaves. The low groan of rutting red deer or *żubry* drifted on the faint breeze from the depths of the forest. As lovers we felt like outlaws seeking a brief asylum in this refuge as generations of outlaws had done before us. A branch occasionally fell to earth as if an animal was crashing through the undergrowth. A strange inner peace took hold. We held hands touching the helmet and looked into each other's eyes.

'We promise to do everything to keep our love alive even if we are forced apart.'

'Yes.'

'And we will work so that we can be together always.'

'Yes, we will.'

We sealed this admittedly rather unsentimental pledge with a passionate kiss and a sip of Ukrainian brandy from the silver lid of my hunter's flask. The perfumed spirit enfolded us. This simple compact

---

193 *Pan Tadeusz*, Adam Mickiewicz trans. Watson Kirkonnell (New York 1981) Bk.IV 53–5

made in that ancient forest has survived many years of trial and separation.

As the dense damp chilled us to the bone and the ants began to bite, we rose reluctantly, the spell broken. Just two kilometres from the Belarusian border, we drove through the old village of Białowieża with its streets of wooden peasant cottages in washed-out greens and blues with carved and columned entrance porches. Old ladies in colourful headscarves took the air with their cats as the day drew in.

The villagers, the forest and the animals suffered greatly from the depredations of foreign invaders, particularly after the final partition of Poland in 1795. After the Kościuszko Insurrection had been suppressed, the Empress Catherine II rewarded her generals with huge estates, forests, and entire villages with their resident 'souls' stolen from the conquered lands. Poaching was rife and the forest lost a third of its area to the shipbuilding industry, timber being the crude oil of those times. During Napoleon's retreat from Moscow Białowieża became the anarchic scene of peripheral campaigns between the French, the Austrians, the Saxons and the Russians. In 1820 Tsar Alexander I in an access of ecological vision made Białowieża a protected reserve but over the next sixty years successive tsars plundered it. By 1888 Tsar Alexander III had become the sole owner of Białowieża. He built a 'palace' of dubious architectural provenance to accommodate hunting parties of the European aristocracy invited each October for sport. Large amounts of game were introduced, which unbalanced the ecology – everything green in sight was nibbled by fallow deer. Tsar Nicholas II continued the tradition of the annual hunt riding out over a specially constructed 'silent road' in a troika. We wandered the extensive and beautiful English park laid out with lawns, copses and ponds between the riverbeds of the Narewka.

During the Great War the German military machine savaged the forest and, as that war failed, the famished troops butchered the forest animals for food. Ironically it was an English company, the Century European Corporation, that caused the greatest havoc when it was given a concession in 1924 to cut four million cubic metres of timber over a period of ten years. The wholesale destruction was finally stopped by the Ministry of Agriculture and under the Piłsudski government part of the forest was declared one of Poland's first national parks. Now this area is a designated World Heritage Site and Biosphere Reserve.

The summer of 1934 saw the arrival of the strangest of all the corpulent figures to stalk the creatures of Białowieża: Herman Göring, 'the monstrous, jewel-encrusted hippopotamus of the Third Reich'.[194] The First World War air ace and operatically costumed *Reichsjägermeister* came to Białowieża to satisfy his compulsion to hunt. He was an expert in the arcane art of interpreting animal droppings and the effect of testicles *in situ* on the taste of venison and antler growth. In his novel *The Erl-King* Michel Tournier paints an unforgettably vivid picture of Göring the hunter with his 'enormous white rump pointing skywards'.

> It was wonderful to see him running heavily from one [dead stag] to another waving his hunting spear. He parted the warm legs of the still palpitating bodies and plunged both hands in. With the right he made a rapid sawing movement, with the left he groped in the scrotum for the testicles, pink, opalescent eggs of living flesh. It is commonly believed that unless a stag is emasculated as soon as possible after it is shot, its flesh becomes musky and inedible.[195]

Dressed in a pale blue silk kimono he would share a haunch of roast wild boar with his pet lion seated beside him at the dinner table, the bleeding meat passing lethargically to and fro between them. By 1941 the Nazis had taken over the forest but, with their mythical German reverence for the primeval, Göring and Himmler declared it a *heiliger Hain* or holy domain. 'The Teutonic knight, reborn for the ages, would wipe out the shame of Grunwald.'[196]

The Nazis felt justified in extending the frontiers of East Prussia as far east as possible and in Germanizing the landscape as an ideal hunting preserve. Two hundred villages around Białowieża were burnt and the farm animals slaughtered. Thousands of men were

194 *Landscape and Memory*, Simon Schama (London 1995) p. 67
195 *The Erl-King*, Michel Tournier (London 1972). A compelling portrait of Göring the hunter is painted in the chapter *The Ogre of Rominten* pp. 169–205
196 Op.cit., Schama p. 69

shot in the 'Teutonic Wood' and buried in pits; the Jews were cleared as vermin from the land. Nazi officers slept in Alexander's palace and stalked the now suitably Aryanized elk and bison. As they retreated they burnt the palace. Following on, the communists demolished it completely to build a ghastly concrete hotel. This has now fortunately been replaced with a superb museum devoted to the natural history of the forest.

In a laudable move in 1991 the Belarus Cabinet declared a huge area (close to a hundred thousand hectares) of their section of the Belovezhskaya Pushcha a National Park and are managing it well. In contrast Poland has become embroiled in a seemingly inescapable conflict between national and local interests operating under strong international pressure. The situation was recently exacerbated when the Director of the National Park was arrested on corruption charges. The extension of the park under differing levels of protection remains a contentious issue. It would restrict the collection and sale of wild mushrooms, a passion in Poland of deep cultural, even political, significance. Millions of Poles regularly pick mushrooms. An old Polish proverb declares 'Flowers are the children of the sun, mushrooms the children of the moon.' Adam Mickiewicz celebrates the activity in *Pan Tadeusz*:

> All to the woods, for mushrooms, who are able!
> And he who brings the finest to the table
> I will have sit beside him the prettiest girl;

The forested province of Podlaskie provides the greatest quantity of mushrooms in Poland. There are some three and a half thousand species, a knowledge of which is vital if one is not to be poisoned. The supporters of sustainable exploitation of the Polish section are local people, predominantly from Hajnówka where the Belarusian minority comprise a quarter of the community. These rural folk obtain around eleven per cent of their annual income from forest fruits, mushrooms, and herbs.[197]

---

197 *The Regionalisation of Harvesting of Non-wood Forest Products in Poland*, Anna Barszcz, Agricultural University of Kraków, Poland in *Electronic Journal of Polish Agricultural Universities* 2006 Vol. 9 Issue 4

All of which serves to remind us that, when forests are destroyed, it is not only the accumulated history of natural growth that vanishes. A preserve of cultural memory also disappears.[198]

On a recent visit to the forest the former international lawyer, Justice Minister, Prime Minister and Minister for Foreign Affairs Włodzimierz Cimoszewicz greeted me at the entrance to his remote wooden cottage *Darz Bór* (a warm greeting among hunters and foresters) deep in the Białowieża Reserve near Hajnówka. I had always regarded him as one of the most impressive members of the government and was disappointed when he withdrew from the presidential campaign in autumn 2005. The house was a ruin, which he restored with a friend who was also keen on shooting ducks.

'Our little dachshund fell straight through the floor into the basement!'

He had been a farmer for some years and as a man of the land had formed a close relationship with nature and the forest. 'You know, only about eight per cent of the forest of Białowieża is actually primeval and protected, the rest is replanting.'

'Yes, I've read that it compares with primary Amazon rainforest in its biodiversity.'

'Yes! Some twelve thousand species of fauna alone are here! You know, Michael, I think people have lived near my house for a long time. The growth pattern of that old oak shows an open cleared space has existed here for about two hundred years.'

The house was modestly furnished with photographs and memorabilia of his time holding the highest offices in the land. He was clearly an unpretentious man of simple tastes, of significant achievements and political commitment.

'Are you happy about Poland joining the European Union?'

'Absolutely! The thing I was most proud of in my career was signing the Treaty of Accession to the European Union together with Prime Minister Leszek Miller. A great moment. That and Poland joining NATO, which I was also involved in.'

---

198 *Forests: The Shadow of Civilisation*, Robert Pogue Harrison (Chicago 1992) p. 62. A profound and rich study of the cultural history of forests in the Western mind. Unique and indispensable.

His study had a huge bison skin on the wall, antlers and a gigantic bison head fixed precariously above a massive computer screen. During the tea and ubiquitous Polish cakes served by his charming wife a number of deer timidly approached the house. We watched them from behind the curtains without moving, lest they flee. His face was radiant with pleasure at the sight.

'Why did you leave politics? Were you tired of it or was there another reason?'

'There was a personal vendetta against me and my family. As soon as they were brought into this world of black propaganda I knew where my loyalties were – to them first. They had already put up with me being a career politician and rarely seeing me. Then to be drawn into a seedy smear campaign. Enough is enough.'

'So you withdrew from the presidential race?'

'Yes. But I had great support, you know, around forty per cent. I was completely exonerated, but the intended damage had been done. A terrible business, Polish politics. Full of disillusionments.'

As the details of falsified documents, stolen rubber stamps and mechanics of the 'plot' emerged, his eyes drifted distantly above me as he spoke, focusing on the feeding deer. In the end, as the hours passed, I felt he was addressing himself rather than me, carefully arranging his memory of events as a justification for his self-imposed 'exile'.

'And *lustracja*?' He became heated at the mention of this word.

'Oh yes, I was put through that particular mill and they found nothing. Nothing! But I did discover a friend had informed on me. I felt depressed, betrayed and disillusioned for days afterwards. But what am I supposed to do with this information? What's the point of knowing? My friend has since died and I am left with the ashes. Now I will never know why he informed on me. They want to create a climate of fear just like the old days. I refuse to sign any more vetting statements.'

I felt we needed to change the subject away from this inflammatory topic.

'Hajnówka near here has a fine Orthodox Church and a wonderful Orthodox music festival, I believe.'

'Yes. There is a significant Belarusian population in this area.' He sighed. 'The Polish minority in Belarus, close on half a million, have a hard life. They mainly settled there between the wars. There's a lot of discrimination against them.'

With great enthusiasm he showed me many photographs of wildlife, particularly bison and deer.

'The bison come to the gate to feed during the winter. It is a wonderful sight to see these magnificent creatures against the snow. The ancient *Puszcza* Borecka and Romincka not far from here are excellent too for watching bison and wolves in winter. My friend King Juan Carlos comes hunting with me in Poland. We have a lot of visitors but many of them are frightened of the forest. Isn't that strange?'

'Well, city people are much the same everywhere. I'm sure there's no shortage of mushrooms in this forest. I expect that attracts them!'

'Actually we lost the election because the electorate were out picking mushrooms that day. Huge traffic jams prevented them getting to the polling booths.'

'Seriously? I know mushroom-picking is deep in Polish culture, but mushrooms in politics? Just out of interest, what Polish artist would you say lies at the spiritual heart of Poland, expresses the real soul of the country?'

'Ah, that's easy! The music of Chopin expresses everything about the Polish spirit. Everything. That and the Polish poetry by our great poets. Not translatable at all. Have you read Szymborska?[199] I still read a great deal of poetry.'

As I left, a group of deer had massed at the end of the long avenue of trees leading to the house. I could not help reflecting that in many ways he resembled one of the wounded animals he cared for. Traumatized, he had taken refuge, sought asylum in the depths of a primeval forest from a more primitive and vengeful external world. Increasingly alarmed at the direction he sees the country moving in, he recently left this forest fastness to return to politics as an independent Senator.

*

199 The remarkable Polish poet Wisława Szymborska was awarded the Nobel Prize for Literature in 1996 'for poetry that with ironic precision allows the historical and biological context to come to light in fragments of human reality'. She was born in Kórnik near Poznań in Western Poland in 1923 and lives in Kraków.

There was no fresh horse blood on the menu at the Tatar restaurant. Delicious dumplings were recommended by the two beautiful young teenage girls who served me. One was a descendant of the Tatars who settled in Kruszyniany three hundred years before. She was of a markedly eastern appearance with jet black, straight hair. The other girl was a blonde Pole with flowers in her hair. As they stood smiling, waiting to take my order, I could not help reflecting on the harmony that existed between Islam and Christianity for centuries in this region during the period of the religiously tolerant Polish–Lithuanian Commonwealth and comparing it with the lamentable world situation today. During the sojourn of Adam Mickiewicz among the Crimean Tatars in 1825, he developed 'oriental' enthusiasms reflected in his beautiful *Crimean Sonnets*. He was able to effortlessly reconcile his great reverence for Islam with his Catholic faith. At this time he also developed an enduring respect for the Jews, to the point of attempting in 1855 to raise a Jewish legion in Istanbul, the Hussars of Israel.[200] The story of the 'Lipka Tatars'[201] is an extraordinary one full of passion and exoticism.

The villages of Bohoniki and Kruszyniany are east of Białystok close to the border with Belarusia and both possess tiny mosques. As one passes through the magnificent *Puszcza Knyszyńska*, it is easy to imagine the small sturdy horses of the Tatars scything across the broad, open plains. The car passed silently over a thick carpet of fallen leaves as there was virtually no traffic in this remote place. Kruszyniany is a hamlet of rustic, mainly wooden houses that straggle along a muddy road. The mosque set among birch trees is a small eighteenth-century weatherboard building painted green. If it were not for the tiny golden star and crescent glittering on the top of twin cupolas, it would be almost indistinguishable from a Christian parish chapel. Fortunately I arrived as one of the Tatar descendants was locking up. His face had a distinct Mongol cast from the central Asian steppe and he was extraordinarily friendly. Turkish and Persian rugs covered the floor.

200 For a full account of the respect Mickiewicz held for the Jewish capacity to fight and resist (as against the cliché of servility) and his attempts to raise a Jewish legion see the readable and fascinating *Black Sea*, Neal Ascherson (London 1995) pp. 171–5

201 The name 'Lipka' comes from the old Crimean Tatar name for Lithuania and is possibly a corruption of the Polish meaning 'small lime tree'.

'Do come in! You are most welcome, sir. Did you know there were still Tatars like me in Poland?' He gave a terrific grin.

'Yes, I did actually. I came to this village to see the mosque. I've just had a delicious lunch of Tatar specialities.'

'Ah! You like the Tatar foods! So you know everything about us, but you do not know the Islamic features in here, I think.'

'No, you're right. I certainly don't know enough about Islam.'

'The small room there is for the women, separate from the men. Here is the *Mihrab* that indicates the passage to Mecca. The *Minbar* is this small platform where the Imam delivers prayers and addresses the congregation. On the walls there are *Muhirs,* ornamental hangings with embroidered verses from the Koran.' The mosque was diminutive in scale but had a definite atmosphere of holiness and peace.

'I see. Is the mosque still used?'

'Yes, but not so often. There are only three Tatar families left in the village now. All the young people are in the city. But I like it here and talking to interesting visitors like you, my good sir!'

Islam has had a long, relatively peaceful relationship with Poland of a unique character. Polish Sarmatians claimed descent from Iranian 'barbarian' tribes from the Black Sea steppe. The Lipka Tatars have been living on the lands of the old Polish–Lithuanian Commonwealth since the fourteenth century. The Tatar warlord Tokhtamysh and his clan were permitted to settle in Lithuania by the Lithuanian Grand Duke Vytautas (1352–1430) after being defeated by the legendary Turco-Mongol warlord Tamerlane. They were permitted to maintain their tribal organization and given the religious freedom to practise Islam. Many fought as light cavalry against the Teutonic Knights at Grunwald and subsequently defended the Polish-Lithuanian Commonwealth from attack. Cooperation lasted through successive reigns until the Counter Reformation, when restrictions of their long-held privileges caused them to appeal to the Sultan Murad III in Istanbul. They finally rebelled and went over to the Turks when the Polish–Ottoman war erupted in 1672.

The Polish author Henryk Sienkiewicz, himself descended from Christianized Lipka Tatars, won the Nobel prize for literature in 1905. His great historical *Trylogia* (Trilogy) written in the late nineteenth century described and in many ways helped forge the national character of Poles, inspiring them to resist under foreign occupation and the Nazis. The Tatar rebellion was immortalized in the last novel of the trilogy – *Pan Wołodyjowski* (Colonel Wolodyjowski, or Fire in the Steppe):

> The young Lipka raised his proud head, cast his lynx-like glare over the gathering and, having suddenly torn open his tunic to reveal his broad chest, he exclaimed "Behold, the blue fish tattoos! I am the son of Tuhaj-Bej!" The room was stunned to silence. The very name of such a terrifying warlord curdled the blood.[202]

Only a year later the Lipkas had become disaffected by their new masters and after the Polish victory at Chocim in 1673 their privileges were restored in an amnesty.

They then fought alongside the winged cavalry of King Jan Sobieski III at the great Battle of Vienna in 1683, wearing straw in their helmets to distinguish themselves from the Tatars fighting on the Turkish side. The famed 'Tatar tactics' of a feigned retreat followed by reverse and attack contributed greatly to victory that day. Sobieski wrote to his wife Marysieńka, 'Our Tatars are entertaining themselves with falcons they have brought with them . . . and are proving to be loyal and trustworthy.' After this victory they were rewarded with land, noble status and exemption from taxes. The ennobled Lipka cavalry units (some astonishingly sharing the same Nałęcz coat of arms as Joseph Conrad) lived like *szlachta*, took part in uprisings after the partition of Poland, fought in the Napoleonic army and finally against the Nazis.

I followed the advice of my Tatar descendant to visit the *Mizar* or Tatar cemetery set in woodland on a slight rise, a place eloquent of the remarkable mixture of cultures in eastern Poland. The gravestones near the entrance were clearly Christian, but these gave way to older Tatar headstones, overgrown and tilted at crazy angles, topped with iron crescents and stars, some with Russian or Arabic inscriptions. Names such as Mustapha Bogdanowicz or Ismail Jankowski

202 *Pan Wołodyjowski*, Henryk Sienkiewicz trans. Jakub Mirza Lipka

reflect the marriage of Pole and Tatar. The origins of Jewish Tatars however are hidden in the mists of time. Families clearly of Asian origin were clearing graves of leaves and tangled overgrowth in preparation for All Saints' Day, a custom they have adopted from their Christian neighbours. One particularly strong Tatar physiognomy sent my mind reeling straight back to the fourteenth century.

Hundreds of rarely visited lakes and ancient forests dominate the regions north of the Tatar villages along the Belarusian frontier up to the Lithuanian border. The *Puszcza Augustowska* and the *Suwalszczyna* possess some of the most remote, beautiful and undeveloped countryside in Europe. Lake Wigry is a labyrinthine network of creeks, forest, marsh and water with many varieties of fish, beaver, game and birds. The outrageously pink Camadolese monastery dominates the lake. Pairs of storks perch and clack conjugal bills on haystacks. Carts pulled by lusty horses are loaded with laughing children sitting on piled leaves of green tobacco. Deserted roads of a blessed rural past.

West of Augustów and eighty kilometres from the Russian border near the Teutonic Knights' castle of Kętrzyn (Rastenburg), Hitler built his megalomaniacal *Führerhauptquartier Wolfschanze* (Wolf's Lair) in the forest of Gierłoż (Görlitz). The forests of East Prussia satisfied the Nazi desire for criminal concealment and secrecy. The ancient *silva Hercynia,* the dark forest that had proved such an impenetrable barrier to the Romans, satisfied all the myths of *Germania.* The headquarters were surrounded by trees, lakes, marsh and river which presented an excellent defence against any concerted Russian drive. The ethnic German population were largely sympathetic towards Hitler.

The compound covered eight square kilometres and consisted of massive concrete bunkers for each member of the Nazi High Command. The complex was surrounded by a minefield, had its own airfield, railway station, power station, water and air purification plants to accommodate some two thousand people. These massive structures were built by Polish slave-labour (the workers executed after completion) by the notorious *Organisation Todt.* The ferro-concrete roof of the comfortably furnished *Führerbunker* was over eight metres thick. 'Wolfie' spent almost two and a half years here conducting the war and no doubt contemplating his inheritance from the Teutonic Knights. A failed attempt on Hitler's life (one of forty-two by the little-studied German resistance movement) was made at *Wolfschanze* on 20 July 1944 by the charismatic Colonel Count Claus von Stauffenberg and is celebrated in a memorial.[203] He came from a distinguished Catholic Swabian family, had recently recovered from terrible war wounds and was a truly heroic figure in the mould of T.E. Lawrence. His last shout of defiant resistance before he was shot was *'For sacred Germany!'* *Wolfschanze* was blown up in January 1945 in the face of the Russian advance. Cyclopean blocks of concrete lie strewn about in a testament to the failure of vaunting paranoia, the outcome of a mind turned in upon its own phantastical constructions. Exploring these immense claustrophobic labyrinths, the smell of decay and incursion of forest vegetation into the ruins echo ancient devastated pyramids settling into the forests of South America.

I headed back to Warsaw on All Saints' Eve. Roadside cemeteries burned with thousands of candles. One cemetery built on uneven land was transformed into small hillocks of fire; in the hollows drifts of candles moved like a tide of flame. Unknown graves, crosses and angels were traced against a sky of deepest rose, the living hovering over the dead. Many people covered tomorrow's remembrance chrysanthemums with newspapers to protect against the night frost. A family of fifteen piled onto a slow horse and cart crossed them-selves in unison when they passed a candle-lit altar, having paid their respects to their relatives.

'Will you come with me to clean the grave of my aunt's husband and her mother? She can't leave her flat these days,' Zosia asked me the morning of All Saints' Day, November 1. 'We've left it a bit late!'

---

203 The briefcase bomb, although it exploded, failed to kill Hitler. Before the meeting it was irrita-bly pushed behind one of the massive oak supports of the table by a general who barked his shin on it. This shield, together with the thickness of the oak table itself, protected Wolfie from the blast. His hair was set on fire, his eardrums perforated, and his trousers shredded. He did not remain the same man and the nervous tremor in his hand worsened. After Hitler survived the blast Stauffenberg watched the strength of his attempted coup ebb away. He was apprehended and hastily shot two days later in a courtyard by the headlights of some parked vehicles. A remarkable and fascinating account of the plot and of the complex aristocratic temperament of Stauffenberg himself is given in *Secret Germany: Claus von Stauffenberg and the Mystical Crusade Against Hitler*, Michael Baigent and Richard Leigh (London 1994). A novel, *The Song Before It Is Sung*, Justin Cartwright (London 2007) deals movingly and thoughtfully with the 1944 bomb plot. A new movie about Claus von Stauffenberg called *Valkrie*, starring Tom Cruise and directed by Bryan Singer, is to be released sometime in 2008.

'Well, I suppose so,' I replied rather reluctantly. Visiting graves on a feast day or as a recreational activity is popular in Poland, but seemed far too melancholic to me.

'Oh, and bring your camera. You can take a picture for her after we have decorated it.'

The original fabric of eighteenth- and nineteenth-century Warsaw has almost disappeared except paradoxically among the dead at Powązki cemetery. In many respects it is an extension of the tombs at Wawel in Kraków. Particularly eminent citizens are buried there among the legions of the forgotten. An autumn funeral at Powązki is particularly moving. The mourner emerges into a chill sun from under the cupola of the cemetery church of St Charles Borromeo. The last leaves of summer flutter down like flakes of gold from an azure sky. One follows the coffin drawn by men dressed in eighteenth-century livery of gilded black behind the priest and swaying cross along far-reaching allées to the waiting vault.

We packed gardening gloves and plastic rubbish bags into a basket. Outside the gates we bought funeral candles in coloured-glass containers of various shapes and sizes, candles that would burn for three days. We bought wreaths of dried and fresh flowers from the acres of blooms on display.

'Well, hold open the bag while I put the dead leaves in, then!' Zosia was impatient as I stood impotently moving from foot to foot. I took a few photographs in the golden light after we had cleared the grave of leaves, washed and buffed it with Hades, the favourite polish for marble tombs.

On this day Poles not only honour departed members of their own families but all who have contributed to the national identity – in politics, the military, the arts and liberal professions. Entire dynasties of architects such as the Merlinis, who built the palaces of Warsaw, lie buried here. A fierce patriotism and intimate relationship with the dead imbue Polish society with rare cohesion. Solitary figures sit hunched on seats cemented to the foot of a grave, rising now and then to adjust just a fraction their arrangements of flowers and candles. The beautiful weather meant Varsovians were in a buoyant mood and an almost festive atmosphere pervaded the golden-leaved necropolis. I found myself purchasing candles and searching out the graves of my favourite

Polish musicians and artists with an unaccustomed feeling of what one might fancifully call 'sepulchral elation'. These gestures of a communal belief in the immortal soul of man were deeply affecting. At dusk the cemetery took on a true metaphysical atmosphere as the temperature fell and the mists of autumn descended. The dome of the church dissolved in fog as I joined the human tide passing through the Gate of Great Silence. The dark paths were illuminated by innumerable points of light, swathes of candles in an expression of fervent theatricality. Poles filtered past the graves in silence or in soft-whispering groups.

A million or so dead have been buried here over two centuries and countless graves robbed or lost. The 'catacombs' are normally long, gloomy galleries with six vertical rows of vaults for wealthier citizens, but that night they were a river of candlelight in red, yellow and white. A complete wheeled fortress gun-carriage adorned the grave of Major-General Jędrzej Węgłowski who invented it and died in 1861. A propeller was fixed to the grave of the Polish aviator Major Ludwik Idzikowski who died attempting to fly the Atlantic in 1929. Tram rails formed a cross for a tramwayman killed when a boiler exploded in 1917. This cemetery was the only place leading sculptors could work without police interference from the partitioning powers, which resulted in superbly sculptured figures.

The funeral processions of Varsovian high society usually departed from the home where the body had been lying for three days. Chopin himself left the instruction, 'Open my body that I may not be buried alive.' The body would then pass to the Holy Cross Church in Krakowskie Przedmieście (where Chopin's heart lies) and then the considerable distance through the pungent and colourful Jewish ghetto quarter to Powązki. The coffins of two Polish racing airmen, Żwirko and Wigura, were mounted on top of the fuselage of their wrecked plane to be transported through the city.

I placed my own candles on the graves of the great pianist Witold Małcużyński, whom my uncle knew and admired, the national composer Moniuszko as well as the violinist and composer Henryk Wieniawski. Chopin's teachers Wojciech Żywny and Józef Elsner were buried here and more recently the Polish film director Krzysztof Kieślowski. His grave has a bronze sculpture of two hands framing a scene before shooting on film. As I wandered down long avenues among nuns, lovers, families, priests and the elderly, glass containers shattered intermittently releasing small seas of flame that were hastily extinguished by passers-by.

The cemetery harbours many fascinating stories. Theatrical melodrama is seldom absent from the death of a Polish artist. Maria Wisnowska was a vivacious actress at the Variety Theatre. Radiantly promiscuous, she became slavishly obsessed (but not in love) with Alexander Bartenev, a glamorous Russian cornet in a regiment of hussars stationed in Warsaw. They decided on a mutual suicide pact. After shooting her with his revolver his nerve failed when it came to turning the gun on himself. Bartenev was demoted in disgrace and imprisoned in a fortress. Impoverished, he faithfully visited his lover's grave until death. More macabre was the result of a bomb which fell on Powązki from a Soviet aircraft. A coffin was thrown up from the depths of a tomb and on the hands of the skeleton were seen a pair of white kidskin gloves. The right hand held a wave of long golden hair, which fell from the skull to the bony knees and rippled in the breeze like a bizarre resurrection of life.[204]

The memorial to the Katyń massacre is illuminated by a veritable sea of candles. The massacre at Katyń forest on the banks of the Dnieper river near Smolensk was one of the most notorious and controversial atrocities suffered by Poles during the Second World War. After the outbreak of hostilities over 20,000 Polish reserve officers and other ranks (doctors, scientists, engineers, teachers, businessmen and other occupations – 'the cream of the class enemy') were detained in Russian camps in September 1939. After a few months of correspondence with their families an ominous silence descended. In April 1943, over 4,000 corpses were exhumed from a mass grave by the Nazis. Each had his hands tied behind his back but had a Russian bullet lodged in the base of his skull. The Nazis blamed the Soviets and the Soviets blamed the Nazis.

Soviet guilt was established beyond doubt when President Gorbachev admitted the crime and revealed the location of the other

204 For a warmly patriotic, anecdotal and profusely illustrated account of the history of Powązki Cemetery see *The Rest Is Silence: The Powązki Cemetery in Warsaw*, Jerzy Waldorff trans. Chester Kisiel (Warsaw 1992)

two mass graves containing the remainder of the corpses. This outrage remains a symbol for Poles of the many atrocities committed against Poland by the USSR. The issue continues to smoulder and has affected generations of Poles with a negative stance towards Russia. Katyń is a weeping sore that can never heal.[205]

Some distance on from Powązki is the Military Cemetery, where the military of the last two hundred years are buried. Here are the anonymous graves of Home Army soldiers who fought in the Warsaw Uprising of 1944, casualties of the Battle of Warsaw or the 'Miracle on the Vistula' in 1920 and soldiers who died valiantly fighting the German invasion of 1939. The extensive open nature of this section set among birches recalls the heartbreaking and bloody resistance of Poland to unmerited aggression. Contemplating the serried ranks of military crosses, each with a candle winking in the night, it is as if the cloth of heaven has been laid upon the earth. After independence in 1918 many of the most notable citizens of Warsaw were buried here, including the pianist Władysław Szpilman.[206]

A visit to the Jewish Cemetery adjacent to Powązki in Okopowa Street is a powerful and melancholic reminder of the tremendous historical presence of Jews in Warsaw and the central contribution they made to the life of the city. From 1527 to 1795 Jews were not permitted to live in Warsaw. The cemetery was founded in 1806, at that time outside the walls, and covered a massive eighty acres. Up to 1939 it contained the bodies of some 200,000 Jews in marked graves. Much of it is a sad and neglected place, finely carved gravestones overgrown and awry, decorative wrought iron rusting in piles, doors to mausoleums gaping as if the soul has fled. Despite this, clearance and dedication by volunteers has improved sections immeasurably over the years. Most moving are the common mass graves to the Ghetto Insurgents (overgrown grassy depressions surrounded by a circle of white marble standing stones with a simple

---

205 For a more detailed examination see *The Murderers of Katyń: A Russian Journalist Investigates*, V. Abarinov (New York, 1993). The website by the Australian historian David Mirams – www.katyn.org.au – is well researched (in both Polish and English).

206 The hero of Polanski's film *The Pianist* died in Warsaw in July 2000 after a distinguished postwar musical career and the composition of over five hundred popular songs. Ironically one of his loveliest songs is called *W małym kinie* [In a Little Cinema] which laments the loss of small, intimate cinemas so popular in the past in Poland.

black band) and memorial graves erected by Jewish families living abroad to honour family members murdered but never met. An inscription reads 'In memory of one million Jewish children murdered by Nazi German barbarians 1939–1945.'

A statue of the renowned Janusz Korczak 'The King of Children'[207] gently accompanies a few of his charges from his orphanage to their joint annihilation. Of the numberless descriptions I have read of the horrors of the Holocaust, this passage, describing the final journey of 200 children to the Treblinka extermination camp, is the most heart-rending of all. It comes from Władysław Szpilman's *The Pianist*.

One day, around 5th August, when I had to take a brief rest from work and was walking down Gęsia Street, I happened to see Janusz Korczak and his orphans leaving the ghetto.

The evacuation of the Jewish orphanage run by Janusz Korczak had been ordered for that morning. The children were to have been taken away alone. He had the chance to save himself, and it was only with difficulty that he persuaded the Germans to take him too. He had spent long years of his life with children, and now, on this last journey, he could not leave them alone. He wanted to ease things for them. He told the orphans they were going out into the country, so they ought to be cheerful. At last they would be able to exchange the horrible, suffocating city walls for meadows of flowers, streams where they could bathe, woods full of berries and mushrooms. He told them to wear their best clothes, and so they came out into the yard, two by two, nicely dressed and in a happy mood.

The little column was lead by an SS man who loved children, as Germans do, even those he was about to see on their way into the next world. He took a special liking to a boy of twelve, a violinist who had his instrument under his arm. The SS man told him to go to the head of the procession of children and play – and so they set off.

---

207 Janusz Korczak (1878–1942) was the pseudonym of Henryk Goldszmit, the heroic Polish-Jewish paediatrician, children's author and educational theorist. Andrzej Wajda made a film of his life in 1990 called *Dr Korczak*. Orphanages inspired by his ideals are still in operation today.

When I met them in Gęsia Street the smiling children were singing in chorus, the little violinist was playing for them and Korczak was carrying two of the smallest infants, who were beaming too, and telling them some amusing story.

I am sure that even in the gas chamber, as the Zyklon B gas was stifling childish throats and striking terror instead of hope into the orphans' hearts, the Old Doctor must have whispered with one last effort, 'It's all right, children, it will be all right,' so that at least he could spare his little charges the fear of passing from life to death.[208]

Such public and collective acts of celebration and mourning, both glorious and humbling, morally impeccable and unashamedly artistic, bind Polish society together. Such gestures guarantee the continuity of the Polish psychological inheritance. As I finally left through the clammy autumnal mist, gathering my coat about me, I realized that All Saints' Day in Poland was not a quaint, even macabre foreign custom, but a unique spiritual contribution to the soul of Europe and a triumph of humanity.

208 Władysław Szpilman, The Pianist trans. Anthea Bell (London 2000) pp. 95–96

CHAPTER 26

The Moving Toyshop of the Heart

A flame of a less spiritually uplifting type was lit as I performed the sad task of burning my private papers one evening behind the tennis courts. The call I dreaded had eventually come.

'Michael, I'm afraid we will have to ask you to pack your bags and come home.'

As I watched the flames consume the old accounts, faded agreements and official letters, I felt this moment was one of final sacrifice. This really was the end of my work in Poland, signs and memories going up in smoke. I stirred the partially burnt embers with a stick.

My last picnic was alone on the banks of the river Pilica. The scene made me nostalgic for the long summer afternoons spent lethargically drinking and talking with Polish friends, watching the pheasants rise in a flurry of beating wings, an old lady leading her muddy cow home on a chain, murmuring softly to it.

The sale of the FSO was almost as complex as the purchase and I would need to drive it some four hundred kilometres to Wrocław. I drove to my local Porno Car Wash to spruce it up. This blatantly sexist confection survived but a short time during the heady first days of the market economy. It fitted well with the sudden influx of foreign luxury. Scantily clad girls in bikinis washed your car with large quantities of foam while the smoking punters watched the labouring nymphets sliding over the bonnets of their grimy Mercedes or BMW. A small coffee bar with table and chairs had been thoughtfully provided on a dais. The customer could smoke, have a cappuccino, leaf through various pornographic magazines while the erotic ballet was in progress. I discovered it had sadly been closed down by the intervention of the local priest so I optimistically followed a tortuous series of arrows down a lane in the direction of another Myjnia Non-Stop (24-hour car-wash). After a number of false leads the final arrow pointed to an old man expectantly standing against a wall with a cloth and bucket.

The driving conditions to Wrocław in teeming rain were foul and the sparkling FSO was soon covered in mud. The road was covered in detritus – pieces of wood, gravel, rocks, dead dogs and huge puddles of indeterminate depth. Monstrous *Tatra* lorries with inward-cambered front wheels towing trailers of coal, sand or pigs threw up clouds of spray that blocked vision for several heart-stopping seconds. A lorry had jack-knifed into a ditch scattering hundreds of small cardboard boxes across the road.

The tall, slender tower of the fortified Pauline Monastery of Jasna Góra at Częstochowa came into view through the miasma. Driving through the acres of crumbling concrete estates before arrival it is difficult to reconcile this with the powerful, mythical status this monastery complex has achieved over a period of six hundred years. The shrine has become one of the most important places of European Christian pilgrimage. The focus of this metaphysical and religious power is the image of the Czarna Madonna or Black Madonna.

The monks came to Jasna Góra or 'Bright Mountain' in 1382 at the behest of Władysław, Duke of Opole, who was related to Louis of Anjou, King of Hungary. Legend holds the icon was originally a portrait of Mary painted by St Luke the Evangelist on the wooden table of her house in Jerusalem. Ownership passed eventually to the Emperor Constantine. Sometime in 1384, during his return to Poland carrying the icon, Władysław camped the night at the monastery on Bright Mountain. Here he supposedly had a dream where the Virgin Mary told him she wished to travel no further. The next morning he had entirely forgotten this hallucination but his horses stubbornly refused to move. This reminded him of her words and he left the painting with the monks.

The original icon is thought to be Byzantine from between the fourth and ninth centuries. The painting had already come to be considered miraculous when it was smashed to pieces, trampled in the dust, stabbed with daggers and cut with swords in Holy Week of 1430 by Hussite iconoclasts. Attempts to repair the picture shortly after were unsuccessful as the ancient techniques had already been lost. Much of the original icon was removed and a new painting done over the old at the court of King Władysław Jagiełło in Kraków. Two slashes were added to her cheek symbolizing the defilement. In 1655 the monastery and the Virgin resisted a six-week Swedish siege by greatly superior forces, leading eventually to their expulsion from the country. A spectacular defence in 1770 against the Russian siege forces of Catherine II was led by the charismatic firebrand Kazimierz Pułaski. The roof of a cupola was taken down, melted and made into bullets. Enemy cannon balls were seen to 'bounce away from the walls'. Siege ladders suddenly became shorter when the miraculous painting was invoked.

A trumpet fanfare and drums accompanies the rising and falling of a chased gold and silver screen that unveils and covers the icon each day. Groups of pilgrims are transfixed on their knees at this extraordinarily theatrical ceremony. Poles have prayed to this haunting image through all the ill-fated insurgencies of the nineteenth century and two world wars. It became a potent symbol during *Solidarność* and under the influence of Pope John Paul II. The walls of the chapel are lined with votive offerings, crutches and jewels. I too placed a message card among them and prayed for its fulfilment. To my astonishment, with the passing years all those wishes have been granted.

The roads of Wrocław threatened to demolish the suspension before I could sell the car. The city had originated in the distant past as a Slavic settlement. In 1259, known as Breslau, it became an independent duchy later to fall under Bohemian, Habsburg and Prussian rule. Wrocław grew into the most important Prussian city next to Berlin with a celebrated university and a distinguished intellectual and cultural history. The Germans made a desperate last stand there against the Red Army in 1945, with the result that over seventy per cent of this historic city was devastated. Silesia was surgically removed from Germany and awarded to Poland by the 'Big Three' powers at the Potsdam Conference in 1945. Much of the population and many of the institutions of L'viv (Lwów) were bodily transported west and resettled in the rubble of the abandoned city.

Ludwika Chopin kept a travel diary of her journey with her brother Fryderyk to Bad Reinerz (Duszniki Zdrój) and published a 'moral novella' based on it for children called *Józio's Journey*. She describes shopping in the enormous and bustling market square of Breslau lined with fine merchants' and burghers' houses and the great Gothic Town Hall. Most of all she was taken with the beautiful River Odra that flows through the city, as well as the parks, the gardens and the charming music. She mentions the picturesque bridges that cross the many canals and waterways and watching the gliding swans. Despite the destruction of war, Wrocław is rapidly returning to her lyrical historical portrait, developing into one of the most vibrant and attractive cities in Poland.

As I walked away from the Polski Fiat after having passed it over to its new owner, I could not help reflecting how perfectly the car suited Polish conditions. In my hotel room I drank a bottle of chilled Russian champagne as the penultimate step of the Polish campaign drew to a close. The entries in my diary describe my feelings as the curtain finally came down.

Warsaw
11 November 1992

Most of the day spent packing. Numerous calls from Zosia. We have discovered over time that we complement each other like a piece of fine engineering. The vacuum within my heart at the prospect of parting from her withers my ability to act. My Polish still prone to error. Trying to make an appointment for a haircut today I asked 'Could I make an appointment to have myself dry-cleaned?' Rather appropriate.

So many papers, books, materials and memories accumulated. The loss of the project and my Polish mistress at a stroke almost too much to bear ... I am in anguish over this separation. Unfulfilled promise seems endemic in this part of the world. The directors in Bath were not keen on the Polish way of doing business. The peculiarly Polish concept of *exile* has crept in like an insidious guest. I worked in a desultory fashion on the Final Report on the Warsaw Project. No way to avoid the painful fact that the debacle could have been avoided with better business planning.

Late evening

I lie on the stripped bed looking at the bare room. The papered walls show the stippled evidence of my decorative schemes. The cell is mute as steam from the kitchen pipes drifts across the flat roofs past the window and is absorbed by the air without a trace. The vibrations of various passions have dwindled to a barely perceptible pulse. The nightly dog fugue continues afar off in the forest by the Vistula.

Bath
13 November 1992

The day I was finally to leave Poland dawned. Emotions in upheaval. The weather was sunny, clear and cold with the achingly blue sky of the north. It must be admitted that hovering over this loss is the bird of freedom and relief. It is over. Disappointing that the Polish staff expressed no regrets. After all, it was a joint project. They were told our costs had ruined it. They have too many jobs to have any loyalty to one, I suppose. A hollow in my heart even so. I had read somewhere that Poles 'lend' themselves to you. Even Lech Wałęsa once said they rarely express gratitude. My great leaders thought me 'too emotionally involved' with the country so no sympathy there either. Probably glad the plug has been pulled. I stood in the empty room with half a bottle of warm mineral water looking at the empty shelves.

I kept thinking of the beautifully unresolved Chekhov story 'The Lady with the Little Dog'. Gurov, in despair over the sordid secrecy of their impossible love, wonders, with his head in his hands, how they can be together always. 'And it seemed as though in a little while a solution would be found, and then a new and glorious life would begin; and it was clear to both of them that the end was still far off, and that what was to be most complicated and difficult for them was only just beginning.'

Intense half-hour of promises with Zosia. At the airport amusing wrangle with the customs officer who refused to believe that the

Sarmatian helmet was a reproduction. On the plane I bought three small bottles of Veuve Cliquot to celebrate my physical survival. This period has opened up historical perspectives of great richness and diversity. While Zosia remains an occupant of my heart I can never really leave this noble country. As an 'honorary Pole in exile' am I entitled to be particularly moved when a Chopin mazurka, polonaise or nocturne sounds in an English concert hall?

From my rooms in Bath overlooking Robert Adam's elegantly Palladian Pulteney Bridge and the magnificent weir on the Avon, my mind is drawn back to the subtle beauty of the Mazovian plain in spring and the lugubrious willows by the slow-moving Vistula. Although pleased to be back in England I am not the same man. I have learned what it is for a nation to profoundly suffer and yet find the courage to reconstruct itself. The *karacena hełm* glints on an old leopard-skin. This curious object over which such an intense pledge was made will contain and preserve my connection with Zosia and the country.

CHAPTER 27

A Yellow Sleigh for the Departing Guests

Zosia drew me back to Poland many times over the years that followed. But no visit was more moving and memorable than that at the turn of the millennium. We spent Christmas Eve in Warsaw under a heavy blanket of snow, the heaviest for many years. The Vistula lay half-frozen under a crusted blanket of white ice. A group of nuns were gathered around the swings in the park, giggling and laughing in arcs of joy, their habits like the wings of bluebirds against the snow.

Preparations for the last Christmas of an epoch were complete. Zosia and her mother seemed to have been cooking for hours, days, weeks. The tree was dressed and lit, piles of presents placed under the branches and the traditional empty place laid at the table should an unexpected wanderer call. The pets had begun to speak in tongues (different languages) – well, that is the folk tale anyway. Twelve dishes are served, symbolizing the twelve apostles. Red *barszcz* (beetroot soup), carp in jelly, mushroom and cabbage *pierogi* (similar to ravioli) and other dishes too numerous to list. The blessed *opłatek* (Christmas wafer) embossed with a Nativity scene was broken and shared among the family with good wishes for the future. Presents were opened and carols sung.

'Put some fish scales in your wallet, Michałku! It will bring you luck and money!'

For that special New Year's Eve we headed into the High Tatra mountains in the south to stay at the great Renaissance castle of Niedzica. This mysterious frontier castle, perched on its limestone crag above a frozen lake had lured me to the region. The eyrie had originally been built by the noble Polish–Hungarian Berzeviczy family above the gorge of the wild Dunajec river early in the fourteenth century.

Zosia and I spent the previous night listening to odd noises in our room, the *Komnata* '*z duchami*' or Ghost Room, located in one of the corner towers of the castle, formerly a chapel. The irrational was soon forgotten as the New Year's Eve ball began with a sumptuous feast. Opulent jewellery, bright in the flickering candles, rose and fell on the low-cut gowns of women breathless with dancing and amorous laughter. Polish mazurkas and polonaises together with Hungarian gypsy music accompanied flurries of snow whispering past the icy windows. A fierce fire burned in the fireplace below the ballroom, the walls covered in antlers and artless Polish family portraits.

By midnight it had begun to snow heavily as we climbed the castle keep with a bottle of champagne and sparklers. The spotlights illuminating the turrets created remarkable effects on the clouds of rushing snow. Champagne toasts were drunk and impossible Slavic promises were made for another thousand years. I pulled my sheepskin jacket over my dinner suit, made a brief excuse to Zosia, my Polish princess, and wandered alone into the snowy courtyard beneath the golden clock to smoke a celebratory cigar. At 2.00am the heavy tapestry curtains of the entrance hall were suddenly flung wide and three flaming piglets were wheeled in on silver trolleys. Cheers filled the vault as carafes of vodka glowed once more on the tables. Portions of the succulent meat were carved with a flourish.

The scintillating ball was meandering to its close as we emerged into the night. A yellow sleigh was drawn up waiting for departing guests, its curved sides decorated in crimson banding. A horse covered in a rustic blanket munched some hay carelessly thrown on the ice. Torches burned on either side of the driver, who appeared to be asleep. Flames glittered off the steel runners as I leaned against it and loosened my bow tie.

'Have you seen the ghost of Umina walking by the lake?' A disembodied voice emerged from the recess of the driver's fur-lined hood. I could scarcely reply from the surprise of hearing a human voice cracking the silence.

'No. Umina? Who was she?'

'Ah, a visitor who comes to the castle and does not know the story of the haunting. Shall I tell you some of it? I used to be a guide here. But now my legs . . . the steps to the dungeon . . . too old now.'

He pushed back the cape to reveal a weathered face, the face of a mountain dweller. His Pieniny dialect was difficult to understand at times, but the tale he told me on that millennium eve has fascinated me ever since.

It was a confused account, as he delivered it, involving an impoverished eighteenth-century Polish–Hungarian nobleman, his voyage to Peru and marriage to the last princess of the Incas. The narrative was rudely interrupted by the arrival of some fifteen *sanie* (sleighs) with flaming torches for the *kulig* (sleigh ride) and bonfire in the forest which would conclude that magical evening. Pale blue light reflected off the moonlit snow, limestone crags and wooden cottages as we bowled along, each sleigh a pool of warm light, the occupants laughing and chattering as sparks from the bitumen torches flew onto their clothing and lodged in their hair or fur caps. The torches blew wildly in the wind and suddenly we were racing. Passing and re-passing on the narrow icy road, the faces of the occupants bathed in light were gleeful, urging the driver on to even greater efforts, the excited horses' hooves slipping, sparks from the torches speeding in long trails now.

It was 5.00am when we finally passed under the stone cross and crawled into bed in the ghost room of the castle. It was noon when I awoke with Zosia in my arms and decided to move to Poland for good. I could not have known then it would take another six years.

CHAPTER 28

Ghosts

The finest castles all have a resident wraith but the ghosts of the past that haunt the individual mind or a nation state are a more insidious species.

Four new lags are talking in a bleak Siberian cell:

'Why are you here ?'

'Well my friend, I was *against* Popov.'

'And you, why are you here?'

'Me? I was *for* Popov.'

'And you, my sad friend in the corner?'

'I *am* Popov.'

The twenty kilometres of secret personal files accumulated in Warsaw during the communist period were stored at the Institute for National Remembrance (IPN) when the Służba Bezpieczeństwa (Security Service of the Ministry of Internal Affairs or SB) was disbanded. Since the fall of communism, the process of vetting suspected collaborators or informers (known as *lustracja*) has been a major arena of domestic conflict. Initially the liberal and more intellectual factions advocated reconciliation between the administrators of the People's Republic and their enemies by drawing what was known as a *gruba kreska* ('thick line') under the past without reprisals. Today they are more in sympathy with vetting but discuss the methodology rather than the principle itself. The more populist faction adopts a rigorous moral stance and insists upon exhaustive vetting of a wide range of figures.

This 'cleansing' process has received a wide measure of popular support but vituperative opposition from many in the professional middle classes who see it as state coercion and an erosion of democracy and their civil rights. In the pursuit of justice the files have been declassified revealing a nest of dead scorpions. The 'urge to purge'[209] has raised many difficult and serious questions of apportioning guilt which will continue to exercise the public mind. Who assisted the Security Services in spying on colleagues, neighbours, even family members? Why did I suddenly lose my job or find it impossible to gain entrance to a university despite good results at school? Should 'punishment' be meted out? How, in a liberal democratic society, does one deal with those who 'without being guilty, cannot be called innocent'[210]? What is to be done with the resented '*nomenklatura* capitalists' who simply changed ideological horses to munch increasing amounts of hay? How to regulate the process in order to avoid blackmail, condemnation without due examination and other forms of abuse? With characteristic Polish bluntness one minister likened informers to 'a fart in the drawing-room'. The guests feel uncomfortable and the perpetrator remains unknown. Another minister more ominously commented, 'There are no innocent people, just inefficient methods of interrogation.'

As a university lecturer Zosia was asked to sign a vetting statement and threatened with dismissal if she refused. She was deeply angry at this perceived threat and coercion.

'Why would I ever have had dealings with the Security Services? I never needed a passport because my family never had the money to travel abroad. Even under communism this type of pressure was never applied. Zealots!'

A professor friend refused to sign. Highly-placed faculty members promised him support if the worst happened.

'You are presumed guilty until you can prove yourself innocent. My gut feeling is not to sign. Compliance to authoritarian directives is not in the Polish character!'

---

209 Much assistance in clarifying this complex topic was derived from '*Explaining Lustration in Eastern Europe: A Post-communist politics approach*' Kieran Williams (SSEES/UCL, University of London) Aleks Szczerbiak (Sussex European Institute) Brigid Fowler (Centre for Russian and East European Studies, University of Birmingham) SEI Working Paper No 62

210 Ved P. Nanda, 'Civil And Political Sanctions as an Accountability Mechanism for Massive Violations of Human Rights', *Denver Journal of International Law and Policy*, 26 (1998), p. 391.

Most priests courageously refused to 'collaborate' with the communists, including the Primate of Poland Cardinal Wyszyński. This remarkable man and fine writer, mentor to Pope John Paul II, went to prison 'separated from the world by thickets of wires, cables, barbs, walls, sentries ... there is nothing around that does not smack of a mission to censor my mind, my work, my life ...' But he warned 'The future belongs to those who love, not those who hate.'[211] The power of religion can never be overlooked in Poland. The contentious radio station Radio Maryja – 'The Catholic Voice in Your Home' – established in 1991, has a strong following and influence, attracting just over a million listeners, mainly in the poorer rural areas of the country. Its controversial founder Fr. Tadeusz Rydzyk, a priest from the Redemptorist order, maintains significant political influence.

Raising the ghosts of the communist past has disillusioned many young Poles with politics. Perhaps such a catharsis is psychologically, even practically, necessary for the older generation to move forward but its relevance to young Poles who grew up in freedom is questionable. They want to move forward out of the provincial and conspiratorial political atmosphere of the past. Economic difficulties after European Union accession have led to unprecedented mass emigration in search of better wages, higher education and more rewarding employment.

Two young friends of mine, Mirek and Ania, worked in Glasgow in a factory making cables for Jaguar cars. I was at a family 'name-day party', loud with Polish festive cheer, friendliness and raucous singing of popular songs. In Poland celebrating the saint after which you were named is vastly more important than your mere birthday. The tables groaned with huge quantities of food. Vodka proliferated. Classic pop music of the sixties and seventies, much loved in Poland, blared.

'What made you go to Glasgow? Why not London?' I shouted, forced to raise my voice over Led Zeppelin's 'Communication Breakdown'.

'We know Polish friends there. We went to make some money to finish university studies in Warsaw. We saved a lot.'

211 *A Freedom Within: The Prison Notes of Stefan Cardinal Wyszyński*, trans. B. Krzywicki-Herburt & Rev. W.J. Ziemba, foreword by Malcolm Muggeridge (New York 1983) p. 157

'Was life difficult?'

'Not for us. But there are bad Poles in England and Scotland. They cheat their own people. But we were with good agency.'

'So what surprised you most about working there?' I asked.

'Many drunken young people on street. Particularly young girls. It is very bad. And drugs,' Ania said.

'Yes. They work like ants, the young people, busy busy from Monday to Thursday then on Friday night – bang! Heavy drinking and wildness in clubs and bars through to Sunday.' Mirek shook his head.

'Why do you think this might be?' I persisted.

'There is no family life like we have in Poland. At Christmas many of my friends could not go back to Warsaw to be with family, brother, sister, and *babcia* [grandmother]. They cried and cried non-stop. For days they cried.'

The gifted young former Polish Minister of National Defence (now Foreign Minister) Radosław Sikorski,[212] who is one of the most intelligent and stylish members of the government, generously made time to talk to me despite the sudden onset of the Middle East crisis in Lebanon. At Oxford he had been a member of the bellicose Bullingdon Dining Club ('The Buller'), a secret drinking society founded in the nineteenth century as a cricket and hunting club and immortalized by Evelyn Waugh as the Bollinger Club in *Decline and Fall*. On a day of fierce heat in Warsaw, dressed in a purposeful open-necked cream shirt and wide brown braces, he was clearly pre-occupied with the fortunes of the Polish civilians trapped in Lebanon and Polish troop deployments in the Middle East. My vague 'civilian' questions based on his engaging book *The Polish House*, which describes the pressures of growing up in Poland under communism and the restoration of the family manor house or *dwór*

---

212 Radosław Sikorski was born in Bydgoszcz in 1963. Involved in the Solidarity movement as an activist in the early 1980s he remained in Britain after martial law was declared in Poland in 1981. He took a BA and MA degree in Philosophy, Politics and Economics at Pembroke College Oxford followed by work as a war correspondent in Afghanistan in the mid 1980s. For a short time he served as deputy defence minister in the first democratically elected government after Communism. He became Polish Minister of National Defence for the Law and Justice Party (PiS) in 2005 and resigned in February 2007 citing irreconcilable differences with the Director of the Military Counter-Intelligence Agency over the security of troops deployed in Afghanistan. He is now Foreign Minister in the new Civic Platform (PO) government elected in October 2007.

at Chobielin, suddenly appeared distinctly inappropriate at that tense time. As with the manor, he had wanted to restore traditional values, modernize the armed forces and rehabilitate the upright and honourable stance of former patriotic officers.

Moving away from the merely personal and knowing his strong anti-communist stance, I put to him the danger of social disharmony arising from the ongoing *lustracja* process. He made an observation that should be understood by those seeking to judge social behaviour in modern Poland.

'Michael, as an outsider you cannot possibly understand what it was like living under communism. People would like to know who for years reported on members of their families, colleagues, and caused them suffering and loss. In fact I published my own file. However, I would never agree to humiliate those who are dismissed. There are limits.'

A Westerner can only imagine with an inadequate degree of empathy life under communism or any other of the brutal autocratic regimes Poland has laboured beneath over the centuries.

In Ibsen's tragedy *Ghosts* the destructive past profoundly inhabits the present. In a pivotal speech the major character Mrs Alving perceptively comments on the tragic consequences of her own haunting:

> I am half inclined to think we are all ghosts, Pastor Manders. It's not just what we inherit from our mother and father that lives on in us. It's all kinds of old, dead ideas, all kinds of old, dead beliefs and suchlike . . . They're not actually *alive* in us, they're just stuck there, and we can't get rid of them. I've only to pick up a newspaper, and I seem to see ghosts lurking between the lines. There must be ghosts the whole country over. Packed tighter than grains of sand.[213]

It is not difficult to draw an analogy between her son Osvald's inherited syphilis lying at the heart of this play, the man himself a tragic figure 'worm-eaten from birth', and the rot at the heart of

213 From Act II of Henrik Ibsen's (1828–1906) *Ghosts* (1881) trans. Stephen Mulrine (London 2005) pp. 123–4

communism. The ghosts of the communist mentality in Poland are more tenacious than most and the odour of their decomposition difficult to dispel.

'Ghosts? My dear, their appearance is so much against them,' commented the acerbic Lady Margot Asquith, wife of Herbert Henry Asquith, ill-fated Prime Minister of Britain during the Great War, in quite another context.

CHAPTER 29

Full Circle

The prejudice against 'Eastern' Europe as a world of underdeveloped, barbarous and backward people had begun long before the Nazi nightmare and their invention of the debased concept of the *Untermensch*. The English traveller William Coxe wrote in the 1780s of the 'swarms of Jews' surrounding his carriage in Poland and Lithuania. He says he had never seen 'a road so barren of interesting scenes as that from Cracow to Warsaw – for the most part level . . . with tracts of thick forest; . . . The Polish peasants are cringing and servile in their expressions of respect.'

During the myopic eighteenth-century Enlightenment, Paris replaced Florence as the centre of the civilized world. 'Civilized' Europe now mentally divided the continent along an East–West axis rather than the North–South of the Italian Renaissance. In 1766 the seventy-year-old Madame Geoffrin, who ruled over the most fashionable salon in Paris, made a celebrated journey to Warsaw to visit King Stanisław Augustus Poniatowski. Although he affectionately referred to her as *chère maman* and she sympathized with his appalling political dilemma, Madame Geoffrin later shuddered: 'When someone speaks about Poland I would like to have my head in a sack.'

The prevailing European attitude to the country was succinctly expressed in Paris in 1896 by the surrealist Alfred Jarry when he staged a play called *Ubu Roi*, beginning the artistic movement known as the Theatre of the Absurd. He explained the setting to the audience: 'The action takes place in Poland, that is to say, nowhere.' Empathy for Poland and its fraught history remains a rare commodity in today's world of realpolitik.

Where is the dividing-line between those generations who paid
   too little
And those who paid too much?[214]

Since beginning my musical studies under the influence of my
uncle, I had always wanted to visit the land of Fryderyk Chopin to
try the layers of his soul in the landscape of his birth. Quite unexpectedly I found myself seduced by a far wider canvas, the slow
revelation of a rhapsodic and romantic cultural history, a land of
surreal emotions and theatrical gesture, a place of warmth and generosity, a passionate past of oriental magnificence and sublime
excess, moments of the utmost patriotic heroism in the face of
impossible odds, a life rich in spontaneity and individual character.
This is a history without the illusion of victory, a history of magnificent defeats resisting vast forces. But it is also a land of deepest
tragedy and a domain of human degradation.

The metaphysical amalgam of Orthodox, Uniate, Jewish,
Muslim, Protestant and Catholic faiths has given rise to a complex
and paradoxical culture, the remnants of which are still preserved in
wooden iconostasis, Muslim mosque and Gothic brick, Renaissance
marble and Modernist concrete. The felt absence of the Jews continues to haunt the naked air of town and murderous forest. The
wariness of a wounded nation prevails. But during the present
period of transition, exponential change and democratic freedom, I
have discovered far more to Poland than the tortured, justifiably
overwhelming memories of the Second World War and the castration of the country by the communists.

It was a slow process of growth. I rediscovered a unique piece of
that great mosaic which is the European mind and culture, a piece
that represents the heroic power of patriotic resistance, honour
above all and individualism at its most concentrated in the face of
the impossible and the unimaginable. After the collapse of the communist ideology I was given the rare opportunity of discovering a
wilfully erased part of my own European heritage, as if a long-lost
member of the family had returned from exile.

214 *Poems 1998*, Karol Wojtyła – Pope John Paul II

Yet 'return' is an inappropriate word for the critical contribution Poland has made to the formation of modern Europe. This unacknowledged legislator has influenced the course of European history from the early establishment of permanent Christianity in the pagan Slav lands in the year 1000, through the Battle of Legnica in 1241, when the Mongol invasion of the continent was halted. The victory over the Teutonic Knights at the battle of Grunwald (Tannenberg) in 1410 and the lack of political consolidation was to have long-term and unimaginable consequences for twentieth-century Europe. The defeat of the Turks at the gates of Vienna in 1683 frustrated the seemingly inexorable Ottoman drive West. Intense patriotism enabled the country to survive the partitions of the eighteenth century which inspired the French Enlightenment to use the country as a laboratory for contesting political philosophies. The first written constitution in Europe was promulgated in Poland on 3 May 1791, emerging from a peculiarly Polish obsession with the notion of national sovereignty and personal freedom. 'For your freedom and ours!' was the cry in many foreign engagements on the side of liberty. The Battle of Warsaw in 1920, popularly known as the 'Miracle on the Vistula', in which the Poles defeated the Soviet army, determined the course of European history for the next two decades. The more recent rise of *Solidarność* led to the collapse of communist regimes like a pack of cards throughout East Central Europe. These are profound influences of a high order, forgotten or never fully acknowledged.

The successful peasantry and the nationalist working class of modern communist Poland largely supplanted the intelligentsia and professional élite who had been methodically murdered or removed from positions of influence. Hundreds of thousands of teachers, lawyers, architects, doctors and scientists were systematically eradicated by the Nazis and Soviets. Their aim was to destroy Polish culture, to put a bullet in its heart. A middle class or bourgeoisie as defined in the West has not really existed in Poland since the Renaissance. There was insufficient time for it to develop under the nineteenth-century partitions or the Soviet hegemony. Yet modern Poland with its large population and significant influence is once again taking its proper place as a member of the European community. The country is bringing to bear those particular critical and creative faculties honed to a fine point during skilful survival under oppression. 'Making again the fish out of fish soup', as Lech Wałęsa so pithily observed.

Significant changes in the expectations and living standards of many Poles have taken place following the exercise of entrepreneurship, brilliant business acumen and substantial foreign investment. The phrase 'from Poland to Polo' was used satirically in America years ago to describe the transition from poverty to the wealth of the self-made immigrant from 'Eastern' Europe. The phrase has now become anachronistic. Although there are only a handful of matches each year, polo is actually played in clubs outside Warsaw that field teams of fine Anglo-Arab ponies. The glitter of expensive cars fills the city streets even as social services, education, the health service and state bureaucracy desperately need reforming. Salaries in nearly all occupations remain cripplingly low. Development that has taken half a century to complete in Western Europe has been telescoped in Poland into a mere fifteen years. The achievement is remarkable, but as with the forced feeding of any organism, unnatural growths have appeared during this unnaturally accelerated process.

Accession to the European Union involves cooperative behaviour, shared values, meaningful contribution to the community and constructive diplomacy worthy of a sophisticated modern state. Formal talks with Poland on enlargement of the EU began on 30 March 1998. Robin Cook, the British Foreign Secretary and President of the meeting, commented, 'Today we are starting the process of finally putting behind us the division of Europe into East and West which has scarred Europe for the last half of this century.' Financial assistance is not a one-way street. 'For the first time there are no excuses: no Russians, no Communists, no Jews can plausibly be blamed for failure.'[215]

However, bearing in mind Poland's turbulent history petrified by generations of autocratic control and victimization, the 'prickly Pole' appellation by patronizing modern Western Europeans is more than a little inappropriate. In the face of the astonishing

215 *The Polish House*, Radek Sikorski (London 1997) p. 239

phenomenon of Polish independence, this superficial attitude betrays a wilful ignorance of the history of the nation, a nation without peer in its dedication to freedom. The country is like any individual that has been beaten and tortured over time – wary and unpredictable in response to the outside world.

The unique contribution Poland has made to the European psyche is resistance to oppression whatever the cost, a universal human emotion rarely expressed with such intensity as here. The political philosopher in Edmund Burke would have been astonished at the extraordinary transformations of this 'brave and haughty nation, long nursed in independence'.[216] Poland is no longer his 'country in the moon'.

Zosia and I were finally married a couple of years ago in a simple ceremony in Warsaw Old Town. Her civil divorce had taken months of bureaucratic wrangling and being a Catholic she was forbidden to remarry in church. She had chosen 'a foreigner'. Ghosts of the old inquisitorial past rose up at the immigration office. 'The Interrogation' tested whether our individual accounts of the relationship matched. Answers were noted and filed by a Kafkaesque secretary.

I had fought this relationship for twelve long years but, however clichéd it may sound, 'true love' did prove triumphant in the end. The pledges made to Zosia and my uncle had been finally redeemed. I was very happy. Yet it was with the greatest reservations that I sold up in England and left my friends and the Palladian glories of Bath for life in a plain capital of questionable charm that has witnessed more human suffering than any other in Europe. My musical studies continue apace as I explore Chopin's '*espaces imaginaires*'[217] on my Pleyel piano. My Polish is slowly improving and my geographical explorations continue further east.

I sometimes wonder if I am in love with an illusion, a Poland that no longer exists or has never existed, an historical chimera, but even if that is so, I know I am the richer for that dream. Personal reality is a choice after all and memory notoriously selective. As Voltaire wrote, 'History is merely accepted fiction.' The composer Robert

216 *The Annual Register* 1769, i. 4.
217 His expression in French from a letter to his family in Polish, July 1845

Schumann once described Fryderyk Chopin's music as 'cannons hidden among flowers'. He could have been speaking of the Polish soul.

Grief rose from the stones of the city. Radio stations and television channels cancelled their scheduled programmes and selected the most lugubrious music of Chopin and Bach. The death vigil of the first Polish Pope was one of silent waiting and many tears. I saw three skinheads with prominent tattoos swagger into a church, machismo dissolving before the golden tabernacle as they knelt and prayed. In the words of a Vatican announcement, this saintly figure, the great patriot, the man of political controversy was 'closer now to God than to man'.

The measure of this selfless humanist is illustrated by the story of the cat. On the day he was to return to Rome in 1978 for the second Papal Conclave, an elderly lady knocked at the door of his residence in Kraków. In a state of great distress she told him she had lost her cat and believed the neighbours had stolen it. Could Cardinal Wojtyła help her? He immediately drove to the neighbour's house, commandeered the cat and returned it to the ecstatic old woman, only minutes later pressing on to the airport and the immortality of the papacy.

I wandered the streets of Warsaw in the small hours pondering the spiritual and political revolution Pope John Paul II had catalysed in Poland on his first pilgrimage to the country in the summer of 1979. It was then he uttered the eloquent biblical phrases 'Be not afraid' and 'Renew the face of the earth', which were taken deep into the hearts of the millions of Poles who joined him in prayer in the open fields outside town and city. He transformed this fragmented society. The regime feared him as a dangerous enemy although paradoxically they assisted their own suicide by helpfully planning his pilgrimage. During the celebrations a miner was asked the use of religion in a communist state and succinctly replied, 'To praise the Mother of God and to spite those bastards!'

The force of the Pope's own language and faith unified the fractious Poles and inspired *Solidarność* to action. He transfigured their consciousness. He returned to them a sense of fidelity and honour. He had learned the power of words to alter the world while studying Polish literature and during the Nazi occupation as a member of the clandestine Rhapsodic Theatre. Any young man who could write subversive plays and remain imperturbable during a clandestine performance of the national epic *Pan Tadeusz* while Nazi propaganda blared in the streets below was not going to be ruffled by mere communist commissars. As Archbishop of Kraków he had ordered that George Orwell's *1984* be read in churches. As Pope he used Christian metaphors to impart his revolutionary message. Lies had made it impossible for the communists to rule the country effectively. 'Fifty per cent of the collapse of communism is his doing,' commented Lech Wałęsa, the leader of the Solidarity movement that overturned communism in Poland, the beginning of an irreversible process.

A candle burned in the window of the Pope's Vatican residence as an outward and very public sign of his spiritual bond with the nation. The people no longer felt humiliated by foreign domination but moulded 'the inalienable rights of dignity' from traditional Polish cultural values of sacrifice and resistance. These same spiritual values had preserved their country in the mind's heart over hundreds of years.

Bells tolled and sirens wailed through the reconstructed streets of the Old Town at the final moment. It was 2 April 2005. Six days of official mourning followed. Bank websites were edged in black and everything was cancelled that smacked of pleasure. Consumption of alcohol and ice-cream was forbidden. Shrines began to materialize in parks and at war memorials. The infatuation of this society with death was at its most intense, the supermarkets piled high with funeral candles. Entire streets were lined with them enclosed in the characteristic glass funnels of red, yellow and white – the national colours of Poland and the Vatican. Knots of people, curiously lacking an air of expectancy, stood silently behind these flickering rows of light waiting for a procession that would never pass. Entire squares and window ledges shimmered in the darkness. Simply being together in the national family 'nest' at this moment appeared of overriding importance. This 'Polish Pope' was symbolically far more significant to Poles than simply head of the Church of Rome. He was a conspicuous example of that rare species, a successful Pole of world power and influence.

Polish eagles and the national flag, entwined with that of the Vatican, were draped in black ribbons. Established wartime traditions returned to life in this unprepossessing yet most courageous of capitals. SMS messages were sent in a mysterious and secret communication network. A directive for the population to meet at this or that place, line with candles this or that street associated with John Paul II, extinguish all the city lights at a particular moment. I obeyed my SMS message to switch off my home lights at 11.00pm. However I noticed on my estate many lights still burning at the appointed time. 'Bloody foreigners!' I found myself muttering as I attended to the funeral candle on the terrace.

His successor Pope Benedict XVI made a pilgrimage to Poland in May 2006 following in the footsteps of his mentor, the man he assured the assembled hundreds of thousands would very soon be canonized as a saint. Outside the Presidential Palace in Warsaw I found myself among a group of nuns bobbing about in the breezy showers like so many raucous gulls. All around me massive crowds of Poles were willing the German Benedict to be the reincarnation of John Paul.

At Oświęcim (Auschwitz) a grim, determined German in windswept robes of white and gold walked alone towards the infamous Black Wall where mass executions took place. This reluctant former member of the Hitler Youth was visibly straining to support an intolerable burden of history. In a formidable act of reconciliation, he kissed and caressed a group of survivors who were assembled in an orderly row.

At prayers in the extermination camp of Birkenau the rain ceased and a rainbow appeared over the barracks, the crematoria and the symbolic watchtower penetrated by the railway line leading to the loading ramp of death. The spring sun shone full upon him as he sat listening to the singing of the mournful Hebrew lament for the dead. The Middle Ages would have deemed it a miracle.

BRIEF CHRONOLOGY OF POLISH HISTORY

850–1385 *THE PIAST KINGDOM*
      966 Baptism of Mieszko I – Poland created a Christian realm
     1226 The German Order (Teutonic Knights) installed in Prussia

1385–1572 *JAGIELLONIAN PERIOD*
     1410 Battle of Grunwald between the Teutonic Knights and a combined Polish–Lithuanian army
     1569 Union of Lublin uniting the Kingdom of Poland and the Grand Duchy of Lithuania

1569–1795 *POLISH–LITHUANIAN COMMONWEALTH*
           'Rzeczpospolita' – 'First Republic'
1587–1632 Reign of Zygmunt III Vasa
1620–1621 First Turkish War (Chocim 1621)
1632–1648 Reign of Władysław IV Vasa
     1652 First *Liberum Veto*
1654–1660 First Northern War with Sweden
1655–1667 Muscovite War
     1672 Second Turkish War
1674–1696 Reign of Jan Sobieski
     1683 Siege of Vienna
1697–1764 Reign of the Saxon Kings: August II (to 1733) August III (to 1764)
1700–1721 Great Northern War
1764–1795 Reign of Stanisław Augustus Poniatowski
     1772 First Partition of Poland

1791   Constitution of 3rd May
1793   Second Partition of Poland
1794   Tadeusz Kościuszko's insurrection
1795   Third Partition of Poland

1795–1918   *PERIOD OF THE PARTITIONS*
1807–1815   Grand Duchy of Warsaw created by Napoleon
1830–1831   November Uprising
1855   Death of the national poet Adam Mickiewicz
1863–1864   January Uprising

1918–1945   *PERIOD OF INDEPENDENCE (Second Republic)*
1918   Józef Piłsudski assumes power (November 11 celebrated as Independence Day)
1920   Battle of Warsaw ('The Miracle on the Vistula' – August 13–19)
1926   Piłsudski Coup d'État (May 12)

1939–1945   *SECOND WORLD WAR*
1939   Poland partitioned by Germany and USSR (September 28)
1941   Nazis begin implementation of the 'Final Solution'
1943   Warsaw Ghetto Uprising (April)
1944   Warsaw Uprising (August 1–October 2)

1944–1990   *'PEOPLE'S POLAND' under Soviet hegemony*
1952   Constitution of the Polish People's Republic (July 22)
1978   Election of Cardinal Karol Wojtyła as Pope John Paul II
1979   First Papal Visit (June)
1980   General Strike and formation of Solidarity in Gdańsk
1981   Declaration of Martial Law by General Jaruzelski
1984   Murder in Gdańsk of Father Jerzy Popiełuszko, pro-Solidarity priest
1989   Round Table Talks between ruling communists and

	Solidarity – Partially free elections – Fall of the Berlin Wall and communist regimes in Czechoslovakia and Hungary
1990	Lech Wałęsa elected President in free elections – Soviets admit guilt over Katyń massacres
1991	Balcerowicz plan of financial and economic shock therapy
1999	Poland joins NATO
2001	Secret communist files opened to public scrutiny
2004	Poland admitted to the EU (May)

[Compiled in part from *God's Playground: A History of Poland* Volume I pp. xxvii–xxx and Volume II pp. xxi–xxiii (Oxford 2005) Norman Davies]

SELECT BIBLIOGRAPHY AND RECOMMENDED FURTHER READING

Abarinov, V. *The Murderers of Katyń: A Russian Journalist Investigates* (New York 1993)

Ascherson, Neal *Black Sea* (London 1995)

Baigent, Michael and Leigh, Richard *Secret Germany: Claus von Stauffenberg and the Mystical Crusade Against Hitler* (London 1994)

Balzac, Honoré de *La Cousine Bette* (1846) trans. James Waring (London 1991)

Borowski, Tadeusz *This Way for the Gas, Ladies and Gentlemen* (London 1976)

Bromke, A. *Poland's Politics: Idealism versus Realism* (Cambridge, Mass. 1967)

Brzeziński, Richard *Polish Winged Hussar 1576–1775* (Oxford 2006)

Butterwick, Richard *Poland's Last King and English Culture* (Oxford 1998)

Cairns, David *Mozart and his Operas* (London 2006)

Cartwright, Justin *The Song Before It Is Sung* (London 2007)

Casanova, Giacomo Girolamo *Memoirs Volume 5e Russia and Poland* 1765

Chłapowski, Dezydery *The Memoirs of a Polish Lancer* (Chicago 1992)

Christiansen, Eric *The Northern Crusades* (London 1997)

Claridge, Laura *Tamara De Lempicka: A Life of Deco and Decadence* (London 2000)

Clark, Alan *Aces High: The War in the Air Over the Western Front 1914–18* (London 1999)

Conrad, Joseph *A Personal Record* (London 1912)

Cooley, Timothy J. *Making Music in the Polish Tatras: Tourists, Ethnographers and Mountain Musicians* (Bloomington 2005)

Crowley, David *Warsaw* (London 2003)

Curry, Jane Leftwich trans. & ed. *The Black Book of Polish Censorship* (New York 1984)

Czaplicki, John ed. *L'viv: A City in the Crossroads of Culture* (Harvard University 2000)

Davies, Norman *White Eagle, Red Star* (London 1972)

— *Rising '44: The Battle for Warsaw* (London 2003)

— *God's Playground: A History of Poland* Volume I and II (Oxford 2005)

— *Europe East & West* (London 2006)

Eigeldinger, Jean-Jacques *Chopin: Pianist and Teacher as Seen by His Pupils* trans. Naomi Shohet with Krysia Osostowicz and Roy Howat ed. Roy Howat (Cambridge 1988)

Koch, John W. *Daisy, Princess of Pless 1873–1943: A Discovery* (Edmonton 2003)

— *Schloss Fürstenstein* (Edmonton 2005)

Garliński, Józef *Fighting Auschwitz: The Resistance Movement in the Concentration Camp* (London 1975)

Garrard, John and Carol, *The Bones of Berdichev: The Life and Fate of Vasily Grossman* (New York 1996)

Garton Ash, Timothy *The Polish Revolution: Solidarity* (revised edition, London 1999)

Gerould, Daniel ed. *The Witkiewicz Reader* (Illinois 1992)

Goldberg, Halina ed. *The Age of Chopin: Interdisciplinary Inquiries* (Bloomington 2004)

Gomułka, Stanisław and Polonsky, Antony eds. *Polish Paradoxes* (London 1990)

Grossman, Vasily, *Life and Fate* (London 1985)

Gruber, Ruth Ellen *Upon The Doorposts of Thy House* (New York 1994)

Grynberg, Michał ed. *Words Outlive Us: Voices from the Warsaw Ghetto* trans. Philip Boehm (New York 2002)

Harrison, Robert Pogue *Forests: The Shadow of Civilisation* (Chicago 1992)

Hoberman, J. *The Red Atlantis: Communist Culture in the Absence of Communism* (Philadelphia 1998)

Kalinowska, Izabela *Between East and West: Polish and Russian Nineteenth Century Travel to the Orient* (New York 2004)

Kallberg, Jeffrey *Chopin at the Boundaries; Sex, History and Musical Genre* (Harvard 1998)

Klee, Ernst; Dressen, Willi; Riess, Volker eds. *Those Were the Days: The Holocaust As Seen by the Perpetrators and Bystanders* trans. Deborah Burnstone (London 1993)

Konwicki, Tadeusz *The Polish Complex* (New York 1982)

— *A Minor Apocalypse* (New York 1983)

Kozakiewiczowie, Stefan and Helena, *The Renaissance in Poland* (Warsaw 1976)

Lanckorońska, Countess Karolina *One Woman's War Against the Nazis* (London 2005)

Lasker-Wallfisch, Anita *Inherit the Truth 1939–1945: The Documented Experiences of a Survivor of Auschwitz and Belsen* (London 1996)

Levi, Primo *If This Is A Man* re-titled for later editions *Survival in Auschwitz* (London 1996)

Lifton, Robert Jay *The Nazi Doctors: Medical Killing and the Psychology of Genocide* (New York 2000)

Lorentz, Stanisław *Neoclassicism in Poland* (Warsaw 1986)

Mann, Thomas *Doctor Faustus* (London 1968)

Maurois, André *Prometheus: The Life of Balzac* (London 1965)

Micińska, Anna *Witkacy Life and Work* trans. Bogna Piotrowska (Warsaw 1990)

Mickiewicz, Adam *Pan Tadeusz* trans. Watson Kirconnell (New York 1981)

Miłosz, Czesław *The Captive Mind* trans. Jane Ziolonko (London 1953)

Najder, Zdzisław ed. *Conrad Under Familial Eyes* trans. Halina Carroll (Cambridge 1983)

Narodowy Instytut Fryderyka Chopina *Chopin in Performance: History, Theory, Practice* (Warsaw 2005)

Niecks, Frederick *Frederick Chopin as a Man and Musician* Volume, I and II (London 1888)

Nowicki, Ron *Warsaw: The Cabaret Years* (San Francisco 1992)

Nykolyshyn, Yuri *The Elegies of L'viv* (L'viv 2003)

O'Connor, Martin *Air Aces of the Austro-Hungarian Empire* (Mesa, Arizona 1986)

Olson, Lynne & Cloud, Stanley *For Your Freedom and Ours: The Kościuszko Squadron: Forgotten Heroes of World War II* (London 2003)

Passent, Agata *Pałac Wiecznie Żywy* (Long Live the Palace!) (Warsaw 2004)

Paulsson, Gunnar S. *Secret City: The Hidden Jews of Warsaw 1940–1945* (New Haven 2002)

Pless, Daisy von *The Private Diaries of Daisy, Princess of Pless 1873–1914* (London 1950)

Potocki, Jan *The Manuscript Found in Saragossa* trans. Ian Maclean (London 1995)

Powell, David A. *While the Music Lasts: The Representation of Music in the Works of George Sand* (London 2001)

Pratt, Michael and Trumler, Gerhard *The Great Country Houses of Central Europe* (New York 1991)

Rees, Laurence *Auschwitz: The Nazis and the 'Final Solution'* (London 2005)

Rink, John and Samson, Jim eds. *Chopin Studies 2* (Cambridge 1994)

Rosen, Charles *The Romantic Generation* (London 1996)

Samson, Jim *Chopin: The Four Ballades* (Cambridge 1992)

— *Chopin* (Oxford 1996)

Schama, Simon *Landscape and Memory* (London 1995)

Sebald W.H. *On the Natural History of Destruction* (London 2004)

Sienkiewicz, Henryk *Pan Wołodyjowski* trans. Jakub Mirza Lipka as *Fire in the Steppe* (New York 1992)

Sikorski, Radek *The Polish House* (London 1997)

Singer, Isaac Bashevis *The Magician of Lublin* (New York 1960)

Snyder, Timothy *The Reconstruction of Nations: Poland, Ukraine, Lithuania, Belarus 1569–1999* (New Haven & London 2003)

Speer, Albert *Inside the Third Reich: Memoirs by Albert Speer* (London 1970)

State Museum, Oświęcim *KL Auschwitz Seen by the SS: Autobiography of Rudolf Hoess* (1991)

Sutherland, Christine *Marie Walewska: Napoleon's Great Love* (London 1979)

Sweeney, Jane ed. *Land of the Winged Horseman: Art in Poland 1572–1764* trans. Krystyna Malcharek (New York 1999)

Szpilman, Władysław *The Pianist* trans. Anthea Bell (London 1999)

Szulc, Tad *Chopin in Paris* (New York 1998)

Teter, Magda *Jews and Heretics in Catholic Poland: A Beleaguered Church in the Post-Reformation Era* (New York 2006)

Tomaszewski, Mieczysław *Fryderyk Chopin: A Diary in Images* trans. Rosemary Hunt (Warsaw 1990)

Tournier, Michel *The Erl-King* (London 1972)

Turnbull, Stephen *Crusader Castles of the Teutonic Knights* Volume I The red-brick Castles of Prussia 1230–1466 illustrated by Peter Dennis (Oxford 2003)

— *Tannenberg 1410: Disaster for the Teutonic Knights* illustrated by Richard Hook (Oxford 2003)

Urban, William *The Teutonic Knights: A Military History* (London 2003)

Vigée-Le Brun, Elizabeth-Louise *The Memoirs of Elizabeth-Louise Vigée-le Brun* trans. Siân Evans (London 1989)

Waldorff, Jerzy *The Rest Is Silence: The Powązki Cemetery in Warsaw* trans. Chester Kisiel (Warsaw 1992)

Wasilkowska, Anna *Husaria: The Winged Horseman* (1998)

Weigel, George *Witness to Hope: The Biography of Pope John Paul II* (New York 1999)

Wilson, Edmund *To the Finland Station* (New York 1972)

Winters, Laurie *Leonardo da Vinci and the Splendour of Poland: A History of Collecting and Patronage* (Milwaukee 2002)

Wolff, Larry *Inventing Eastern Europe: The Map of Civilisation on the Mind of the Enlightenment* (Stanford 1994)

Wyszyński, Stefan *A Freedom Within: The Prison Notes of Stefan Cardinal Wyszyński* trans. B. Krzywicki-Herburt & Rev. W.J. Ziemba Foreword by Malcolm Muggeridge (New York 1983)

Załuski, Iwo and Pamela *Chopin's Poland* (London 1996)

Zamoyski, Adam *Chopin: A Biography* (London 1979)

— *Paderewski* (London 1982)

— *The Polish Way: A Thousand-year History of the Poles and their Culture* (London 1987)

— *The Last King of Poland* (London 1992)

— *The Forgotten Few: The Polish Air Force in World War II* (London 1995)

— *Holy Madness: Romantics, Patriots and Revolutionaries 1776–1871*
(London 1999)

— *Poland: A Traveller's Gazetteer* (London 2001)

Żygulski, Zdzisław *An Outline History of Polish Applied Art*
(Warsaw 1987)

The commanding position of Polish film in the history of European cinema needs no elaboration here. In this filmography I have chosen Polish and foreign films that have a direct relevance to my text. A very few unfortunately have no English subtitles. I have selected less well-known films of eminent Polish directors and more obscure work rarely screened outside Poland.

Antczak, Jerzy
Nights and Days (1975) A magnificent film chronicling the shattering of nineteenth-century family life after the failure of the 1863 uprising in Poland.

Bugajski, Ryszard
Interrogation (1982) A woman wakes up in prison after a night out to find she has been charged with a crime she did not commit. One of the most harrowing films ever made of interrogation under communism.

Ford, Alexander
Knights of the Teutonic Order (1960) Massively popular Polish epic film with panoramic battle scenes and tempestuous costume drama.

Has, Wojciech
The Saragossa Manuscript (1965 re-released uncut 2001) Based on the extraordinary eighteenth-century gothic novel by Jan Potocki set in Spain during the Napoleonic Wars.

Hoffman, Jerzy
Pan Wołodyjowski (1968)
The Deluge (1974)
With Fire and Sword (1999)
The magnificent filmed version of Nobel laureate Henryk Sienkiewicz's monumental historical Trilogy

Holland, Agnieszka
Europa Europa (1990) The extraordinary true story of a young Jewish man who passes himself off as an Aryan to the Nazis.

Kawalerowicz, Jerzy
Mother Joan of the Angels (1961) A case of possession in a group of seventeenth-century French nuns – Catholic faith and repression are examined in a quite extraordinary manner.

Kieślowski, Krzysztof
The Scar (1976) His debut film about a loyal party man building a chemical plant against the wishes of the local population.

No End (1985) This film is a highly original blend of ghost story, political drama and a meditation on the nature of love set during the period of martial law in Poland in 1982.

Krauze, Krzysztof
My Nikifor (2004) A masterpiece. A portrait of one of the world's most remarkable naive painters in one of Poland's most honoured films.

Munk, Andrzej
Passenger (1963) A German woman travelling on a ship who was once an SS overseer at Auschwitz recognizes a woman prisoner whose life she saved. A remarkable story unfolds prompted by the selective nature of her memory.

Piwowski, Marek
The Cruise (1970) A Polish cult classic comedy that parodies the communist system through the medium of a weekend river cruise.

Polański, Roman
Two Men and a Wardrobe (1958) A short absurdist parable lasting 20 minutes made while Polański was a student at the Łódź Film School. Two men carrying a large wardrobe are confronted with a number of hostile, blackly humorous encounters. Many of Polański's subsequent themes find their first expression here.

Knife in the Water (1962) A couple heading for a yachting weekend in the Mazurian Lakes pick up a hitch-hiker and play dangerous mind games out on the water.

The Pianist (2002) Polański's personal experience of the Warsaw Ghetto is brought to bear on the memoir of the classical concert pianist Władysław Szpilman who struggles to survive in the 'wild ghetto'.

Skolimowski, Jerzy
Moonlighting (1982) Set during the 1980s and the Solidarity protests it stars Jeremy Irons as the leader of a team of builders working illegally in London.

Ferdydurke (1991) Based on the remarkable novel by Witold Gombrowicz it explores Polish cultural and political mores in a remarkable fashion.

The Career of Nicodemus Dyzma TV mini series starring Roman Wilhelmi (1980) The television series is the finest version. A man walking aimlessly around Warsaw finds an invitation to a party in the street. His meteoric career begins when he decides to attend. More realistic but similar in philosophy to *Being There* (Peter Sellers) from the 1971 novel by the Polish author Jerzy Kosiński.

Severák, Jan
Dark Blue World (2001) This excellent Czech film gives a dramatic depiction (within a love story) of the training of a Czech Spitfire Squadron which was similar to the training, experience and frustrations of many Poles in the RAF.

Siebert, Detlef
Auschwitz – The Nazis and the Final Solution (2004) Outstanding
BBC series based on the book by Laurence Rees.

Szabó, István
Colonel Redl (1985) The Hungarian director's interpretation of the
story of the First World War Austrian spy and intelligence officer
Alfred Redl. This brilliant film starred Klaus Maria Brandauer as
Redl in one of his most powerful and charismatic performances. The
film was a Jury prize winner at Cannes in 1985.

Visconti, Luchino
The Damned (1969) The greatest cinematic study of Fascism at a
major turning point in European history by one of the greatest of
modern directors. The seductive perversion of the mechanisms of
power through the metaphor of Nazism is essential to understanding the horrifying victimisation of Poland.

Wajda, Andrzej
War Trilogy
A Generation (1955) Set in Warsaw in 1942 it relates the destinies of
two young men opposing the Nazis.
Kanał (1956) A brilliant and gruelling film depicting the Warsaw
Uprising of 1944.
Ashes and Diamonds (1958) Arguably the most important Polish
film takes place on the last day of WW II in a small Polish town.
Life's reality is contrasted with its potential.

Lotna (1959) A tribute to the glorious history of the Polish cavalry
and its passing.

The Wedding (1972) Based on a famous play by Stanisław
Wyspiański written in 1901, it depicts the dangers of moves towards
Polish independence through focusing on a wedding between rep-
resentatives of different social classes.

The Promised Land (1975) Based on a novel by the Polish writer
Władysław Reymont it tells the story of a Pole, a German and a Jew

attempting to build a business together in the late nineteenth-century industrial city of Łódź.

Man of Marble (1977) Chronicles the downfall of an heroic socialist bricklayer Mateusz Birkut through the eyes of a young female filmmaker.

The Conductor (1980) A renowned international conductor works with a Polish provincial orchestra and attempts to relive a love affair he once had with the mother of a violinist in the orchestra. The violinist's husband, the resident conductor of the orchestra, objects. Starred Sir John Gielgud.

Man of Iron (1981) Portrays the Solidarity labour movement through a character modelled on Lech Wałęsa

Dr Korczak (1990) This film has a fine script by Agnieszka Holland. It relates the tragic story of the heroic figure of Janusz Korczak who voluntarily went to his death in the gas chambers at Treblinka in August 1942. He chose to accompany to their deaths the two hundred Jewish children from the orphanage he owned and ran in the Warsaw Ghetto. Given a standing ovation at the 1990 Cannes Film Festival, a storm of controversy greeted its general release.

Pan Tadeusz (1999) The film of the Polish national epic by Adam Mickiewicz published 1834

Katyń (2007) A film concerning the iconic Soviet crime for Poles. A bleak portrayal of how thousands of Polish reserve officers – teachers, doctors, lawyers and intellectuals – were imprisoned and then systematically executed in 1940.

Żuławski, Andrzej
The Third Part of the Night (1971) A visionary and influential film set in Poland under Nazi occupation.

Films about Fryderyk Chopin and His Music

Lapine, James
Impromptu (1991) This composer has been poorly served by film directors through exaggeratedly sentimental and clichéd treatment. This entertaining film is the most acceptable of a generally poor lot.

Michelangeli Plays Chopin – Opus Arte – RAI Recordings (1962) No tricky camera work, no hysterical interpretations, no grimacing or appearance of 'visions', no inflated dynamics, no imposition of the personality of the performer but simply magnificent playing of the highest order of artistry. Michelangeli at the height of his interpretative power.

András Schiff plays Chopin plus Documentary 'Schiff on Chopin' (2005) A fine reading of the Preludes accompanied by an interesting full length documentary on the composer's life with many location scenes shot around Poland.

Holocaust – A Music Memorial Film from Auschwitz (DVD; BBC and Auschwitz-Birkenau State Museum 2005) An almost unbearably moving film about the role of music in Auschwitz filmed on location with a number of the world's greatest classical musicians. Reminiscences of survivors including the cellist Anita Lasker-Wallfisch and others who played in the Auschwitz camp orchestras.

INDEX

Acre 261, 264
Adam, Robert 192, 318
Aigner, Christian Piotr 193–4
AK (*Armia Krajowa AK*, Home Army)
    33, 34*n*, 35, 36, 39*n*, 87, 310
Alec Cobbe Collection of Early
    Keyboard Instruments,
    Hatchlands, Surrey 137*n*
Alexander I, Tsar of Russia 123, 124, 296
Alexander III, Tsar of Russia 296, 298
All Saints' Day 305, 306–7, 312
All Souls' Day (*Zaduszki*) 140
amber 167–8, 263, 264
Amber Road 72, 167, 263, 271
Anielewicz, Mordechai 33
Anna Jagiellon, Queen 176
anti-Semitism 90, 182–3
Arkadia 284–5
Augustus III, Elector-King 7, 17, 288,
    293–4
Auschwitz-Birkenau concentration
    camp, Poland (Oświęcim) 19, 54,
    71, 79–90, 167, 179, 182, 269, 335

Bach, C.P.E. 130
Bach, Johann Sebastian 5, 81, 123,
    126*n*, 135, 333
Bader, Group Captain Douglas 207–8
Baltic Sea 69, 70, 167, 271, 276
Balzac, Honoré de 134, 233–4
Balzac, Madame de (Countess Ewelina
    Hańska) 134, 137, 233
Barania Góra (Ram Mountain) 72
Baranów, near Sandomierz 180
Battle of Britain (1940) 87, 205, 206

Belarus 286, 301
Bellini, Vincenzo 124, 137
Bellotto, Bernardo 36
Belovezha forest, Belarus 286
Bełżec extermination camp 179, 219
Benedict XVI, Pope 335
Bentley Boys 214
Berdichev, West Ukraine 232
Berkeley, Richard 131
Berlioz, Hector 23
Berrecci, Bartolommeo 175
Białowieża forest, Poland 47*n*, 166,
    286, 292–301
Białystok 286–9
Bieszczady 234, 244, 245
Black Madonna (Czarna Madonna),
    Częstochowa 314–15
Bletchley Park (Station X),
    Buckinghamshire 209, 210
Bolesław I Chrobry, King 146
Bolko I, Duke 75
Bolko Konrad Friedrich of Hochberg,
    Count 78
Boykos 230, 244
Branicka, Izabela (née Poniatowska)
    288
Branicki, Hetman Jan Klemens 288,
    289
Brooklands racing circuit 214
Bug River 91
Bulgakov, Mikhail 228
Bullingdon Dining Club ('The
    Buller'), Oxford University 325
Burke, Edmund ix, 19, 332
Burlington, Lord 42

Cahill, Edward (1898–1976),'Uncle
    Eddie', Australian concert pianist
    1–3, 5, 24, 125, 222, 308, 329, 332
'Cambridge Pimpernels' 202
Canaletto (Giovanni Antonio Canal)
    36n
Canova, Antonio 222
Caracciola, Rudolf 214, 246
Carlyle, Thomas 18
Carpathian mountains 214, 246
cars
    Aston Martin 214
    Austro-Daimler 246
    Benz 214
    BMW 313
    BNC racing car 245
    Bugatti 214, 246
    buying, registering and insuring a
        Polish car 62–8
    Chitty Bang Bang 214–15
    DKW cabriolet 246–7
    FSO 125p 62, 65, 67, 146, 151, 287,
        313, 314, 316
    FSO Warszawa 247
    Mercedes 32, 200, 231, 246, 313
    Polski Fiat 126p ('Maluch') 26, 89,
        103, 251–2
    reception of MM's Rolls Royce
        Silver Shadow in Poland 237
    repair and blessing of MM's Rolls-
        Royce Silver Shadow 224–7
    Rolls-Royce Phantom II 199n
    Rolls-Royce Phantom II
        'Allweather Tourer' 199
    Rolls-Royce Phantom III Drop-
        head Coupé 199
    Steyr 220 cabriolet 87
    Polish Syrena 21
    Lwów Grand Prix 214
    Tatra Mountain Road Race 214, 246
Casanova: Memoirs of Casanova
    Volume 5e Russia and Poland 47
Catalani, Angelica 24
Catherine the Great, Empress of
    Russia 41, 106, 189, 190, 191, 296,
    315
Catholic Church 146, 176, 182–3, 226,
    236n, 261, 274

cerkwie (tserkvy) 236, 244
Chałubiński, Dr Tytus 247
Charles Edward Stuart, Prince
    ('Bonnie Prince Charlie') 55–6
Chełmno (Kulm) 262–3
Chocim, Battle of (1621) 55, 180–81,
    304
Chopin, Emilka 139
Chopin, Fryderyk 2, 3, 5, 18, 223, 301,
    329
    annual celebrations of his birth 24,
        121
    concert tour of England (1848)
        137–8
    and bel canto song 124, 135
    debate on the spelling of his name
        125n
    difficulties of interpretation 130
    enthusiasm for his music in Asia 134
    festivals 127–30
    and George Sand 23, 28, 130, 134,
        138
    health 137, 139, 140
    improvisations on 'Dąbrowski
        Mazurka' Jeszcze Polska nie
        zginęła ('Poland Has Not Yet
        Perished') 132
    International Chopin Piano Festival,
        Duszniki Zdrój 127–9
    International Fryderyk Chopin
        Piano Competition, Warsaw
        128, 129–30, 134
    his heart is returned to Poland 24,
        141, 308
    and Konstancja 124, 139, 140
    leaves Poland, never to return
        140–41
    memorial 105
    music banned 105n, 120, 133
    Ostrogski Castle museum 23–4
    Paderewski on 133
    personality of 122, 134–5
    piano recitals at Łazienki Park 105
    Poland's national composer 131
    quality of his preferred piano sound
        136, 137
    reception in diverse countries 133–4
    Schumann on 332–3

similarities to François Couperin
125, 125*n*

'takes the waters' at Duszniki Zdrój
126–7

his teachers 122–6

tempo rubato 124, 133, 136

and 'Uncle Eddie'– Edward Cahill
(1898–1976) Australian concert
pianist 1–3, 5, 24, 125, 222, 308,
329, 332

universality of 131

and Tytus Woyciechowski (a close
friend of Chopin) 126, 136,
140

żal 121

  Ballades 132

  Étude in C minor Op.10 No.12
    (Revolutionary) 25

  études 120, 135

  Fantasy in F minor Op.49 132

  Funeral March (from Piano
    Sonata no.2 in B flat minor,
    op.35) 81

  Krakowiak Rondo 140

  Là ci darem la mano variations
    124, 140

  mazurkas 124, 125, 133

  nocturnes 132, 133

  Piano Concerto in F Minor 139

  piano concertos 125, 126*n*

  Polonaise in B-flat major (his first
    at the age of 7) 123

  Polonaise-Fantasie 105, 128

  polonaises 125

  Prelude in D-minor 25

  rondos 125

  variations 125, 126*n*

  waltzes 133, 182

Chopin, Justyna (née Krzyżanowska)
121, 139

Chopin, Ludwika 316

Chopin, Mikołaj 120–21

Cimoszewicz, Włodzimierz 299–301

Claude Lorrain 185, 284

Clay, Catrine 145, 146

Cobham, Lord 193

communism 18, 46, 146, 152, 197,
237

castration of Poland by communists
329

and eating out 57*n*

fall of 22, 96*n*, 131, 150, 181, 322,
334

leads to a complete erosion of ethics
282

and the lie as governing principle 20,
196

moderate in Poland 273

production figures 'massaged' 61

prostitution of nature to industry 71

as reality for an entire generation 48

rot at the heart of 326–7

Conrad, Joseph 15*n*, 19, 98–9, 145,
232, 247–8, 250, 304

Copernicus, Nicolaus *see* Kopernik,
Mikołaj

Czartoryska, Izabela 192–3, 194

Czartoryska, Princess Marcelina 129,
141

Czartoryski, Prince Adam Kazimierz
192, 194

Czerwińsk nad Wisłą 262

Częstochowa 314–15

Daisy of Pless (Mary-Theresa Olivia
Cornwallis-West) 74–9, 222

Dashwood, Sir Francis 41

David, Jacques-Louis 51, 56

Dębno Podhalańskie: Church of St
Michael the Archangel 246

Delacroix, Eugène 23, 137

Dnieper River 15, 106, 309

Dulwich Picture Gallery, London
191

Dunajec River 245

Duszniki Zdrój (Bad Reinerz) 126–9,
139, 316

dwór (manor house) 30, 119, 120, 122,
245, 325–6

'Eaglets of Lwów, The' 240, 241

East Central Europe 5, 15, 38, 96*n*,
145, 217, 228*n*, 230*n*, 240

East Prussia 276, 283, 297, 305

Elsner, Józef 123–6, 140, 308

Enigma code broken by Poles 209, 210

European Union 261
Poland as its longest eastern frontier
228
Poland's accession to 19, 176, 299,
324
Poland's 'difficult' behaviour
towards 210
and Poland's 'heroic failures' 191
Poland's strong negotiating style 142
and political ideals 216
and regeneration of Warsaw 45
talks with Poland on EU
enlargement 331

Familia, the 192
Feuchtwangen, Grand Master
Siegfried von 264
Field, John 126, 134
Frank, Generalgouverneur Hans 170,
269
Frederick II, Emperor 201, 262
Frombork 276
Führerhauptquartier Wolfschanze
(Wolf's Lair), Gierłoż (Görlitz)
305, 306

Galicia (Western Ukraine) 19, 230, 231,
239, 247
Gameren, Tylman van 23, 221
Gamerra, Giovanni di 157
Gdańsk (Danzig) 69, 117, 144, 146,
185, 230, 260, 263, 264, 271–4
Bay of Gdańsk 72, 271
Lenin Shipyard, Gdańsk 273
German-Polish reconciliation
(December 1970) 33
Gestapo 39, 203, 269, 293
Gładkowska, Konstancja 124, 139, 140
Gniezno 146–7
Goczałkowickie, Lake 72, 76
Goethe, Johann Wolfgang von 251
'golden freedom' 15, 16
Golden Horde 29, 168, 182, 267
górale (highland folk culture) 247, 248
Göring, Hermann 3, 297
Góry Świętokrzyskie (Holy Cross
Mountains) 57
Grudziądz (Graudenz) 265, 266

Grunwald (Tannenberg, Zalgris),
Battle of (1410) 99, 266–9, 290,
293, 303, 330
Gucci, Santi 176, 180

Haber, Fritz 83
Hajnówka 298, 299, 300
Hallé, Charles 134, 135
Hans Heinrich XV, Baron, Prince of
Pless 74–8
Hejnał Mariacki trumpet signal
(Kraków) 170
Hellfire Club and the last king of
Poland 41
hełm karacenowy (helmet of Karacena
armour) 294, 295, 318
High Tatra mountains 245, 247, 319
Himmler, Heinrich 56, 90, 203, 270,
297
Hitler, Adolf 34, 75, 78, 90, 203, 230,
270, 272, 283, 305–6
Hoess, *SS Hauptsturmführer* (Captain)
Rudolf 80, 82, 86
Holocaust 35, 83, 229, 232*n*, 311
Home Army *see* AK
Horowitz, Vladimir 128, 130, 232
Hummel, Johann Nepomuk 126, 134,
136
Husaria (cavalry) 174

Institute for National Remembrance
(IPN) 322
Islam and Poland 302, 303

Jagiellonian kings (1385–1572) 168, 175
James Francis Stuart, Prince ('The Old
Pretender') 55
Jan Sobieski III, King 43, 55, 173–4,
175, 304
Janowiec, castle of 186–7
Jasna Góra (Bright Mountain)
Monastery, Częstochowa 314–15
Jelenia Góra 73, 74
Jewish Cemetery, Okopowa Street,
Warsaw 310–11
Jews
in Berdichev 232
in Białystok 288

clandestine community in Warsaw 33
Hungarian 87
Jewish Tatars 305
in Kraków 178–9
in Lublin 216
in L'viv 240
Mickiewicz and 302
murder of 19, 32, 33, 35, 71, 179, 216, 219, 232, 240, 291, 311
number of deaths in Warsaw during Second World War 36
and the painting in Sandomierz cathedral 182–4
renewal of religious/cultural life 90, 264
Ukrainian 229
in Vilnius 290
Volhynian 230
in the Warsaw Ghetto 31–3
in Zamość (Himmlerstadt) 219
John Paul II, Pope 146, 175, 183, 204, 236, 274, 315, 324, 329n, 333–5
Jungingen, Grand Master Ulrich von 267, 268

Kamsetzer, Jan 106
Karkonosze Mountains (*Riesengebirge*, Giant Mountains) 73
Kaszuby ('Polish Switzerland') 275
Katyń massacre (1940) 99, 155, 196, 309–10
Kazimierz III 'the Great', King 178, 182
Kazimierz Dolny 184–7
Kent, William 193
Kepler, Johannes 201
Kętrzyn (Rastenburg) 305
Kieślowski, Krzysztof 308–9
Kiev 14, 228, 231–2
Knights of the Cross (*Krzyżacy*) *see* Teutonic Knights
Kolumna Zygmunta III (Sigismund Column), Warsaw 36–7
Konrad, Duke of Mazovia 262–3
Konstantin Pavlovich, Grand Duke 123
Kopernik, Mikołaj (Nicolaus Copernicus) 263–4, 276
Korczak, Janusz (Henryk Goldszmit; 'The King of Children') 311, 312

Kórnik 145
Korzeniowski, Apollo Nałęcz 98, 99
Kościuszko, Tadeusz 56, 168, 169, 176, 190, 204–5
Kościuszko Squadron, Polish Air Force 204, 206, 209, 210
Kościuszko Uprising (1794) 290, 296
Kraków 29, 57, 99, 130, 182, 241
  Act of Insurrection (1794) 190, 204
  capital transferred to Warsaw 167
  Cloth Hall (*Sukiennice*) 169, 269n
  'Golden Age' 168
  Jagiellonian University 168, 177
  Jama Michalika café 172
  Zielony Balonik (Green Balloon) satirical cabaret 172
  Kazimierz district 90, 178–9
  Kościół Mariacki (St Mary's Church) 177
  Lenin in 247
  Muzeum Czartoryskich 173
  market square 169–70, 269n
  more chic than Warsaw 169
  Pod Kopcem (Under the Mound) hotel 168
  Wawel Castle 168, 170–71, 172–3
  Wawel Cathedral 167, 168, 175–6, 307
  Sigismund Chapel, Wawel Cathedral 175
  Wawel Hill 168, 172, 175
  Dragon of Wawel Hill 171–2
Krasiczyn Castle 236

Łańcut palace 221–3, 224, 253
Lemkos 230
Lenin, Vladimir Ilyich 8, 19, 247
Lenz, Wilhelm von 132–3
Leonardo da Vinci: *Lady with an Ermine* 173, 194
Leschetizky, Theodor 222–3
liberum veto 16, 17
Lidzbark Warminski (Heilsberg) 277
Lipka Tatars – Kruszyniany Village 302, 303, 304
Liszt, Franz 2, 126n, 128, 134, 136, 137n, 138, 201
Lithuania 261, 289–90, 303

Louis I the Great, King of Hungary (King Ludwig Węgierski; Louis of Anjou) 263, 314
Louis XIV, King of France 98n, 125
Lower Silesia 73
Lublin 32, 215–17, 269
Lubomirska, Aleksandra 56
Lubomirska, Elżbieta (née Czartoryska) 221–2
Lubomirska, Izabela 56
Luftwaffe 202, 203–4, 205
lustracja process 196, 300, 322–3, 326
L'viv (Lwów, Lemberg), Ukraine 133, 184, 218, 230, 238, 239–43, 316
Lychakiv cemetery, L'viv 240

Majdanek concentration camp 216
Małachowski Palace, Nałęczów 108, 109–10
Malbork (Marienburg) 260, 264, 265–6, 268, 269–70
Malinowski, Bronisław 249, 250
Mann, Thomas 77, 81
Marie-Casimir de la Grange d'Arquien ('Marysieńka') 173, 175, 304
Matejko, Jan 177, 188
    The Battle of Grunwald 269
    Prussian Homage 269n
Mazovian plain 37, 40, 44, 147, 292
Mazury 276
Mendelssohn, Felix 127
Mengele, Dr 81, 85, 88, 90
Merlini, Domenico 42, 154
Michelangeli, Arturo Benedetti 130
Mickiewicz, Adam 132, 167, 171, 172, 176, 194, 230, 302
    Crimean Sonnets 304
    Pan Tadeusz 30n, 99, 131n, 194–5, 289–90, 298, 334
Mieszko I, King 144, 146
Miłosz, Czesław 30, 40–41, 99
monarchy – election of kings 16, 188, 189
Morando, Bernardo 218
Mozart, Wolfgang Amadeus 3, 122, 123, 124, 126n, 129, 141, 157
    in Warsaw 154–9
mushroom-picking 298, 301

Musicae Antiquae Collegium Varsoviense 155

Nałęcz coat of arms 98, 145, 304
Nałęczów 108, 109, 110
Napoleon Bonaparte 70, 152, 194
    creates Duchy of Warsaw 19
    David's portrait 51
    France seen as the cradle of Napoleon 205
    love for Maria Walewska 147, 148–9
    on Polish women 37, 164
Napoleon III, Emperor 149
Narew River 148, 292
Nazis 39, 89, 170, 220, 236, 290, 304, 328
    Améry's analysis 83–4
    and The Battle of Grunwald 269
    Białowieża area 293, 297–8
    children stolen by 145
    Chopin banned by 105n, 133
    concentration/extermination camps 18–19, 80, 84, 85
    eradication of Polish intelligentsia and professional élite 330
    and German music 81
    and the Katyń massacre 309
    murders by 35, 40, 229, 240, 309, 311
    Poland neither surrendered to nor collaborated with Nazis 210
    summary executions of their own men 21
    and the Teutonic Knights 270
    theft of artworks 29, 194
    unique among absolute regimes 82
    vilification of Jews and Poles 229
    Warsaw Ghetto established 31
    and the Wolf's Lair 305
Nicholas I, Tsar of Russia 24
Nicholas II, Tsar of Russia 105n, 296
Nieborów 284
Niedzica castle 319–20
NKVD (Narodnyï Komissariat Vnutrennikh Del; People's Commissariat of Internal Affairs) 36, 155, 230, 293
Nogat River 264, 265

Nohant 130, 137
nomenklatura 96, 112, 114, 256, 323
Northern Crusades 261, 264, 266

Oliwa 275
Operation Vistula 230–31, 237
Ostrogski Castle, Warsaw 22–3, 27–8

Paderewski, Ignacy Jan 1, 30, 110, 133, 144, 223
Pałac Branickich (Branicki Palace), Białystok 286, 288–9
Paleczny, Piotr 128
Paradowski, Dariusz 158
Petit Trianon, Le, Versailles: Jardin Anglais 193
Philip IV the Fair, King of France 264
pianos
    Broadwood 137*n*
    Bucholtz 136
    Erard 136
    Graf 136
    Pleyel 23, 136, 137, 332
    Steinway 136, 138
Piast dynasty 144, 146, 182, 200
Pieniny mountains 245
Pilecki, Witold 87
Pilica River 232, 313
Piłsudski, President Józef 144, 191, 199*n*, 204, 248, 260, 297
Plersch, Jan Bogumił 106
Płock 262
Podhale region 245
Podlaskie 298
Poland
    becomes ethnically homogeneous 19
    emigrants to the United Kingdom 142
    final partition (1795) 18, 19, 144, 145, 188, 190–91, 193, 296
    first partition (1772) 19, 239
    German invasion of (1939) 202
    Great Poland Uprising (1918) 144
    January Uprising (1863) 25
    November Uprising (1830–31) 24, 132
    and Palladianism 154, 194
    the 'Polish Pope' 333–5

Second Partition (1793) 190, 272
    start of Russia's domination 17
    supports Ukraine's 'Orange Revolution' 241
    under the Russian yoke again (1831) 25
    Warsaw Ghetto Uprising (1943) 31, 33
    Warsaw Uprising (1944) 23, 31, 33–6, 40, 99, 155, 196, 208
Polish Air Force 204, 205, 206, 210, 220
    Squadron 303, 'Kościuszko', 204, 206, 209, 209*n*, 210
Polish Armed Forces 33*n*, 199
'Polish attic' (architectural feature) 169
Polish character 20, 47, 227, 279
Polish Christmas (1999) 319, 325
Polish Constitution (1791) 189–90, 191
Polish eagle 12, 40, 120, 146, 335
Polish Easter 185–6, 187
Polish embassies 15–16
Polish food 226–7
Polish Government-in-Exile 34, 146, 199, 206, 209
Polish intelligentsia 192, 245, 248, 249, 274, 291, 330
Polish language 10, 47, 92–4
    pronunciation guide xv–xvi
Polish legions 274
Polish New Year's Eve (1999) 319
Polish patriotism 99, 131, 132, 169, 193, 194, 274, 307
Polish-Lithuanian Commonwealth 14, 16, 17, 188, 216, 221, 230, 286, 287, 289, 302, 303
Polish-Ottoman war (1672–6) 303
Polish-Soviet War (1919–20) 260
Polish-Ukrainian War (1918–19) 240
Pomorze Wschodnie (Eastern Pomerania) 275
Poniatowska, Irena 128–9
Pope, Alexander 41–2, 284
Popiełuszko, Father Jerzy 274
Potocki, Alfred 223
Potocki, Jan – *Manuscript Found in Saragossa* 222
Potocki, Wojciech 35, 36

Potsdam Conference (1945) 200, 315–16

Poussin, Nicholas 284

Poznań 14, 142, 143–5, 203

Prussia 261, 262, 264, 270, 272

Prus, Bolesław author of *Lalka* ('The Doll') 110

Przemyśl 234, 235

Puszcza Augustowska 305

Pułaski, General Kazimierz 232, 255, 315

Puławy 192

Pułtusk 148

Puszcza Białowieska 286

Racławice, Battle of 190

Raczyński, Count Edward Bernard 146

Radio Marya 324

Radziwiłł, Prince Antoni 126–7

Radziwiłł, Princess Helena 284

Radziwiłł, Karol 17–18

Radziwiłłówna, Barbara 101

Redl, Colonel Alfred 234–5

Ries, Ferdinand 134, 154

Rogalin 145, 146

Rousseau, Jean-Jacques 194
    Considérations sur le gouvernment de la Pologne 189

Roztocze National Park 220

Rubinstein, Artur 30, 130, 134, 232, 247–8

Salza, Grand Master Hermann von 262

Sand, George (Aurore Dudevant) 23, 28, 130, 134, 137, 138

Sandomierz 180, 181–4

Sanok 225, 236–7

Sapieha, Prince Adam Stefan, Cardinal 236

Sarmatism, Sarmatians 14–15, 55, 56, 98*n*, 132–3, 173, 174, 207, 218, 236, 293, 294, 303

Schloss Fürstenstein (Zamek Książ; Rock of Princes) 74–8

Sienkiewicz, Henryk 110, 194, 303–4

Sikorski, Radosław 325–6

Sikorski, General Władysław 199, 206

Silesian Beskid Mountains 69, 72, 76, 271

Służba Bezpieczeństwa (Security Service of the Ministry of Internal Affairs; SB) 322

Śmielów, near Poznan 194–5

Śmigły-Rydz, Marshal 199

Sobibór extermination camp 219

Sobieski-Stuart family 54

Sokolov, Grigory 128

Solidarność (Solidarity) 226, 273–4, 315, 325*n*, 330, 333, 334

Solina 234

Sopot 271, 276

Speer, Albert 89–90

Stalag Luft III, Żagań (Sagan) 200, 202, 208, 210–11
    Great Escape 202–4, 210–11
    Wooden Horse escape 210

Stalin, Joseph 33, 44, 208, 209, 230

Stanisław Augustus Poniatowski, King 36*n*, 41–2, 47*n*, 106, 147, 154, 155, 188, 189, 191, 192, 222, 288, 293, 328

Stauffenberg, Colonel Count Claus von 306

Stendhal (Marie-Henri Beyle) 211–12

Strzelecki, Sir Paul Edmund (Polish explorer of Australia) 18

Stoss, Veit 177–8

Stowe, Buckinghamshire 193, 284

Sutkowski, Stefan 155, 156, 157, 159

szlachta (Polish nobility) 15, 16, 17, 30*n*, 101, 121, 188, 189, 190, 192, 236, 245, 304

Szpilman, Władysław 32, 310 *The Pianist* 32, 311–12

Szymanowski, Karol 248, 250

Szymborska, Wisława 301

Talleyrand-Périgord, Charles de, Prince de Bénévent 148, 200, 211

Talleyrand-Périgord, Dorothée 200–201

Tannenberg, Second Battle of (1914) 268

Tatars 19, 29, 31, 168, 170, 173, 181, 184, 188, 267, 302–5

Tatra mountains 110, 246, 247
Telemann, Georg Philipp 51, 76
Teutonic Knights 194, 260–68, 270,
 271, 275, 293, 297, 303, 305, 330
Toruń (Thorn) 263–4
Treblinka extermination camp 31, 32,
 39*n*, 311
układ (network of contacts) 59, 107, 112
Ukraine 44, 228, 239, 242, 243
Ukrainian-Polish civil war 230
Ukrainians 19, 229, 230
 resettlement of 230–31
Union of Lublin (1569) 216, 286
Upper Silesia 72, 74, 76, 77–8

Versailles, Treaty of (1919) 144, 272
Viardot, Pauline 129, 138
Vienna, Battle of (1683) 55, 173, 194, 304
Vigée-Le Brun, Elizabeth-Louise 191
Vilnius (Wilno), Lithuania 230, 289, 290
Vistula River 6, 7, 15, 24, 41, 47, 69–72,
 79, 87, 101, 104–5, 191, 193, 231,
 259, 260, 265, 318
 central role in Polish history 70
 at Christmas 319
 delta 275
 estuary 271
 a favourite playground in the past 71
 and the finest view of Warsaw 21
 the finest vista of the river 262
 gives Warsaw a unique setting 22, 104
 and the Holocaust 71, 89
 at Kazimierz Dolny 184–5
 at Kraków 168, 170, 172, 176, 178, 179
 as the main artery of trade and travel
  264
 maturing of 180
 Mermaid of Warsaw 70–71
 pollution 68, 71, 72
 sandbars 22, 69, 104
 source of 72
Vistula Lancers 70, 199
vodka 10, 11, 12, 48*n*, 95–6, 231, 256, 324
 Żubrówka 47, 166, 213, 293

Wałbrzych (Waldenburg) 75, 79
Waldorf, Jerzy 45
Wałęsa, Lech 43, 273, 274, 317, 331, 334

Walewice 147, 148
Walewska, Countess Maria 147,
 148–50
Walpole, Horace 77
Warsaw
 becomes the capital of Poland 37
 Bar Mleczny (Milk Bars), Old Town
  57
 buildings and gardens 41–5
 destruction in Second World War
  31, 36
 Election Field of Kings, Wola 188
 Kościół Świętego Krzyża (Holy
  Cross Church) 24, 141, 308
 Łazienki Palace and Park 41–4,
  105–6, 156, 190
 Mały Powstaniec ('Little Insurgent')
  40
 Palace of Culture and Science 22, 44,
  93, 97, 104
 Pawiak Gestapo prison, ulica Pawia
  39
 Pavilion X museum, Cytadela 25–6
 Piłsudski Square 215
 Pod Krokodylem (Under the
  Crocodile) café 107, 108
 Powązki cemetery, Warsaw 45,
  307–10
 St Charles Borromeo, cemetery
  church of 307
 St John's Cathedral 191
 Stadion Dziesięciolecia, Praga 253
 Royal Castle 36, 37, 139, 148, 154, 191
 Saxon Palace 121, 123
 Umschlagplatz (Shipment Square)
  32, 33
 Wedel Chocolate House 97–8
 Wilanów Palace (*Villa Nuova*) 54,
  55–6
 inter-war cultural and artistic scene
  30–31
 intimations of a glorious past 29
 Old Town 36, 39, 40, 45, 70, 107,
  332, 334
 rebuilt 36–41
 Zajazd Napoleoński restaurant 51
Warsaw, Battle of ('Miracle of the
 Vistula') (1920) 260, 310, 330

Warsaw Ghetto 31–3, 90
Warsaw Uprising (1944) 23, 31, 33–6, 40, 99, 155, 196, 208
Warszawska Opera Kameralna (Warsaw Chamber Opera) 99, 154–9
Watteau, Jean-Antoine 285
Wieliczka salt mine 251
Wielkopolski Park Narodowy (Great Poland National Park) 147
Wieniawski, Henryk 223, 308
wieszcz (prophetic seer) 131, 132
Wilhelm II, Emperor of Germany 75, 76, 77
Williams, Sir Charles Hanbury and Stanisław Augustus, the last king of Poland 41, 288
Winston, David 137*n*
Witkiewicz, Stanisław 248–9
Witkiewicz, Stanisław Ignacy ('Witkacy') 248–9, 250
Władysław II Jagiełło, King 266, 267, 268, 293, 315
Wojciech, St (Adalbert) 146–7
World War I 77, 105*n*, 144, 234, 235, 241, 250, 296
World War II 14, 18, 31–6, 37, 105*n*, 117, 144, 170*n*, 178, 181, 195, 202–11, 228–30, 231, 236, 240, 263, 272, 329

Wrocław (Breslau) 83, 190, 230, 313, 314, 315–16
Wyszyński, Cardinal 324

Yalta accords (1945) 36, 146, 208, 210, 230, 236*n*, 239

Zakopane 110, 245–51
Zamek Krzyżtopór, Ujazd 251
Zamek Pszczyna (Pless) 74, 76–7
Zamość 184, 217–20, 269*n*
Zamoyski, Grand Hetman Jan 217, 218, 219
Zug, Szymon Bogumił 193, 284
Zygmunt I Stary (Sigismund I the Old), King 175, 269*n*
Zygmunt II August, King 101, 173
Zygmunt III Vasa, King 36–7, 155
Zyklon B pesticide 83, 84, 88

Żagań (Sagan), Silesia 200–212
Żelazowa Wola 3, 119–22, 134, 284
Żeleński, Dr Tadeusz 'Boy' 172, 240–41
żubry (Lithuanian bison) 292–5, 298, 300, 301
Żywny, Wojciech Adalbert 122–3, 308